Transactions of the Royal Historical Society

SIXTH SERIES

VII

CAMBRIDGE
UNIVERSITY PRESS

Published by the Press Syndicate of the University of Cambridge
The Edinburgh Building, Cambridge CB2 2RU, United Kingdom
40 West 20th Street, New York, NY 10011–4211, USA
10 Stamford Road, Oakleigh, Melbourne 3166, Australia

First published 1997

A catalogue record for the book is available from the British Library

Library of Congress cataloguing in publication data applied for

ISBN 0 521 62262 X hardback

SUBSCRIPTIONS. The serial publications of the Royal Historical Society, *Royal Historical Society Transactions* (ISSN 0080–4401), Camden Fifth Series (ISSN 0960–1163) volumes and volumes of the Guides and Handbooks (ISSN 0080–4398) may be purchased together on annual subscription. The 1997 subscription price (which includes postage but not VAT) is £50 (US$80 in the USA, Canada and Mexico) and includes Camden Fifth Series, volumes 9 and 10 (published in July and December) and Transactions Sixth Series, volume 7 (published in December). Japanese prices are available from Kinokuniya Company Ltd, P.O. Box 55, Chitose, Tokyo 156, Japan. EU subscribers (outside the UK) who are not registered for VAT should add VAT at their country's rate. VAT registered subscribers should provide their VAT registration number.

Subscription orders, which must be accompanied by payment, may be sent to a bookseller, subscription agent or direct to the publisher: Cambridge University Press, The Edinburgh Building, Shaftesbury Road, Cambridge CB2 2RU, UK; or in the USA, Canada and Mexico: Cambridge University Press, 40 West 20th Street, New York, NY 10011–4211, USA. Prices include delivery by air.

SINGLE VOLUMES AND BACK VOLUMES. A list of Royal Historical Society volumes available from Cambridge University Press may be obtained from the Humanities Marketing Department at the address above.

Printed and bound in the United Kingdom by Butler & Tanner Ltd, Frome and London

CONTENTS

TRANSACTIONS OF THE
ROYAL HISTORICAL SOCIETY

PRESIDENTIAL ADDRESS

By R. R. Davies

THE PEOPLES OF BRITAIN
AND IRELAND, 1100–1400:
IV LANGUAGE AND HISTORICAL MYTHOLOGY

READ 22 NOVEMBER 1996

SINCE the beginning of the nineteenth century language has come to occupy a prominent place, often a provocative and intolerant one, in the ideology and rhetoric of nations. 'Every people (*Volk*)', so Herder asserted, 'has its own language as it has its own culture (*Bildung*).'[1] Bishop Stubbs spoke with equal certainty, if only to vindicate the Germanic character of the English people and to clear it of the charge of being infected with Roman or Celtic traits. Language, he pronounced roundly, is 'the nearest approach to a perfect test of national extraction'.[2] It is a sentiment whose certainty and content would command almost no historical support today. We are much more likely to agree with Eric Hobsbawm's opinion that 'language was merely one, and not necessarily the primary, way of distinguishing between cultural communities'.[3]

Many reasons help to explain the retreat from the linguistic nationalism of the nineteenth century. Some of them rest in a realisation of the complexity and fluidity of languages in our modern world and the artificiality of some of the language classifications which have been created by modern states for their own ideological ends. But for the historian equally important has been the recognition that language appears far less prominently in the evidence, especially perhaps the

[1] Quoted in Benedict Anderson, *Imagined Communities* (revised edn, 1991), 67–8.
[2] William Stubbs, *The Constitutional History of England* (1906 edn), I, 7.
[3] E. J. Hobsbawm, *Nations and Nationalism since 1780* (Cambridge, 1990), 58.

medieval evidence, than our own modern presuppositions suggest it should. Indeed the very word language, *lingua*, has an ambivalence, both in Latin and in many vernacular languages, which is itself suggestive.[4] Let me instance a few examples from contemporary evidence to illustrate the point. When Adam de Feypo in the late twelfth century referred to his brother as 'the first of our language' (*primum omnium de lingua nostra*) who was ordained in the bishopric of Meath', it is not language but ethnic affiliation and loyalty which are referred to.[5] Gerald of Wales showed a greater sensitivity to, and curiosity about, language than most of his contemporaries; but in one of his most famous stories in *The Description of Wales*—that of the interview at Pencader between Henry II and an old Welshman about the future of Wales—he likewise identified people and language, *gens* and *lingua*.[6] It was common in official correspondence and chronicle alike to refer to the Welsh as 'men of the Welsh tongue', and though such a phrase could be construed as excluding English-speaking settlers in Wales its general connotations were again clearly those of ethnicity and political loyalty, rather than being specifically and narrowly a language descriptor.[7] One might object that all these examples are taken from ethnic and political borderlands where language identity was a short-hand formula for cultural, and thereby political, affiliations; but the word language can have the same capacious connotations in well-developed and centralised states. When Edward I in 1295 informed his subjects that the king of France had a detestable plan to wipe the English language (*lingua*) from the earth, his hysterical tone makes it clear that what he was referring to was the genocide of the English people rather than mere linguistic annihilation.[8]

We may draw rather different, and indeed contradictory, conclusions from this apparently inexact and loose usage of the word language in medieval sources. The identity of language and people, *gens* and *lingua*, may have been regarded as so complete that the two were in effect synonymous. It is a view to which we must return, because there are clear echoes of it among medieval writers and theorists themselves. On the other hand, language appears as but one, and by no means the most important, of the attributes which defined a people; laws and

[4] Cf. Robert Bartlett, *The Making of Europe. Conquest, Colonization and Cultural Change 950–1350* (1993), 201; J. A. Watt in *A New History of Ireland, II: Medieval Ireland 1169–1534*, ed. Art Cosgrove (Oxford, 1987), 346.

[5] *Chartularies of St. Mary's Abbey, Dublin*, ed. J. T. Gilbert, Rolls Series (1884–6), II, 21–2.

[6] 'gens ... haec Kambrica, aliave lingua', Giraldus Cambrensis, *Opera*, ed. J. S. Brewer *et al.*, Rolls Series (1861–91), VI, 227 (Description of Wales, Book II, chap. 10).

[7] *Royal and Other Historical Letters ... of the Reign of Henry III*, ed. W. W. Shirley, Rolls Series (1862–6), II 230 (1262). Many other examples could be cited.

[8] W. Stubbs, *Select Charters of English Constitutional History* (9th edn, 1913), 480.

customs, life-styles and origin legends often figure much more prominently. Most important, language is not apparently high on the agenda
of issues of conflict between the peoples of the British Isles, between
conquerors and conquered. Thus neither in Wales nor in Scotland in
the thirteenth and early fourteenth centuries does language figure at
all in the propaganda wars with the English. Rather is it laws and
customs, feudal dependence and liberty which are the issues *par excellence*.

Several reasons suggest themselves why language, strictly speaking,
figures so apparently rarely as an issue of contention between peoples.
Language, after all, was a universal human attribute; differences in
language were divinely ordained and so much part of social life, at
different levels, that they were hardly worthy of comment, let alone the
focus of loyalty or hostility. So it is, for example, that scholars still find
it difficult to determine the degree of bilingualism in Anglo-Norman
England and the extent to which Anglo-Norman was spoken.[9] The
matter rarely excited comment; it is only in the fourteenth century,
notably with the writings of Robert Manning of Brunne, that we can
apparently witness the beginnings of a linguistic nationalism in England
and the sense that the English language had been one of the victims
of the Normans.[10] In a world in which Latin and French were such
effective *linguae francae* for the clerical and aristocratic elites, it would
have been strange indeed had vernacular languages attracted much
comment or loyalty from those who were socially powerful and literate;
that would have been to question the very social exclusiveness which
was the hallmark of those two international languages.

Furthermore in what was overwhelmingly an oral culture, there was
far more fluidity of language zones and far greater dialectical differences
within a single language than we, so used to universal education and
the standardising impact of print-culture and easy travel, often recognise.
John Trevisa, translating Higden's *Polychronicon*, commented that there
were 'diverse manners of English in the realm of England' and quoted
the view that 'we southern men may scarcely understand' the language
of Northumbria and especially of York which, for good measure, he
explained was 'scharp, slitting and frotynge and unschape'.[11] In such a

---

[9] Ian Short, 'On Bilingualism in Anglo-Norman England', *Romance Philology*, 33 (1979–80), 467–80.

[10] T. Turville-Petre, 'Politics and Poetry in the Early Fourteenth Century: The Case of Robert Manning's Chronicle', *Review of English Studies*, new series 39 (1988), 1–28; *idem*, 'The "Nation" in English Writings in the Early Fourteenth Century', in *England in the Fourteenth Century*, ed. N. Rogers (1993), 128–39; *idem*, *England the Nation. Language, Literature and National Identity 1290–1340* (1996)

[11] Ranulph Higden, *Polychronicon*, ed. C. Babington and J. R. Lumby, Rolls Series (1865–86), I, 160–3. Cf. the distinction between the speech of south-country Englishmen, north-country Englishmen and English-speaking Scots referred to in a lawsuit of 1360: D. M. Owen, 'White Annays and Others', in *Medieval Women*, ed. D. Baker (1978), 332, 343–4.

world the notions of a standard 'national language' and of a single linguistic community which could close ranks against outsiders did not easily take root. This did not mean, of course, that there was no sense of linguistic pride and anxiety to defend the purity and antiquity of language. The learned classes in Ireland, for example, used a single literary language whose origins date back to at least the sixth century and was practised throughout the whole of Gaeldom for a millennium and more.[12] In Wales the classical poets of the twelfth century likewise made much of their 'good, learned, refined' and 'uncorrupted' Welsh.[13] Yet such references should not mislead us: in both Wales and Ireland a consciously elevated and frequently archaic literary language was deliberately fostered by the professional poets and jurists. The professional cultivation of such an esoteric language is quite a different matter from a popular commitment to a language among the people at large as a manifestation of their ethnic unity and individuality.

There was, of course, another reason why the totemic and uniformist assumptions which tend to cluster around 'national' languages in our world were so slow to develop in medieval society. As in all pre-print societies the language situation was much more complex and fluid than we are used to; diversity and multiplicity of languages were taken as the norm. Language uniformity was taken as an indication of weakness rather than of strength. So it was that Etienne de Conti mocked the little kingdom of England which had only one language.[14] But the English were not minded to take such Gallic insults lying down. Thomas Polton, a member of the English delegation to the council of Constance, indeed took the argument directly into the enemy's camp: 'Where the French nation, for the most part, has one vernacular which is wholly or in part understandable in every part of the nation, within the famous English or British nation, however, there are five languages, you might say, one of which does not understand the other.'[15] Thomas Polton was scoring a point and doing so outrageously when it is recalled that his list of the languages of the 'English or British nation' included Gascon. But the general point that he was making—that Britain was a land of rich linguistic diversity—was certainly valid, and much more valid and

(I owe this reference originally to G. W. S. Barrow, *Kingship and Unity. Scotland 1000–1306* (1981), 145.)

    [12] Cf. F. J. Byrne, *Irish Kings and High Kings* (1973), 8.

    [13] J. E. Caerwyn Williams *et al.*, eds., *Gwaith Meilyr Brydydd a'i Ddisgynyddion* (Cardiff, 1994), 29, l. 5 and 30, l. 30; Nerys A. Jones and Ann P. Owen, *Gwaith Cynddelw Brydydd Mawr*, I (Cardiff, 1991), 85, l. 31. Morfydd Owen *et al.*, eds., *Gwaith Llywelyn Fardd ac Eraill* (Cardiff, 1994), 444, ll. 136, 139.

    [14] Quoted in Colette Beaune, *Naissance de la nation France* (Paris, 1985), 297.

    [15] The passage is published at length in C. M. D. Crowder, *Unity, Heresy and Reform 1378–1460* (1977), 121; for a recent comment, J.-P. Genet, 'English Nationalism: Thomas Polton at the Council of Constance', *Nottingham Medieval Studies*, 28 (1984), 60–78.

significant in the early twelfth century than it was three centuries later in Polton's own day. Scholars may differ on the vexed question of how long a form of French remained an actively spoken language in Norman and Angevin England; but there can be no doubt that French came to be cultivated for literary, documentary and legal purposes in the higher echelons of English society, thereby further enriching an already complex linguistic map. 'Twelfth-century England,' it has been observed, '... was a cultural and linguistic melting pot ... Multi-lingualism ... was its overriding characteristic.'[16]

If this was so of England, it was even more true of other parts of Britain, such as Wales.[17] Welsh was, of course, the dominant language in almost every part of Wales and indeed well beyond Offa's Dyke. When Archbishop Baldwin went on his crusading tour through the country in 1188 he found that he needed interpreters at the very borders of the country, at Radnor, Usk and Llandaff.[18] Indeed later evidence makes it clear that Welsh was the language of at least the peasantry within areas of what were then, or were to become, western Shropshire and Herefordshire.[19] Yet in lowland Wales the linguistic map was by no means simple or unitary. Many of the older place-names of north-east and east central Wales were undoubtedly Anglo-Saxon, however much they may have been subsequently dressed up in the most respectable Welsh clothes. English was overwhelmingly the language of the small boroughs which came to pepper the coastal lowlands of south Wales. It was in English that Henry II was given a stern moral lesson on the need for strict observance of the Sabbath at Cardiff in 1172 and it was a local settler, Philip of Marcross, who was able to bridge the linguistic gap between the French-speaking Henry and his English-speaking critic.[20] Further west in Pembroke and south-west Wales, the very substantial Flemish settlement clung on to its native language until at least the opening years of the thirteenth century; while the evidence of close links with Ireland and the common appearance of the word

[16] Ian Short, 'Patrons and Polyglots: French Literature in Twelfth-Century England', *Anglo-Norman Studies*, 14 (1992), 229–49 at 244. See also R. A. Lodge, 'Language Attitudes and Linguistic Norms in France and England in the Thirteenth Century', *Thirteenth-Century England*, 4 (1992), 73–85.

[17] For Wales see in general Llinos Beverley Smith, 'Pwnc yr iaith yng Nghymru, 1282–1536', in *Cof Cenedl I*, ed. G. H. Jenkins (Llandysul, 1986), 3–33; *idem*, 'Yr Iaith yng Nghymru'r Oesoedd Canol', *Llên Cymru*, 18 (1994–5), 179–91.

[18] Giraldus Cambrensis, *Opera*, VI, 14, 55, 67 (Itinerary through Wales Book I, chaps. 1, 5, 7).

[19] B. G. Charles, 'The Welsh, their Language and Placenames in Archenfield and Oswestry', *Angles and Britons. O'Donnell Lectures* (Cardiff, 1963), 85–110; M. Richards, 'The Population of the Welsh Border', *Trans. Cymmrodorion Society* (1970), part I, 77–100.

[20] Giraldus Cambrensis, *Opera*, VI, 64–5 (Itinerary, Book I, chap. 6). Gerald repeated the story in *Expugnatio Hibernica*, ed. A. B. Scott and F. X. Martin (Dublin, 1978), 108–11.

Gwyddel (Irish) in Welsh personal and place-names suggests that there may have been some Irish-speaking colonists in the far west of Wales.[21]

We must, of course, not exaggerate. Over most of Wales, Welsh was the sole language of the vast majority of the population; in most of the country it was only the small ruling elite which had command of a different language or languages. What happened at Brecon in 1302 provides a rare vignette of a world which normally lies beyond the reach of the stylised French or Latin documentation.[22] When the royal commissioner visited the area to take seisin of the lordship he found over two thousand Welshmen assembled before him. 'Because they did not know how to do fealty in English,' so his report ran, 'I took one Latimer, a clerk, and made him swear to do loyally what I should command on your part and told him the words of fealty, and he charged the others in Welsh.' Yet in and around Brecon town itself and in river valleys to the east, deeds and accounts make it clear that English must have been extensively spoken, for the field names and other highly localised toponyms are English. And the same was true of many parts of lowland eastern and southern Wales. This was a society of two, or more, languages rather than a bilingual society. But it was a society, at least in these frontier areas, which took the diversity of language in its stride and did not make a fuss about it. The English government and the Marcher lords often had professional interpreters on their pay-rolls and must of necessity have used them far more frequently than the documentation suggests.[23] The frequency with which place-names appear in both Welsh and English forms in deeds within a few years—Philipston in Brecon as Tre Philip, for example—or the way in which Welshmen adopted, and no doubt discarded, English aliases when it suited them—Rheinallt ab Ieuan ap Thomlyn, for example, masquerading as Reynold son of John Broughton—suggests a relaxed and realistic attitude towards the coexistence of languages and the problems it raised.[24] There was no need for the Welsh to be

---

[21] Flemish: Giraldus Cambrensis, *Speculum Duorum*, ed. M. Richter *et al.* (Cardiff, 1974), 37; Lauran Toorians, 'Wizo Flandrensis and the Flemish Settlement in Pembrokeshire', *Cambridge Medieval Celtic Studies*, 20 (1990), 99–118; the Irish: see comments of D. Simon Evans, *Historia Gruffud vab Kenan* (Cardiff, 1977), cix–cxiii.

[22] *Calendar of Inquisitions Miscellaneous 1219–1307*, no. 1870.

[23] In the southern half of the Principality the interpreter was called *walstottus*: R. A. Griffiths, ed., *The Principality of Wales in the Later Middle Ages, I: South Wales 1277–1536*, 72. Examples of interpreters on Marcher pay-rolls: Public Record Office SC6/1234/2, 5 (Chirk, Bromfield and Yale); Shrewsbury Public Library 9777 (Oswestry); G. T. Clark, ed., *Cartae... de Glamorgan* (Cardiff, 1910), III, no. 920 (Kilvey). For employment of interpreters in Ireland see, for example, 'The Irish Pipe Roll of 14 John, 1211–12', ed. O. Davies and D. B. Quinn, *Ulster Journal of Archaeology*, 3rd series, 4, supplement (1941), 44–5.

[24] Philipston/Trephilip: National Library of Wales, Tredegar Park 137/91–2 (1446–53); Rheinallt ab Ieuan ap Thomlyn: *Catalogue of Ancient Deeds*, VI, C.6935.

defensive about their language; it is only from the sixteenth century that such a sentiment begins to manifest itself, even in the conservative poetry. On the contrary, there is evidence from the late medieval Wales, as there is from late medieval Ireland, that the native vernacular was making major advances at the expense of English in areas such as Glamorgan and that families such as the Stradlings, Turbervilles, Hanmers or Sourdevalles of ancient English or Anglo-Norman stock were now at the very least bilingual. The same impression of relaxed acquiescence in the diversity of languages is evident from the native Welsh side: a notable Welshman such as Llywelyn Bren, the leader of revolt in Glamorgan in 1315–16, could pride himself on being the owner of a French copy of the *Roman de la Rose*, and the Welsh poets, rather than bemoaning the seductive advance of English, as they would from Tudor times onwards, could compliment their patrons on the bilingualism of their households.[25]

In these circumstances it is hardly surprising that language scarcely figures as an issue between the English and the Welsh. Nor does it do so in Scotland in the very generations when the struggle for the identity and liberty of Scotland was at its height. This of course, is in no way surprising: the identity of the Scots as people was not, and could not be, based on the cultivation and defence of a common language, for there was none such. There was, it is true, a marked revival of and pride in Gaelic institutions and traditions in the thirteenth century, as is witnessed most famously in the presence of an aged highland *shennachie* reciting the royal genealogy in Gaelic at Alexander III's inauguration in 1249.[26] Many generations later Walter Kennedy could indeed put about the claim that Gaelic was 'the good language of this land'.[27] But such a view was, of course, a total distortion. The land that we know as Scotland was even more a patchwork, or melting pot, of languages than either England or Wales, especially in the twelfth and thirteenth centuries. Several distinct varieties of Celtic, Scandinavian and English languages were to be found within its borders, and to these was added in the twelfth century the French which the Norman settlers brought in their wake and which, as the chroniclers tell us, the Scottish monarchy and its circle so sedulously cultivated from the reign of David I onwards. Nowhere was this linguistic diversity more obvious and more kaleidoscopic than in the areas immediately to the north of the border. In the east a form of Old English had in effect largely swept the board

[25]J. H. Matthews, ed., *Records of the County Borough of Cardiff* (Cardiff, 1898–1911), IV, 57–8; Smith, 'Pwnc yr iaith yng Nghymru', 13.

[26]John Bannerman, 'The King's Poet and the Inauguration of Alexander III', *Scottish Historical Review*, 68 (1989), 120–49.

[27]Quoted in D. Murison, 'Linguistic Relationships in Medieval Scotland', in *The Scottish Tradition*, ed. G. W. S. Barrow (1974), 71–83 at 80.

in the lowlands as far as the Forth estuary; but in the west speakers of an ancient Brythonic or P-Celtic language lived cheek by jowl with those who spoke varieties of English and Scandinavian languages, while in Galloway proper Gaelic speech prevailed.[28]

By the fourteenth century the linguistic map of Scotland had, doubtless, been considerably simplified; but the most dominant feature of that simplification had been the triumph of a form of the English tongue. The remarkable wave of town foundations appears to have been a key factor in the triumph of English, especially as the language of business and commerce; but even in rural lowland areas north of the Forth—in Fife, Angus and Gowrie—it was likewise making remarkable strides.[29] It is not the least of the paradoxes of the period that in the years of the Wars of Independence Scotland, or rather lowland and eastern Scotland, and England were closer together linguistically than they had ever been. The Scots of Roxburgh found that the English of Wark had no difficulty in decoding and imitating their English password; the monk of Westminster explained that part of the reason for the English disaster at Otterburn in 1388 was that it was impossible to distinguish English from Scots because they spoke a 'single language'; while in a famous letter to Henry IV in 1400 the Scottish earl of March excused himself from writing in French because 'the Englishe tonge is maire cleare to myne understanding'.[30] In these circumstances language could not be an issue which divided English from Scots or a bulwark of Scottish national identity. Indeed as James I put it provocatively but correctly in 1604, 'a communitie of Language, the principall meanes of Civil Societie' was a bond which should pull the two kingdoms and peoples together.[31] Within Scotland itself language was an issue which divided rather than united the country. When John of Fordun in the later fourteenth century made his famous and derogatory analysis of the distinction between the peoples of the highland and lowlands he was quite convinced that the difference in customs and habits between them ran clearly along a profound linguistic fault-line between Scottish and Gaelic and what we would call Scots.[32] As Geoffrey Barrow

[28] G. W. S. Barrow, 'The Anglo-Scottish Border: Growth and Structure in the Middle Ages', in *Grenzen und Grenzregionen*, ed. W. Haubrichs and R. Schneider (Saarbrücken, 1994), 197–212, esp. 202–3; Daphne Brooke, 'Gall-Gaidhil in Galloway', in *Galloway. Land nd Lordship*, ed. R. D. Oram and G. P. Stell (Edinburgh, 1991), 97–116.

[29] See briefly Ranald Nicholson, *Scotland. The Later Middle Ages* (Edinburgh, 1974), 24–5, 73–4, 274–5 and Map A; G. W. S. Barrow, *Scotland and its Neighbours* (1992), 106–8.

[30] G. W. S. Barrow, *Robert Bruce and the Community of the Realm of Scotland* (3rd edn, Edinburgh, 1988), 69; L. C. Hector and B. F. Harvey, eds., *The Westminster Chronicle 1381–94* (Oxford, 1982), 348–9; *Royal and Historical Letters during the Reign of Henry IV*, ed. F. C. Hingeston, Rolls Series (1860–1965), I, 24.

[31] Quoted in Jenny Wormald, 'The Creation of Britain: Multiple Kingdoms or Core and Colonies?', *ante*, 6th ser., II (1992), 175–94 at 177.

[32] John of Fordun, *Chronica Scottorum*, ed. W. F. Skene (Edinburgh, 1971–2), I, 42. Cf.

has observed 'a linguistic ambiguity was built into the fabric of the medieval Scottish nation'.[33]

From all of this we might well be entitled to conclude that language played no part in the identities of peoples, least of all in the British Isles. But it would be premature to rush to such a conclusion. After all any theory of language in the middle ages would have taken the eleventh chapter of Genesis as its point of departure with its description of the Tower of Babel and the deliberate divine decision to mix the languages and to make them mutually incomprehensible.[34] That division, like all divine actions, was carefully calculated; it produced, so it was thought, exactly seventy-two languages corresponding to the ancient cosmological symbolic number. The division of languages was, therefore, no human accident; but a divine plan which had served to shape the peoples of the world and which explained their relationship to each other. Isidore of Seville put the point with characteristic crispness: 'Peoples have arisen from different languages, not languages from different peoples.'[35] Another thinker expressed it even more telegraphically: language makes a people, *gentem lingua facit*.[36] If that indeed was the theoretical orthodoxy, then language was truly primary in the making, and thereby in the definition, of a people. If so, language was as much a hallmark of a people as were its laws, customs and life-style. Language was not merely a matter of vocabulary, grammar and syntax; rather was it the expression of the soul or character of a people. So it was, for example, that William of Malmesbury observed that the mode of expression in a language varied according to the customs or character of a people, *iuxta mores gentium*.[37] It was this same assumption that language was an essential part of ethnic identity which persuaded the Scots to try to win over the Irish to an alliance in the 1320s by insisting that their friendship was naturally based on common language and common life-style (*lingua communis quam ritus*).[38]

If peoples were indeed shaped by language, then language was as much a source of pride and loyalty as were their laws. This was perhaps particularly evident in those societies where hereditary learned orders

Calendar of Papal Registers. Papal Letters, IV, 1362–1404, 56; *Acts of the Lords of the Isles 1336–1493*, ed. J. and R. W. Munro, Scottish History Society (1986), lviii.

[33] G. W. S. Barrow, *The Anglo-Norman Era in Scottish History* (Oxford, 1980), 147.

[34] A. Borst, *Der Turmbau von Babel* (Stuttgart, 1957–63); and for an English summary of some of his views, idem, *Medieval Worlds, Barbarians, Heretics and Artists in the Middle Ages* (Oxford, 1991), esp. chap. 2.

[35] Isidore of Seville, *Etymologia … libri xx*, ed. W. M. Lindsay (Oxford, 1911), 9.1.1. (Quia ex linguis gentes, non de gentibus linguae exortae sunt.)

[36] Claudius Marius Victor, quoted in Bartlett, *The Making of Europe*, 198.

[37] William of Malmesbury, *Gesta Regum*, ed. W. Stubbs, Rolls Series (1887–9), I, 31.

[38] *Regesta Regum Scottorum v. The Acts of Robert I, 1306–29*, ed. A. A. M. Duncan (Edinburgh, 1988), no. 364.

of poets and jurists took it upon themselves to defend the purity and archaism of an ancient language. Such, for example, were Ireland and Wales. It was in that spirit that an Irish scholar-monk in the eleventh century expounded his views of the origins and superiority of the Irish language: 'ten years after that there was discovered by Fénius Fasard the speech which is melodious and sweet in the mouth'.[39] Elsewhere in Europe the dominance of Latin and of classical culture may have inhibited the development of such a measure of curiosity about the vernacular. Even so, it was readily recognised that language could be a powerful bonding agent for a people. So it is that the phrases 'mother language' and 'natural language' come to figure increasingly in discourse from the twelfth century onwards. People sharing the same language, so it was believed, formed natural communities in life and governance. 'Just as animals with the same language live peaceably together by nature,' as one observer put it rather charmingly, 'likewise men of the same language lead a common life together more easily.'[40] From that general observation two conclusions might be readily drawn. The first suggested that language communities formed natural political and governmental communities likewise. The point was put with particular force in a Slavic context, for example, in 1300: 'for it is fitting that those who do not differ much in speaking the ... language should enjoy the rule of a single prince'.[41] The corollary was, of course, disturbing: not only was the very diversity of languages so characteristic of medieval Europe thereby seen as a major hindrance to effective unitary rule, it was also a threat to relations between different language communities. For as Edmund Spenser was to put it with disarming directness, 'it is unnatural that any people should love another's language more than their own'.[42]

The implication of Spenser's statement was, of course, ultimately very sinister. Language, according to such a definition, was not only a bond of affection and focus of loyalty; it could also readily become the basis of demarcation, exclusion, contempt and hostility. That could be so even within well-built and centralised kingdoms. We must, it is true, tread with great care here especially in England. Notions of the suppression and stigmatisation of English after the Norman conquest— notions which owe more to the seductive appeal of Sir Walter Scott

[39] *The Book of Leinster*, ed. R. I. Best *et al.* (Dublin 1954–83), III, 573, quoted in D. Ó Corráin, 'Nationality and Kingship in Pre-Norman Ireland', *Historical Studies*, II (1978), 1–35 at 6. One early Irish tract, *Auraicept na nÉces*, emphasised that the common origin of the Irish lay in their language rather than in an eponymous ancestor.

[40] Quoted in Borst, *Der Turmbau*, 785.

[41] Quoted in Bartlett, *The Making of Europe*, 202.

[42] Edmund Spenser, *A View of the Present State of Ireland* (1596), ed. W. L. Renwick (Oxford, 1970), 67.

and Charles Kingsley than to the historical evidence itself—no longer command support. Likewise images of a great cultural divide between Anglo-Norman and Middle English cultures and literatures are being replaced by an awareness of a continuum of patronage and under-standing across the languages.[43] There is no need on such a view to go looking for language-conflict or a deliberate downgrading of the vernacular in a society where Latin and, increasingly, French were the dominant literary, academic and governmental languages of the ruling elite but where some, and probably extensive, knowledge of English was the norm among all social classes, probably by at least the mid-twelfth century. Furthermore, it is now much more clearly recognised than it was even half a generation ago that a strong sense of English-ness—of the 'English of England', as Jordan Fantosme calls them[44]—could be adequately and indeed almost raucously expressed from at least the 1130s in neoclassical Latin or tripping Anglo-Norman verse. Englishness was not tied to the literary cultivation of the English language or to hang-ups about its status.

We may readily concede the force of this case and yet recognise that the issue of the status and cultivation of the English language did become an increasingly prominent issue in the development of English identity in the thirteenth and fourteenth centuries. Ignorance of English was already apparently regarded as almost a disqualification for high office in England by the late twelfth century: at least such was the interpretation of the particular contempt in which William Longchamp was apparently held.[45] As English xenophobia grew by leaps and bounds in the thirteenth century, the English language and mastery of it became an item, though by no means a prominent one, in the catalogue of true Englishness—witness the conscious use of the language in public documents during the critical years 1258–65. Our knowledge is, of course, based overwhelmingly on a very restricted political elite; it is, therefore, all the more interesting to catch a glimpse of what popular sentiment may have been like in the revealing comment of the chronicler that 'whoever did not know the English tongue was despised by the masses and held in contempt'.[46] Contempt is a negative feeling; pride a more positive one. And it is pride in the English language as the natural and indeed the sole language of true-born Englishmen which comes to figure increasingly as the fourteenth century progressed. 'As everich Inglische can', was the assumption of one poet; 'that kan eche man understand, that is boren in Engelande', was the sentiment of

[43] See generally Short, 'Patrons and Polyglots'.
[44] *Jordan Fantosme's Chronicle*, ed. R. C. Johnston (Oxford, 1981), l. 631.
[45] *Gesta Regis Henrici Secundi*, ed. W. Stubbs, Rolls Series (1867), II, 219.
[46] *Flores Historiarum*, ed. H. R. Luard, Rolls Series (1890), II, 481.

another about the English language.[47] As our period closes we are on the edge of the age of Gower and Chaucer and Lydgate, of wills and deeds in English, the age of 'the triumph of English', of growing public declarations that English was the natural and national language of England and of the English. Language and national sentiment were to be increasingly yoked together in the propaganda of the English state.

If in England—and, as it happens, almost simultaneously in Scotland[48]—the English language was becoming increasingly the language of government and being cherished for its own sake, it is from the borderlands of the British Isles that at an earlier period we can see how important language could be in defining ethnic identities. This is how we would expect it to be: it was precisely where two peoples met and overlapped that language sensitivities were most likely to be acute, especially where the division of language and political power and privilege more or less coincided. Wales was such an area. Native Welsh society was a profoundly conservative and status-conscious society, deeply mindful of the need for purity of extraction for qualification as a free-born Welsh nobleman. It is little wonder, therefore, that in Welsh circles inability to be able to speak Welsh (*anghyfiaith*) should be equated with being an alien (*estron*).[49] Such sentiments became increasingly more strident in the thirteenth century as the temperature of political confrontation rose sharply: one poet could scarcely conceal his contempt for the English as a 'foreign, alien-tongued people'; another prided himself on knowing no English or French and looked forward to returning to Gwynedd where fluent Welsh was spoken under its native prince.[50]

But it was in Ireland above all that tension about language became an important ethnic identifier. Ethnic tension was more crudely confrontational in Ireland from a fairly early date of English settlement and colonisation than it had been in Wales, and language was part of the explosive mixture. It was partly a matter of contempt for what was seen as a backward and barbarian civilisation which needed to be dragged into the brave international world of Latin Christendom. As Abbot Stephen of Lexington put it famously in 1229: 'How can anyone

[47] The first quotation is from 'Of Arthur and of Merlin', cited in Turville-Petre, 'Politics and Poetry' 27; the second is from *Historical Mss. Commission. Manuscripts of Lord Middleton* (1911), 239.

[48] For a recent review of the chronology of the adoption of the vernacular in Scottish documents, see Hector MacQueen, *Common Law and Feudal Society in Medieval Scotland* (Edinburgh, 1993), 93–5.

[49] *Historia Gruffud vab Kenan*, 25, 30–1; A. W. Wade-Evans, ed., *Vitae Sanctorum Britanniae et Genealogiae* (Cardiff, 1944), 17.

[50] *Llawysgrif Hendregadredd*, ed. J. Morris-Jones and T. H. Parry-Williams (Cardiff, 1933), 218; Gerald Morgan, 'Nodiadau ar destun Barddoniaeth y Tywysogion yn Llsg. NLW 4993', *Bulletin of the Board of Celtic Studies*, 21 (1964–6), 149–50.

love the cloister or learning who knows nothing but Irish', and decreed accordingly that no one was henceforth to be admitted to the Cistercian Order unless he could confess his sins in French or in Latin.[51] Much more serious was the assumption that knowledge of Irish and political disloyalty to the English establishment went inevitably hand in hand. Such a view had been expressed from early days especially in ecclesiastical appointments, because (as it was said) 'Irishmen ... maintain their own language [= nation]'; the good citizens of Cork put it even more bluntly, declaring that 'those of Irish speech are enemies of the king and his subjects'.[52] Above all, as English control in Ireland faltered and as isolated English communities made increasing compromises with their Irish habitat, the defence of the English language came to be seen as one of the crucial frontier guards against contamination and degeneracy. A letter of 1360 analysed the situation: 'Men of the English race in that land study and speak the Irish language and foster their children among the Irish ... so that our country dwellers of English stock for the most part are becoming Irish in language.'[53] The Statutes of Kilkenny generalised the answer to the problem, decreeing that every Englishman henceforth use the English language and be named by an English name, and sternly warning the English living among the Irish from using the Irish language among themselves.[54] Language barriers were being legislatively, if ultimately ineffectively, erected. Nor was the attitude of the Irish very different. The abusive language of the *Triumphs of Turlogh (Caithréim Thoirdhealbhaigh)* directs much of its contempt for the English at their speech, calling them 'stuttering stammerers', 'tongue-tied strangers' and 'lisping English'.[55] It would be easy to believe that they would subscribe to the Irish view of the English language as expounded by a later English commentator: 'for language, they do so despise ours as they think themselves the worse when they hear it'.[56]

All this suggests that language, after all, was not unimportant as an ethnic identifier especially in frontier societies. It also surely suggests that the significance of language in this respect was growing apace in the later middle ages and with it a growing intolerance of language

[51] Stephen of Lexington, *Letters from Ireland 1228–9*, ed. B. W. O'Dwyer (Kalamazoo, 1982), 68, 91, 162.

[52] J. A. Watt, 'English Law and the Irish Church: The Reign of Edward I', in *Medieval Studies to Aubrey Gwynn* ed. J. A. Watt *et al.* (Dublin, 1961), 137–67 at 150–1; G. O. Sayles, ed., *Documents of the Affairs of Ireland before the King's Council* (Dublin, 1979), 28 (Cum igitur Hybernica lingua vobis et vestra sit inimica), 72 (Irish and Scots described 'come ceux qi heont lange engleise').

[53] *HMC 10th Report*, App. V, 260–1.

[54] *Statutes ... of Ireland, John to Henry V*, ed. H. F. Berry (Dublin), 434–5.

[55] *Caithréim Thoirdhealbhaigh*, ed. S. H. Grady, Irish Texts Society (1929), 26–7, 30–1.

[56] Quoted in D. B. Quinn, *The Elizabethans and the Irish* (Ithaca, 1966), 88.

diversity. This is indeed exactly what we find in the British Isles. We can touch here only briefly on two facets of it. The first we may characterise as the cultivation of language as an instrument of exclusion and for the deliberate promotion of ethnic hysteria. We get an early hint of it in the report in a contemporary English chronicle that in his raids into northern England William Wallace spared no one who used the English language;[57] but it is perhaps during Owain Glyn Dŵr's revolt in Wales that the issue came most menacingly into view. There are so many reports that it was the intention of the English and the Welsh alike to destroy each other's language that there can be no doubt that language had become part of the rhetoric of hysteria during the revolt.[58] Particularly interesting in this context was Adam of Usk's comment that when the men of Cardiganshire were pardoned for their revolt in 1401 they were allowed to use Welsh 'though its destruction had been decreed by the English'.[59] Such stories are unlikely to be true; but they lift a veil on the anxieties of contemporaries. Those anxieties come into even clearer focus, and from a much more credible source, when we learn for example in the charter granted to the borough of Welshpool in 1406 that proceedings in the town's court are henceforth to be in French or English only or note the privilege that was granted to Simon Pulford when he took land in Moldsdale that he would not be judged except by Englishmen and in the English, not in the Welsh, language.[60]

We might ascribe all this to the paranoia produced by revolt; but even without the pretext of revolt there was throughout later medieval and early modern Europe a detectable shift towards regarding linguistic uniformity as a necessary precondition for a strong and unified state. Language, from being one of the identifiers and prerogatives of each and every people, was being turned into an instrument of state power and uniformity. An early articulation of the new orthodoxy comes, interestingly enough, from late fourteenth-century Ireland, where language had already become a touchstone of loyalty and Englishness. 'Experience teaches us', so it was observed, that 'diversity of tongues' caused 'wars and diverse tribulations.'[61] By the sixteenth century the

[57] 'Annales Londonienses', *Chronicles of the Reigns of Edward I and Edward II*, ed. W. Stubbs, Rolls Series (1882), I, 41.

[58] Examples: Public Record Office, Chester 25/25 m. lv; Chester 30/17 m. 23; *Proceedings and Ordinances of the Privy Council*, ed. N. H. Nicolas (Record Commission, 1834–7), II, 55; *Select Cases in the Court of King's Bench*, ed. G. O. Sayles (Selden Society, 1936–71), VII, 114–17.

[59] *Chronicon Adae de Usk*, ed. E. Maunde Thompson (1904), 71.

[60] M. C. Jones, *The Feudal Barons of Powys* (1865), 49; British Library Additional Charter, 51498.

[61] E. Perroy, *L'Angleterre et le grand schisme d'occident* (Paris, 1933), 395, 403.

new orthodoxy was fully in place. 'It hath ever been the use of the conqueror to despise the language of the conquered and to force him by all means to learn his.' That spelt out the philosophy of language domination and uniformity brutally in terms of power. But earlier in his treatise Edmund Spenser had made it clear that he recognised that the battle about language was ultimately about hearts and minds and the very identities of peoples. 'The words are the image of the mind,' he commented, '... so that the speech being Irish, the heart must needs be Irish, for out of the abundance of the heart the tongue speaketh.'[62] Never has the centrality of language to the psyche and identity of a people been more acutely analysed. The message was clear: if the peoples of the British Isles were to be united in loyalty to a unitary crown and state, then diversity of language must ultimately be eradicated. The Act of Union of England and Wales in 1536 said it all: Welsh was dismissed as 'a speche nothing like ne consonaunt to the naturall mother tonge used within this Realme'; all courts should henceforth be held in English and no one using Welsh should henceforth hold any office in England or Wales. In Ireland, likewise, in 1541 the adoption of English language and customs was one of the conditions imposed on Gaelic chiefs in the policy of surrender and regrant.[63] Historians have rightly bent over backwards to emphasise that no intentional language annihilation was involved in such legislative declarations. But what surely was involved—as Edmund Spenser so readily conceded— was a recognition that individuality of language could be one of the crucial keys to the identity of a people; regnal solidarity thereby ultimately required, at least at the official level, as broad a linguistic uniformity as possible. After all, as medieval pundits had said: language made a people; therefore a single people should be satisfied with a single language.

Above all a people must have a shared history if it is to be a people. Just as with individuals, so with communities there can ultimately be no identity without memory. Ethnic communities are constituted by

---

[62] Edmund Spenser, *A View of the Present State of Ireland*, 67–8.

[63] 27 Henry VIII, c. 26; Steven G. Ellis, *Tudor Ireland 1470–1603* (1985), 138. It was in the same spirit that an Act was introduced in 1536–7 enjoining clerks in Holy Orders in Ireland to do their best 'to learn the English tongue and language and use English order and fashions', D. B. Quinn, 'The Bills and Statutes of the Irish Parliament of Henry VII and Henry VIII', *Analecta Hibernica*, 10 (1941), 71–169 at 156. It was for the same reason that the SPCK two centuries later advised against preaching in Irish, because it would 'keep up the distinction of their people from ours to make us one people and of one religion, which would have but one language', 'Rawlinson Manuscripts (Class C)', *Analecta Hibernica*, 2 (1931), 1–44 at 27.

myths and memories; without them they are mere aggregations of population contained within boundaries. It was Ernest Renan who made the famous comment that getting its history wrong is part of being a nation; but without a shared memory of the past, however 'wrong' it may be, a people will lose its identity. As one sociologist has put it, it is historical mythology which provides 'emotional and aesthetic coherence to undergird social solidarity and social definition'.[64] It literally makes sense of the past, and thereby of the present and its relationship to the past. It is significant in this context that the Latin world *historia* is translated into the Middle Welsh term *ystyr*, literally 'meaning' or 'significance'. 'Thus the history of something explained its meaning; and its meaning was to be found in its history.'[65] Of nothing was this more true than of a people. And since peoples are in a state of constant flux and redefinition—and, arguably, much more so in the middle ages when many of them were not corseted within the framework of a state organisation—their historical mythology is for ever evolving. Thus in early Ireland the history of a particular Irish people, the Féni, was apparently gradually transformed into a history of the Irish people as a whole; in Scotland, likewise, a deliberate attempt seems to have been made to unify the country, notably the Scots and the Picts, 'by obliterating the memory of the different ethnic origins of the people'.[66] New ethnic communities similarly created a new historical mythology for themselves; without it they would lose their identity and so be absorbed into existing historical mythologies and peoples. Nowhere is this more clear than in Ireland: there the English community asserted its identity in a whole host of ways; not the least important was the articulation and elaboration of its own history from the time of Henry II onwards.[67]

Many of these mythologies were already age-old when the twelfth century opened: it is their remarkable resilience, and adaptability, across more than a millennium in many cases, which is one of their most distinctive features and makes our how historiography look remarkably shallow and ephemeral. This is particularly true of medieval Ireland

[64] Anthony D. Smith, *The Ethnic Origins of Nations* (Oxford, 1986), 25.

[65] P. P. Sims-Williams, 'Some Functions of Origin Stories in Early Medieval Wales', in *History and Heroic Tale. A Symposium*, ed. T. Nyberg *et al.* (Odense, 1988), 97–131 at 98.

[66] D. Ó Corráin, 'Irish Origin Legends and Genealogy: Recurrent Aetiologies', in *History and Heroic Tale* ed. Nyberg *et al.*, 51–96; E. J. Cowan, 'Myth and Identity in Early Medieval Scotland', *Scottish Historical Review*, 63 (1984), 111–35. The quotation is from T. F. O'Rahilly, *Irish History and Mythology* (Dublin, 1946), 194.

[67] *Documents of the Affairs of Ireland*, 99–100. For comment, Robin Frame, 'England and Ireland, 1171–1399', in *England and her Neighbours 1066–1453. Essays in Honour of Pierre Chaplais*, ed. M. Jones and M. Vale (1989), 139–57 at 152–3; *idem*, 'Overlordship and Reaction, c. 1200–c.1450', in *Uniting the Kingdom? The Making of British History*, ed. A. Grant and K. J. Stringer (1995), esp. 78–9.

which has the largest corpus of early surviving vernacular literature in Europe.[68] The *Lebor Gabála Érenn*, the book of the taking of Ireland, was not composed in its present form until the later eleventh century at the earliest, but it draws on traditions which go back at the very least to the eighth or even the seventh centuries.[69] It provided a history of the Goidels from the creation and, crucial for the present argument, it was based on the assumption that all the people of Ireland were descended from a single ancestor and thereby truly formed a single people. It was the canonical interpretation of the history of the Irish and as such was unquestioned until the seventeenth century. It was truly one of the crucial bulwarks of Irish identity. The Welsh, or rather the Britons, cannot perhaps match the Irish in the proven chronological span of their historical myths; but several of their essential features are already to be found in the ninth-century *Historia Brittonum* or in the tenth-century poem *Armes Prydein*; they had not lost their appeal, even if they had changed their form and content, more than six centuries later.[70] The Scottish situation, one suspects, was not dissimilar. Scholars may differ—as is inevitable given the nature, and absence, of evidence—as to how much of the various, and sometimes conflicting, interpretations of the early history of the *Scotti* to be found in John of Fordun's *History* in the later fourteenth century draw on ancient traditions and as to how old those traditions are.[71] But given the close links and similarities between Irish and Scottish Gaeldom and their respective learned classes, it is not difficult to believe in 'the ancient and splendid histories of the Scots' to which the clergy of Scotland referred in their declaration in 1319.[72] After all, one of the few early sources for Scottish history is the text known as 'An explanation of the history of the men

---

[68] See in general Kathleen Hughes, *The Early Celtic Idea of History and the Modern Historian* (Cambridge, 1976); F.J. Byrne, 'Senchas: The Nature of the Gaelic Historical Tradition', *Historical Studies*, 9 (1970), 137–59; John Carey, *The Irish National Origin-Legend. Synthetic Pseudohistory* (Cambridge, 1994).

[69] Kathleen Hughes, *Early Christian Ireland. Introduction to the Sources* (1972), 282–3; D. Ó Corráin, 'Nationality and Kingship in pre-Norman Ireland', *Historical Studies*, 11 (1978), 1–35, esp. 5–7.

[70] B. F. Roberts, 'Geoffrey of Monmouth and Welsh Historical Tradition', *Nottingham Medieval Studies* 20 (1976), 29–40; J. B. Smith, *The Sense of History in Medieval Wales* (Aberystwyth, 1989).

[71] For differing emphases on the antiquity or otherwise of Scottish historical traditions, see, on the one hand, Bannerman, 'The King's Poet', and D. Broun, 'The Origin of Scottish Identity', in C. Bjørn *et al.*, *Nations, Nationalism and Patriotism in the European Past* (Copenhagen, 1994), 35–56, and, on the other, R. James Goldstein, *The Matter of Scotland. Historical Narrative in Medieval Scotland* (Nebraska, 1993). Cf. also A. A. M. Duncan's trenchant comment (*Cedpath 90*, 8): 'Scotland was a political creation without any attested early mythical history to service the kingship.'

[72] E. L. G. Stones, ed., *Anglo-Scottish Relations 1174–1382. Some Selected Documents* (2nd edn, Oxford, 1970), 284–5.

of Scotland'. It may be as old as the seventh century; but what is striking for us in the present context is its title with its self-proclaimed purpose of providing an explanatory historical mythology for a people.[73] When Alexander III was inaugurated as king at Scone on 13 July 1249, the king's poet recited his genealogy right back to Guidheal Glas, son of the king of Athens, and Scota his wife, daughter of Pharaoh of Egypt. We might dismiss this famous episode as a manifestation of cultural antiquarianism (which can certainly be traced in other spheres in later medieval Ireland and Scotland); but when we couple it with the remarkable efflorescence of historical writing, much of it about the very distant past, in fourteenth-and fifteenth-century Scotland we must surely recognise how important historical mythology was to a people, more especially perhaps a people which lived under the shadow of the power that was the kingdom of England.

In Ireland, Wales and Gaelic Scotland the preservers and presenters of historical mythology were pre-eminently a mandarin and often hereditary literate caste, whose expertise ranged across poetry, myth-ology, story-telling and genealogy and who drew few distinctions between these various categories. They were the conservative keepers and remembrancers of highly conservative and past-oriented societies, drawing upon a vast corpus of triads, genealogies, foundation-legends and a mass of literary, toponymic and onomastic lore. It is the absence of such a class of professional remembrancers, and likewise of a professional caste of hereditary jurists, in England by at least the twelfth century, which is one of the profound and profoundly significant cultural divides between England and the societies to its north and west. We might speculate that this was so because at the higher secular and ecclesiastical levels England was now firmly part of a north-west European cultural orbit; we might also wonder whether the precocious governmental unity of the country did not mean that its regnal solidarity found ample expression in a whole host of practical ways, without the need to be upheld by a dominant and intrusive historical mythology. It is arguable that it is only societies uncertain of their present status and even more unsure of their future prospects which need the self-assurance of nostalgia and historical mythology.

This did not mean that the English did not cultivate their own historical mythology. On the contrary, it is the astonishing success of their particular historical mythology which is one of the clearest expressions of the growing English domination of Britain. This is not the occasion to dwell on this theme: historians such as James Campbell, John Gillingham and Patrick Wormald have made it very much their own of late. It is a theme which, in terms of written history, starts with

---

[73] J. Bannerman, *Studies in the History of Dalriada* (Edinburgh, 1974), 27–157.

Bede. Here we need only note that his topic is the history of the English people, *gens Anglorum*: it is no accident that Aelfric of Eynsham refers to his work simply as the *Historia Anglorum* or that William of Malmesbury likewise regularly calls Bede's masterpiece *gesta Anglorum*.[74] It was much more than that, of course; but in a real sense it created the English as a single people by giving them a single historical mythology, by emphasising their common Germanic origins, by converting the *adventus Saxonum* into the chronological break in the history of Britain, and by consigning the Britons to a historical oubliette. The task of constructing a canonical historical mythology for the English was resumed by a remarkable group of historians in the twelfth century, self-consciously building on the achievement of Bede and bridging the gap between his day and theirs.[75] What needs to be emphasised here is that these historians were quite clear what they were about; they were constructing an image, a historical mythology, of the past of the English people. It was not accidental that they gave their books titles such as *Historia Anglorum* or *Estoire des Engleis*. William of Malmesbury declared his intention to write 'a continuous history of the English' and to record 'the deeds of the English from their arrival in England'; Henry of Huntingdon likewise proclaimed his wish to chronicle 'the deeds of this kingdom and the origins of our people' (*nostrae gentis*) and punctuated his work with periodic announcements of further stages in the evolution of the English nation; while later in the century William of Newburgh proclaimed it his intention to compose 'the history of our people, that is the English'.[76] It might have been considered desirable by William of Newburgh's day—though William himself did not think so—to extend the history of Britain to include the luxuriant detail of Geoffrey of Monmouth's history of the Britons and their kings, but that was ultimately no more than a curtain-raiser for the history of the English. The English historical myth was self-satisfyingly and self-absorbingly English. It was also arguably one of the most resilient and successful mythologies ever created. It does not require much imagination to construct a bridge from the Venerable Bede across to William of Malmesbury's determination to write 'the continuous history of the

[74] Quoted in H. E. J. Cowdrey, 'Bede and the "English People"', *Journal of Religious History*, 11 (1981), 523; William of Malmesbury, *Gesta Regum*, I, 1, 30, 56, 67, 260, etc.

[75] See in particular James Campbell's seminal study, 'Some Twelfth-Century Views of the Anglo-Saxon Past', *Peritia*, 3 (1984), 131–50, reprinted in his *Essays in Anglo-Saxon History* (1986), chap. 13.

[76] William of Malmesbury, *Gesta Regum*, II, 518; Henry of Huntingdon, *Historia Anglorum*, ed. Thomas Arnold, Rolls Series (1879), 3, 47–8, 52, 134, 163, 172; ed. D. Greenway (Oxford, 1996), 4, 96–8, 106, 264, 317, 334–6; William of Newburgh, 'Historia Rerum Anglicarum', *Chronicles of the Reigns of Stephen, Henry II and Richard I*, ed. R. Howlett, Rolls Series (1884–9), I, 28.

English' and thence across the centuries to the conviction of the founders of academic history in Britain to build the syllabus of history in Britain around the corner-stone of continuous English history. It is when corner-stones are removed that buildings soon begin to totter.[77]

'Continuous' is the crucial word in this context. The historical mythology of a people is ultimately concerned to show that the people in question is literally aboriginal and that its unbroken history as a people validates such a claim. A people's place in today's sun depends on it being able to show that it is immemorially a people and can construct the past to show that is so. The exercise could take a variety of forms. In a society dominated by kings and kingship, regnal and dynastic continuity was bound to be one crucial facet of historical mythology. So it was that the famous Irish Remonstrance of *c.* 1317 concluded with a thumping declaration that 'a hundred and ninety seven kings of our blood have reigned over the whole of Ireland'. The Scots could not quite compete with the Irish in the regnal numbers game: they modestly confined their unbroken kingship to a mere one hundred and thirteen kings, but added defiantly 'the line unbroken by a single foreigner'.[78] Kings were certainly important; they and their dynasties required their own validating charters in the form of regnal lists; but as the declaration of Arbroath made abundantly clear—and as the *Lebor Gabala Erenn* and *Henry of Huntingdon's History of the English* in their very different ways likewise demonstrate—it is the unity, the identity and the ethnic homogeneity of a people which above all needs to be underpinned by an appropriate historical mythology. So it was that the most wondrous historical mythologies of the peoples of the British Isles, as of all the other peoples of Europe, were concocted largely out of biblical and classical materials, spliced with local vernacular traditions and further spiced from Geoffrey of Monmouth's inventions.[79] Such origin legends of peoples had, of course, to be regularly revised to cope with changing current circumstances; but that only goes to prove how crucial was the sense of being a community of common descent through time to the identity and credibility of a people. A people without a history was a contradiction in terms; only an unbroken history, preferably from Noah's or even Adam's day, could eventually demonstrate that a people was a people because it had always been a people. A late eleventh-century Welsh scholar, Ieuan ap

[77] I have explored the theme of this paragraph more fully in *The Matter of Britain and The Matter of England. An Inaugural Lecture* (Oxford, 1996).

[78] Remonstrance: Walter Bower, *Scotichronicon*, ed. D. E. R. Watt *et al.* (Aberdeen, 1987), VI, 384–403; Declaration of Arbroath: A. A. M. Duncan, *The Nation of Scots and the Declaration of Arbroath 1320*, Historical Association (1970).

[79] See in general Susan Reynolds, 'Medieval *Origines Gentium* and the Community of the Realm', *History*, 68 (1983), 375–90.

Sulien, made the point forcefully even if the chronological span of his claim was modest: 'I am born of the famous name of Britons who once withstood the Roman army energetically....'[80]

Ieuan ap Sulien spoke for a conservative, clerical elite in south-west Wales. That should prompt us to ask, finally, how deeply rooted in popular consciousness was the historical mythology of a people? Was it rather something that was effectively confined to a tiny group of professional remembrancers—be they the *filid* of Ireland, the *cyfarwyddiaid* and court poets of Wales, the *shennachie* of Gaelic-speaking Scotland, and the handful of monks and canons who composed most of the histories which have come down to us from twelfth-and thirteenth-century England? The honest answer is that we shall never know; for popular memory was oral memory and thereby lies beyond the reach of the historian. What we know of popular social memory in more recent times should make us very chary of believing that some of the complex historical mythology which we find recorded in the books of the literati could ever have been digested and remembered at a popular level. Popular memory latches on to emblems and ceremonies, to local cults and topographical lore, rather than to a sustained and ordered memory of the past.[81] Indeed those familiar with Le Roy Ladurie's *Montaillou* or with Carlo Levi's *Eboli* will readily sympathise with Levi-Strauss's view of peasants dwelling in 'an island of time' with little memory beyond a generation or two, and even then a highly selective one.

Yet that is not the whole truth. The popular memory may have been highly selective and often very short in its span; but it could be surprisingly retentive and specific (if factually often very wayward) especially where its own interest, status and privileges were at stake. The peasants of north-east Wales in the 1270s for example could apparently recall the expulsion of the English from the Prestatyn area in the later twelfth century, even if their exact dating of the event and the personnel involved was garbled.[82] Likewise the peasants of St Albans in the fourteenth century called on the evidence of 'the most illustrious king Offa' in their struggle with the abbot.[83] But it is in kinship-dominated societies such as Wales and Ireland that we can best witness what remarkable feats of genealogical memory could be performed by men whose nobility of blood was in their eyes their title to status but

---

[80] M. Lapidge, 'Welsh Latin Poetry of Sulien's Family', *Studia Celtica*, 8–9 (1973–4), 68–106 at 83.

[81] See in general Paul Connerton, *How Societies Remember* (Cambridge, 1989); James Fentress and Chris Wickham, *Social Memory* (Oxford, 1992).

[82] J. Conway Davies, ed., *The Welsh Assize Roll 1277–84* (Cardiff, 1940), 161–2.

[83] Rosamond Faith, 'The "Great Rumour" of 1377 and Peasant Ideology', in *The English Rising of 1381*, ed. R. H. Hilton and T. H. Aston (Cambridge, 1984), 43–74.

whose economic standing must often have been no more than that of ordinary peasants. It has been calculated that pre-twelfth-century genealogies and origin-legends in Ireland contain upwards of 20,000 names.[84] In Wales Gerald observed that 'people know their family tree by heart and can readily recite from memory the names not only of their grandfathers, great-grandfathers, and great-great-grandfathers but their relatives up to the sixth and seventh degree and beyond'. And when the record evidence and the genealogical evidence begin to become abundant from the fourteenth and fifteenth centuries, it is clear that Gerald is not exaggerating.[85]

Genealogies, it might be objected, are a highly personalised and restricted form of historical memory. But not only is it clear that genealogical knowledge was remarkably widespread in medieval Wales and Ireland—in stark and significant contrast with contemporary England—genealogy also only acquired its full meaning when it was located, as ultimately it was, in a broad-based historical mythology. Nor should we underestimate the degree to which an often no doubt bowdlerised form of that mythology was communicated to the population at large by oral transmission. Thus when we hear of the English government banning the 'rhymers and wasters' whose propaganda incited the Welsh to revolt, or of the monks of a Cistercian monastery wandering through Wales propagating Welsh chronicles and prophecies, or of the hill-top assemblies so common in Wales and Ireland, we are catching further glimpses of the way that the historical mythology was being disseminated among the population at large.[86] Two vignettes from Wales from well beyond our period may help to reinforce that image. The first comes from a well-known report on the state of north Wales in Elizabethan times:

> Upon the Sondaies and hollidaies the multitude of all sorts of men woomen and childrene of everie parishe doe use to meete in sondrie places either one some hill or one the side of some mountaine where theire harpers and crowthers singe them songs of the doeings of theire auncestors, namelie, of theire warrs againste the kings of this

[84] Ó Corráin, 'Irish Origin Legends', at 55.

[85] Giraldus Cambrensis, *Opera*, VI, 200 (Description of Wales, Book I, chap. 17); F. Jones, 'An Approach to Welsh Genealogy', *Transactions of Cymmrodorion Society*, (1948), 303–466; M. H. Brown, 'Kinship, Land and Law in Fourteenth-Century Wales: The Kindred of Iorwerth ap Cadwgan', *Welsh History Review*, 17 (1995), 495–519; A. D. M. Barrell and R. R. Davies, 'Land, Lineage and Revolt in North-East Wales, 1243–1441: A Case Study', *Cambrian Medieval Celtic Studies*, 29 (1995), 27–51.

[86] For 'rhymers and wasters' etc. in Wales, see R. R. Davies, *The Revolt of Owain Glyn Dŵr* (Oxford, 1995), 92–3 and sources cited there; for similar assemblies in Ireland, see Katherine Simms, *From Kings to Warlords. The Changing Political Structure of Gaelic Ireland in the Later Middle Ages* (Woodbridge, 1987), 72–5.

realme and the English nac'on, and then doe they ripp upp theire petigres at length howe eche of them is discended from those theire ould princes. Here also doe they spende their time in hearinge some part of Thalaassyn [Taliesin], Marlin Beno Pybbye [Myrddin pen beirdd], Jeruu [?Iorwerth], and suche other the intended prophetts and saincts of that cuntrie.[87]

There could be no more convincing picture of the cultivation and transmission of a historical mythology, and its natural link with genealogy, amongst the population at large. When Daniel Defoe came on his tour of Wales in the eighteenth century, this historical mythology was already attenuated and the professional bardic order which had sustained it in terminal decline. Even so Defoe found that 'stories of Vortigern and Roger of Mortimer are in every old woman's mouth' in Radnorshire; and he concluded with this general observation about the Welsh:

> They value themselves much upon their antiquity: the ancient race of their houses, and families, and the like; and above all, upon their ancient heroes: their King Caractacus, Owen ap Tudor, Prince Llewelin, and the like noblemen and princes of British extraction; and as they believe their country to be the pleasantest and most agreeable in the world, so you cannot oblige them more than to make them think you believe so too.[88]

For the Welsh at least, the cultivation of their own historical mythology was one of the few means that they could exploit to hang on to their identity as a people. Their laws had been formally buried in 1536 and their customs, as Higden had already observed in the fourteenth century, were approximating increasingly to those of the English. As to language, it was scarcely the badge of separateness and survival that it has become, for some, in the late twentieth century. So long as it cultivated an identifiable historical mythology, a people may still claim to be a people. Even the proponents of uniformity recognised that creating a unitary past was a prerequisite for creating a united kingdom. In the wake of the union of the crowns in 1603 Francis Bacon emphasised the need for 'this island of Great Britain, as it is now joined in monarchy for ages to come be so joined in history for times past, and ... *one* [my italics] just and complete History [be] compiled for both nations'. Unfortunately he spoilt the impact of such irenic notions, and let the cat out the bag, by referring to 'the worthiness of the history

---

[87] Edward Owen, ed., *A Catalogue of Manuscripts relating to Wales in the British Museum*, Cymmrodorion Record Series (1900–22), I, 72.

[88] Daniel Defoe, *A Tour through England and Wales (1724–6)* (Everyman edn, 1928), II, 54, 67–8.

of Britain ... and the partiality and obliquity of that of Scotland'.[89] Bacon's comment is not without contemporary relevance, as the furore over the National Curriculum in History suggests. The fact that England, Scotland, Wales and Northern Ireland have their own separate syllabuses in history suggests that it is the interpretation of the past that is one of the best guides to the sensitivities and aspirations of the present. It might also suggest that the concept of a people—hopelessly elusive and possibly illusory as it is, and lacking that documentary and archival solidity which are the prerequisites of modern academic historiography—is not one altogether unworthy of our attention as historians.

---

[89] Quoted in Jenny Wormald, 'The Creation of Britain: Multiple Kingdoms of Core and Colonies', *ante* 6th series, II (1992), 175–95 at 179.

THE LIMITS OF TOTALITARIANISM: GOD, STATE AND SOCIETY IN THE GDR[1]

By Mary Fulbrook

READ 26 JANUARY 1996

HISTORY is not an exact science. In describing and seeking to resurrect—or at least reconstruct—past societies, historians make use of concepts which bear a double freight of meaning. Unlike the elements, atoms and molecules of natural science, which—however much they are artefacts of the inquiring scientist's mind rather than natural 'givens' of the outside world—cannot answer back, the terms which historians use to describe the human world are themselves not only part of the way in which that past world was lived and experienced by the historical actors, but are also part of the way in which historians see, experience and act in their own social and political world. Historical concepts at any level of abstraction beyond the most basic and immediate empirical reference are also part of broader contemporary debates.

This is very clearly the case with the historiography of the GDR, which raises profound issues concerning the relationship of scholarly inquiry to political and moral values. Since the fall of the Wall and the opening of the riches of the East German archives, all attempts at understanding the character of the East German dictatorship have been accompanied by vehement and often very bitter controversies at a variety of levels. These debates have ranged from specific questions concerning alleged 'guilt' and 'responsibility' for maintaining or sustaining a dictatorship, as in the debates on former Stasi informers (IMs) or the evaluation of West German *Ostpolitik* in the 1970s, to the much more general level of whether history should, in principle, seek to be an objective, value-free form of inquiry.[2] The exploration of GDR

[1] Much of the research on which the substantive argument in this paper is based was supported by grants from the British Academy and the UCL Deans Fund, for which I am very grateful. A fuller account of my own overall interpretation of the GDR can be found in *Anatomy of a Dictatorship: Inside the GDR, 1949–1989* (Oxford, 1995). This paper attempts to deal with some of the broader theoretical issues raised in attempts to interpret and compare modern dictatorships, and was in part provoked by the reception of my book. I am grateful to my colleagues Judith Beniston, Stephanie Bird, Herbert Grieshop, Bill Larrett, Timothy McFarland and Martin Swales, for informal discussions which helped me clarify my ideas while writing this paper.

[2] Cf., for example, Jens Hacker, *Deutsche Irrtümer* (Berlin, 1992); Klaus Schroeder, ed., *Geschichte und Transformation des SED-Staates* (Berlin, 1994).

history raises to attention once again classical methodological debates over concept formation and ethical neutrality in history and social science which raged in Germany a century ago (and received explicit critical discussion in the work of Max Weber), and which again exploded in the neo-Marxist critiques of the late 1960s and 1970s, but which had fallen into a form of exhausted consensus in the more pragmatic empiricist mood of western academia in the 1980s.

This sea-change in atmosphere and evaluation is at its most obvious with the concept of 'totalitarianism'. In its heyday, the concept served the Cold War purpose of conflating dictatorships of the Right and the Left under a common global label: the Soviet Union under Stalin and Germany under Hitler could be equated and castigated with scholarly impunity. The ideological differences in the contents and aims of communism and Nazism could be designated as secondary and relatively unimportant, while the allegedly striking structural and organisational similarities in the two dictatorships were at the forefront of attention. What became most important was the contrast with pluralist democracy.

The political uses of such an approach in the Cold War era, particularly in West Germany in the 1950s and 1960s, were all too obvious. Conservative West Germans could seek to establish their newly found democratic credentials by hiding behind their long-standing hatred of communism: it took only a little mental sleight of hand for former Nazis or *Mitläufer* to produce a simple equation along the lines of 'I am anti-Communist = anti-totalitarian = anti-Nazi = democratic = good'. (One is tempted to throw into this equation somewhere, on Orwellian lines, something about 'four legs good, two legs bad'.) This legitimatory political function was soon subjected to vigorous critique by the more radical thinkers of the late 1960s, who sought to replace totalitarianism by notions such as 'fascism'. The more far-left of these radicals ended up in a similar form of conflation, although with rather different contents, seeing virtually any form of the (hidden or open) 'dictatorship of the bourgeoisie' under 'late monopoly capitalism' as essentially 'fascist'.

Once the dust had settled a little on the more extreme word-slinging of the late 1960s, a sober scholarly aftermath was characterised by an implicit agreement to drop the concept of totalitarianism from the centre stage of academic vocabulary. While still used for purposes of political castigation, it was deemed to be not very illuminating for academic and scholarly inquiry. In the more relaxed era of *Ostpolitik* and detente, only the apparently antediluvian Right would still refer to the notion of totalitarianism, while the majority of would-be 'objective' scholars groped for new concepts of understanding and comparison. The change in political climate correlated too with advances in academic historical research. More detailed empirical investigation into structures of power in the Third Reich, for example, revealed the essentially polycentric or polycratic, indeed chaotic, structures of power in the Nazi dictatorship. The more historians poked around in the entrails of Hitler's state, the more it appeared to be a multi-headed hydra rather than the streamlined beast portrayed in both Nazi propaganda and later political diatribe.[3] For most academic historians in the 1980s, the concept of totalitarianism appeared at best to be an outdated model of yesteryear, to be played around with as a straw man for demolition in undergraduate lectures but not to be used a serious tool of research. If anything, the career of this concept could confirm the view that history approached the natural sciences in making real advances, with paradigm changes providing radically new and better insights into the subject matter under analysis.

This comfortable emerging consensus was exploded with the changing climate after the historical watershed of 1989/90. Suddenly the notion of totalitarianism was back in fashion. As eastern Europe emerged from decades of dictatorship, so the political uses of a label of castigation became more relevant. Former victims of oppression were of course more than entitled to indulge in diatribe against their erstwhile oppressors. What is somewhat more surprising, however, is the speed with which the concept sped back to the centre stage of academic and scholarly debate. Contemporary history is perhaps more peculiarly politicised than most eras of history, although all periods have their recurring battles and peculiar lines of trench warfare. Nevertheless, for a theoretical concept which had been so thoroughly done to a thousand scholarly deaths over the previous two decades, this sudden resurrection in academic circles was little short of miraculous.

It is worth therefore explicitly reflecting on the concept, and the degree to which it is of genuine scholarly use. In this paper, I seek to analyse the 'limits of totalitarianism' in two senses: first, the extent to which the East German dictatorship was in any sense (yet to be defined) 'totalitarian'—i.e. the limits of any attempts at total control; and secondly, the extent to which the concept itself is useful as a tool of academic historical inquiry, irrespective of its political purposes. I shall pursue these questions with particular reference to God: the role of religion, and in particular of the Protestant churches, was both highly important and highly ambiguous in the historical dynamics of the stabilisation and destabilisation of the East German dictatorship. The Protestant church was both numerically the most important, and arguably politically the most significant, religious organisation in the

[3] For an excellent discussion of the state of debate, see Ian Kershaw, *The Nazi Dictatorship* (3rd edn, 1993).

GDR. But its political significance is highly ambiguous. The prominence of pastors and other Christians in the events of autumn 1989 have led the 'gentle revolution' to be dubbed, in some quarters, a 'Protestant revolution'. On the other hand, with the opening of the archives and the revelations of the Stasi informers at even the highest levels of the church, there was a rapid reaction in the other direction: the Protestant churches were accused of having—once again in German history— acted in a politically subservient, state-sustaining manner, subordinating freedom in the realm of the spirit to obedience in the world of power (*Macht* and *Geist*).[4] An exploration of relations between church, state and society in the GDR can help to illuminate the complex patterns of domination in the East German dictatorship. I shall finally return to the wider questions concerning the use of the concept of totalitarianism, and the issue of politics and value freedom in historical interpretation.

Towards operationalisation: the totalitarian project

In order to examine the usefulness of a concept, we have to know what it means. Clearly, if we use totalitarian not as a 'natural' category, with a taken-for-granted, 'common sense' meaning, but rather as an analytically constructed ideal type, then we can define it in a (limited) variety of ways.

The classical definition of totalitarianism by Friedrich and Brzezinski stressed six features: a single mass party, with a single ideology, exercising a monopoly of the use of force and of the news, with central control of the economy, backed up by the use of a secret police.[5] Obviously, if one operates with this list of features, the exercise becomes purely classificatory: did or did not any given regime possess all or most of these features? If the answer is yes, then one can engage in a little political diatribe: look at how different that regime is from the pure model of democracy/America/West Germany (or wherever). But it does not get one much further, unless one assumes that these features together explain the stability of the dictatorship—in which case it is very difficult to explain change, let alone ultimate collapse. As a list of

---

[4] Cf., for example, G. Besier, *Der SED-Staat und die Kirche* (Munich, 1993); Erhart Neubert, *Vergebung oder Weißwäscherei? Zur Aufarbeitung des Stasiproblems in den Kirchen* (Freiburg: Herder, 1993); G. Rein, *Die Protestantische Revolution 1987–1990* (Berlin, 1990); Ralf Georg Reuth, *IM 'Sekretär'. Die 'Gauck-Recherche' und die Dokumente zum 'Fall Stolpe'* (Frankfurt/Main and Berlin, 1992).

[5] Carl Friedrich and Zbigniew Brzezinski, *Totalitarian Dictatorship and Autocracy* (Cambridge, MA, 1956).

central characteristics, this definition simply highlights aspects of the political system without exploring the extent to which these features actually affected, or interacted with, 'society'.

Others have tried alternative definitions. Hannah Arendt in particular emphasised the moment of terror as a definitive feature of totalitarian regimes, combined with a high degree of mass popular support.[6] Recent writers have sought to render the concept more flexible in a variety of ways. Eckhard Jesse, for example, building on the work of Juan Linz, distinguishes 'totalitarian' dictatorships from both 'authoritarian' dictatorships and earlier autocratic states, seeing totalitarian dictatorships as 'post-democratic', as 'political systems which try to form citizens through ideology, to control them completely, and at the same time to mobilise them'.[7] This attempt at mass mobilisation and total control is obviously the 'modern' post-democratic aspect differentiating them from the autocratic states of early modern Europe. Sigrid Meuschel emphasises rather the attempts of totalitarian dictatorships to reduce the autonomy of separate spheres of society and economy, to excise the differentiation which is deemed to be a constituent element of 'modern' societies.[8] In this sense, too, the concept is used to emphasise some form of 'post-modernity'.

As Ralph Jessen has recently pointed out, depending on one's set of categories for operationalisation of the concept, one can come to very different conclusions.[9] If Hannah Arendt's emphasis on terror is taken to be the key feature, then clearly Hitler's Auschwitz and Stalin's Gulag outdid any deaths on the Wall, any Stasi deceit and subterfuge, however reprehensible, by a long way; any attempt to argue otherwise would, in Jessen's view, be to trivialise the atrocities of the mass murder of millions of people. Thus Nazi Germany and the Soviet Union under Stalin would have to be seen as more 'totalitarian' than the GDR. Similarly (as Jessen fails to point out) if general mass mobilisation and apparently spontaneous popular support is the key criterion, then the Third Reich would clearly score higher than the GDR. If, on the other hand, a centralised, streamlined political system is prioritised, as in the Friedrich and Brzezinski model, then the GDR would score as more 'totalitarian' than would the more chaotic political structures of the Third Reich.

Moreover, as some critics of the model of totalitarianism have pointed

[6] Hannah Arendt, *The Origins of Totalitarianism* (New York, 1951).

[7] Eckhard Jesse, 'War die DDR totalitär?', *Aus Politik und Zeitgeschichte*, B 40/94, 7 Oct. 1994, 12–23 at 15.

[8] Sigrid Meuschel, 'Überlegungen zu einer Herrschafts- und Gesellschaftsgeschichte der DDR', *Geschichte und Gesellschaft*, 19 (1993), 5–14.

[9] Ralph Jessen, 'DDR-Geschichte und Totalitarismustheorie' (unpublished MS, Feb. 1995).

out, it is an essentially static concept. It allows for little differentiation or change over time, but is, rather, a merely descriptive label, a preliminary means of categorising certain types of regime. Some supporters of the concept have regarded this criticism as less than devastating, however, suggesting that one can define phases in which a particular state was more or less totalitarian. Thus Eckhard Jesse, for example, distinguishes between the early, Stalinist phase of the GDR under Ulbricht, and the later, authoritarian phase under Honecker, the former period being deemed to be 'more totalitarian' than the latter.[10] Other analysts of the GDR have, however, employed totalitarian as a blanket term to denounce the East German dictatorship in its entirety, with little distinction between different phases. On this view, the apparent changes in the post-Ostpolitik period of detente reflect, not so much changes in reality, but rather politically coloured changes in the perceptions of western observers.[11] We shall return at some length to this interpretation below.

In a very interesting discussion of the usefulness of the concept as applied to Stalinist Russia and Hitler's Germany, Ian Kershaw has suggested that totalitarianism is less useful as a description or model of the *actual* relations between state and society than as an encapsulation of certain *aspirations* on the part of the leading party. As Kershaw points out, 'the totalitarianism concept always held that there were special features—unprecedented inroads into society through new techniques of mass mobilisation and new levels and types of repression—which distinguished it from other categories of modern dictatorship'.[12] In Kershaw's view, there are two key aspects to totalitarianism. First, there is the 'total claim' made by rulers on ruled: the regime seeks 'through a varied combination of manipulation and terror to homogenise and mobilise the population in the interests of revolutionary goals ... and [allows] no space for any alternative'; totalitarian regimes try 'to win soul as well as body'.[13] Secondly, totalitarian regimes replace ' "politics"—as a rationally expedient pursuit of limited goals—by ideological vision and unprecedented levels of state-sanctioned violence towards the societies they [rule]'.[14] Thus, on Kershaw's model, it is the project of

---

[10] Jesse 'War die DDR totalitär?'.

[11] As in the Schroeder/Staadt interpretation, discussed further below: see Klaus Schroeder and Jochen Staadt, 'Der diskrete Charme des Status Quo. DDR-Forschung in der Ära der Entspannunspolitik', in *Geschichte und Transformation des SED-Staates*, ed. Schroeder.

[12] Ian Kershaw, 'Totalitarianism Revisited: Nazism and Stalinism in Comparative Perspective', *Tel Aviver Jahrbuch für Deutsche Geschichte*, 23 (1994), 23–40 at 25.

[13] *Ibid.*, 32.

[14] *Ibid.*, 33.

the rulers, rather than the system of rulership, which should be at the heart of the analysis.[15]

At this point, one might be tempted to give up, and pronounce a plague on all their houses. Should one not simply enter a plea for a return to empiricism, pragmatism and all the alleged virtues of the legendary British anti-conceptualism? However, there are several reasons why this is a less than useful response—quite apart from the fact that in any event, even the most committed empiricists use, whether explicitly and consciously or otherwise, analytic concepts which are not 'empirical givens'. First, as mentioned at the outset, the concept of totalitarianism has attained such current popularity among certain academic circles that it must be addressed clearly and analytically, and not simply denounced as an outdated tool of political diatribe. Secondly, and perhaps more importantly, despite all the differences among the approaches briefly reviewed above, there are some common elements—and these common elements refer to something in the real world, for which historians are struggling to find an expression. The debate is, in short, about something real; it is about a particularly intrusive type of dictatorial modern politics that goes beyond what is implied by the concepts of autocracy and authoritarianism. And the very virulence of the controversies partly relates to the fact that many participants in these debates have a personal experience of some aspect of that reality which they are seeking to grasp and reconstruct in an abstract concept. We must therefore continue to take it seriously, but seek to address it from another tack.

For the purposes of this paper, I shall take the current model of totalitarianism prevalent among certain scholars with respect to the GDR, leaving aside the somewhat separate debates on the Soviet Union and the Third Reich. This currently prevalent model is in fact not a single definition of what does or does not constitute a totalitarian regime, but is rather an interlinked bundle of metatheoretical as well as empirical arguments which I shall seek to disaggregate and address separately.

The arguments have been developed explicitly, for example, in an influential attack on pre-1989 GDR research by Klaus Schroeder and Jochen Staadt; they have been expressed in a less conscious manner in general interpretations of the GDR, such as that by two prominent East German historians, Arnim Mitter and Stefan Wolle; and they have

---

[15] Nevertheless, Kershaw also sees the concept as in some sense describing the whole: he suggests that 'the concept of totalitarianism should be used to depict an unusual revolutionary, violent and transitional phase in the life of a regime' (*ibid.*, 40) or 'a dynamic, but transitional phase ... [which] can give way either to complete collapse, or to systematisation' (*ibid.*, 32). It is not entirely clear why this should be the case, unless one assumes that no party or leader can sustain an attempt at mass mobilisation for very long for some intrinsic reason which is not made explicit in the model.

been taken up polemically by British scholars such as Timothy Garton Ash.[16] For purposes of brevity, I shall call this general bundle the 'pro-totalitarian' school of thought, or 'pro-to' for short.

The package deal consists essentially of three major substantive and metatheoretical strands. First, as far as the substantive interpretation of the GDR itself is concerned, pro-tos criticise all GDR research which fails to prioritise the repressive and coercive elements of the political dictatorship. Implicit in this line of criticism are two assumptions: (a) that repression and coercion are key explanatory features which are central to understanding the history of the GDR throughout its forty years of existence; and (b) that apparent changes discerned by western scholars in the 1970s and 1980s are more a function of changes in western perceptions in the era of detente than of real changes in the political system itself. I shall deal with this point at some length in what follows. Secondly, pro-tos criticise what they call the *Immanenzansatz*, or the attempt to understand political systems and beliefs in the par-ticipants' own terms, rather than employing some external criteria of evaluation (*Fehlen von eigenen Bewertungsmaßstäben*). This is allegedly what led left-liberal scholars in the 1970s and 1980s to take at face value some of the East German regime's claims to be a different kind of industrial state, with different solutions to the problems of modern society, rather than continuing to denounce it as an illegitimate and repressive political system. And thirdly, pro-tos criticise the notion of value freedom in social and historical research, suggesting that pro-ponents of value freedom are simply employing it to camouflage their own values and prejudices. The precise position of the pro-tos on this is a little underdeveloped theoretically, but they imply that because research which claims to be value-free in fact tends to support a regime which pro-tos attack, then value freedom as such is neither possible nor desirable. The logic of this position would of course be that there is no empirical means of adjudicating between conflicting historical interpretations of the same phenomena, but the pro-tos do not actually draw this conclusion.

I shall address their three points in turn. I shall seek to argue a more differentiated and qualified case, with respect both to the general theoretical positions and the substantive interpretation of the GDR. I shall begin by assuming that the third point does not hold water, because I shall reconsider the history of the GDR in the light of

---

[16] See Schroeder and Staadt, 'Der diskrete Charme'; A. Mitter and S. Wolle, *Untergang auf Raten* (Berlin, 1993), and my comments on this in M. Fulbrook, 'Methodologische Überlegungen zu einer Gesellschaftsgeschichte der DDR', in *Die Grenzen der Diktatur*, ed. R. Jessen and R. Bessel (Vandenhoek and Ruprecht, 1996); T. Garton Ash's highly polemical and misjudged review of my book, *Anatomy of a Dictatorship*, in the *TLS*, 13 Oct. 1995, and my reply in *TLS*, 20 Oct. 1995.

empirical evidence, in order to provide what I believe to be a substantive account of the establishment, stabilisation and destabilisation of the dictatorship in terms which do not accord with the emphasis on repression in the pro-tos' view. I shall then return to the wider theoretical questions raised by the second and third points.

The substantive argument: plus ça change, plus c'est la même chose?

The main substantive argument advanced by the pro-tos is that the GDR was, and was throughout its history, totalitarian in the sense of being ultimately based on repression and force. Any attempt to argue otherwise is seen, essentially, as falling prey to SED propaganda or trying to present a rosier picture of conditions in the GDR in order to legitimise *Ostpolitik*.

There are, as indicated above, two parts to this argument. One is that the GDR's essential nature never really changed. All apparent changes are the product of successful SED propaganda and influence on western sympathisers and woolly-minded academics who were taken in by what the regime wanted to let them know, and overlooked or dismissed any evidence contrary to their own preconceptions. The other is that the key to explaining the stability and longevity of the GDR is repression and force. To suggest anything else is to engage in what the Germans call *Verharmlosung* or *Verschönerung*—rendering less vicious, more acceptable, and in the process assisting the SED in its project of effectively presenting itself as a wolf in sheep's clothing.

Despite the pro-tos' views on value freedom, this tenet is, I think, susceptible to empirical test. In what follows, I shall present a picture of the development of state and society in the GDR, with particular reference to the role of the churches and religious dissent, which would, I suggest, run counter to the pro-to picture.

Let me start this by suggesting that we can agree that the SED/communist state was characterised by a totalitarian project, in the sense of an *attempt* to gain total control over the minds and actions of the whole populace (as in Kershaw's definition). The ruling communist party in the GDR, the SED, certainly sought to extend its ideological and political control over the population. In this sense, it is legitimate to speak of an *aspiration towards total domination* in the GDR, and it is this project of *total penetration and mobilisation of society* which requires examination. We can then analyse the extent to which such a project is or is not successful: we can begin to explore the reasons for stability and instability over forty years, and can seek to delineate the rocks on which the aspiration founders.

There were essentially three phases to the history of the GDR, which seem to me rather different in terms of all manner of factors and parameters. The first is the period in which the structures of the dictatorship were being established and developed, from 1949 to the construction of the Berlin Wall in 1961. The Berlin Wall provides a convenient and striking end point for this period, but, arguably, other processes—such as patterns of social mobility and generational shifts— were in many respects equally significant in changing patterns of political orientation and behaviour in the ensuing years. The second is a phase of relative stabilisation, from the 1960s through to the mid-1970s; the end point here is nowhere nearly so clearly and simply demarcated, but a bundle of concurrent processes (economic, political, social, cultural, international) in the later 1970s presented serious challenges to the system, to which Honecker and his comrades in the SED leadership failed to develop adequate solutions in the course of the 1980s. This final phase is one of clear destabilisation, although the ultimate collapse in 1989 was precipitated by the changes in external circumstances in the Soviet bloc under Gorbachev. Let me consider aspects of relations between God—or at least his representatives on earth—state and society in each of these phases, to illuminate certain features of the patterns of domination and challenges to dictatorship in each phase.

God was a most formidable opponent for the totalitarian project. While Marxism-Leninism had only a few decades of political insti-tutionalisation, and was implanted into exceedingly unpromising soil in post-Nazi Germany, Christianity had nearly two thousand years of organisational and ideological experience on which to draw. The communists who flew into Germany from Moscow at the end of the war were a tiny minority of people supported by a military, occupying power, facing a largely hostile, defeated population, while the Protestant churches in the GDR counted around 15 million members (out of a total population of around 17 million) with around 1 million Catholics and, relatively speaking, mere handfuls of other religious groups. In the psychological aftermath of defeat, the Churches were an important locus of solace, comfort and meaning; moreover, given the resistance of certain Christians, they stood out as a symbol of some integrity and opposition to Nazi rule. On the other hand, the communists had the might of the Soviet military occupation behind them, and held the balance of real power in the emergent state. While processes of secularisation assisted them in their battles against Christianity, never-theless the power of religious faith should not be underestimated. The balance remained ambiguous throughout.

For all the twists and turns of the story, it was not a simple matter of outright, constant, visible repression. And in the subtleties of the story lie the seeds both of the interim successes and the ultimate failure of the totalitarian project. Religious belief, the 'sigh of the oppressed creature', the 'heart of a heartless world', in the event evinced a remarkable capacity to survive in the actually existing socialism of the GDR—but, ironically, as we shall see, its survival had quite a lot to do with the means which the state used to try to excise it. And—odd though it might seem to have to remind historians of this fact—there was a history to the GDR: things changed over nearly half a century.

Battles for the soul: God and the SED in the early period

The period from 1949 (or 1948) to 1961 was characterised by the most outward, visible repression in the GDR's history. It was also, curiously, the period during which the regime could least depend on its own repressive and even political forces. Ulbricht was wary of calling out the Kasernierte Volkspolizei in June 1953, for fear that his own armed police would simply join forces with the demonstrators.[17] The supposed political allies of the SED—the bloc parties and mass organisations— were often equally unreliable, as indeed were some SED functionaries themselves. The records are full of complaints about the unreliability of functionaries, their difficulties in maintaining the party line in face of criticisms from colleagues and workmates, their own 'Schwankungen' (hesitations, doubts) in the face of unpalatable policies or sudden changes in party line.

At the same time, the SED faced formidable problems with respect to the populace and popular attitudes. The June Uprising of 1953 indicated, despite its rapid suppression, the extent of widespread social and economic unrest, political hostility and downright opposition to the communist regime. Although most workers retreated into a form of grumbling, sullen resentment and conformity in the following years, many skilled young adults simply voted with their feet while the border was still permeable in Berlin: over 3 million people left the GDR for the West before 13 August 1961. The vast majority of those who stayed behind were predominantly concerned about their own material survival, and lived in a state of uncertainty about the future which, with the supposed benefit of hindsight, we may find it hard to imagine

[17] Cf. Torsten Diedrich, *Der 17. Juni 1953 in der DDR. Bewaffnete Gewalt gegen das Volk* (Berlin, 1991).

today. Rumours about another war, the movement of troops, startling changes in government, were rife, particularly in moments of heightened tension such as 1956. Moreover, the strength of pre-existing belief systems was still extremely powerful.

What then, specifically, of communist and Christian battles for the soul in this period? Communists in the Soviet Zone of Occupation after 1945 were quick to try to combat the transmission of Christian doctrine, although they were very much more circumspect with regard to the churches as institutions. The churches alone were exempt from what was euphemistically called land reform—the expropriation of estates over 100 hectares in size—and hence retained their property intact. They were also allowed to engage in their own denazification, which meant, effectively, that there was almost total continuity in church personnel. This did not, however, mean a completely homogeneous and united church; not only were the eight different regional churches rather different in theological and political character from each other, but within the regional churches there were often very bitter hostilities between those pro-Nazi Christians who had supported the *Deutsche Christen* and those who had opposed Hitler and belonged to the Confessing Church (*Bekennende Kirche*). The *Kirchenkampf* of Nazi Germany rumbled on in the late 1940s and 1950s. Moreover, a wide range of political opinions could be found among people who were united only by a common Christian faith. On the other hand, however, they were certainly not atheistic communists.

In the following years, a variety of strategies were deployed by the SED, in differing combinations and to differing degrees over time, to try to help along the predicted 'withering away' of religion under communism. First, there was the gradual and insidious removal of the means through which religious education, belief and practice could be propagated, combined with considerable pressures on individuals who continued to profess a Christian faith. In 1946, the Law for the Democratisation of Schools abolished denominational schools, and religious education in schools was made more difficult through time-tabling and other mechanisms. With the 'building of socialism', insidious undermining was complemented by outright battle. In the Cold War atmosphere of the 1950s, the churches were seen as the ultimate in fifth-columnism, outposts of the capitalist–imperialist west, 'supported financially, politically and ideologically by the western world', and committed to 'deadly enmity' against the GDR and all it stood for.[18] Many of the highest church functionaries were (allegedly) overpaid theologians and lawyers 'who had played a dishonourable role ... as

---

[18] Bundearchiv Potsdam, O-4 1918, 'Analyse der Kirchen-Hierarchie und ihrer Tätigkeit nach 1945', n.d., *c.* 1955, p. 6.

members of the Nazi party'[19] and had subsequently escaped denaz-ification. Doubly damned as former fascists and current agents of western imperialism, these church functionaries were pursuing 'the totalitarian project (*Anspruch*) of taking into their grip, penetrating and dominating every aspect of the life of their church members, in all matters whether great or small'.[20] (Clearly the SED was suffering from a degree of mirror image vision; and note that the term totalitarian is used in a perjorative sense, a point to which I shall return later.)

Given the extraordinary paranoid world view of the SED, it is hardly surprising that they now engaged in what was more or less perceived as a battle to the death, particularly with respect to the rising generation. Groups of Young Christians (the *Junge Gemeinde*) were accused of belonging to an illegal organisation, and, when this campaign had to be called off in the aftermath of the June Uprising of 1953, a new tactic was adopted to distinguish between the conformist sheep and the Christian goats. The introduction in 1954 of a secular state ceremony for young adolescents, the *Jungendweihe*, was a new form of pressure against young people who professed a religious faith. Initially, the church leadership mounted a vigorous battle against the *Jungendweihe*, denouncing it as incompatible with confirmation in church. Similar qualms were expressed by the church leadership with respect to the state youth organisation, the FDJ, the new statutes of which revealed it to be committed to a materialist world view. As Bishop Dibelius put it in a circular of August 1955 to all young Christians, to be read out by all pastors to their congregations, 'A person who is committed to God cannot at the same time support and profess this sort of world view.'[21]

Eventually, however, the church leadership had to give way. The church/state communique of 1958, accompanied by a subtle alteration in the text of the *Jugendweihe*, led to a calling off of the campaign in the following year. This softening of the church/state relationship was related to a visible distancing of the GDR churches from their West German brethren, who had been dubbed the 'NATO-church' following their agreement to provide ministry to the new West German army— and this distancing, or stiffening of attitude, was closely related to the state's pressures on, and infiltration of, the East German churches. It should however be noted that although the former battle was lost, and the church renounced its position of outright opposition to the *Jug-endweihe* and the FDJ, a more general pressure on young Christians

[19] *Ibid.*, p. 93.
[20] *Ibid.*, p. 6.
[21] Bundesarchiv Potsdam, O-4 1918, circular letter from Bishop Dibelius of 2/8/55, fol. 130.

continued throughout the existence of the GDR, making it very difficult for Christians to study for the *Abitur* (the academic school leaving exam, a prerequisite for university entrance) or to go on to study any subject other than theology at university.

This visible battle was complemented by a more insidious, invisible infiltration of the church. The concept of totalitarianism, with its stress (on whichever definition) on a combination of mass mobilisation, terror and repression, fails to capture the subtlety and ambiguity of the means which the SED used to attempt to disrupt, undermine and destroy organisations, families, even individuals, from within. As far as the church was concerned, the SED made a very well-informed and tactically astute series of attempts to sow discord where there was harmony (to adapt a famous phrase), and particularly to foment already existent differences of opinion among the different wings of the church— between the German Christians and adherents of the Confessing Church, for example. A great deal of attention was paid to examining the attitudes and past records of particular individuals, differentiating between those 'negatively minded' spirits who were determinedly pro-western, and those more regime-friendly or at least pliable types who might be harnessed to the state's cause. Groups of the latter, the potentially 'state-approving' (*staatsbejahende*) Christians were to be built up and links developed between these and state or SED bodies. The League of Pastors (*Pfarrerbund*) was one outcome of this; and so was something altogether more sinister.

The SED also sought to co-opt individuals in key positions into working for the State Security Police, more popularly known as the Stasi. Such work could range from rather limited informing to much more pro-active, strategic interventions in inner-church politics and procedures which vitally affected the character of the church and the major decisions it took in its relations with the state.[22] Thus, for example, it was possible to ensure through the work of a Stasi informant in the Thuringian church, Herr Lotz, that the successor to Bishop Mitzenheim of Thuringia was one Ingo Braechlein, himself a Stasi informant. The Thuringian church led the way in finding new forms of accommodation with the state, playing a role in the communique of 1958 and related amelioration of church/state relations, the rather forced 'Christian-Marxist' dialogues of the 1960s, and most, crucially, the decision to split from the West German churches in 1969 and form—finally—the League of Protestant Churches in the GDR. This Stasi infiltration was thus crucial to the transformation of the Protestant churches from outright opponents of the regime to, in their new guise,

---

[22] Cf., for example, G. Besier and S. Wolf, eds., *'Pfarrer, Christen und Katholiken'. Das Ministerium für Staatssicherheit der ehemaligen DDR und die Kirchen* (2nd edn, Neukirchen, 1992).

a relatively compliant if uncomfortable and subordinate partner by the early 1970s. In some senses, this transformation could be interpreted not so much as either indoctrination, or repression, of an alternative ideology, but rather as a form of somewhat incomplete and porous incorporation within actually existing socialism.

There were also, perhaps surprisingly, less insidious means of seeking to assist the withering away of Christianity in the GDR. Although the 1950s was the decade in which outright use of visible terror in the classic Stalinist sense was at its most evident, the SED at the grass roots could be very much less crass in its approach. Given all we have been told about the extent to which the Third Reich had succeeded in cutting away the luxurious undergrowth of German social and leisure organisations so typical of Imperial and Weimar Germany, it is remarkable how much self-organised activity persisted under the auspices of religious life in the GDR of the 1950s. Particularly in rural areas, there was a very real form of what may be described as 'civil society'—to dignify it with a theoretical term few contemporaries would have recognised. Yet, despite the relatively paranoid tone of most of the documents from the 1950s, it is quite surprising to find the SED recommending improved social offerings to young people, in order to entice them away from the social, cultural, musical, and even culinary offerings of the church (one pastor, who had told children that Russian soldiers did not go to heaven, allegedly enjoyed great popular support because he invited everyone home to coffee and cake).[23] Moreover, the local records are full of indications that even SED functionaries and (less surprisingly) functionaries of the affiliated parties, such as the self-professedly Christian CDU, were sympathetic to the religious beliefs and practices of their colleagues and neighbours. It is clear that the central policies of the SED could not always be translated easily into local practice. In the course of the 1950s and 1960s, the SED devoted a great deal of attention to building up its mass organisations and its functionary system of rule, in order to organise, control and effectively drench every aspect of social life and leisure time.

---

[23] SAPMO-BArch IV 2/5/322, report of SED Stadtleitung Plauen to the Central Committee of the SED, 30/1/56. Cf. also SAPMO-BArch, IV 2/5/322, letter of W. Barth to Genosse Kleinert, Abteilung Leitender Organe, 28/9/55.

From coercion to control and compliance: the 1960s and 1970s

The SED was in fact remarkably successful in organisational aspects of this strategy, although less so in relation to the relative attractiveness of the activities which were on offer. An opinion poll carried out by the Central Institute for Youth Research in 1969 revealed that only half the young people questioned were willing to say that they found the FDJ interesting—the obviously desired response which they should have given—while as many as a quarter admitted that they had attended only one or indeed no FDJ meetings in the previous six months.[24] What is striking in the records, however, is the way in which the functionaries of the parties, the state trade union and other mass organisations, themselves became more reliable, and the ways in which the system itself became established and ever more taken for granted. Particularly after the erection of the Berlin Wall in 1961, and aided by generational and social factors such as enhanced social mobility for the previously less privileged, and for willing political conformists and apparatchiks, the GDR became, to all outward appearances, a system capable of smoothly reproducing itself. The routinisation of the structures of the dictatorship correlated with increasing stability, and with patterns of grumbling conformity rather than political uncertainty and sporadic opposition.

At the same time, if we examine the other side of the equation—not so much state strategies and structures, as patterns of religious immunity and resistance (in the passive, 'medical' sense of *Resistenz*, adopted by Martin Broszat with respect to the Third Reich)—we find that God's strongholds were in what might be called the biologically and socially doomed sectors of the population. An analysis of religious faith and practice by a GDR sociologist in the late 1960s found that religious faith correlated directly with age: 41.6 per cent of those aged under 14 were without religious affiliation; in the 25–40 age group, it was 36.9 per cent; in the 50–5 age group, it was 26.8 per cent; and among the over-70s, it was a mere 13.5 per cent.[25] Similarly, religious faith was more resistant to withering away in the old communities of the countryside than in the growing urban areas, and there were strong correlations with 'declining' social classes: a third (33.7 per cent) of the

[24] SAPMO-BArch, A 2/2021/370, 'Kurzfassung über Probleme und Folgerungen zur Bewußtseinsentwicklung Jugendlicher in der DDR, die vom Zentralinistitut für Jugendforschung anläßlich der "Umfrage 69" vorgelegt wurden', p. 11.

[25] Bundearchiv Potsdam, O-4 459, 'Der Prozeß des Absterbens von Religion und Kirche in der DDR' (Feb. 1968), p. 9.

working class were without religious affiliation, compared to a mere 12.8 per cent of independent traders, 12.5 per cent of private artisans and 11.1 per cent of peasants. The working class was obviously at least fulfilling its historically progressive role with respect to religion, even if it continued to evince a degree of false consciousness concerning its enthusiasm (or otherwise) for actually existing socialism. But, as usual, the party would need to assist the scientific laws of history along a little: as Professor Klohr pointed out at the end of his analysis of declining religious affiliation in the GDR, many thousands of GDR citizens were still religious; and this 'demands ... our greatest mass-political interest and appropriate state measures'.[26]

Despite the growing political compliance of the church, it nevertheless fought to maintain its religious and spiritual presence, with some degree of success in certain respects. Uniquely among communist states, the introduction of military conscription in the GDR in 1962 was followed two years later by a decree permitting a form of alternative military service, without bearing arms, as 'construction soldiers' (*Bausoldaten*). Many young people with a pacifist conscience thus came under the wing of the church through the route of serving as *Bausoldaten*. The adoption by some churches of new forms of music and worship—such as the Jazz, Beat and Blues masses of the later 1960s—and church outreach work among 'asocial elements' of the population (dropouts, drug addicts) in the 1970s ensured that it maintained a vital social presence that would not die away so easily.

Moreover, in the post-*Ostpolitik* era of detente, following the churches' separation from the West German churches, the church was no longer seen as quite such a threat. There were different interpretations of the new situation. Bishop Schönherr's famous formulation of 1971—we want to be a church not against, not alongside, but *within* socialism—was sufficiently vague as to allow a range of modes of accommodation with the regime.[27] Although there were some Christians who objected to its political implications and chose to interpret it in a very narrow, almost purely geographical sense, there were others, particularly in a slightly younger generation of more pro-socialist Christians, who were prepared to see the GDR as the peculiar stamping ground in which they were to act in God's name. A generous interpretation of the controversial church functionary Manfred Stolpe, who has been the focus of intense controversy for his refusal to withdraw from political and public office in united Germany despite his undisputed and close contacts with the Stasi, for example, would tend towards this view.

---

[26] *Ibid.*, p. 11.
[27] For a rather hostile interpretation, cf., for example, Reinhard Steinlein, *Die gottlosen Jahre* (Berlin, 1993).

Just as the churches were changing, seeking new modes of survival and adaptation, so too was the state. The early Honecker period was characterised by an outward display of would-be toleration—the policy of no taboos in culture, the signing of the Helsinki agreement, and so on—and the official line at this time was that Marxists and Christians should walk 'hand-in-hand', united by common humanistic goals, working together to improve the human condition in the here and now, irrespective of where they thought they might be heading in any conceivable afterlife. The churches' valuable contribution to the East German welfare state—through hospitals, old people's homes, orphanages, work with the sick and disabled—was explicitly recognised and welcomed, as—less explicitly—were the hard currency contributions of the West German churches to certain projects dear to the state as well as the churches in the GDR.

How this form of state/church accommodation, or unequal partnership, should be evaluated within the concept of totalitarianism is hard to gauge. Despite such dramatic protests against the continuing lack of real freedom as the self-burning of Pastor Oskar Brüsewitz in 1976, this situation was hardly an instance of naked state repression of an alternative ideology. Nor was it a case of indoctrination; even though there was a high degree of Stasi infiltration, state coercion and subtle pulling of the strings, nevertheless the balance suggests that the church was pursuing relatively vigorously a committed policy of maintaining space for Christian faith and practice in a state committed to atheism. Outer compliance, if awkward and partial, combined with a limited scope for spiritual freedom, hardly amounts to mass mobilisation, indoctrination or repression through terror. The equation is a complex and quite ambiguous one. Moreover, it seems quite clear to me that the situation in the 1970s was qualitatively different from the more visible battles of the 1950s; this difference is present in reality, and not merely in the would-be objective eye of this observer.

The final phase

A number of interrelated developments suggest a progressive destabilisation from the later 1970s. The oil crises of 1973 and 1979 had effects throughout the industrial world, and the reverberations within the East German economy in terms of mounting indebtedness and environmental damage were visible in general contours, even if not in precise details. The Helsinki agreement had raised expectations among the population which the regime failed to fulfil. The western decision on nuclear missiles in 1979 and the Soviet invasion of Afghanistan heightened international tensions in a new mini-Cold War, fuelled by Reagan's powerful rhetoric in America and Kohl's new nationalism in West Germany. Within the GDR, Honecker's regime appeared ever more sclerotic, as he relied increasingly on a close circle of advisers and refused to recognise the signs of impending crisis; at lower levels of the political system, increasing frustration with Honecker's gerontocratic leadership was tempered by habits of iron party discipline and the decision to wait—as Egon Krenz famously put it—for a 'biological solution' to Honecker's leadership.[28]

As far as the role of the religion is concerned, the complexities and ambiguities proliferated with the church/state agreement of 6 March 1978. This has been variously interpreted as a major achievement for the church in securing a degree of official recognition and permitted space within communism, and a move towards a degree of limited pluralism by the now apparently more tolerant Honecker regime. It was, however, from the SED's point of view, intended as something rather more insidious: a form of *Gleichschaltung*. It is clear from the documents now available that the state perceived the agreement as a means of co-opting the church leadership as, effectively, the long arm of the state, a means of controlling the parts the party could not reach. Repeatedly, over the following years, state and SED officials reminded church leaders of 'the spirit of 6.3.78', and dropped heavy hints that the concessions granted to the church on that day could be endangered if activities within the church were allowed to get out of control in any way.[29] Although many dissident spirits within the church interpreted the agreement as enlarging their area of freedom to discuss and organise, for the next several years—at least until the mid-1980s—the church leadership was relatively dutiful in maintaining dissent within bounds and sustaining the awkward compromise in which it was caught. The church leaders had not quite sold their soul for a mess of pottage—rather, they thought they had bought the conditions in which they could preserve their soul, but at the expense of supping with the Devil (to mix a few metaphors).

This unstable compromise did not last for long, however, for a combination of reasons. First, the church leadership could not control its flock through the mechanisms of democratic centralism which the SED had mistakenly imputed to its new partner. Seeds were sown which grew in unexpected directions. Under the protection of the

[28] Quoted in Peter Przybylski, *Tatort Politbüro. Band 2: Honecker, Mittag und Schalk-Golodkowski* (Berlin, 1992), 74.

[29] For more detailed discussion, documentation and source references, see *Anatomy of a Dictatorship*, chs. 4 and 8.

church groups began to discuss issues concerning peace, the environment, human rights. In the early years, a growth of self-confidence and capacity to articulate alternative points of view was perhaps the most important outcome; by the mid-1980s, there were key organisational developments, such as the formation of national networks and the production of newsletters. There were also significant changes in the international situation, particularly after the accession of Gorbachev to power in the Soviet Union in 1985. The growing demand for reform within the GDR could appeal to Gorbachev in ways which were rather uncomfortable for the SED leadership. Finally, in the later 1980s the more unruly spirits within the church began to grow increasingly restive with the constraints imposed by a cautious church leadership, and, having been nurtured under its protective wing for several years, finally outgrew the dependence on their metaphorical step-parent. In some cases, such as that of a leading light in the unofficial women's peace initiatives of the 1980s and a founder member of New Forum in 1989, Bärbel Bohley, who was not herself a Christian, there was always a sense that one day dissent would free itself from the church. As she put it already in 1984, according to a Stasi report, ideally she would like 'to break with the "tutelage and regulation" of the church' but she had no idea 'whether and how an "independent women's group" outside the church could exist'.[30] In other cases, such as that of Vera Wollenberger, committed Christians had to go through a period of personal disillusionment before they could break free from obedience to the authorities above, as they did, for example, in the foundation of a 'Church from Below' (*Kirche von Unten*) in 1987.[31]

The agreement of March 1978 had appeared to the state to be the culminating victory in its policies regarding the church; but, in the event, it proved to be the beginning of the end. Despite the processes of secularisation which Professor Klohr had noted with some satisfaction a decade earlier, the church/state agreement lent the church a new political relevance in the GDR of the 1980s. In addition, earlier state policies had unintentionally produced a class of carriers of the new dissident currents: those who had refused to conform as children, but were determined to study, had ended up as theologians and pastors; others who had been fired from their jobs for political nonconformity had often only gained employment in some capacity with the church; *Bausoldaten* started to meet for annual reunions in the 1970s, and very soon formed a coherent group of alternative peace activists. Within the general penumbra of certain churches, where pastors were appropriately inclined, alternative cultural subcurrents began to grow, seeking new

---

[30] Ministerium für Staatssicherheit (MfS), ZAIG, Z 3396, No. 368/84, 27.9.84.
[31] Vera Wollenberger, *Virus der Heuchler: Innenansichten aus Stasi-Akten* (Berlin, 1992).

ways to live within, and change for the better, the actually existing socialism of the GDR.

Those participating in these new subcurrents were in some respects themselves products of the GDR. This was true generationally: the adherents of alternative peace and human rights initiatives, the environmentalists and activists of the new social movements of the 1980s, were young adults who had been born into or predominantly socialised within the GDR. It was true also structurally: such subcurrents could not have emerged—or their emergence is at least hard to understand—without the peculiar relations between church and state described above. These 'quasi-Christians' of the 1980s had little in common with the older members of those religious islands of immunity in the parishes of the 1950s described earlier. They also had very little in common with the kinds of spontaneous disaffection and political opposition expressed in the 1953 June Uprising, and, on a smaller scale, in numerous unofficial work stoppages, acts of sabotage and sporadic insubordination which occurred persistently throughout the history of the GDR. And it is true also in a much more specific and banal sense: many of the dissident grouplets of the 1980s had a high percentage of Stasi informers in their midst, swelling their numbers and often egging the groups on into ever more daring and risky acts of opposition. One of the major surprises after (and intermittently during) the *Wende* was the sheer number of Stasi informers who had played prominent roles in the dissident movements of the summer and autumn of 1989 (Ibrahim Boehme, Wolfgang Schnur, even Lothar de Maizière). But, leaving aside the Stasi infiltrators, the new nonconformists of the 1980s were very much the products of Ulbricht and Honecker. And they were the ones who spearheaded the demonstrations of 1989, with banners proclaiming, defiantly, 'We are staying here!' (*Wir bleiben hier!*). Unintentionally, the successful co-option of a compliant church by the state had begun to sow the seeds of its own internal destruction.

The reason the churches were so important in the growth of the dissenting movements of the 1980s had to do with a number of factors. The structural production of a dissenting class in the environs of the church was achieved slowly, unintentionally, over many years of segregating nonconformists and conformists through the *Jugendweihe*, alternative military service, and the like. The unique structural location accorded to the church by the agreement of 6 March 1978 then provided the key space for organisation and politicisation in the course of the altered circumstances of the 1980s. Had this not been the case, it is doubtful whether the oppositional eddies and currents concerned with peace, human rights, the environment, would have gained as much ground as they did in the following years. The GDR would still have collapsed, as its outer limits were removed with the loss of the

Iron Curtain in the late summer of 1989, but its inner implosion would, arguably, have been very much less peaceful. One cannot understand the 'gentle revolution' without reference to the fact that demonstrators started from churches, and that they practised a positive, active, stance of non-violence—a factor which was crucial to the eventual withdrawal of violent repression as a political option for the state.

The metatheoretical arguments: the *Immanenzansatz* and value freedom

Before considering the broader implications of this account for substantive interpretations of the GDR as a totalitarian state, let me return to the more general theoretical issues raised by the pro-totalitarian school. The 'package deal' introduced briefly above includes two metatheoretical riders.

The first is the critique of what the pro-tos call the *Immanenzansatz*, or, more specifically, the attempt to understand the East German political system within the participants' own terms rather than evaluating it from the standpoint of western democracy. The pro-tos claim that one should not take the SED's own assertions at face value, and that the deficiency of much pre-1989 research lay in the fact that western researchers were taken in by the regime's own propaganda. In a banal sense, this general line of argument has a point: all historical sources must of course be subjected to appropriate critical analysis, including references to the conditions of origin, the intentions of the producers of the sources and the target audience; to reproduce SED propaganda as though it were true would be to do bad history. But the pro-tos confuse bad practice with mistaken principles. They inflate this point to argue that one should not seek to enter into the world view, understand the ideology and mindset, of the historical protagonists, but rather that one should explicitly evaluate them from one's own external standpoint.

This is to confuse empathy with sympathy. As Max Weber pointed out in his conception of interpretive sociology, what distinguishes the explanation of human action from explanations in natural science is that one cannot understand human behaviour without understanding the meanings which actors attach to their actions; what is rational from one point of view may appear very non-rational from another. A Buddhist or a Hindu will have very different notions of how to lead the holy life than a medieval Catholic monk or a Reformation

Protestant—and these differences in belief will have vital consequences for their behaviour in and impact on this world.

To understand the GDR, we do have to understand the projects and beliefs of those living in it and seeking to establish and maintain, or to protect and defend, very different and often wholly opposing world views. There is no point whatsoever in applying the pro-tos' 'external measure of evaluation' (*Bewertungsmaßstab*) as a means of denunciation, if we want to explain what actually happened as the communists sought to achieve their goals. It is also, as I have sought to demonstrate, quite pointless remaining at the level of denouncing political repression if we want to understand the changing mechanisms thorough which the communists sought to achieve their goals—whether we accept the latter or not, and whether we accept their public documents at face value or not.

It may be noted that the pro-tos do not denounce any reference to Christian faith or democratic beliefs as failing to pass the *Immanenz* test. I have referred to God, even in the title of this paper, as though God exists as a real historical force; while many people may believe this to be true, probably many more (at least among western academic audiences) do not, and consider that God is a historical force only insofar as historical actors have strong religious beliefs on which they act. I see no reason whatsoever to bring in any 'external measures to evaluate' Christian faith, and, similarly, fail to understand why this should be applied to communism. We can and must take the actors' own beliefs at their face value in exploring their patterns of action and effects. In particular, we must look at the social and political bases, the patterns of organisation and the configurations of forces in order to understand communist attempts at domination and Christian patterns of resistance to these.

Related to the *Immanenzansatz* is the question of value freedom and objectivity. The pro-tos denounce the 'left-liberal' interpretations of the GDR as erecting a pretence of value-neutrality in order to camouflage their own left-wing sympathies and alleged blindness to the deformities of communism. It is pointed out that those West German scholars developing what they claimed were more differentiated analyses of the GDR during the 1970s tended to be sympathetic to the political aims of their paymasters, the Social–Liberal coalition government in Germany, and that their academic interpretations of changes in the GDR buttressed the SPD's concepts of *Ostpolitik*, detente and 'rapprochement through change'. On this interpretation, the claim to objectivity and 'value-freedom' was only a renunciation of criticism as far as communism was concerned, and actually acted in the SED's interests.

This is a subtle and nasty criticism. It again conflates two things: a general methodological point, and an instance of arguable bad practice. The general point—whether or not in principle it is possible for historians and social scientists to pursue research which is ethically neutral—is collapsed into a specific accusation that the findings of these left-liberal researchers were inaccurate and distorted because of their own political biases, rather than because of lack of sufficient empirical material in certain areas, or for other 'objective' reasons. It also presupposes that the picture which they drew of the GDR was in fact wrong, and that the totalitarian model with which the pro-tos seek to replace it is more accurate. This latter should, of course, be a point which is open to empirical adjudication rather than political mud-slinging, and I have sought to make some contribution to this empirical debate above. But the pro-tos allege that political preferences determine the section of those aspects of reality that are seen or dismissed as irrelevant.[32]

The limits of totalitarianism revisited

What conclusions may be drawn? It seems to me that this analysis of the GDR can lead to some rather clear conclusions, with respect both to the concept of totalitarianism and the broader questions raised by this debate.

The concept of totalitarianism has a limited degree of usefulness in (a) characterisation of a particular type of political project on the part of a ruling party and (b) denunciation of that project on the part of those who disagree with it for political and moral reasons. It does grasp a particular type of totalising aspiration on the part of a ruling party. But it is a perjorative term for denouncing that aspiration from a pluralist or democratic perspective. As a perjorative term—in a way which other analytic concepts are not, or at least not to such an extent—it must, I think, be queried from the standpoint of a would-be value-free historical science. This presupposes that there can be such a thing, a point to which I shall return in a moment.

The concept does not, however, have a useful role as an explanatory device. In order to explain the degrees of success of the totalitarian project, one cannot have reference solely to the elements of coercion, repression, indoctrination; one must consider both a wider range of

---

[32] Notably, they do not apply this kind of interpretation to their own substantive views of the GDR. One is led to wonder whether, in the pro-tos' view, value freedom may be possible on the right but not on the left of the spectrum?

mechanisms of domination, and take into account the structural contours and landscape of those seeking to resist this domination. A history of political repression alone explains nothing without an analysis of the penetration of society by the state, and a social history of patterns of partial accommodation, grumbling compliance, nonconformity, more active dissent and opposition. The complexities and ambiguities of these processes cannot be adequately captured by an essentially dichotomous approach in separating cleanly between repressive, totalitarian 'state' and innocent, oppressed 'society'.

Here too it is possible to reach some specific substantive conclusions. In particular, the totalitarian project of domination is more likely to meet its limits when there is a combination of a structurally permitted relatively autonomous institution with an alternative emotive, all-encompassing and powerful world view, capable of generating commitment and enthusiasm beyond any passing intellectual fashion. Religious faith—of many varieties—has proved itself across the centuries to be a much more powerful force than the secular theories of Marxism-Leninism would have given it credence (unless they are willing to concede that the conditions for the 'the sigh of an oppressed creature, the heart of a heartless world' continued to exist under actually existing socialism). Any attempt to eradicate this force from East German communism would have been better advised to have removed the institutional bases of religious practice at the outset, rather than to have tolerated and then tried to co-opt the churches—an attempt which rebounded dramatically in the events of 1989.

On the other hand, the failure to convince vast numbers of the population of the revolutionary ideals of Marxism-Leninism as interpreted by the SED was not a significant barrier to regime stability over the years. Popular discontent, so long as it remained fragmented, isolated, a private matter of grumbling, retreating into the private sphere (or to the West, should the opportunity arise) was not, while the Wall remained intact, a destablising force. Deep state penetration of social organisation and social behaviour, if not quite of the soul, was sufficient to ensure that, while the essential outer conditions obtained, the GDR was a dictatorship capable of routinisation and (increasingly sclerotic) adaptation and change.[33]

In examining the limits of totalitarianism in the GDR, it has become apparent that the primary emphasis on a combination of terror and

---

[33] Here, it should be noted, it is not sufficient to examine popular attitudes in isolation from the context of their expression. The behaviour to which these attitudes give rise is a product, not only of opinions, but of perceived opportunities and risks. Grumbling discontent is a quite different thing when leaving for the west implies—pre-1989—the chance of being shot on the Wall, or when it means—in summer/autumn 1989—being met with 100 DM 'greetings money', balloons and bananas.

indoctrination fails to capture some of the more subtle means by which the SED sought to achieve social and political control. In addition, the rather dualistic, top-down emphasis on state control of society obscures both some of the more interesting complexities of the patterns of partial penetration, and of the ways in which the SED's failure to achieve total penetration or real mass mobilisation did not necessarily entail destabilisation of the dictatorship. Quite the contrary: the regime was perhaps at its most stable when people were allowed to live as outwardly conformist, passively grumbling subjects. On the other hand, some apparent great successes had Achilles heels (or were Trojan horses, depending on what metaphor one prefers): the remarkably successful infiltration and co-option of the Protestant church actually accelerated the ultimate downfall of the SED.

To summarise this point: the concept of totalitarianism is too global to capture adequately changes in political strategies and balance over time. It lacks sufficient subtlety in exploring the variant means of domination. There is a failure to appreciate the importance of different aspects of political organisation and political structure for stabilisation and change in a dictatorial regime. The primary focus on ideology and repression misses the crucial importance of *Anpassung*, grumbling conformity and the isolation of dissent, as key aspects tending towards political stability despite lack of commitment, as well as failing to explore the conditions for the organisation of alternative movements which can mount effective challenges to the regime under particular conditions. In short, an analysis of the SED's relations with the Protestant churches illustrates, not only the limits of the totalitarian project, but also of the concept of totalitarianism as a means of understanding the political dynamics of the East German dictatorship.

There are two possible more general conclusions with respect to the concept of totalitarianism to be drawn from this. One is that the concept of totalitarianism be allowed to stand as a plausible concept for describing 'somewhere else' (be it Stalin's Russia or Hitler's Germany), and that the GDR simply does not constitute an instance of it. On this view, Hitler's Germany and Stalin's Soviet Union may remain the only two historically existent cases—granted that one accepts the applicability of the concept to these two cases, which is itself not uncontentious. The second possible conclusion is that the concept should be jettisoned as being, even in its most restricted form, fruitful only in the sense that hitting your head against a wall for long enough will begin to reveal some of the features of that wall, but possibly at the expense of the contours of your head. Whichever of these conclusions one adopts, I would argue that totalitarianism is in any event an inappropriate concept for understanding GDR politics and society.

The question then remains: how is the GDR best characterised, and can this characterisation be done at a sufficient level of abstraction as to include other cases of comparable political types? We need a more specific, qualified concept with respect to the type of dictatorial regime we are concerned with here. In contrast to the Third Reich, the GDR was not an instance of charismatic domination: neither Ulbricht nor Honecker had either the personal qualities, or the structural position, of Adolf Hitler. Nor was it a rational-legal system of domination, to continue with Max Weber's typology: the arbitrary and politicised character of important aspects of the GDR's legal system should not be dignified with this term. And it clearly was not a form of traditional authority. But it was certainly bureaucratic.[34]

In pursuing this question, we should perhaps reflect for a moment on the need for a system of classification. I think we need to distinguish between two different levels at which concepts are needed. There is the broader level determining the selection of cases for comparison and contrast, without suggesting that, by the use of a blanket term, they are in some essential way identical. Thus we could as easily select cases for comparison in terms of being (for example) instances of communist states, or advanced industrial states, or modern dictatorships, or post-communist states—or whatever. Similarly, we can choose comparable periods of transitions—or failed transition—under different rubrics (transitions to dictatorship, transitions to democracy, successful and failed revolutions, and so on). We need concepts at this level of abstraction in order to group together similar beasts and distinguish those belonging to one type from others. But the way in which this is done will depend on the questions informing the inquiry. Thus we could as easily compare 'German dictatorships' (Third Reich and GDR), or 'communist dictatorships' (Soviet Union and its satellite states, other communist states) as we could the divergent developments of dictatorial East and democratic West Germany.[35] Unlike animal and plant species, or the chemical elements and compounds of the natural world, there simply are no clearly bounded lines for classification of the social and political world. (One cannot, for example, test which

---

[34] I have elsewhere, not entirely flippantly, sought to develop the 'Octopus theory' of the GDR, using the analogy of an octopus seeking to extend its tentacles into every last aspect of society, developing a remarkable, but never quite complete, degree of penetration of 'society' by 'state': see M. Fulbrook, 'Reckoning with the Past: Heroes, Victims and Villains in GDR History,' in *Rewriting the German Past*, ed. P. Monteath and R. Alter (New York, 1997). It would however have to be an octopus with permeable membranes, or perhaps an ink-spraying squid, to capture the real impact of state on society in what Jürgen Kocka has aptly termed a 'durchherrschte Gesellschaft': H. Kaelble, J. Kocka and H. Zwahr, eds., *Sozialgeschichte der DDR* (Stuttgart, 1994).

[35] This might appear to be belabouring the obvious, but in certain quarters recently there have been noises to the effect that the latter form of comparison is in some way politically illicit; cf., for example, Garton Ash, *TLS*, 13 Oct. 1995.

societies would or would not produce fertile offspring, if mated, in order to determine genus and species.)

But there is a second level for more differentiated comparison within any set of cases. These more partial concepts will have to do with factors such as dissent, opposition, forms of accommodation—and here already a very good analytic vocabulary is being developed with respect to the Third Reich, which can fruitfully be transposed to discussions of the GDR, as well as employed in comparative analyses of modes of response and resistance in modern dictatorships.

I have argued above that the project of the rulers in the GDR was a great deal more sophisticated and complex than the concept of totalitarianism will allow; their strategies of domination were complex and ambiguous; the limits of the attempt at total control illuminate the limits of the concept itself. I would suggest that the emotional rights of erstwhile victims to denounce the repressions of the regime be respected, while historians remain within a more complex framework of partial analytical concepts, seeking to do more justice to the complexities and ambiguities of reality—whatever their personal views and sympathies with respect to the range of historical actors in the regimes they observe.

BRITISH POLITENESS AND THE PROGRESS OF WESTERN MANNERS: AN EIGHTEENTH-CENTURY ENIGMA

By Paul Langford

READ 23 FEBRUARY 1996 AT THE UNIVERSITY OF WALES SWANSEA

IN March 1802, the peace treaty of Amiens was signed, resulting in a two-way flow of travellers across the English Channel. Among those arriving at Dover was Joseph Fiévée, printer by trade, *littérateur* by vocation, and latterly politican by profession. It is said that he was commissioned by Bonaparte himself to report on affairs in London. In any event, his findings were published in the *Mercure* and reprinted in a work whose title, *Lettres sur l'Angleterre, et réflexions sur la philosophie du XVIIIe siècle*, challenged comparison with the most famous of French commentaries on England, that of Voltaire. It reads as polemic rather than analysis, confronting what Fiévée took to be serious errors made by his countrymen when they wrote about Britain. But little of the book was what one might expect of such a work. Fiévée was not primarily interested in British politics, law and government, but in the character and manners of the people. His conclusions may be summed up in one of his many generalizations. 'If civilization ... is the art of rendering society pleasing, agreeable and congenial, the English constitute the least civilised nation of Europe.'[1]

We may not want to attach weight to such judgements. Fiévée was a Jacobin turned Royalist turned Bonapartist who was later to become a violent Ultra and in his declining years a constitutional monarchist. His *Lettres sur l'Angleterre* plainly formed part of the First Consul's propaganda campaign, attacking at once the licence of the ancien régime and the degeneracy of the national enemy. None the less, Fiévée's strategy, blaming the *philosophes* for selecting Britain as a model of progress, retains a certain interest. So does his belief that the conclusive proof lay in the realm of what he called 'civilization'.

It was true that Britain had been regarded as something of a model, and not merely in terms of the transitory fashions and tastes that appealed to an increasingly cosmopolitan market of polite consumers.[2]

---

[1] (Paris, 1802), 193.
[2] Anglomania has a considerable historical literature; see Jacques Gury, 'Une excentricité

The reasons for this are not hard to find. Britain's success as a commercial and military power made it the outstanding example of a society that seemed to have translated economic potential into strategic muscle. Moreover its peculiar form of government, Montesquieu's republic hidden beneath monarchy, transformed the reputation of a country formerly known for its political instability. And not least there was that tradition of intellectual innovation celebrated by Continental admirers of Newton and Locke, making it what the German economist Philipp Nemnich hailed as 'most enlightened Nation in the Commercial World'.[3]

Politeness or as Fiévée called it civilization (the two were then synonyms in French[4]) would not appear to provide the obvious testing bench for these achievements. But there was a logic to his reasoning, even if it requires careful definition of what constituted politeness to make sense. Today, politeness is a subject of much interest, linking a number of fashionable themes, including the transition from a discourse of civic virtue to one of benevolent sensibility, and the emergence of that trans-national public sphere which has turned historians of politics into students of political culture. But politeness covers a multitude of meanings. In one it figures primarily in the history of ideas, a complex of values that expressed the eighteenth-century's faith in the altruism of human beings liberated from irrational beliefs. This is the politeness of Shaftesbury, or of Hume.[5] It is politeness at its most fundamental. At the opposite extreme is politeness at its most superficial, a code of conduct that regulated social behaviour from the way to make a bow to the proper manner of holding a tea-cup. Politeness in this sense was often described by the obsolescent term civility; later it was to be labelled etiquette. It is the concern of the conduct manuals and numerous other writings, sacred and profane.[6]

à l'anglaise: l'anglomanie' in *L'excentricité en Grande-Bretagne au 18e siècle*, ed., Michèle Plaisant, (Lille, 1976), 189–211; Josephine Grieder, *Anglomania in France 1740–1789: Fact, Fiction, and Political Discourse* (Geneva, 1985); Claude Nordmann, 'Anglomanie et anglophobie en France au xviiie siècle', *Revue du Nord*, 66 (1984), 787–803; Frances Acomb, *Anglophobia in France, 1763–1789: An Essay in the History of Constitutionalism and Nationalism* (Durham, NC, 1950); Michael Maurer, *Aufklärung und Anglophilie in Deutschland* (Göttingen, 1987); A. G. Cross, *'By the Banks of the Thames': Russians in Eighteenth Century Britain* (Newtonville, MA, 1980).

[3] Philipp Andrew Nemnich, *An Universal Dictionary of Merchandise* (1799), preface.

[4] Peter France, *Politeness and its Discontents: Problems in French Classical Culture* (Cambridge, 1992), 2, 54ff.

[5] Larry Klein, *Shaftesbury and the Culture of Politeness* (Cambridge, 1984); N. Phillipson, *Hume* (1989).

[6] Two accounts spanning the period are Fenela Ann Childs, 'Prescriptions for Manners in English Courtesy Literature, 1690–1760, and their Social Implications', (DPhil thesis, Oxford University, 1984), and Marjorie Morgan, *Manners, Morals and Class in England, 1774–1858* (1994).

There is, however, a third area of meaning, linking these two, located within what contemporaries called manners in English, *moeurs* in French, *Sitten* in German, by which they meant social customs as they reflected the character of distinct cultures. In the travel literature of the late eighteenth century and early nineteenth century especially, this pre-occupation made for interesting empirical comparisons. Tourists of Fiévée's generation had been brought up to see themselves as philosophic travellers, students of history as revealed by the facts of contemporary life, every man, and many women, their own Montesquieu.

How did such self-appointed experts approach British manners? From the mid-eighteenth century at least, with high hopes. Former generations had regarded the British as latecomers in the history of European civility and landed at Dover expecting what the German Uffenbach called a 'general lack of courtesy'.[7] Even well-disposed commentators felt there was much to apologise for. Thus Prévost, in the preface to his translation of Grandison, explained the changes he had felt it necessary to make:

I have suppressed or reduced to the common usages of Europe, whatever in the manners of England might be shocking to other nations. It has seemed to me that those traces of the ancient British grossness, to which only the force of habit can still blind the English, would dishonor a book in which politeness must go hand in hand with nobleness and virtue.[8]

But as Prévost's language implied, perspectives were changing even in his time. Barbarians might have a contribution to make to a modern civility. Politeness as defined by its eighteenth-century proponents was supposed to move away from the court-based culture of Louis XIV's France and adopt a more open, even more egalitarian tone.[9] Moreover if the successes of Britain had been correctly described, they were precisely those that might be expected to give rise to progressive forms of social interaction. It was an axiom of the philosophers and conjectural historians that commerce, making the British what John Millar called 'an active and polished people', brought in its wake a superior sociability.[10] So did the famed liberty of Britons. 'A free people', it was said, 'are a social people, fond of friendly intercourse. Cheerful converse and unreserved communication of sentiment soften the nature, refine the

---

[7] *Oxford in 1710 from the Travels of Zacharias Conrad von Uffenbach*, ed. W. H. Quarrell and W. J. C. Quarrell (Oxford, 1928), 10.

[8] R. Cru, *Diderot as a Disciple of English Thought* (New York, 1913), 339–40.

[9] See Daniel Gordon, *Citizens without Sovereignty: Equality and Sociability in French Thought, 1670–1789* (Princeton, 1994).

[10] *An Historical View of the English Government, from the Settlement of the Saxons in Britain to the Revolution in 1688* (4 vols., 1803), IV, 249.

manners, expand the heart, and enlarge the understanding. Freedom of speaking and acting is the source of civilization.'[11] Gothic liberty in this sense was an opportunity not a disqualification, and as Archenholz put it 'no polished nation was ever so free as the English are at this day'.[12]

Within Britain itself there was lively debate about the way that liberty might promote a distinctive code of manners, especially from mid-century. George III's favourite bishop, Richard Hurd, explicitly challenged the superiority of the Continent in his *Dialogue concerning the Uses of Foreign Travel* of 1764, accusing the most celebrated of English authorities on taste and manners, the third earl of Shaftesbury, of capitulating to cosmopolitan courtliness. Hurd offered by way of correction a patriotic version of politeness.

'The manners of each state are peculiar to itself, and best adapted to it. The civility, that prevails in some places on the Continent, may be more studied and exquisite than our's, but not therefore to be preferred before it. Those refinements have had their birth from correspondent policies; to which they are well suited, and from which they receive their whole value ... We have a country to embrace, not a court to adore.'[13]

This became a common theme thereafter, articulated for example in a manifesto for the new-model gentleman written by Thomas Macdonald: *Thoughts on the Public Duties of Private Life*. Macdonald admitted that the gentleman was not an English invention, but as he put it, 'there are circumstances in the manners, situation, and government of Great Britain which are peculiarly favourable to its perfect and complete formation'. The result was the definitive model for modern civility, combining 'temperate and well-ordered freedom', 'independence of person and equality of right'.[14]

Foreigners may not have read Hurd and Macdonald but they did have a growing familiarity with English literature. It is paradoxical that at a time when the social and intellectual elites of Continental Europe were drenched in French culture, so much of what they read had originally been published in English. Moreover much of that, especially from the pen of novelists who 'made all Europe weep or smile', was the literature of manners.[15] Foreigners often came to Britain with a pre-formed picture of English life drawn from this source. Fanny Burney's

---

[11] W. Eton, *A Survey of the Turkish Empire* (1798), 245.
[12] *A Picture of England* (2 vols., 1789), I, 9.
[13] 35, 159.
[14] (1795), 31–2.
[15] Robert Mattlé, *Lamartine voyageur* (Paris, 1936), 285.

novels were described by a German enthusiast as a 'History of National Manners in themselves.'[16] The Italian Agosto Bozzi thought he had collected from Smollett and Fielding 'not only vast stores of English words and colloquial expressions, but of English manners and peculiarities, the knowledge of which converted me almost into an Englishman at once'.[17] Considering that Bozzi did not arrive in England until half a century after the time of Smollett and Fielding, this says something about the pace of change among Englishmen, or at least among the naval officers who constituted most of his early acquaintance. At any rate others went further still, attributing to the English language as well as literature, a peculiar capacity for social improvement. The Swede Geijer noted that no other language had so many words for nuances of feeling and character. 'Therefore it is that English politeness is in so many respects a true politeness.'[18]

It has to be said that these experiences were not the common one. English literature may have enriched the mental world of many who came to Britain, but few of them found what they had been led to expect. Steele had boasted that the English genius was for 'Free, Open and Unreserv'd' manners,[19] and the standard claim of many after him was that this resulted in a certain 'rough civility'. Unfortunately it seemed to outsiders to have more of roughness than civility about it. The Russian Karamzin observed in the 1790s: 'To live here for the enjoyment of social life would be like seeking flowers in a sandy desert. All the foreigners in London with whom I have become acquainted and talked agree with me.'[20] Travel literature is itself, of course, a problematic source, and at best we are in a world of perceptions. But the place of British politeness in eighteenth-century Europe was precisely a matter of perception, and in the following century, as travellers sought to relate it to the changing values of their own time, it retained its perceived importance. This is a rich subject and I do not pretend to do more than select three themes that seem to have significance. They are the means by which social life was regulated, the degree of openness that it permitted and the hierarchies that it engendered.

Foreigners looked first for the supposed liberty that characterised every kind of activity in Britain. The stereotype was of freedom-loving egotists whose social life like their politics resisted dictatation and even direction. For Anglomaniacs it was the freedom of English mores that was so attractive, especially when, for example in matters of dress and

[16] C. A. G. Goede, *The Stranger in England; Travels in Great Britain* (3 vols., 1807), II, 148.

[17] P. B. Granville, ed., *Autobiography of A. B. Granville* (2 vols., 1874), I, 273.

[18] Erik Gustaf Geijer, *Impressions of England 1809–10*, intr. Anton Blanck (1932), 154.

[19] *The Correspondence of Richard Steele*, ed. Rae Blanchard (Oxford, 1941), 445.

[20] *Letters of a Russian Traveller 1789–1790*, trans. and abridged by Florence Jones (New York, 1957), 335.

deportment, it took a form that could be imitated without recourse to government. The famous frock coat, adapted to every occasion and permitting freedom of movement whether on foot or on horseback, was seen as an emblem of the British constitution.[21] Other commonly cited examples were the right to wear one's hat where one wished, perfunctory forms of acknowledgement, which avoided the implied deference of a courtly bow, and the familiarity of the handshake. All were considered signs of a society dedicated to equality and mutual self-respect.[22]

Liberty implied acting naturally and lack of ceremony might be considered synonymous with Englishness, as the Swiss Zimmermann argued in an influential tract of 1759.[23] The tendency was to assume a simple correlation between concentration of power and elaborate protocol on the one hand, and the diffusion of power and easy-going manners on the other. The crippling etiquette of Spanish and German courts could be contrasted with the informality that reigned in English high society, even at the court of St James itself. Foreigners were impressed by the visibility of English royalty, which sometimes approached what we might call Scandinavian levels. George II is not thought of as a popular monarch, yet tourists observed him and his queen walking among the crowds in the Mall with only half-a-dozen yeomen of the guard to attend them.[24] In the next reign Georg Lichtenberg was still more startled at Kew to see spectators at a boxing bout completely ignoring George III and Queen Charlotte when the royal phaeton drove among them.[25] It was tempting to conclude that this was the way of the future. By the 1780s, as Continental monarchies recognised the advantages of a less stifling formality, they were thought of as adopting the English model. When Mirabeau found at Brunswick a German palace shorn of etiquette, he attributed it to the duchess of Brunswick who, he noted, was 'wholly English, as well in her inclinations and her principles as in her manners'.[26] Generally shifts in manners

---

[21] Nora Waugh, *The Cut of Men's Clothes, 1600–1900* (1964), 105.

[22] Louis Simond, *Journal of a Tour and Residence in Great Britain, during the Years 1810 and 1811, by a French Traveller* (2 vols., Edinburgh, 1815), I, 21; Edouard de Melfort, *Impressions of England* (2 vols., 1836), II, 204; Joan Wildeblood and Peter Brinson, *Polite World: A Guide to English Manners and Deportment from the Thirteenth to the Nineteenth Century* (London, 1965), chap. 10, where less formal fashions are treated as characteristic of the nineteenth century, though all of them had been practised in some degree in the eighteenth.

[23] J. G. Zimmermann, *Essay on National Pride*, trans. Samuel Hull Wilcocke (1797), 78–9. See also John Alexander Kelly, *England and the Englishman in German Literature of the Eighteenth Century* (New York, 1921), 61.

[24] *The Memoirs of Charles-Lewis, Baron de Pollnitz* (2nd edn, 2 vols., 1739), II, 436.

[25] *Lichtenberg in England*, ed. Hans Ludwig Gumbert (2 vols., Wiesbaden, 1977), I, 309.

[26] *Histoire secrète de la cour de Berlin* (2 vols., Alençon, 1789), I, 251.

were attributed to the infectious nature of trade-borne liberty. Visitors to Hanover often reported the improvement that resulted from contact with the British.[27]

Of course, not everyone was impressed by English freedom of manners. The Flemish patrician the Prince de Ligne called it the liberty to have a piss at dessert.[28] Polite Frenchmen of the old school criticised their countrymen for adopting the 'mannières grossières' of a barbarous nation.[29] There were also less biased objections, many of them from Germans who admired the English but were taken aback by their manners. Lack of ceremony could look like inhospitality and inattentiveness, as the Anglophile Heinrich Watzdorf regretfully concluded.[30]

But more interesting than these reservations is the challenge to widely held assumptions. Many visitors did not find life in Britain at all what they expected it to be. Abroad British Grand Tourists seemed idiosyncratic in dress, bearing, manner. At home they appeared highly conformist. In any public place one blue or blackcoated gentleman looked and behaved much like another. Nor was the lack of ceremony indisputable. Johanna Schopenhauer, who learned to venerate all things British from expatriate families in Danzig in the 1780s, including what she called 'greater freedom in company, without transgressing any of the rules of good behaviour', soon found in Britain itself that its inhabitants were far from unceremonious. This seemed to her an etiquette-ridden nation, seeking routine and ritual in private and in public.[31] Her experience was primarily of middle-class life but others who moved in higher circles were also surprised by the artifice they found there. The English derided the formality of court life in European capitals, yet foreigners found West End life almost as rule-bound. Friedrich von Gentz, who certainly knew his diplomatic protocol, described the practice of everyday visiting in London as a kind of state affair.[32] His contemporary the French printer Crapelet considered a London visit much more severe in point of etiquette and ceremonial than one in Paris. The very terminology of English politeness seemed

[27] John Moore, *A View of Society and Manners in France, Switzerland, and Germany* (2 vols., 1779), II, 91.

[28] *Mémoires, lettres et pensées*, préface de Chantal Thomas (Paris, 1989), 632.

[29] Alfred Franklin, *La civilité, l'étiquette, la mode, le bon ton du XIIIe au XIXe siècle* (Paris, 1908), 148–9.

[30] *Briefe zur Characteristik von England gohörig; geschrieben auf einer Reise im Jahre 1784 von Heinrich von Watzdorf* (Leipzig, 1786), 156.

[31] Johanna Schopenhauer, *Reise durch England und Schottland* (2 vols., Leipzig, 1818), II, 16–17.

[32] Friedrich von Gentz, *Briefe von und an Friedrich von Gentz*, ed. Friedrich Karl Wittiche (3 vols., Munich and Berlin, 1909–13), II, 392.

bizarre. Where else would one 'pay' someone a visit as if it were the settling of a debt or the purchasing of a service?[33]

A feature of the system was the extent to which these rules were unspoken yet none the less binding. The Baronness Riedesel, in London during the War of American Independence, was used to the routine of court life in a petty German state and found London confusing, as she learned to distinguish between the outer framework of regulation constituted by visiting cards, at homes, routs, and so on, and the inner core of informal codes that determined who was acceptable where.[34] It was easy to fall foul of a system which like the British Constitution itself was unwritten yet intimidatingly authoritative. One subject that features frequently in the accounts of visitors to London was the seemingly trivial yet evidently perplexing matter of door-knocking, something that did not feature in conduct manuals. Servants were trained to respond to a hierarchy that extended from the single and almost silent touch of a milkman to the five deafening onslaughts of a duke or his footman. Foreigners initially adopted a hesitant, deferential approach which brought humiliation at the hands of servants. In due course the practice found its way to other cities, reminding visitors that learning to knock like a gentleman was an essential art in Britain.[35]

A further concern was the hypocrisy that afflicted English life. With so much attention to the 'convenances', the conventions of society, the penalty for nonconformity was high. 'The terrible interdiction of the popes, in the Middle Ages, is scarcely more to be feared than the anathema of the beau monde in England' it was reported.[36] Forms of social exclusion ranged from the 'cut', an expression that gained currency in the 1770s, to the excommunication imposed by the great hostesses in alliance. With such penalties the likelihood of deceitful trangression was very high. The kind of hypocrisy that resulted was of concern to moral reformers at home as well as visitors from abroad. A manservant could be dismissed for refusing to tell the direct lie that 'the London custom, of denying one's self' required when his mistress chose not to be at home.[37] A maidservant's sexual peccadillos would certainly not be tolerated for the sake of politeness, yet, as was remarked, 'an adulterous intercourse in low life is an unfortunate partiality in high

[33] Crapelet, *Souvenirs de Londres en 1814 et 1816* (Paris, 1817), 44.

[34] *Baroness von Riedesel and the American Revolution: Journal and Correspondence of a Tour of Duty 1776–1783*, revised trans. Marvin L. Brown, jr (Chapel Hill, 1965), 10ff.

[35] Léon de Buzonnière, *Le touriste écossais, ou itinéraire général de l'Écosse, ouvrage indispensable au voyageur* (Paris, 1830), 32.

[36] Prosper Mérimée, *Etudes Anglo-Américaines*, ed. Georges Connes (Paris, 1930), 1–2.

[37] C. Jenner, *The Placid Man: Or, Memoirs of Sir Charles Beville* (2nd edn, 2 vols., 1773), II, 142.

life'.[38] Considering that candour and sincerity were boasts of the British and considering too their horror at what they took to be Continental forms of hypocrisy such as the French masquerade or the Italian cicisbeo, these criticisms were damaging.

Another concern was the power conferred on individuals. At Almack's, the most celebrated of all London assemblies between the 1760s and the 1830s, this was exercised by a group of women whose word was law. It was described by Marianne Spencer-Stanhope in her novel of the same name.

> Almack's is a system of tyranny which would never be submitted to in any country but one of such complete freedom that people are at liberty to make fools of themselves. No government would ever have had the effrontery to suppose that people would, on their knees, crave permission to pay their money to a junto, self-elected, whose power exists but by courtesy; who make laws, and enforce them too, without any sort of right.[39]

In the resorts another kind of arbitrary power could be encountered. Visitors came to Bath rightly expecting not to be bothered by the armed guards in attendance at Continental spas. But what they found seemed an alternative kind of despotism. Bath was ruled by a Master of Ceremonies whose powers would never have been tolerated in a king or a minister. As the marquis de Bombelles put it in 1789, 'The English, so fanatical about liberty, ... like sheep obey a pollicon who after misconducting himself elsewhere comes seeking a job which every other man of good society would decline.'[40] What was really English about it of course was the fact that neither court nor government had any say, the Master of Ceremonies being freely elected by those who patronised his assemblies. It was a microcosm of English public life, a voluntary association imposing on itself a considerable degree of subjection.[41] However, this was not what outsiders had traditionally thought of as English freedom, and suggested the need for a radical reappraisal.

This petty tyranny was not only erected on home ground. As tourists multiplied in the late eighteenth century, their etiquette went with them. It was observed with great rigour in cities where there were sufficient

---

[38] F. Mac Donogh, *The Hermit in London: Or, Sketches of English Manners* (5 vols., 1819–20), II, 118–19; *Town Talk: Or Living Manners* (n.d.), I, 375.

[39] *Almack's: A Novel* (3 vols., 1826), II, 209–10.

[40] Marc de Bombelles, *Journal de voyage en Grande Bretagne et en Irlande 1784*, ed. Jacques Gury (Oxford, 1989), 293.

[41] Luigi Angiolini, *Lettere sull'Inghilterra*, ed. Guido di Pino (Milan, 1944), 108ff.

British residents or passers-through to make it viable.[42] In such places the best that the bemused foreigner could hope for was to be entertained on terms devised for London rather than Rome or Geneva. English settlements were rarely appreciated in this respect however welcome their money. When Madeira became a favourite resort for invalids at the end of the century, even the English admitted that the contrast with Portuguese manners was unflattering. The same thing happened at another health centre, Montpellier. From a German standpoint it seemed that society there had been ruined by English ways.[43]

So much for unceremoniousness. What of accessibility? The first and most striking impression that foreigners gained was exclusiveness. Exclusiveness did not necessarily signify snobbery. It seemed to be something more fundamental, something that affected all ranks, making for a constant sense of retreat, of compartmentalism. Here was an obsession with the maintenance of privacy in public places, which, if such accounts are correct, would make a nonsense of the portrayals of eighteenth-century sociability offered by modern sociologists such as Richard Sennett or Habermas.[44] The English manner was described as setting a kind of ring around everyone.[45] Such an enclosure could even be incorporated in the physical structure of places of recreation; hence the booths and cubicles to be found in taverns and coffee-houses.[46] At inns people sought a private room if they had the money and expected a booth if they had not. The table d'hôte of Continental inns was a mark of inferior accommodation in Britain, associated at best with commercial hotels. The English diner could be likened to a hermit, completely inaccessible to strangers.[47] George Canning cheerfully admitted to the charge when he commended eating 'as silently and shortly and sulkily as you please, without interfering one with another'.[48] Even Covent Garden actors, congregating in nearby taverns, made it a rule to dine at separate tables before assembling to exchange pleasantries over their port.[49]

[42] Christopher Hervey, *Letters from Portugal, Spain, Italy and Germany, in the Years 1759, 1760, and 1761* (3 vols., 1785), I, 425.

[43] Christian August Fischer, *Letters during a Journey to Montpellier* (1806), 65.

[44] Richard Sennett, *The Fall of Public Man* (Cambridge, 1977); Jurgen Habermas, *The Structural Transformation of the Public Sphere: An Inquiry into Category of Bourgeois Society*, trans.Thomas Burger (Cambridge, MA, 1989).

[45] Erik Gustaf Geijer, *Impressions of England 1809–10*, 126.

[46] Karl Philipp Moritz, *Journeys of a German in England in 1782*, trans. and ed. Reginald Nettel (1965), 72.

[47] William Austin, *Letters from London: Written during the Years 1802 and 1803* (Boston, 1804), 173.

[48] *The Letter-Journal of George Canning, 1793-1795*, ed. Peter Jupp, Camden Fourth Series, vol. 41 (1991), 160.

[49] Amédée Pichot, *Historical and Literary Tour of a Foreigner in England and Scotland* (2 vols., 1825), I, 231.

There was general agreement that the mania for peace and privacy made the English unique. It was predictable that Italian cafés would provide havens of Latin warmth, exuding hospitality and openness to strangers, but even the smoke-filled infernos of Dutch and Germans placed communality first.[50] This was not true at all in England. There were no billiards or backgammon tables, no noise, only the reading of newspapers and speaking in low tones.[51] The modern belief that 'anyone sitting in the coffee house had a right to talk to anyone else, to enter into any conversation, whether he knew the other people or not, whether he was bidden to speak or not' is far indeed from the truth as recorded by those who lived through its golden age.[52] In this respect the West End club did not represent a break with the past, a premonition of Victorian seclusion, so much as an institutionalization of Augustan sociability. Introverted clubbishness had apparently always been a feature of these establishments. Nor was it restricted to men. That famous Augustan tea table that featured in Addison and Richardson and which has excited modern historians of gender, was found wanting by Continental visitors. It was brutally condemned for its mindless tedium in a celebrated scene of Madame de Stael's novel *Corinne*, one which provoked much public and private discussion among English readers.[53]

The celebrated English cult of the home also provided evidence of the need to protect private space. Bonstetten thought it generally a north European phenomenon, the result of climatic conditions. Home for a northerner resembled a snail's shell, so vital was it to his existence. To a southerner it had nothing like the same significance.[54] In fact in the English instance the metaphor of the snail seemed quite appropriate. It was often used by those who observed the English Grand Tourist, travelling in a coach which contained every conceivable home comfort, down to Harvey's sauce and the equipment for cooking beefsteaks.[55] In any event, home implied a rejection of sociability. Helvétius seised upon it as the key to understanding the difference between the French and other nations. Paris was one great house and Parisians, indeed all French people, one great family. Other cities were collections of houses.[56] London presented the extreme case.

[50] Louis Antoine, marquis de Caraccioli, *Voyage de la raison en Europe; par l'Auteur des lettres récréatives et morales* (Compiègne, 1772), 164.

[51] Johann Wilhelm von Archenholz, *A Picture of England*, II, 107–8.

[52] Richard Sennett, *The Fall of Public Man*, 81.

[53] *Corinne ou L'Italie* (2 vols., 1807), II, 369.

[54] Charles-Victor de Bonstetten, *The Man of the North, and the Man of the South; or the Influence of Climate* (New York, 1964), 25.

[55] Washington Irving, *Tales of a Traveller. By Geoffrey Crayon, Gent* (2 vols., 1824), II, 75.

[56] *Oeuvres complètes de Diderot* (20 vols.,Paris, 1875), II, 383.

Visitors found it puzzling that the homes of the elite were entered only on specific invitation.[57] Politeness presupposed a certain accessibility to other polite people. This stopped short at an Englishman's door. Foreigners complained that it was out of the question to call at the dinner hour and expect dinner.[58] Indeed to attempt to do so was a breach of manners. Elsewhere the reverse would have been the case. Not cordially to welcome a chance visitor would have been grossly discourteous.[59] Even more surprising was the care with which the humblest Briton guarded his home. Sheltering from the rain in the nearest cottage was not welcomed as it was on the seigneurial Continent.[60]

The physical appearance of town housing especially was one of the first things on which newcomers to London commented. French visitors spoke of living in boxes, cubicles or cells. A witticism often repeated was that the English had driven out the monks under Henry VIII only to turn their cities into gigantic convents.[61] The impression was reinforced by the sight of iron fences which, as the Swiss Henri Meister commented, made London houses veritably the castles an Englishman's home was said to be.[62] And when London, along with some provincial towns, started spilling beyond its suburbs in the late eighteenth century, spawning a new villa-England, travellers were intrigued by the pains taken to protect its owners from the gaze of passers-by with a high paling, or a thick hedge.[63] But the examples could be multiplied. Even the Englishman's religious observances were affected. Where else in Europe did one commonly see churches packed with boxed and locked pews?[64] It was the sight of such pews that was finally to make the historian Michelet conclude when he visited England in 1834, that the definitive English maxim must be 'no pleasure if not exclusive'.[65]

These tendencies gave rise to numerous reflections on the peculiar nature of life in Britain. Perhaps after all public association, that most characteristic of English activities, for all kinds of purposes from celebrating an anniversary to founding a hospital or reforming the constitution, had its origin not in open sociability but rather in a limited kind of collaboration. Tavern booths, it was remarked, symbolised

[57] Prince Pückler-Muskau, *Tour in England, Ireland, and France, in the Years 1828 and 1829* (4 vols., 1832), IV, 185.

[58] Louis Dutens, *Memoirs of a Traveller, Now in Retirement* (5 vols., 1806), IV, 243.

[59] *Londres et les anglais par J. L. Ferri de St.-Constant* (4 vols., Paris, An XII [1804]), I, 191.

[60] Pückler-Muskau, *Tour in England, Ireland, and France, in the Years 1828 and 1829*, IV, 185.

[61] *Londres et les anglais par J. L. Ferri de St.-Constant*, I, 23.

[62] *Letters Written during a Residence in England Translated from the French of Henry Meister* (1799), 189.

[63] Nathaniel Hawthorne, *Our Old Home* (2 vols., 1863), I, 151.

[64] *Letters from London: Written during the Years 1802 and 1803* (Boston, 1804), 30.

[65] *Sur les chemins de l'Europe* (Paris, 1893), 41.

'separation in union—the type of English life'.[66] Still more disconcerting was the discovery that in the most commercial of all societies, the ultimate ambition was not so much shared consumption as comfort in isolation: private travelling, private dining, private drinking, private reading.

The third concern, the fundamental matter of sociability, followed naturally from such questioning. Were the British as individuals easy of address and familiar of manner? In particular had the cult of the gentleman made it possible for all classes to enjoy a degree of companionship unattained elsewhere. At least until the 1790s the conventional picture of the British aristocracy was of a body that had accepted the constraints of an egalitarian society. Visitors to Britain expected to find that rank counted for far less in Britain than elsewhere, and sought blue-ribboned noblemen consorting with mechanics at bowls and cock-fighting.[67] Numerous stories were told of the social humiliations that individual noblemen underwent. The snag is that very often they were the same story, repeated by one traveller after another. In this genre the most popular anecdote concerned the fourth duke of Bedford who was said to have been horse-whipped by a commoner.[68] There was some truth to this story in that Bedford had certainly as a young man found himself in difficulties in a Jacobite riot at Lichfield races in 1747. Even so the sociological significance that this episode was made to bear seems rather excessive.

This is not to deny that the British nobility was indeed in many respects differently positioned from its Continental counterparts, but when commentators did attempt to substantiate the idea that the British were unusually egalitarian in their treatment of each other, they were frequently confounded. Social life did not abound in easy familiarity and natural bonhomie, and least of all did it do so where relations between different classes were involved. It was one of the commonest of all observations by foreign visitors that servants in England were more reserved than those elsewhere. Familiarity between employer and employees hardly existed. Moreover people who enjoyed the rank of gentlemen, whatever that meant, for it was entirely self-bestowed, did not engage in ready communication. To make the acquaintance of an Englishman or even to talk with him was notoriously difficult. As a German tourist remarked,

---

[66] Alphonse Esquiros, *The English at Home*, trans. and ed. Lascellese Wraxall (2 vols., 1861), I, 272.

[67] [Anon.], *Remarks on the Letters, concerning the English and French* (London, 1726), 23, in reply to Béat Louis Muralt, *Letters Describing the Character and Customs of the English and French Nations* (1726), 39.

[68] Johann Wilhelm von Archenholz, *A Picture of England*, I, 40–1.

What contributes much to the 'dullness' of English society, is the haughty aversion which Englishmen ... show to addressing an unknown person; if he should venture to address them, they receive it with the air of an insult. They sometimes laugh at themselves for this singular incivility, but no one makes the least attempt to act differently when an opportunity offers.[69]

It was a common assertion that conversation, the very essence of politeness, hardly existed under such conditions. On the Continent 'une conversation anglaise' was a silence and the stage Englishman a tongue-tied stutterer.[70] Numerous travelogues record heroic attempts to penetrate the social reticence of the English, most unavailing. Reserve, coldness, mauvaise honte, various terms were employed, but all confirmed the impression that however rewarding it might be to get to know the English well, the easy sociability so prized by the eighteenth century was beyond them, at any rate on home ground. Grand Tourists who had learned Continental manners abroad were accused of abandoning them when they returned home. 'The English who disembark at Dover are not the English who were at Paris and in Italy', wrote Alessandro Verri.[71] Anecdotes on this subject abounded. Typical is a story of the Neapolitan diplomat Caracciolo. Caracciolo had been a bosom companion of Lord Malton, heir to the marquessate of Rockingham, when Malton toured Italy. Some years later, he came to England as envoy, naturally expecting a friendly reception. Instead, encountering his former companion, now Lord Rockingham, he met only 'cold, formal politeness'. He got his own back in due course when he found himself dining in the company of Rockingham with a royal prince, the duke of Cumberland. On this occasion it suited Rockingham to demonstrate his Continental connections by reminding Caracciolo of their acquaintance in front of Cumberland. Caracciolo responded by remarking that he could only recall a young nobleman named Lord Malton.[72]

These three sets of closely related observations offered a fundamental challenge to the notion that modern manners à l'anglaise were what enthusiasts for the new informality of the English gentleman and gentlewoman thought they were. How was one to explain the seeming coldness of a nation that possessed all the qualifications for true politeness yet woefully failed to translate them into practice?

[69] Pückler-Muskau, *Tour in England, Ireland, and France, in the Years 1828 and 1829*, III, 381.

[70] Christopher Hervey, *Letters from Portugal, Spain, Italy and Germany*, II, 498–9.

[71] *Lettere e Scritti inediti di Pietro e di Alessandro Verri*, ed. Carlo Casati (3 vols., Milan, 1879–80), I, 384–5.

[72] *Memoirs of the Life and Peregrinations of the Florentine Philip Mazzei 1730–1816*, trans. Howard R. Marraro (New York, 1942), 117.

One answer lay supposedly in national character, itself a major preoccupation of late Enlightenment thinking. Foreigners were not very good at distinguishing between Britishness and Englishness in general, but many began to do so in the late eighteenth century. Tourists were increasingly drawn to Celtic regions, attracted by the forces that drew the English themselves, improved communications, enthusiasm for romantic scenery and fascination with the cultural survivals of pre-commercial Britain and Ireland. The superior politeness of the Scots, Welsh and Irish constitutes one of the most hackneyed themes of the resulting literature. Typically they were described as 'more urbane, more self-possessed, more obliging than the Englishman'.[73] It is significant that these claims were not made simply on behalf of the peasantries that might have been expected to preserve outmoded manners, but also of more self-consciously modern communities, at any rate in Scotland and Ireland where there were places large enough to be compared with English cities. In Edinburgh and Glasgow, Dublin and Belfast, foreigners claimed to find agreeable society. Moreover Celtic exiles maintained their native politeness on English soil. The American Benjamin Silliman, entertained to dinner in Liverpool, went out of his way to explain that the tedium of the occasion was exclusively English. 'Before dismissing this dinner, I ought to observe that the reserve and coldness which marked the manners of most of the gentlemen were strongly contrasted with the polite and attentive hospitality of our host, (a Scotchman,) who suffered no one of his guests to remain unnoticed.'[74] Similiarly, the Count Kielmansegge reported of Bath,

> The quantity of Irishmen here ... without doubt contributes very much to make this place especially pleasant to foreigners. They are easy of access, and take pleasure in showing civility to strangers; ... For these reasons, as well as on account of the prevalence of the social customs of Dublin, which are said to have many advantages, the place was decidedly agreeable.[75]

Britons who were not English naturally concurred. For Mrs Grant of Laggan, who spent portions of her life in North America and England, and was read throughout the English-speaking world, 'the land of cakes' was 'the land of social life and social love' untainted by the 'cold and close attention to petty comforts and conveniences which absorbs the English mind'.[76] A whole genre of Irish stories emerged,

[73] *Lettere sull'Inghilterra*, ed. Guido di Pino (Milan, 1944), 361.

[74] *A Journal of Travels in England, Holland and Scotland, and of Two Passages over the Atlantic, in the Years 1805 and 1806* (2 vols., New York, 1810), I, 56.

[75] Friedrich Kielmansegge, *Diary of a Journey to England in the Years 1761–1762*, trans. Countess Kielmansegg [née Philippa Sidney] (1902), 125–7.

[76] *Memoir and Correspondence of Mrs. Grant of Laggan*, ed. J. P. Grant (3 vols., 1844), I, 68.

my own favourite being the remark a Dublin shoeblack is said to have uttered by way of rebuke to an unpleasantly haughty English customer: 'All the *polish* you have is upon your boots, and I gave it you.'[77]

Significantly, the English themselves did not dissent from such judgements. Characteristic comments described the Scots as 'infinitely more civil, humanised, and hospitable, than any I ever met with', the Welsh as a 'very joyous social people'.[78] In Ireland, too, visitors thought they were in the presence of a superior civility which could not simply be attributed to outdated modes. Sir John Carr, in his tour of 1805, defied his reader to attend an Irish ball without being struck by 'the spirit, good-humour, gravity, and elegance, which prevail in it: in this accomplishment they may rank next to the animated inhabitants of Paris'. But this was no monopoly of the middle class; the most degraded of the peasantry seemed to have it. 'Their native urbanity to each other is very pleasing; I have frequently seen two boors take off their hats and salute each other with great civility.'[79] Dublin became as proverbially cheerful as Paris. To say as the actor-manager Wilkinson said of Hull that it was the 'Dublin of England'[80] was the ultimate accolade.

But while the English might seem generous in conceding Celtic sociability, they were less ready to admit that it conferred superiority. Irish cordiality was often taken to be insincere or at least superficial. Particularly after the Irish Union, Irish politicians encountered considerable prejudice on this score, to say the least.[81] Welsh civility was also found intrusive, 'perhaps too inquisitive'.[82] Scots were regarded slightly more favourably. But compliments were likely to be of the backhand variety, somewhat resembling those paid to French manners. No self-respecting Englishman would actually have wanted to emulate them. He merely admitted that there were some frivolous arts in which other nationalities were more accomplished precisely because they were more frivolous. By the turn of the eighteenth and nineteenth centuries, when Saxonism was becoming a cult, this could be tied in with the superior virtues of the English race, solidity, gravity, decency, and so on. The Celtic side of Britannia's coin provided evidence of an excess

[77] John Carr, *The Stranger in Ireland; or, a Tour in the Southern and Western Parts of that Country, in the Year 1805* (1806), 300.

[78] *Letters from Edinburgh; Written in the Years 1774 and 1775* (London, 1776), 66ff; *A Tour through the Northern Counties of England, and the Borders of Scotland* (Bath, 1802), 56; P. W. Clayden, *The Early Life of Samuel Rogers* (1887), 184.

[79] *The Stranger in Ireland; or, a Tour in the Southern and Western Parts of that Country, in the Year 1805*, 236, 251.

[80] Claire Tomalin, *Mrs. Jordan's Profession: The Story of a Great Actress and a Future King* (1994), 33.

[81] *Autobiography of Henry Taylor, 1800–1875* (2 vols., 1885), I, 212.

[82] *A Tour in Wales, and through Several Counties of England, including both the Universities, Performed in the Summer of 1805* (1806), 46.

of familiarity, a garrulousness, a want of decorum, that could be contrasted with English social life.

National character aside, there seemed good reason to question the underlying analysis that had created great expectations of the English. In this respect Joseph Fiévée may be taken as representative of a trend. It is not in retrospect a surprising trend. The twin pillars of British modernity, commerce and liberty, both looked rather shaky when re-examined in the light of early nineteenth-century realities. It was all too easy to portray the British merchant not as a bringer of prosperity and progress but as an agent of monopoly and imperialism. Continental resentment of the cynicism with which free trading arguments were employed to reinforce British supremacy bred a train of thought that went with growing alarm at the consequences of industrialization. Comments like those of Stendhal and Heine on British materialism, which turned the whole of society into at best money-grubbing phi-listines, at worst mindless drudges, reveal how far the Continental intelligentsia had travelled since Voltaire.[83] Evidence of stunted socia-bility fitted readily in the resulting picture.

By this time, of course, English opinion itself had become more sceptical about the way that commerce affected manners. One line of argument was that in a society of potential customers, a stranger was in the first instance a commodity whose worth needed calculating.[84] Unfortunately, estimating wealth in so fluid a society was extremely difficult. Traditional courtesy literature attached much significance to the way one should treat superiors and inferiors. But this assumed that one knew pretty clearly who were one's superiors and inferiors. In other countries the cringing manners of the peasant or lackey, on the one hand, or the overbearing familiarity of a great magnate or a rich bourgois, on the other, told their own tale. Englishmen being both free and equal under the law had no occasion to give away their status. Appraising each other accordingly became a complicated, nuanced task.

This argument was to take on additional sophistication and force in the hands of de Tocqueville, who also analysed what he called 'This English avoidance of English people' in terms of the difficulty of estimating social status.[85] But in this at least de Tocqueville was not original. As Mrs Piozzi put it, 'if our persons of condition fail even for a moment to watch their post, maintaining by dignity what they or

---

[83] F. W. J. Hemmings, 'Stendhal: anglophile ou anglophobe?', in *Stendhal et l'Angleterre*, ed. K. G. McWatters and C. W. Thompson, (Liverpool, 1987), 5; S. S. Prawer, *Coal-Smoke and Englishman: A Study of Verbal Caricature in the Writings of Heinrich Heine* (1984).

[84] William Austin, *Letters from London: Written during the Years 1802 and 1803*, 16–17.

[85] Philip Gilbert Hamerton, *Human Intercourse* (1884), 226, paraphrasing de Tocqueville's *Democracy in America* II, book 3, chapter 2.

their families have acquired by merit, they are instantly and suddenly broken in upon by the well-employed talents, or swiftly-acquired riches, of men born on the other side the thin partition'. In Italy she noted the problem simply did not arise because 'birth alone can entitle man or woman to the society of gentlemen and ladies'.[86] Heinrich von Watzdorf offered corroboration from a Saxon perspective. English noblemen lacked legal provileges and accordingly sought to preserve their status by means of a certain stiffness.[87]

An interesting twist was given to this interpretation by Francis Jeffrey, who as a Scotch Reviewer was not known for his mercy to Englishmen. In the *Edinburgh Review*, he argued that reserve was a consequence of the wealth creation and redistribution that had taken place from about the 1770s, precisely the time when growing numbers of foreign commentators were dismayed by the constricting nature of English society. 'So many persons now raised themselves by their own exertions, that every one thought himself entitled to rise; ... a herd of uncomfortable and unsuitable companions beset all the approaches to good company, and seemed determined to force all its barriers.' There had been, he claimed,

> an incredible increase of forwardness and solid impudence among the half-bred and half-educated classes of this country—and ... there was consequently some apology for the assumption of more distant and forbidding manners towards strangers, on the part of those who were already satisfied with the extent of their society. This, we have no doubt, is the true history of that awful tone, of gloomy indifference and stupid arrogance, which has unfortunately become so striking a characteristic of English manners.[88]

So much for freedom and the creation of wealth as generators of politeness.

Sources of the kind I have been employing are not to be taken at face value. They doubtless tell us as much about the needs of those who compiled them as the qualities of those they describe. Some of the puzzlement and dismay that they expressed might be traced to changing European perspectives, unsurprisingly in a period dominated by two Revolutions and rapid economic growth. But there is substantial agreement among them on the salient points and they do have the advantage that they describe rather than prescribe. Much of the

[86] Hester Lynch Piozzi, *Observations and Reflections Made in the Course of a Journey through France, Italy, and Germany* (2 vols., 1789), I, 107.

[87] Heinrich Maximilian Friedrich von Watzdorf, *Briefe zur Charakteristik von England gohörig; geschrieben auf einer Reise im Jahre 1784 von Heinrich von Watzdorf* (Leipzig, 1786), 56–7.

[88] *Edinburgh Review*, 37 (1822), 310–12.

material that historians have used to identify unifying European values and practices was, on the contrary, designed to improve and amend. It as at least worth considering Jeffrey's belief that polite society was developing in quite the opposite direction from that predicted by earlier generations and recommended in such advice.

Two caveats: I do not mean to imply that the influence of British manners was played out. In fact in the cult of the English gentleman they offered a model that was long to have a marked interest and even appeal, well into the present century. However, the nineteenth-century gentleman was far removed from the ideal of the eighteenth and seen by other Europeans as evidence of the survival of aristocratic influence rather than of a refreshingly egalitarian code. The expression used by Fiévée's employer, Napoleon Bonaparte, to describe it was 'morgue aristocratique'. This would have saddened Sir Andrew Freeport and his creators but it reflected a common perception of English gentility. And by the early nineteenth century it was one that many critically minded Englishmen entertained of themselves.

> The same aristocratic feeling pervades all ranks—the same dread of being contaminated by acquaintanceship, and of losing one's place in society by the least connection with an inferior. Englishmen all seem like cast away mariners, clinging to a wreck; each unfortunate is absorbed in considerations of the fate he can scarcely hope to escape.
> Walk our streets, enter our saloons; there is mistrust in every face, and even in the greeting of every friend there lurks a reserve behind the show of friendship, that is chilling to the heart that cares for aught beyond itself.[89]

Finally still less do I mean to imply any lessening of the extraordinary attention devoted to British life generally after the turn of the eighteenth century. In fact the wonderment of foreigners who came to Britain as the full effects of industrialization took effect, mounted rather than diminished, and of course they were fascinated by the resulting culture, material and intellectual. They criticised much more than their predecessors of a century before, but they did not deny that Britain's development was a phenomenon, nor did they deny its historic significance. When Edouard de Montulé glimpsed the white cliffs of Dover from Boulogne in 1821, he exclaimed (so he says), 'there is the centre of civilization', using words imitated by numerous of his and the following generation.[90] But civilization in the 1820s did not mean what

---

[89] C. H. Phipps, later marquis of Normanby, *The English in Italy* (3 vols., 1825), II, 296.
[90] Edouard de Montulé, *Voyage en Angleterre et en Russie, pendant les années 1821, 1822 et 1823* (2 vols., Paris, 1825), I, 11.

civilization had meant to Fiévée's and earlier generations and that is rather the point, is it not? The British might have helped to transform the term. They might even have redefined the nature of progress. But as the new cosmopolites of the commercial era they had only flattered to deceive, and for the democratisation of manners western society was to look elsewhere.

HISTORY AS DESTINY:
GOBINEAU, H. S. CHAMBERLAIN AND SPENGLER
By Michael Biddiss

READ 26 APRIL 1996

THE novel which won the 1987 Booker Prize was Penelope Lively's *Moon Tiger*. Its central character is an historian whom, on the opening page, we find already near to death. Even so, she is meditating about the completion of a new work: 'A history of the world. To round things off. I may as well—no more nit-picking stuff about Napoleon, Tito, the battle of Edgehill, Hernando Cortez ... The works, this time. The whole triumphant murderous unstoppable chute—from the mud to the stars, universal and particular, your story and mine.' And she adds: 'I'm equipped, I consider; eclecticism has always been my hallmark.'[1]

That is certainly one narrative to read. The somewhat comparable history which I propose to analyse here might well be introduced with the familiar formula that there was once a Frenchman, an Englishman and a German. If that signals a certain unreliability on the part of the protagonists, then this may well be an appropriate caution with regard to the cases of Arthur de Gobineau (1816–82), Houston Stewart Chamberlain (1855–1927) and Oswald Spengler (1880–1936). No one would any longer rate the *Essai sur l'inégalité des races humaines*, nor *Die Grundlagen des neunzehnten Jahrhunderts*, nor even *Der Untergang des Abendlandes* as a major contribution to scholarship. However, in the earlier twentieth century, the three systematisers and eclectics who wrote those curious chronicles did enjoy—albeit only posthumously in the first case—a certain vogue that remains of substantial interest to the intellectual historian. Part of the explanation for their prominence relates to the views which they expressed about the past development of the Teutonic peoples. But the matter is also bound up with a second, and closely connected, issue. This concerns the different extrapolations which the members of our trio made from that history towards certain predictive visions of the destiny which must lie ahead for Germany, and indeed for Europe and the world at large. Here, I propose to consider each of the three writers in turn, while also developing cumulatively certain patterns of comparison and contrast between them.

[1] P. Lively, *Moon Tiger* (Harmondsworth, 1988), 1.

73

The four volumes of Gobineau's *Essai* appeared in 1853–5.[2] Their author was a young and talented autodidact of legitimist political background, whose career as a diplomat had been launched under the patronage of Alexis de Tocqueville in the aftermath of the 1848 revolutions. Yet the response which Gobineau's treatise offered to that wave of disorder in France and far beyond was much more starkly reactionary than anything ever voiced by his distinguished friend.[3] The *Essai* sought to justify the kind of conclusions which its preface outlined as follows:

> I have become convinced that the race question dominates all the other problems of history, that it holds the key to them, and that the inequality of races from whose fusion a people is formed is enough to explain the whole course of its destiny ... It is now my belief that everything great, noble, and fruitful in the works of man on this earth, in science, art, and civilization, derives from only one starting-point, develops from the same seed, is the result of a single thought, and belongs to one family alone, whose different branches have dominated all the civilised countries of the globe.[4]

It must be said at once that the subsequent vindication of this position by means of a universal history relies heavily on circular argument. The hypotheses about racial causation which the past is supposed to confirm are themselves used to settle many doubtful historical points, and the course of the narration is all too often directly dependent upon the assumed accuracy of a theory that must eventually be interpreted as having been conceived arbitrarily and *a priori*.

Central to Gobineau's account was the notion of three original stocks, arranged in hierarchy.[5] Each was alleged to possess characteristics that were permanent, except insofar as alterations ensued from inter-breeding with rival races. Lowest were the Blacks, dominated by animal passion and equipped with very limited intellectual and moral capacities. Next came the Yellows, devoted to the achievement of material sat-

---

[2] A. de Gobineau, *Essai sur l'inégalité des races humaines* (4 vols., Paris, 1853–5). Subsequent references are to the best modern edition: A. de Gobineau, *Œuvres*, ed. J.Gaulmier, vol. I (Paris, 1983), 133–1174 (text) and 1216–471 (notes). For overall analysis, see M. Biddiss, *Father of Racist Ideology: The Social and Political Thought of Count Gobineau* (1970), especially Part Two.

[3] See A. de Tocqueville, *Œuvres complètes*, IX: *Correspondance d'Alexis de Tocqueville et d'Arthur de Gobineau*, ed. M. Degros (Paris, 1959); and M. Biddiss, 'Prophecy and Pragmatism: Gobineau's Confrontation with Tocqueville', *Historical Journal*, 13 (1970), 611–33. Much of the *Essai* was composed during a diplomatic posting to Berne, where Gobineau found himself exposed to what he interpreted as the excesses of Swiss democracy.

[4] Gobineau, *Œuvres*, I, 138–9.

[5] The matter is most succinctly summarised *ibid.*, 339–48.

isfaction, but otherwise typified by apathetic acceptance of mediocrity in all things. Superior to both were the Whites, characterised by an 'energetic intelligence' that sustained their love of liberty, order and honour. Even within this third category Gobineau identified a super-elite of Aryans (a term ever more in vogue since the Indo-European philological revolution around 1800),[6] comprising those who had kept freest from mixture with other races or with debased Whites.

The *Essai* did not, however, preach any simply theory of racial purity. The tragic element in Gobineau's drama—the key to its nemesis—was that civilization arose only by mixture between Aryan stock and some modicum of alien blood. Thus miscegenation is not only a stimulant towards achievement but also the principal agent of eventual decay. Gobineau traced world history passing across ten civilizations, through whose course the Aryan creative power had become ever more exhaus-ted. Originating in Central Asia, the great race had moved from India to Egypt and Assyria; it had fostered the Alleghanian, Mexican and Peruvian cultures of America, as well as that of China; it had under-pinned the glories of Greece and Rome, and had enjoyed its concluding triumphs in the medieval Germanic realms. For Gobineau, as for Tacitus, the Aryan-Teutons were certainly heroic figures characterised by vigour, idealism and love of war and honour; they held themselves in high esteem, eschewed urban settlement and stressed the dignity of woman. But now these old warriors had long been gone, and their modern descendants were deemed to be a stock debilitated by Celtic and Slavonic influences. In short, the *Essai* argued that contemporary Europe, despite pockets of vestigial vigour in some of its northern regions, was in irreversible decline.

As for the USA, Gobineau declared that, if hope could not be found there in the land of Crèvecoeur's 'new man', then civilization was indeed doomed. And he found no hope, for across the Atlantic too the Anglo-Saxon virtues were being swamped by the influx of new breeds: 'This people which calls itself young', wrote Gobineau, 'is in reality the old European stock, less restricted because of more favourable laws, but not better inspired ... A simple change in geographical location cannot regenerate races which are more than half-exhausted.'[7] Thus the author's anxieties about contemporary France became universalised into a proclamation of total despair—into a vista of utter racial exhaustion. On that basis, perceptive but isolated figures like himself were now fated to be merely the impotent observers of an ineluctable descent into the barbarism of miscegenated mass mediocrity.

<hr />

[6] See L. Poliakov, *The Aryan Myth: A History of Racist and Nationalist Ideas in Europe* (1974), 188–92.

[7] Gobineau, *Œuvres*, I, 1142.

The *Essai* was far from being Gobineau's only book. Alongside other historical and philosophical works, he wrote not only verse and drama but also a number of travel-accounts, short stories and novels. Since the mid-1960s much of his avowedly imaginative literature, in prose at any rate, has come to be well regarded by many literary critics, especially for an elegance of irony reminiscent of Stendhal.[8] Such habilitation for Gobineau's talent as story-teller is fair enough. But that is not true of whatever part of his rescue has relied upon two related misperceptions: the first involves viewing the *Essai* as dealing more with the richness of human diversity than with the scale of congenital inequality and doomed decay, while the second involves the assumption that Gobineau's literary reputation needs to be preserved by under-playing the significance of racism within the overall corpus of his writing. These are approaches which have been challenged, in a largely convincing manner, by Pierre-Louis Rey. For him, it is the theme of racial hierarchy which gives the whole range of the mature *œuvre* that broad untiy which Gobineau himself often stressed; and it is this same theme which severely restricts the effectiveness of that concern for the individual so eloquently professed in the later imaginative works. On this view, such writings have their own fundamentally didactic intent, and demand assessment as an integral part of a philosophy which, even across the diverse genres of its utterance, remains, in Rey's words, 'stubbornly directed towards the mastering of positive truths'.[9]

This broad consistency of racial determinism affects the gloss that must be put on the vitalist rhetoric embodied in those works—especially the novel *Les Pléiades* (1874) and the drama *La Renaissance* (1877)—which form the summit-area of Gobineau's creative achievement. Heroicity survives here as the prerogative of a few gifted individuals who stand out as isolated instances of 'ethnic persistence'. It is precisely the dilemmas facing such *esprits d'élite* which are central to *Les Pléiades*. As Gobineau himself put it, the novel is based on the idea 'that there are no longer classes, that there are no longer peoples, but only—in the whole of Europe—certain individuals who float like wreckage upon the flood'.[10] The natural nobility of these *fils de roi* bears little positive correlation with the corrupted schemes of hierarchy still encountered in societies which are deemed now to have lost all grasp of their proper racial bearings. Four hundred years ago—so Gobineau, like Jacob Burckhardt believed—there had been, within the Italian states, some

---

[8] J. Gaulmier, *Spectre de Gobineau* (Paris, 1965), proved to be particularly seminal in this development.

[9] P.-L. Rey, *L'univers romanesque de Gobineau* (Paris, 1981), 22.

[10] Letter of 7 October 1872, in *Correspondance entre le comte de Gobineau et le comte de Prokesch-Osten*, ed. C. Serpeille de Gobineau (Paris, 1933), 361.

scope left for men of worth to strive for control over events. But even there, as *La Renaissance* portrays, the tide of decadence had been rising, so that figures such as Caesar Borgia and Pope Julius II—heirs to the Aryan legacy even amidst latinization—found themselves able only to delay rather than to avert the coming triumph of herd-values.

Through such later writings Gobineau made even more patent the duality of moral evaluation which was already present in the *Essai* as between Aryan and non-Aryan, elite and mass. Increasingly he attacked, as Nietzsche also was beginning to do, that Christian pity-ethic which had weakened creative egoism. Such admiration as Gobineau admitted in *La Renaissance* for Pope Alexander VI related precisely to the latter's readiness to repudiate an enervating tradition. The drama depicts that pontiff advising Lucretia Borgia in these terms: 'For the kind of person whom destiny calls to dominate others, the ordinary rules of life are reversed and duty becomes quite different. Good and evil are transferred to another and higher plane . . .'[11] This projection of morality *jenseits von Gut und Böse* involved Gobineau not simply in proclaiming the merits of the few but also in denying all ethical significance to the remaining mass of debased beings. The classification of the latter into 'fools', 'scoundrels' and 'brutes' constitutes the climax of one of the chief set-pieces within *Les Pléiades*, and demonstrates the author's skill in manipulating figures of speech derived from images of animality and pestilence so as to express hostility towards what Baudelaire had called 'zoocracy'.[12] In this way Gobineau contributed to that diverse and self-revealing literature of metaphor through which fear of the crowd was vented in the later nineteenth century.[13] By means of this same rhetoric of the bestial and the bacillar he also began to disclose something of that progression which exists, at least potentially, within all racist ideology—from the depersonalization of its victims into an even more destructive state of utter dehumanization, where a campaign for their physical obliteration becomes a conceivable sequel to their moral nullification.

Let me stress, however, that this was not the logic which Gobineau himself pursued. His restraint stemmed not from any belief about some better available policy, but rather from a conviction about the pointlessness of all future public striving. From the *Essai* onwards, he withdrew increasingly from the whole business of manufacturing pol-

[11] Gobineau, *Œuvres*, vol. III (Paris, 1987), 657.
[12] See *ibid.*, 14–20. Baudelaire's remark 'From freedom cherished impiously is born a new tyranny, the tyranny of beasts – zoocracy' is quoted in A. E. Carter, *The Idea of Decadence in French Literature, 1830–1900* (Toronto, 1958), 9.
[13] See S. Barrows, *Distorting Mirrors: Visions of the Crowd in Late Nineteenth-Century France* (New Haven, 1981), especially ch. 2; and J. S. McClelland, *The Crowd and the Mob: From Plato to Canetti* (1989), especially chs. 4–7.

itical prescriptions, genocidal or otherwise. Racist ideologues commonly condemn themselves, albeit unwittingly, to a paralysis of real moral judgement as between the circles of the chosen and of the repudiated; much rarer are the instances where they refrain from making recommendations about positive action aimed at consolidating the ascendancy of the former or at saving civilization from the encroachments of the latter. Yet, for Gobineau, not even Pope Alexander's Machiavellianism remains relevant to the contemporary world. Nor does the ruritanian state of Burbach, in which much of *Les Pléiades* is set, retain any function beyond that of a refuge where the heirs of the culture-bearers may constellate to observe the course of decadence. Henceforth their task is not to master destiny, but only to contemplate from afar (with something akin to the Nietzschean *Pathos der Distanz*) the sad enactment of such fate. Minerva's owl brings them understanding—yet only of their impotence. Their remaining obligations are not public but private, being focused on a duty towards their own personal self-fulfilment, or, at most, towards the *petit cercle* of their fellows.

In a new preface to the *Essai*, prepared shortly before his death, Gobineau conceded nothing to the critics of his despair.[14] Similarly, in his very last article—a global overview highlighting the peril rising from Slavic and Mongoloid hordes—he apologised only for having earlier underestimated the speed of civilizational decay.[15] Repeatedly during these final years Gobineau depicted humanity as a ruminant herd devoid of regenerative energies, awaiting some centuries hence not simply the extinction of its species but the still worse fate of reaching that annihilation only as degraded beings. Here was the self-styled aristocrat, nostalgic for epochs past, denouncing the nineteenth century's illusions about 'progress'. His own vision was as bleak as any in the tradition of *Kulturpessimismus*. It not only prefigured the anxieties about human purpose that would be encountered in the existentialism of a later period, but also foreshadowed the horrors of dehumanization that would be depicted through the dystopian literature of the age of Zamyatin, Huxley and Orwell.[16]

When Gobineau died in 1882 at Turin, the end came under conditions of loneliness, self-exile and near-obscurity. One consolation, though, was a new friendship. This was an association which proved crucial to the future cult of what became known as 'gobinism'. Here it is worth recollecting that, much earlier, de Tocqueville had suggested to the

---

[14] This appeared in the posthumous two-volume reissue of 1884: see Gobineau, *Œuvres*, I, 1167–74 (text) and 1457–71 (notes).

[15] See 'Ein Urtheil über die jetzige Weltlage', *Bayreuther Blätter*, 4 (May 1881), 121–40. The original French text entitled 'Ce qui se fait en Asie' was later published in the *Revue du Monde Latin*, 6 (1885), 397–418.

[16] See J. Passmore, *The Perfectibility of Man* (1970), especially ch. 13.

author of the *Essai* that, 'Alone in Europe, the Germans possess the talent for getting impassioned about what they see as abstract truth, without any regard for the practical consequences—and it is they who could provide you with a really favourable audience.'[17] And so it was to be, due principally to the link belatedly forged between Gobineau and Richard Wagner. They met first in 1876, and their mutual admiration soon fermented to the point where the Frenchman was writing for the *Bayreuther Blätter* and visiting Haus Wahnfried for the celebration of the composer's own last two birthdays in 1881–2. They died within months of each other, and soon the Bayreuther Kreis around the widowed Cosima Wagner was promoting Gobineau's work as an adjunct to the perpetuation of the Master's own fame.[18] The result was largely distortive, giving to the new *Gobinismus* a more redemptive leitmotif than its originator ever intended. This was the atmosphere in which the Gobineau Vereinigung was established in 1894, and within which its founder, the scholar-librarian Ludwig Schemann, dedicated himself to disseminating the Frenchman's writings and assembling a commemorative archive at the newly Germanised Strassburg.[19] Similarly, the Wagnerite ethos also permeated that cult of revamped, more buoyant, racist Teutonism which was generated by another writer who had also chosen exile from his own native land—the composer's future son-in-law, Houston Stewart Chamberlain.

The author of the *Grundlagen des neunzehnten Jahrhunderts* was born at Southsea in 1855, the same year that the latter two volumes of the *Essai* appeared. Though he was the son of an English admiral and spent some time at Cheltenham College, the delicate Chamberlain received much of his education abroad, at institutions in France and Switzerland as well as from a German private tutor. In 1878 he embarked on his first marriage, with Anna Horst the daughter of a Breslau lawyer, and then proceeded to study biology at the University of Geneva. Henceforth he would survive on private family funds and increasingly through literary earnings, not least as the author of works celebrating many aspects of Teutonic racial achievement. During the 1880s, while residing at Dresden, Chamberlain fell under the spell of Wagnerism. The start

---

[17] Letter of 30 July 1856, *Correspondance Tocqueville/Gobineau*, 267.

[18] See W. Schüler, *Der Bayreuther Kreis von seiner Entstehung bis zum Ausgang der Wilhelminischen Ära: Wagnerkult und Kulturreform im Geiste völkischer Weltanschauung* (Münster, 1971), 235–52. Much revealing information about the importance of Gobineau's friendship and of his influence at Bayreuth can be found in *Cosima Wagner's Diaries: Volume Two, 1878–1883*, ed. M. Gregor-Dellin and D. Mack (1980).

[19] See particularly L. Schemann, *Gobineaus Rassenwerk* (Stuttgart, 1910), and his *Gobineau: Eine Biographie* (2 vols., Strassburg, 1913–16); also, Schüler, *Der Bayreuther Kreis*, 101–6.

of his direct contribution to the Bayreuther Kreis itself can be dated from his first meeting with Cosima in June 1888.[20] Early in the 1890s he moved to Vienna. The writings which he produced there were deeply suffused not just with the whole spirit of Wahnfried but also with his determination now to be more German than the Germans, particularly in a sense orientated towards Hohenzollern rather than Habsburg loyalties. By 1896 he was already the author of three works on Wagnerian themes.[21] With these to his credit, Chamberlain was then invited by his new publisher, Bruckmann of Munich, to prepare an historical study which, as the century reached its close, would take overall stock of the condition of modern civilization. It was this, the *Grundlagen*, which made his name.

The book was issued in 1899, running to two volumes and more than a thousand pages. As Geoffrey Field has observed, it 'turned Chamberlain almost overnight into the prophet of race for educated laymen in Central Europe'.[22] The work embodied what G. P. Gooch would soon call 'a glittering vision of mind and muscle, of large-scale organization, of intoxicating self-confidence, of metallic brilliancy, such as Europe has never seen'.[23] Composed in the capital city of a declining multi-national Austro-Hungarian Empire, Chamberlain's undertaking reflected all too well the place and time of its origination—not least, through its concern with the painful consequences of ethnic intermixture and through its echo of the populist anti-Semitism that was now becoming fundamental to Viennese politics at the epoch of Karl Lueger's mayoralty.[24] The book was intended largely as a preparatory study, covering mainly European history before 1800. The author's desire, never fulfilled, was to follow this with an even more substantial analysis of the nineteenth century itself. By this procedure, Chamberlain declared, 'we should be able to foreshadow the future—no capricious and fanciful picture, but a shadow cast by the present in the light of the past'.[25]

[20] See generally *Cosima Wagner und Houston Stewart Chamberlain in Briefwechsel, 1888–1908*, ed. P. Pretzsch (Leipzig, 1934); also, Schüler, *Der Bayreuther Kreis*, 112–27 & 252–67. Chamberlain's own *Lebenswege meines Denkens* (Munich, 1919) provides the most important autobiographical text concerning his overall intellectual development.

[21] H. S. Chamberlain, *Das Drama Richard Wagners* (Leipzig, 1892); *Richard Wagner: Echte Briefe an Ferdinand Praeger* (Leipzig, 1894); and *Richard Wagner* (Munich, 1896), the last of these being a major biographical account.

[22] G. Field, *Evangelist of Race: The Germanic Vision of Houston Stewart Chamberlain* (New York, 1981), 214.

[23] G. P. Gooch, *Germany* (New York, 1925), 118.

[24] In the growing corpus of relevant literature the most outstanding study is C. Schorske, *Fin de Siècle Vienna: Politics and Culture* (1980).

[25] H. S. Chamberlain, *The Foundations of the Nineteenth Century* (2 vols., 1910 ['1911' on title-page]), I, lxii. Here all citations of the *Grundlagen* are made with reference to this first and only English-language version, taken from the 5th edition of the German text. For further information about the preparation of this translation, see n. 38 below.

What we can discern from the *Grundlagen*, as supplemented by other writings, is at least the rough shape of that projection from history to prophecy. Its leading features depend upon patterns of explanation by reference to race that are, at many points, directly reminiscent of Gobineau whose *Essai* Chamberlain had begun to study (at Cosima's prompting) back in 1893. The 'Introduction' to the *Grundlagen* tells us how advances in science have made the last hundred years 'a century of races', and how, as 1900 approaches, 'the so-called unity of the human race is indeed still honoured as a hypothesis, but only as a personal, subjective, conviction lacking every material foundation'.[26] So, as in the *Essai*, the various races (whose boundaries are defined with opportunistic flexibility) not merely differ from one another but also exhibit a hierarchy; and, again, it is the interplay between these unequal stocks that holds the key to explaining social and political phenomena in all their complexity. No less striking, however, is the way in which Chamberlain cites Gobineau usually in order to criticise him, and thus seeks to present the *Grundlagen* as adapting and improving this whole mode of thinking towards heights of cogency unattained in the 1850s.[27]

Four major points of distinction need highlighting. First, Gobineau's treatment of the Jews, though generally unflattering, was scarcely more negative than his judgement of other contemporary Europeans, whereas that of Chamberlain is altogether more obsessively hostile. Second, the text of the *Grundlagen* gives a much more explicitly Christian (and essentially Protestant) gloss to the racist position than anything that the agnostical author of the *Essai* had ever felt moved to provide. Third, Chamberlain offers some prospect of reversing those patterns of historic movement which in Gobineau had run inexorably from original purity towards debilitating miscegenation. 'The sound and normal evolution of man', so we read in the *Grundlagen*, 'is not from race to racelessness, but on the contrary from racelessness to ever clearer distinctness of race.'[28] Sound and normal, possibly: yet it is also an evolution that the higher races can sustain for themselves only through constant vigilance over their patterns of endogamy (as well as their occasionally creative bouts of exogamy) and through permanent struggle against the threat of infiltration by those lesser breeds who would otherwise swiftly debilitate them. The discourse is not of a racial perfection already attained, but of a process of perfectibility as yet unfinished—a process of *Volkwerdung* (or ethnic fulfilment), echoing the paradoxical Nietzschean imperative that men must become what they are. Thus, as a fourth

---

[26] Chamberlain, *Foundations*, I, xciii–xciv.
[27] See, for example, *ibid.*, I, 263, 280n, 315; II, 206.
[28] *Ibid.*, I, 296.

point of contrast with Gobineau, the author of the *Grundlagen* treats optimistically the potential future destiny of his chosen race, and talks not about despairing resignation to the ills of the world but about a quasi-Wagnerian quest to conquer them through action.

Chamberlain's treatise identifies five fundamental influences on nineteenth-century civilization: the art, literature and philosophy of Greece; the law and statecraft of Rome; the world-redeeming revelation of Christ; the alien and destructive influence of the Jew; and the renerative power of *der Germane*, the hero of the Aryan-Teutonic races. These last peoples, though initially deemed to embrace also the Celts and Slavs, become in the *Grundlagen* ever more emphatically equated with their most illustrious branch—that of *die Deutsche*, or Teutons in the narrower Tacitean sense of the term. And it is upon their destiny, above all, that the work focuses.

According to the *Grundlagen*, it was the birth of Christ which constituted the most significant event in world history. With his appearance the legacy of Greece and Rome began to be changed into a form upon which the Teutons could draw. To bolster that case Chamberlain even indulged in a highly convoluted argument (about the pronunciation of Aramaic gutturals, and much else) directed against any supposition that the Messiah was, in racial terms, Jewish.[29] The Jesus who strides across the pages of the *Grundlagen* is proud, aggressive and self-indulgent— something closer to a Bismarckian Junker than to the paragon of humility found in more conventional descriptions. In this new guise, Christ becomes the God of the young and vigorous Indo-Europeans, among whom the Teutons are best suited to hearing and answering his call. It is even suggested that he had chosen to live amongst the Jews simply for the reason that, there, his particular qualities would stand out most clearly in contradistinction to those about him—a situation amply confirmed by the events leading up to his crucifixion!

The subsequent history of civilization, as presented in the *Grundlagen*, is essentially the tale of the struggle between Teuton and Jew over the legacy of the ancient world, over the survival or destruction of Christianity, and, not least, over the continuing existence of the two races themselves. Just as Marx and Engels had postulated in *The Communist Manifesto* a progressive simplification of class conflict into that of two great forces,[30] so Chamberlain exploited (in contradistinction to

---

[29] See *ibid.*, I, 201–12. Note also *C. Wagner / H. S. Chamberlain in Briefwechsel*, 564–8, for Cosima's letter of 7 May 1899 and his reply of 22 May, each dealing with the author's reluctance to be equally explicit about some matching assertion that Christ must have been an Aryan. The hesitation turns out to be based on the merely tactical consideration that too much frankness on this point might well alienate those whose anti-Semitism was as yet insufficiently developed!

[30] See *Karl Marx: Selected Writings*, ed. D. McLellan (Oxford, 1977), 222.

Gobineau) the dramatic possibilities of pitting the Teutonic breed against one very particular racial enemy. Though he does make some more general reference to the 'Chaos of Peoples' at the end of the Roman Empire and to the threat from 'coloured' stocks in his own time, the narrative of the *Grundlagen* concentrates increasingly upon an explicit polarization of Teutons and Jews. Here are rival races who, each strengthened by their condition of relatively high endogamy, seem locked as the embodiments of Good and Evil in some relentless Manichean struggle to settle great eschatological issues of tribal redemption and damnation. Granted the rising anti-Semitism of the late 1890s, it is perhaps unsurprising that Chamberlain should have devoted his longest chapter to the corruptive influence of the Jews. The strictures that he occasionally registers against crude criticism of them (note, for example, his politeness about the Sephardim)[31] are merely beguiling. Far more typical of the bitter tone of his reflections on Jewishness is the following: 'This alien people has become precisely in the course of the nineteenth century a disproportionately important and in many spheres actually dominant constituent of our life ... Practically all branches of our life have become more or less willing slaves of the Jews.'[32]

As for the Teutons, Chamberlain depicts them very much according to the classic Aryan typology refined by Gobineau and others during the course of the nineteenth century. We find in the *Grundlagen* a familiar discourse concerning blond long-heads, who combine idealism and practicality, and who are lovers of loyalty and freedom, yet of honour above all else. Until the end of the twelfth century, they had been fully engaged in fighting for the very survival of a rejuvenated Christian culture. Only since that time, in 'The Rise of a New World', have they been able to give more positive indications of their own regenerative potential in the fields of science, industry, economics, politics, religion, philosophy and art. The account of recent centuries is certainly one of progress, but not as any universal or inevitable condition. The Teutons have achieved their advances only in the face of unrelenting Semitic enmity, and by recognizing the vigorous challenges—not the complacent certainties—of *Volkwerdung*.

Amongst the greatest of Teutonic achievements was the Protestant Reformation, which is portrayed in the *Grundlagen* as a decisive act of liberation from the vacuous universalism of Rome. Accompanying his text with a line-drawing of the supposedly Germanic features of Martin Luther, Chamberlain conjures up an almost Wagnerian image of the great churchman as a re-embodiment of his epic forebears:

[31] See Chamberlain, *Foundations*, I, 272–3.
[32] *Ibid.*, I, 330.

One can picture this man fifteen hundred years ago, on horseback, swinging his battle-axe to protect his beloved northern home, and then again at his fireside with his children crowding around him, or at the banquet of the men, draining the horn of mead to the last drop and singing heroic songs in praise of his ancestors.[33]

Yet it is not only the Reformation, but also (just as in Gobineau) the Renaissance, that Chamberlain aspires to portray as a flowering of Teutonic genius. Thus the achievements of Leonardo and Michaelangelo are also brought within the fold of the great race. Even Dante, who could scarcely look less like Luther, is included— with the extraordinary argument that it is in the very contrast of their particular physiognomic features that their intimate racial relationship is best revealed.[34] This is one of the most flagrant examples of Chamberlain's opportunistic approach to 'method'. His concept of racial *Gestalt*—here, ideally, the triumph of orderly form over chaos—was a heady cocktail of external physical qualities and inner spiritual ones. Such a mixture could be validated by reference to intuition whenever 'science' in some more conventionally testable sense failed him. Put another way, Chamberlain's habitual procedures remind us sharply of what can happen to the historiographical applications of neo-Kantian idealism once these escape from Dilthey and fall into less scrupulous hands.[35]

Sadly, it must also be recorded that Chamberlain's ambitious synthesis so well epitomised the manner and the aspirations of much German racist thinking around 1900 that, unlike Gobineau in the 1850s, he saw his *magnum opus* credited with a large measure of immediate success. Here recent commentators such as Geoffrey Field and Roger Chickering have focused our attention particularly on the middle-class nationalists: the former observes, for example, that Chamberlain's tone 'captured their buoyant spirit as well as their nagging fears of moral decline'.[36]

---

[33] *Ibid.*, I, 541.

[34] See *ibid.*, I, 538–42.

[35] These problems are also particularly well exemplified in Chamberlain's unfinished and posthumously published work on *Natur und Leben*, ed. J. von Uexküll (Munich, 1928). On the general theme of such philosophical distortion, see R. Stackelberg, *Idealism Debased: From Völkisch Ideology to National Socialism* (Kent, OH, 1981). Similar issues have recently been pursued, within the context of response to the 'Entzauberung' ('disenchantment') analysed by Max Weber, in Anne Harrington's admirable study of *Reenchanted Science: Holism in German Culture from Wilhelm II to Hitler* (Princeton, 1996), and especially in ch. 4 with regard to Chamberlain himself.

[36] Field, *Evangelist of Race*, 2; and see generally R. Chickering, *We Men Who Feel Most German: A Cultural Study of the Pan-German League, 1886–1914* (1984). For the influence of Chamberlain, and Gobineau, on Heinrich Class (the League's president), see F. Stern, *The Politics of Cultural Despair: A Study in the Rise of the Germanic Ideology* (New York, 1965), 124–5n.

The text also appealed to Kaiser Wilhelm II. He read extracts to the imperial family, and received Chamberlain at court. Wilhelm also conducted a correspondence with the self-exiled Englishman that was to last for more than twenty years. One of the Kaiser's earliest letters to the author of the *Grundlagen*, written at the end of 1901, included these words:

> You come along and with one magic stroke bring order into the confusion, light into the darkness. You show the goals for which we strive and work, explain these things which we had sensed only dimly, and reveal the paths which must be followed for the salvation of the Germans and thus the salvation of mankind![37]

This was the atmosphere in which a popularly priced edition of Chamberlain's book appeared five years later, and by 1914 over 100,000 copies of the work had been sold in the German lands. Such was its commercial success that as early as 1907–8 the question of an English version was being raised. Here the prime mover appears to have been Anna Chamberlain—even though she was about to be divorced from her husband, who would himself then move permanently to Bayreuth and swiftly take as his second wife Eva, daughter of Cosima Wagner and of the late Master himself. The resulting translation, which was eventually issued as *The Foundations of the Nineteenth Century* from London towards the end of 1910 with an introduction by Lord Redesdale, met with a mixed, but mainly polite, reception.[38]

By 1914 Chamberlain was one of the leading forces in a Bayreuth Circle which had long been identified with extreme Pan-Germanist ambitions and which had indeed come to form what Frederic Spotts

---

[37] Letter of 31 December 1901, in H. S. Chamberlain, *Briefe 1882–1924 und Briefwechsel mit Kaiser Wilhelm II*, ed. P. Pretzsch (2 vols., Munich, 1928), II, 142.

[38] The enthusiasm of George Bernard Shaw in *Fabian News*, 22 (June 1911), 53–4, is perhaps worthy of particular note. In more general terms, the far from easy route by which the *Grundlagen* became converted into the *Foundations* (see also n. 25 above) is discussed in C. Holmes, 'Houston Stewart Chamberlain and Great Britain', *Wiener Library Bulletin*, 24, 2 (1970), 31–3, and in Field, *Evangelist of Race*, 459–61. Letters relevant to the preparation of the English edition were kept by the first Baron Redesdale—grandfather of 'the Mitford girls' (including Diana who married Sir Oswald Mosley, and Unity who had similar but unfulfilled designs on Hitler)—and these items can now be consulted at the Gloucestershire Record Office: Mitford Papers, D2002[C48]. Among the most interesting holdings is the long autobiographical letter of 25 November 1908 in which Chamberlain comments to Redesdale along lines that are somewhat defensive about the Kaiser's enthusiasm for the *Grundlagen*: 'given the state of feeling in Germany any interest he shows is likely to do quite as much harm as good. I myself am very fond of the Emperor and am grateful for all the kindness he has shown me, but I should not value very highly his opinion on a book.'

has aptly called 'the Krupps of the culture industry'.[39] With the outbreak of international hostilities, Chamberlain turned his talents towards promoting the war effort of the Second Reich and, in particular, towards deriding his native England. His *Kriegsaufsätze*, published at Munich late in 1914, were soon translated for distribution from London as well—but only under a title, *The Ravings of a Renegade*, which neatly reversed the intended trajectory of the polemical salvo.[40] In 1915 his writings won him the award of the Iron Cross, and in 1916 he became a naturalised German. During the rest of the war he continued to produce propagandist works in similar vein—some so imprudently annexationist that the German censors themselves felt obliged to insist on alterations. As Roderick Stackelberg notes: 'If the function of his prewar works had been to provide an ideology for Germany's educated elite, the function of these pamphlets was to mobilise mass support for nationalist and imperialist goals.'[41] In 1917 he was among the founders of *Deutschlands Erneuerung*, which quickly became one of the leading journals of the extreme anti-Semitic and anti-democratic right. Even after the collapse of the Wilhelminian regime, he persisted in corresponding with the exiled Kaiser. However, as an increasingly populist and counter-revolutionary promoter of Pan-Germanic ideas who insisted on the polarization of race and anti-race and on the imperatives of *Volkwerdung*, the ailing Chamberlain would also soon be serving the new Nazi movement as the oracle of Bayreuth.

[39] F. Spotts, *Bayreuth: A History of the Wagner Festival* (New Haven, 1994), 113. It was in 1914 that Winifred Williams (shortly to become the wife of the Wagners' son, Siegfried) began to move into the inner circle around Cosima as yet another Briton keen to be even more German than the Germans: see *ibid.*, 137–8.

[40] See *The Ravings of a Renegade, Being the War Essays of Houston Stewart Chamberlain*, intro. by Lewis Melville [pseudonym for Lewis S. Benjamin] (1915). I have recently presented a more detailed discussion of this episode in a paper on 'The Englishman as German: Text and Counter-Text in Houston Stewart Chamberlain'. This was delivered in September 1996 to a Joint Symposium of the Universities of Düsseldorf and Reading, dealing with the general theme of 'Interkulturelles Verstehen', and it is due to appear in the forthcoming publication of these conference proceedings as edited by Therese Seidel and Cedric Brown for the series 'Kultur und Erkenntnis', issued by Narr of Tübingen. Among Chamberlain's other writings from this period, his pamphlet of 1915 entitled *Who is to Blame for the War?* was also issued in an English (as well as an original German) version. The place of publication for the translated text is unclear: 'Bruckmann' (implying Munich) is pencilled on to the British Library copy, but the source is given as Sweden in J. M. Robertson, 'Herr Chamberlain and the War', *Contemporary Review*, 108 (1915), 299. The preface to the English rendering of the pamphlet states that it is being issued for the benefit of 'readers in neutral countries' (p. 3). However, at that stage in the war, it may well have served to alienate some of the most influential of these same readers through its attack on 'the vilest despotism that has ever existed – the despotism of the American Dollar' (p. 6)! On Chamberlain's war pamphlets in general, see Stackelberg, *Idealism Debased*, ch. 13.

[41] Stackelberg, *Idealism Debased*, 146.

There it was that—early in October 1923, just a few weeks before the failure of the Beer Hall Putsch in Munich—Hitler came to pay his respects to the Germanised Englishman. Their dialogue led Chamberlain promptly to send, in terms that directly echoed the Kaiser's praise of 1901 for the author of the *Grundlagen* himself, an effusive and open declaration of allegiance: 'At one blow you have transformed the state of my soul. That Germany in its hour of greatest need has given birth to a Hitler is proof of its vitality.'[42] As Field has observed: 'With this letter Chamberlain became the first person of national and even international reputation as a writer to align himself with the Nazi movement.'[43] The party's newspaper, the *Völkischer Beobachter*, regularly returned the compliment, and there were four further amicable meetings between Hitler and his newly enrolled supporter before the latter died in January 1927. At the Bayreuth funeral of Chamberlain the presence of Hitler (together with a group of pallbearers from the *Sturmabteilung*) was to prove historically more significant than that of the ex-Kaiser's son, Prince August Wilhelm. A few months later Alfred Rosenberg, the self-styled 'philosopher' of National Socialism, would produce a book which through its very title praised Chamberlain as 'The Prophet and Founder of a German Future'.[44]

Six years later, Bayreuth was also the venue for the one recorded encounter between Hitler and Oswald Spengler. Even the aura of Haus Wahnfried was insufficient to make a success of their long private meeting. The new *Reichskanzler* seems to have been the more disappointed of the two participants, if only because he had harboured the larger number of illusions about potential points of agreement between them.

Spengler's eminence in 1933 was linked to the fact that around the end of the Great War he had registered in Germany an even more striking literary sensation than the one triggered by the *Grundlagen* at the turn of the century. The first half of *Der Untergang des Abendlandes* was published in the late summer of 1918, when its Blankenburg-born author was thirty-eight years old.[45] As another contribution to the

[42] Letter of 7 October 1923, in Chamberlain, *Briefe 1882–1924*, II, 126.
[43] Field, *Evangelist of Race*, 438.
[44] See A. Rosenberg, *Chamberlain als Verkünder und Begründer einer deutschen Zukunft* (Munich, 1927). Note also *Alfred Rosenberg: Selected Writings*, ed. R. Pois (1970), 21–3; and R. Cecil, *The Myth of the Master Race: Alfred Rosenberg and Nazi Ideology* (1972), 12–14.
[45] O. Spengler, *Der Untergang des Abendlandes* (2 vols., 1918–22): the first printing of volume I was originally issued by Braumüller from Vienna, but all subsequent German publication both of this and of volume II was handled by C. H. Beck Verlag of Munich. Here all citations are geared to the standard English 'authorised translation' of C. H. Atkinson, presented as *The Decline of the West* (2 vols., 1926–8).

writing of global history, this was a work breathtaking in its range and in its dogmatism not only about the patterns of the past but also about the way ahead. The arguments underpinning Spengler's doom-laden prophecies met with little sympathy from most academics. But, in regard to a wider public, this hitherto obscure and prematurely retired schoolmaster did manage to fulfil his prediction of 1916 that the work would have the impact of an avalanche rushing down into a placid mountain-pool![46] By 1922, when the second half of the *Untergang* appeared, Spengler was already a cult-figure in Germany, and to some extent beyond. When the English version began to come out in 1926, the German sales of Volume One had already reached 100,000. Arthur Moeller van den Bruck, who was wrong about so much else, may well have been right at least in his judgement that, amidst the extraordinary circumstances of the early 1920s, here indeed was 'the destiny-book of our whole epoch'.[47]

When Spengler began to compose the *Untergang* in Munich around 1911, he was already convinced that a crisis in the affairs of Europe was imminent. By the time that war erupted in 1914, much of the first volume had been drafted. He had predicted the coming of the conflict, but had failed to foresee both its long duration and its disastrous outcome for Germany. Being declared unfit for military service, Spengler promptly made his writing into a contribution towards the national war effort. A vast range of reading supported his project, but he acknowledged two intellectual debts of outstanding importance.[48] One went to a writer whom Chamberlain too had deeply respected, while the other was directed towards a philosopher whom the Englishman had no less clearly condemned. In the first place, Spengler cited Goethe, as his master of method—not so much in literature as in natural science, and in plant morphology above all. Here the author of the *Untergang* was drawing inspiration from the typically romantic impatience with any study of nature which remained merely analytical and dissective, and which thus failed to illuminate the *Urphänomen*, the deeper realities and underlying structures of existence. Spengler's other principal mentor was Nietzsche, whom he admired as a critic of all contemporary complacency. The *Untergang* reflects at many points such Nietzschean themes as the idea of decadence, the will to power, the

---

[46] Letter of 12 July 1916 to Hans Klöres, in O. Spengler, *Briefe, 1913–1936*, ed. M. Schröter and A. Koktanek (Munich, 1963), 54.

[47] Quoted from an article in the *Deutsche Rundschau* as cited by Beck Verlag within a promotional pamphlet of *c.* 1925–6: see the Allen and Unwin files relevant to the preparation of the English edition, which are held in the British Publishing Archives at the University of Reading Library. For more concerning Moeller on Spengler, see Stern, *Politics of Cultural Despair*, 293–5.

[48] See particularly Spengler, *Decline*, I, 49n.

contrast between Apollinian and Dionysian ideals, the transience of the Christian pity-ethic and the concept of eternal recurrence. In Spengler's view, the sage of Sils Maria had been most remarkable for his efforts to destroy the received ideas of the late nineteenth century. Now it was time for even stronger affirmation, however gloomy. This would come from an historian confident that he could see—certainly backwards, but why not forwards too?—far beyond the limited horizons of more myopic contemporaries.

Spengler rejected as parochial any merely Eurocentric historiographical framework based upon ancient, medieval and modern periodization. He made the quite reasonable complaint that this could distort many aspects of past development. However, he then crafted an even more Procrustean bed of his own upon which facts might be tortured. Goethe's *Urphänomen* had inspired Spengler to think of an octet of 'independent and individual plant-like cultures'.[49] The *Untergang* treats five of these (the Egyptian, Indian, Babylonian, Chinese and Mexican flowerings) with relative brevity. Those that receive much fuller attention comprise, first, the Apollinian culture characterizing Greece and Rome; second, the Magian manifestation, associated principally with Islamic societies but embracing also many aspects of Judaic, early Christian and Byzantine experience; and, third, '*die Kultur des Abendlandes*' which has dominated the most recent millennium of European development. This last version, quite strongly Germanic in its emphasis, also receives the ominous label of 'Faustian' culture. The *Untergang* amounts, essentially, to an historical investigation of 'the morphological relationship' between these eight elements, with a view to elucidating the laws and rhythms governing their fate.

For Gobineau and Chamberlain the thrust of historical processes is predominantly linear, moving downward in the one case and (potentially at least) driving upward in the other. With Spengler, however, we move into the world of gyre—vast, looping circles of eternal recurrence. Moreover, although he seems to resemble the other two in his claim that race is 'a decisive element in every question of life',[50] his ideas about what it might actually *be* remain extremely vague. Certainly it never assumes in the *Untergang* that role as the central dynamo of historical movement which it plays throughout the *Essai* and the *Grundlagen*, and neither of these earlier works is directly cited in the later one.

How cultures spring up is indeed a topic about which Spengler, always stronger on sequences than causes, remains more than usually obscure. Still, once it does emerge, each culture then seems destined

---

[49] Letter of 5 January 1919 to Georg Misch, in Spengler, *Briefe, 1913–1936*, 116.
[50] Spengler, *Decline*, II, 130.

to follow a biological pattern of growth, maturity and decay. The author suggests that this process, stretching typically over a millennium or so, may also be expressed according to the rhythm of the seasons from springtime onward. By the stage when autumn gives way to winter, we have also the phase of transition from *Kultur* proper to that of mere *Zivilisation*. As Spengler seeks to explain:

> In this work, for the first time the two words, hitherto used to express an indefinite, more or less ethical distinction, are used in a *periodic* sense, to express a strict and necessary *organic succession*. The Civilization is the inevitable *destiny* of the Culture ... Civilizations are the most external and artificial states of which a species of developed humanity is capable. They are a conclusion, the thing-become succeeding the thing-becoming (*sie folgen dem Werden als das Gewordene*), death following life, rigidity following expansion ... They are an end, irrevocable, yet by inward necessity reached again and again.[51]

The contrast between 'culture' and 'civilization' had been drawn by Nietzsche a generation earlier, and even during Spengler's own era Thomas Mann too was developing a similar theme of tension in order to convey a distinction between the values of Germany and those of 'the west' in a stricter sense.[52] Yet the *Untergang* expresses the point with particular starkness. Its author presents not simply a picture of stagnation and decay but also—for each particular culture-become-civilization—something that amounts, just as sharply as in Gobineau, to an *entropic* vision of energies exhausted and unreclaimable.

The ambitiousness of unifying pattern present in the *Untergang* becomes clearer once we appreciate that Spengler is alleging that tight similarities exist not only through the history of each individual culture but also as between cultures at each analogous stage of the organic process previously sketched. Regarding the first of these structural constraints, the author insists that each culture is suffused by a distinctive spirit, which binds together through 'morphological relationship' all the forms under which it expresses itself. Thus, in an enterprise that involves bold imaginative leaps, Spengler claims to discern a certain harmony across the political, economic, religious, scientific, literary, artistic and

---

[51] *Ibid.*, I, 31.

[52] A measure of similarity between Spengler and the character of Naphta in Mann's *Der Zauberberg* (2 vols., Berlin, 1924) was one of the points noted by J. P. Stern in 'The Rise and Fall of Random Persons', an especially valuable article from 1985 reprinted in his collection *The Heart of Europe: Essays on Literature and Ideology* (Oxford, 1992), 123–39. In his *Betrachtungen eines Unpolitischen* (Berlin, 1918) Mann had already provided one of the most memorable expositions of alleged tension between 'culture' and 'civilization'. For the role of this polarization within the longer tradition of German philosophical idealism, see also the comments by Fritz Stern in *Politics of Cultural Despair*, 246n.

other spheres. All aspects of Apollinian existence, for example, are said to centre upon its dominant concern with the tangible and finite—'the ordering of the "become" in so far as this was present, visible, measurable, and numerable'.[53] On this basis, Spengler draws together the fashion for life-sized nudes and small temples, the emergence of the city-state and the development of coin-currency. As for the contrasting experience of Europe in more recent times, 'the Western, Gothic, form-feeling ... is that of an unrestrained, strong-willed, far-reaching soul, and its chosen badge is pure, imperceptible, unlimited space'.[54] So this is a culture which expresses the linkages between such superficially disparate phenomena as printing, cathedral spires, deep perspective in painting, cheque-books and the credit system, the music of fugue and counterpoint, long-range artillery and the telephone.

The second structural constraint is crystallised best in the three charts on 'the comparative morphology of history' appended to the first volume of the *Untergang*. These illustrate Spengler's conception of the 'contemporaneity' that exists between the phases of all cultures as they each live through their healthy millennium before passing into the span of civilizational decay. Thus 'the new God-feeling' of the springtime produces the parallel between Vedic religion and the Catholic cult of the Virgin Mary; summer brings together Pythagoras and Leibniz as mathematicians of 'number as copy' (*die Zahl als Abbild*), as well as Mohammed and Milton as the champions of puritanical intensity; the characteristic autumnal confidence in the might of reason makes contemporaries of Socrates and Voltaire; Alexander the Great and Napoleon join chilled hands as the harbingers of the politics of winter. In similar vein, Spengler can associate Buddhism, Stoicism and Socialism as morphologically equivalent demonstrations of the proposition that 'each culture has its own mode of spiritual extinction'.[55]

It was precisely this insistence upon sequential regularities which underlay the predictive arrogance of the *Untergang* and fuelled the work's enormous public impact. 'It was not until he got to the twentieth century', writes Stuart Hughes, 'that Spengler revealed the truly original implications of his morphological method, and it was his account of his own time and his predictions for the decades to come that chiefly shocked and alarmed his readers.'[56] And nobody had ever claimed more than he for the prophetic utility of studying the past. 'The central idea', declared Spengler in another text, 'is the concept of Destiny.'[57]

---

[53] Spengler, *Decline*, I, 81.
[54] *Ibid.*
[55] *Ibid.*, I, 356.
[56] H. S. Hughes, *Oswald Spengler: A Critical Estimate* (New York, 1952), 86.
[57] O. Spengler, 'Pessimism?', in *Selected Essays*, ed. D. O. White (Chicago, 1967), 137. This piece was originally published in pamphlet form as *Pessimismus?* (Berlin, 1921).

Just as the very first sentence of the *Untergang* rang out with the claim that 'In this book is attempted for the first time the venture of predetermining history', so did its final words read '*Ducunt Fata volentem, nolentem trahunt.*'[58]

The actual vista offered by the *Untergang* to the twentieth-century west was a thoroughly wintry one. Central to this increasingly desolate landscape was the *Weltstadt*, the menace of 'megalopolis'. Cultural springtime is enjoyed in a predominantly rural setting; summer brings a more urban emphasis, involving a healthily symbiotic relationship with the agrarian hinterland; and autumn witnesses a fully ripened cultural development which is inseparable from the maturing of town life. However, Spengler also sees the autumnal city as the context within which a dangerously paradoxical influence begins to operate. Despite its superficially positive image, 'the spell of personal freedom'[59] upon which urbanization thrives is a force full of negative consequences over the longer term. It develops into a quest for the emancipation, even the divorce, of the town from its hinterland. Just as the city then sucks dry the life-blood of the countryside, so eventually does the 'megalopolis' emerge at the cost not simply of completing the process of rural destruction but also of devouring other urban rivals. As autumn gives way to winter, everything becomes concentrated 'in three or four world-cities that have absorbed into themselves the whole content of History, while the old wide landscape of the Culture, become merely provincial, serves only to supply the cities with what remains of its higher mankind'.[60] Society finds itself drained of all creative diversity, as the great city becomes the monopolistic centre of political, economic, spiritual and artistic control. Here is a universe diminished and shrunken—one such as the Romans experienced when their Forum became the *sole* focal point of the ancient world. For Spengler, the metropolis means death. It is a 'stone-colossus' marking the tomb of every great culture—'the monstrous symbol and vessel of the completely emancipated intellect, the world-city, the centre in which the course of a world-history ends by winding itself up'.[61] From age to age the sequences are chillingly inexorable: 'After Syracuse, Athens, and Alexandria comes Rome. After Madrid, Paris, London come Berlin and New York.'[62]

[58] Spengler, *Decline*, I, 32; II, 507.

[59] *Ibid.*, II, 354.

[60] *Ibid.*, I, 32.

[61] *Ibid.*, II, 98.

[62] *Ibid.*, I, 31–2. Hughes, *Spengler*, 43, aptly quotes Henry Adams's observation of 1894 that, 'If a science of history were established today ... I greatly fear that it would take its tone from the pessimism of Paris, Berlin, London, and St Petersburg.' It is also relevant that in 1922, when the second volume of the *Untergang* appeared, T. S. Eliot's notes on lines 366–76 of *The Waste Land* ('Who are these hooded hordes swarming / Over endless plains, stumbling in cracked earth / ... Falling towers / Jerusalem Athens Alexandria / Vienna London / Unreal') included a telling 'Spenglerian' quotation from

The great cities which Gobineau had condemned as the focal points of debilitating miscegenation are associated by Spengler with a further form of 'race-suicide'. This occurs when the obsessive desire for money which also characterises each era of decline serves to promote the habit of limiting births. Though modern Europe might not yet have experienced the agony of depopulation, Spengler believed that there were already many signs of women starting to undervalue their dignity as mothers: 'Now emerges the Ibsen-woman, the comrade, the heroine of a whole megalopolitan literature from Nordic drama to Parisian novel. Instead of children, she has soul-conflicts; marriage is a craft-art for the achievement of "mutual understanding".' The contemporary epoch is developing, like the Hellenistic centuries, 'an ethic for childless intelligences', and one in which the father of many children is becoming an object of mere mockery.[63] The long-term outcome will indeed be a form of racial suicide, leaving even the great cities ultimately deserted, 'harbouring in their stone masses a small population of fellaheen who shelter in them as the men of the Stone Age sheltered in cave and pile-dwellings'.[64]

Already, for Spengler, the city exists largely as facade. Its exterior has become, albeit on the metropolitan scale, every bit as deceptive as that of a Potemkin village. Behind and beneath the superficial elegance are concealed darker and more dangerous forces: 'Always the splendid mass-cities harbour lamentable poverty and degraded habits, and the attics and the mansards, the cellars and back-courts, are breeding a new type of raw man (*einen neuen Urmenschen*)—in Baghdad and in Babylon, just as in Tenochtitlan and today in London and Berlin.'[65] This is where the tensions of civilization develop, readily exploited by an unscrupulous popular press and clearly reflected in the fatuous forms of recreation through which metropolitan man strives to obtain relief from that stress. Rome in its last days had its own equivalents to the 'cinema, expressionism, theosophy, boxing contests, nigger dances, poker, and racing'[66] which so typify the present epoch. Here Spengler, like Gobineau and Chamberlain too, revealed his indebtedness to what Patrick Brantlinger has called 'the major myth of our time', that of 'negative classicism'[67]—something having at its core an image of deca-

---

the small collection of essays recently produced by Hermann Hesse under the title *Blick ins Chaos* (Berne, 1920).

[63] Spengler, *Decline*, II, 105.

[64] *Ibid.*, II, 107.

[65] *Ibid.*, II, 102.

[66] *Ibid.*, II, 103.

[67] See P. Brantlinger, *Bread and Circuses: Theories of Mass Culture as Social Decay* (Ithaca, NY, 1983), especially 17, and 24.

dence most famously expressed in Juvenal's reference to the rabble's craving after *panem et circenses*.

Spengler is no less keen, however, to blame those who lead that mob by pandering to its depraved desires. It is indeed the points of interaction between the unscrupulousness of the leaders and the mindlessness of the led which inspire some of his most memorably agonised passages. 'To the world-city', declares Spengler, 'belongs not a *Volk* but a mass.'[68] The latter is a force known and feared in every civilization:

> It is the absolute of formlessness, persecuting with its hate every sort of form, every distinction of rank, the orderliness of property, the orderliness of knowledge. It is the new nomadism of the Cosmopolis ... Thus the Fourth Estate becomes the expression of the passing of a history over into the historyless. The mass is the end, the radical nullity.[69]

In writing thus, Spengler was reflecting his debt to Nietzsche and asserting his agreement with many other European intellectuals of the early twentieth century who shared his sense of asphyxiation amidst the herd.[70] He composed the second volume of the *Untergang* while memories of the Spartacist Revolt and the Munich Soviet were still fresh. When he compares explicitly the rising against the Thirteenth Dynasty of Egypt with the events of 1789 and 1871 in Paris, it seems plain that the urban mob's threat to social order in the Germany of the early 1920s has become an even more burning concern. The picture is one of megalopolitan revolution, where the masses have become 'will-less tools' of the ambition of leaders bent on projecting into the external world the chaos which reigns within themselves. 'It is wholly immaterial', declares Spengler, 'what slogans scream to the wind while the gates and skulls are beaten in. Destruction is the true and only impulse. The world-city, the land-devouring demon, has set its rootless and futureless men in motion; and in destroying they die.'[71] As Europe now re-enters a Caesarist age when 'men of force' (*Gewaltmenschen*) will use those metropolitan masses for their own purposes, he urges his contemporaries to acknowledge that 'the age of gigantic conflicts' is imminent.[72]

The prose of the *Untergang* is at its most powerful when Spengler scans these vistas of continuing violence and when, especially in Volume

---

[68] Spengler, *Decline*, I, 33.

[69] *Ibid.*, II, 358.

[70] I have endeavoured to pursue this theme more generally in *The Age of the Masses: Ideas and Society in Europe since 1870* (Harmondsworth, 1977). See also the titles cited in n. 13 above.

[71] Spengler, *Decline*, II, 427n.

[72] *Ibid.*, II, 416.

Two, he denounces the impracticality of liberal-democratic principles as a shield against Caesarism. According to him, everything for which the victors of 'the west' in 1918 claimed to stand was destined soon to go under. This gave readers beyond Germany some food for thought. Even more swiftly, the analysis offered some comfort, a certain paradoxical *Schadenfreude*, to a whole generation of the defeated. Many of them responded favourably to the hints that, if Caesars there were to be, it would be best for Germany herself to provide them—and thus possibly delay the phase when the Russians or the Japanese would lead a new stage of dominance, and even a new cycle of *Kultur*. But to what extent did the *Untergang*, like Gobineau's *Essai*, exclude the scope for real political choice and activism? How far was it vulnerable to Chamberlain's own accusation that the gloom and doom were overdone?[73] Insofar as he could resolve these points, Spengler did so by distinguishing between the longer and the shorter term. His essay entitled 'Pessimism?', published in 1921 between the appearance of the two halves of the *Untergang*, sought to deny that his philosophy endorsed a paralysis of action, at least for the present.[74] As he had previously declared to Hans Klöres, 'first force, then construction', carried through not by majorities but by the few with a real vocation for politics.[75] Far from denying fate, it is men such as these who in the long term will actually fulfil it.[76]

Over the first twenty-five years after its publication, many of the prophecies made in the *Untergang* seemed to come close to being borne out. Writing soon after a second world war, Erich Heller would make this memorable comment: 'The history of the West since 1917 looks like the work of children clumsily filling in with lurid colours a design drawn in outline by Oswald Spengler.'[77] With prediction clearly serving to assist eventual actualization, his book made its own contribution towards undermining the frail Weimar Republic. While he remained peripheral to the regular academic community and did not publicly identify himself with any specific political grouping, Spengler went on to produce a number of smaller works developing variations upon the themes of the *Untergang*, with particular reference to current problems.[78]

---

[73] See H. S. Chamberlain, *Drei Vorworte* (Munich, 1923), 19.

[74] See Spengler, *Selected Essays*, 133–54.

[75] Letter of 18 December 1918 to Klöres, in Spengler, *Briefe, 1913–1936*, 113.

[76] It is noteworthy that, when choosing the title of his major work, Spengler had considered using the term 'Vollendung' (conveying the sense of fulfilment as well as termination) rather than 'Untergang': see 'Pessimism?', in *Selected Essays*, 134.

[77] E. Heller, *The Disinherited Mind* (Harmondsworth, 1961), 159.

[78] On the limits to the pose of Olympian detachment, see especially W. Struve's essay, 'Oswald Spengler: Caesar and Croesus', in his *Elites Against Democracy: Leadership Ideals in Bourgeois Political Thought in Germany, 1890–1933* (Princeton, NJ, 1973), 232–73.

As early as 1919, during the construction of the Weimar constitution, he rushed out a short volume on *Preussentum und Sozialismus*. It warned German youth against endorsing either an illusory parliamentarism, or a betrayal of socialism in its *best* sense. The work's curious mixture of radicalism and conservatism is encapsulated in its conclusion:

> Become men! ... We need hardness, we need a courageous scep-
> ticism, we need a class of socialistic mastertypes. The path to power
> has already been mapped: the valuable elements of German labour
> in union with the best representatives of the Old Prussian state, both
> groups determined to build a strictly socialist state in the Prussian
> manner; both forged into a unit by the same sense of duty, by the
> awareness of a great obligation, by the will to obey in order to rule,
> to die in order to win, by the strength to make immense sacrifices
> in order to accomplish what we were born for, what we are, what
> could not be without us.[79]

Here was an attempt to nationalise socialism that seemed potentially convergent with the aims of Hitler. During the 1920s Spengler published various lectures on political topics, and in 1931 issued some metaphysical and anthropological ruminations under the title *Der Mensch und die Technik*.[80] One of its conclusions—that soon the coloured races would turn the Machine against its inventors for the purpose of destroying the west—not only echoed Gobineau but also re-emerged strongly in Spengler's final work, *Jahre der Entscheidung*.[81]

That book appeared during the first months of the Nazi regime. The assaults upon Weimar made by Hitler and Spengler had been, at many points, similar. However, there was between them only a far more limited agreement about the positive policies needed for the future. Spengler acknowledged, for instance, that there did exist a Jewish problem, but he thought that assimilation was the key to its solution. Further, as Walter Struve notes, 'He believed in German superiority, but not in the racial superiority of Germans.'[82] Spengler's political sympathies went less to Hitler, whose Beer Hall Putsch he had earlier and promptly condemned, than to those traditional conservative nationalists who had tried to treat the Führer as their 'drummer-boy'. The Austrian corporal was plainly not the particular Caesar whom the writer of the *Untergang* had in mind as his *Gewaltmensch*. Stuart Hughes

---

[79] Spengler, *Selected Essays*, 130–1.

[80] O. Spengler, *Der Mensch und die Technik: Beitrag zu einer Philosophie des Lebens* (Munich, 1931); translated as *Man and Technics: A Contribution to a Philosophy of Life* (New York, 1932).

[81] O. Spengler, *Jahre der Entscheidung: Deutschland und die weltgeschichtliche Entwicklung* (Munich, 1933); translated as *The Hour of Decision: Germany and World-Historical Evolution* (New York, 1934).

[82] Struve, *Elites Against Democracy*, 272.

remarks that, once Hitler grasped how little enthusiasm towards the new Reich was evident in the pages of *Jahre der Entscheidung*, 'the Nazis turned on Spengler with the fury of disappointed expectation'.[83] Further sales of the book were prohibited (though only when 150,000 copies were already in print), and until his death in 1936 in Munich its author suffered declining health and official disfavour.

Even today Spengler's *Untergang* stands, alongside Arnold Toynbee's multi-volume *A Study of History*, as one of the most awesome monuments to historical positivism in the first half of the twentieth century.[84] By postulating systems involving recurrent cycles of culture or civilization, Spengler (strongly) and Toynbee (more hesitantly) both came ultimately to mimic the 'repeatability' of the scientist's controlled experiment. The works of Gobineau and Chamberlain are different from this to the extent that with them the patterns of development emerge as more linear and the structures of explanation as more racially determined. But the *Essai* and the *Grundlagen* do share with the *Untergang* a biologically orientated 'scientism', in the pejorative sense stressed by Karl Popper: 'the naive belief that the methods of the natural sciences (or, rather, what many people believe to be the methods of the natural sciences) must produce similarly impressive results in the social field'.[85] Spengler especially would have resisted any such labelling. He had declared: 'Nature is to be handled scientifically, History poetically.' Yet he also had to concede, at once and revealingly:

> There are no exact boundaries set between the two kinds of world-notion. However great the contrast between becoming and the become, the fact remains that they are jointly present in every kind of understanding. He who looks at the becoming and fulfilling in them, experiences History; he who dissects them as become and fulfilled cognises Nature.[86]

Spengler's central weakness is not the fact that he perceives a certain complementarity between the two modes; it is, rather, that his switches

[83] Hughes, *Spengler*, 132.
[84] I sought to examine these works, together with such kindred ones as H. G. Wells's immensely popular *The Outline of History* (2 vols., 1920), in my 1993 Presidential Address on 'World History and World Heritage' given to the Historical Association Annual Conference held at the University of Durham. An enlarged version of this text has now been published as 'Global Interdependence and the Study of Modern World History', in *Politics in an Interdependent World: Essays Presented to Ghita Ionescu*, ed. G. Parry (Aldershot, 1994), 66–84.
[85] K. R. Popper, *The Open Society and its Enemies* (4th edn., 2 vols., 1962), I, 285–6.
[86] Spengler, *Decline*, I, 96–7.

from one to the other are so unrigorous and opportunistic.

That is similarly characteristic not only of Chamberlain, whose almost parodistic version of neo-Kantianism was noted earlier, but also of Gobineau. As Melvin Richter has observed, the *Essai* too required from the past the sort of corroboration 'which could not be supplied by any records then existing or ever likely to be found'; or as Ernst Cassirer put it another way, 'Gobineau's metaphysics claimed to be a natural science.'[87] Whenever the need to establish clear criteria of truth and falsifiability becomes pressing, all three of these authors retreat into mere lyrical assertion. Bearing in mind just where Gobineau and Chamberlain did become popular and just how little success they enjoyed in their own native countries, we might agree all the more readily with the observation made by J. P. Stern on the *Untergang* in particular—that it represents 'a mixture of genres ... intensely *German* in cutting across the distinctions and kinds of French and English theories and literary conventions'. On that basis, he regards the work as embodying 'a pattern of inherently prosy utterances ... which freely cross and re-cross what the arch-Spenglerian, T. S. Eliot, called "the frontiers of metaphysics and mysticism"'.[88]

This may also be broadly the sense in which Spengler was even more *timely* than Chamberlain, and considerably more so than Gobineau—the sense in which he was not just a diagnostician of current intellectual (as well as social) ills, but also a clear symptom of their prevalence. Ludwig von Bertalanffy, an early reviewer of the *Untergang*, got close to the heart of the matter with these words:

> The most vital thing to grasp about Spengler is that he focuses together all the trends of our time. Here his style has the delicacy of language we find in a Hölderlin; there, the prosaic cold tone of a business report. His mind is sometimes full of inward mysticism like Novalis; sometimes as deliberately and clearly reasonable as Voltaire. He is as fanatical as a Russian sectarian, but also as coldly dispassionate, remote, and business-like as a bank director.[89]

The resulting paradoxes are similar in their substance and solution to those which Jeffrey Herf has brought together so stimulatingly under the heading of 'reactionary modernism'.[90] Does not Spengler reflect

---

[87] M. Richter, 'The Study of Man—a Debate on Race: The Tocqueville–Gobineau Correspondence', *Commentary*, 25 (1958), 154; E. Cassirer, *The Myth of the State* (New Haven, 1961), 231.

[88] J. P. Stern, 'The Weltangst of Oswald Spengler', *Times Literary Supplement* (10 October 1980), 1152.

[89] Quoted from an article in the *Kölnische Zeitung* by the pamphlet cited in n. 46 above.

[90] See J. Herf, *Reactionary Modernism: Technology, Culture, and Politics in Weimar and the Third Reich* (Cambridge, 1985).

something of that, not just in his attitudes towards technology but also in the confusing oscillations between positivism and poetry which characterise his whole approach towards historiographical discourse? To press further: does not this ambivalence (shared with Gobineau and Chamberlain) closely parallel perhaps the most important paradox that we encounter when considering Nazism itself as an intellectual construct?

It is clear that Hitler's movement was, in essence, hostile to the free intellect. Yet that did not prevent the Führer from being readier than many of his critics to appreciate the sheer power of ideas—above all, the force of ideas and emotions operating in dynamic interaction. To the extent that Nazism developed its own brand of scientific pretentiousness in a quest for dogmatic security, it revealed its debt to forms of uncritical positivism. But another outstanding feature of Hitler's career was his keenness to exploit the energy of myth and unreason—as a *complementary* force in this drive to close the gap between certainty desired and certainty attained. By the 1930s, everything best in the great tradition of critical rationalism had become imperilled by an alliance between two aspects of Nazism which were only superficially opposed to each another. One was an explicit, if quite undiscriminating, recognition of the claims of science (especially in the biological sphere); the other was an even more evident addiction to crude irrationalism. It is precisely the *liaison* between these aspects—the cerebral and the visceral—which helps to explain Nazism's excess of logicality and illogicality alike. Here also was one of the clearest flaws in Gobineau, Chamberlain and Spengler alike. Although the first had long been dead and had dismissed all future striving, carefully selected parts of his writings became incorporated into school-readers under the Third Reich; as for the second, he had directly welcomed the emergence of Nazism; and the third, despite his own coolness towards Hitler, had been amongst the most influential contributors to that scene of intellectual confusion upon which the Führer's movement could thrive.

Of these three eclectics (very much in Penelope Lively's sense), it is the author of the *Untergang* who continues to haunt us most. Even the titles used for reputable world-historical enterprises by authors such as William H. McNeill or John Roberts can sound like formulae of anti-Spenglerian exorcism.[91] More sympathetically, a monograph of 1989

---

[91] I have particularly in mind W. H. McNeill, *The Rise of the West: A History of the Human Community* (1963), and J. M. Roberts, *The Triumph of the West* (1985). The latter has of course also published *The Hutchinson History of the World* (1976). As for McNeill, other relevant writings include his Prothero Lecture, 'A Defence of World History', *Transactions of the Royal Historical Society*, 5th series, 32 (1982), 75–89; his major biographical study, *Arnold J. Toynbee: A Life* (1989); and his self-revisionist piece on '*The Rise of the West* after Twenty-Five Years', *Journal of World History*, 1 (1990), 1–21.

could still end with the observation that 'Spengler's contributions to history were a new point of departure, possibly analogous to that stage in the history of science represented by Copernicus.'[92] Yet it would surely be wiser for us to see in him less of the heliocentrist and more of the flat-earther. If the *Untergang* is indeed to be praised, let this be done only in Stern's more hesitant and minor key. 'Is there', he asks, 'a reader who, willing to suspend his disapproval of the author's obscure and ambiguous political purpose, can deny the intellectual exhilaration that issues from these sequences of contrasts and similarities?'[93] In the final resort, however, these are surely the kind of sequences that we ought to associate with mere incantation. Certain passages in Spengler—such as those on the arts of the Baroque and the Rococo, or on the city as a form of language and semiotic—can be welcomed for their bracing suggestiveness. None the less the *Untergang*, taken as a whole, betrays far more of the weaknesses than of the strengths that we may properly attribute to fantasy. Here, Cassirer rightly declared, is 'an astrology of history'.[94] In essence, Spengler—like Gobineau and Chamberlain before him—develops the kind of illusion to which men succumb when they indulge what Isaiah Berlin has called that very human yearning to discover 'a unitary pattern in which the whole of experience, past, present, and future, actual, possible, and unfulfilled, is symetrically ordered'.[95] The members of our trio thus become the *terribles simplificateurs* of Burckhardt's deepest fears.[96] If their story offers us any final lesson, this might well be that today's urgent need to provide scholarly global historiography of the highest quality will never be satisfied by leaving the task to writers of such 'destiny-books'—in effect, to authors who believe that grandiose questions about the past should be given some tidy and deterministic answer, and who, failing that, proceed as though almost any answer would be better than none.

---

[92] K. P. Fischer, *History and Prophecy: Oswald Spengler and the Decline of the West* (New York, 1989), 242.

[93] Stern, 'Weltangst of Oswald Spengler', 1152.

[94] Cassirer, *Myth of the State*, 291.

[95] I. Berlin, 'Historical Inevitability', in *Four Essays on Liberty* (1969), 106. To take the case of a more recent publishing success (which temporarily rode the wave of triumphalist Reaganism–Thatcherism), it is arguable that the neo-Hegelian 'Fukuyama thesis' also fell into the kind of error highlighted by Berlin. See Biddiss, 'Global Interdependence', 79–82, for a critique of F. Fukuyama, 'The End of History?', *The National Interest*, 16 (1989), 3–18, and of the same author's *The End of History and the Last Man* (1992).

[96] This is one of the judgements made specifically about Chamberlain in Field, *Evangelist of Race*, 173.

CONSTRUCTING THE PAST IN THE EARLY MIDDLE AGES: THE CASE OF THE ROYAL FRANKISH ANNALS

By Rosamond McKitterick

READ 24 MAY 1996 AT THE UNIVERSITY OF LEEDS

HUMAN beings are in a perpetual dialogue with the past from their vantage point in the present. St Augustine put this most succinctly when he discussed what he thought of as 'three times', that is, 'a present concerning past things; a present concerning present things and a present concerning future things. For these three are in the spirit and I do not see them elsewhere: the present concerning past things is memory; the present concerning present things is perception; the present concerning future things is expectation'.[1]

To record and explain the past, men and women in history have resorted to many means. In calendars, necrologies and martyrologies, for example, past and present time are organised in conjunction with each other, for past time is remembered in terms of the commemoration of anniversaries in the present.[2] Memories may even be heightened and given the impetus to record them in writing by contemporary crises.[3] In our own profession of the writing of history, particular constraints are in evidence. We all construct a past which we try to make as faithful to our evidence as possible.[4] Yet limitations of memory (both our own and that of the authors of our sources)[5] and the chronological framework, quite apart from the nature of the discipline

---

[1] Augustine, *Confessions*, XI, c. 20, ed. M. Skutellaa, H. Jürgens and W. Schaub, *S. Aurelii Confessionum libri XII, Bibliotheca scriptorum graecorum et romanorum* (Stuttgart, 1981), 281; 'praesens de praeteritis memoria, praesens de praesentiis contuitus, praesens de futuris expectatio': Eng. trans. R. S. Pine-Coffin (Harmondsworth, 1961), 269. See Janet Coleman, *Ancient and Medieval Memories. Studies in the Reconstruction of the Past* (Cambridge, 1992), 101–12.

[2] Mary Carruthers, *The Book of Memory. A Study of Memory in Medieval Culture* (Cambridge, 1990).

[3] Gerd Althoff, 'Zur Verschriftlichung von Memoria in Krisenzeiten', in *Memoria in der Gesellschaft des Mittelalters*, ed. D. Geuenich and O.-G. Oexle, Veröffentlichungen des Max-Plancks-Institut für Geschichte 111 (Göttingen, 194), 56–73.

[4] Ruth Morse, *Truth and Convention in the Middle Ages, Rhetoric, Representation and Reality* (Cambridge, 1991).

[5] See Patrick Geary, *Phantoms of Remembrance. Memory and Oblivion at the End of the First Millennium* (Princeton, 1994), on the importance of what is forgotten.

and conventions associated with historiography as a genre, play a crucial role in producing distinctive interpretations of the past of varying degrees of plausibility and conviction.[6]

In constructing an account of the past a writer can either work within the confines of a particular genre or create new conventions of his or her own for the record of memory.[7] He or she is dependent on information within his or her own and other people's memories and the communication of that information in oral or written form. Thus the concerns of literacy, orality and historiography come together as the record of memory.[8] Bearing in mind Halbwach's view that social groups construct their own images of the world by establishing an agreed version of the past,[9] it is the fact that these memories are established by communication that is so important for our understanding of written history in whatever period we historians study. Just as we need to determine the degree to which many of one's own ostensibly private memories are social memories and shared in general terms with many others, so too the apparently individual authorship of an historical text may express a shared social memory of a particular group. Recalled past experience and shared images of the past are kinds of memories that have particular importance for the constitution of social groups. Within these, the creation of accounts of past events that draw on memory but select from it in distinctive ways that become accepted, and thereafter shared, by a group is part of what I have chosen to call 'constructing the past'. Thus the Franks in the early middle ages, their construction of their identity[10] and an agreed version of their past in the form of narrative histories, are a striking illustration of the dialectic between oral and written, and between private and group, memories.

---

[6] See the seminal Jan Vansina, *Oral tradition. A Study in Historical Methodology*, trans. H. M. White (1965), and the suggestions made by Hayden White, *The Content of the Form. Narrative Discourse and Historical Representation* (Baltimore and London, 1987), and Walter Goffart, *The Narrators of Barbarian History* (Princeton, 1986). See also the essays in *Historiographie im frühen Mittelalter*, ed. Anton Scharer and Georg Scheibelreiter, Veröffentlichungen des Instituts für Österreichische Geschichtsforschung 32 (Vienna and Munich, 1994), and *The Perception of the Past in Twelfth-Century Europe*, ed. Paul Magdalino (1992), especially Lars Boje Mortensen, 'The Texts and Contexts of Ancient Roman History in Twelfth-Century Western Scholarship', 99–116.

[7] See the discussion by Lars Boje Mortensen, 'Stylistic Choice in a Reborn Genre. The National Histories of Widukind of Corvey and Dudo of St. Quentin', in *Dudone di S. Quintino*, ed. P. G. A. Degl'Innocenti (Trento, 1995), 77–102.

[8] James Fentress and Chris Wickham, *Social Memory* (Oxford, 1992).

[9] M. Halbwachs, *Les cadres sociaux de la mémoire* (Paris, 1925), and *La mémoire collective* (Paris, 1950).

[10] Discussion of identity, sometimes implicated in ethnicity, in the early middle ages abound: see, for example, the pathbreaking study by Patrick Amory, *People and Identity in Ostrogothic Italy, 489–554*, Cambridge Studies in Medieval Life and Thought (Cambridge, 1997), and his references to the earlier literature.

In the Carolingian period, moreover, a new narrative genre, namely annals, was devised to express these feelings and beliefs about the immediate past by the elite.

These Frankish annals provide a year by year account of events, dated according to the Christian era. Questions of time and the way these written records were produced within a particular chronological framework have all kinds of symbolic resonances; they are a vital part of what I have referred to elsewhere as a taught mode of organising memory.[11] It is taught in the sense that the Franks inherited historical traditions from the Jews, the Romans and the early Christians, but exploited these within their own chronological and political schemes for their own ends. It is on these schemes that I wish to focus in this paper and thereby bring together questions of memory, the construction of the past, and the manipulation of chronology and time, in the context of the Franks and their annals in the eighth and ninth centuries.

Time is something that can be measured, but it is also something that can be controlled and manipulated. This is particularly evident in the construction of the past in early medieval historiography. Indeed, attitudes towards time in Frankish sources are so fundamental a part of our historical evidence that there is a danger that we may omit to consider its significance or implications. To examine time and its functions in the early middle ages, therefore, may yield something very specific about the perception of the past, present and even future on the part of any group. As this is expressed and embodied in writing designed to record the past in one way or another, time, numeracy and literacy become inextricably linked. The concerns of the *trivium* and the *quadrivium*, with writing and speech on the one hand and numbers and calculation on the other, are united.

Let me first give some indication of the perceptions of time in the early middle ages. Bede in his *De temporum ratione* commented that time for all mortals was divided up into moments, hours, days, months, years, centuries and eras.[12] Some of these rhythms of time passing are natural and regulated by the sun and moon, such as years, months and days. The perception of days and months, moreover, is influenced by biological cycles in humans. Superimposed upon this natural base,

<hr>

[11] Matthew Innes and Rosamond McKitterick, 'The Writing of History', in *Carolingian Culture: Emulation and Innovation,*ed. Rosamond McKitterick (Cambridge, 1994), 193–220 at 193 [hereafter Innes and McKitterick, 'Writing of History'].

[12] Bede, *De temporum ratione*, II, ed. C. W. Jones, *Bedae Opera de temporibus* (Cambridge, MA, 1943), 182 [hereafter *Opera de temporibus*]. An English translation and full commentary is in preparation by Faith Wallis with the title *Reason and Reckoning. Ordering Time in the Scientific Works of Bede* [hereafter *Reason and Reckoning*].

however, are the man-made elements of hours, weeks, centuries and eras of the world. These reckonings and their functions have everything to do with human mentalities. Jacques Le Goff chose to describe the early middle ages as observing church time and the later middle ages as merchants' time.[13] This is self-evidently too schematic and too simplistic. It omits to take into account that church time is also *historical* time, in that it orients itself in relation to a specific event. Initially this was the year of the Passion but it subsequently became the year of the Incarnation. Further, Christian time is also *theological* time in that it sees whatever smaller or larger units man may devise in relation to eternity. Thirdly, in terms of specific calculations during the year, Christian time observes variable *liturgical time*, and thus cyclical time, for it is the Christian festivals—Easter, a moveable feast, and Christmas, a fixed day—which determine the cycle of feasts for the entire year. All these are linked to *astronomical time*. On a day to day basis, moreover, Christian time can also be divided up in a specific context, such as *monastic* time, where the division of days into 'hours' yields variable lengths of time according to the season. Further, any particular society could add its own artificial rhythms, related to seasonal, military, administrative or daily needs. The Franks, for example, convened each spring an assembly of the leading men of the kingdom which could also serve as a mustering of the host[14] and the Alemannian laws stipulate that a judicial court should be held once a fortnight (or once a week in troubled times).[15] Thus in the early middle ages we have to consider political time (as well as social and economic time) as separate or separable from Christian time. The obvious instance of this is the use of regnal years for the dating of documents[16] or to record the passing of years in most early medieval historical narratives.

[13] Jacques Le Goff, 'Time, Merchant's Time and Church's Time in the Middle Ages', in *idem, Time, Work and Culture in the Middle Ages*, trans. A. Goldhammer (Chicago, 1980), 29–42.

[14] For example, *Annale regni francorum* s.a. 767, ed. F. Kurze, *Monumenta Germaniae Historica* [hereafter *MGH*], *Scriptores rerum germanicarum* (Hannover, 1895) [hereafter *ARF*], 24.

[15] *Lex Alamannorum*, XXXVI, ed. K. Lehmann, *MGH Legum sectio I. Legum nationum Germanicarum*, I.i (Hannover, 1885), 94.

[16] The earliest original charter preserving the year of the Incarnation in Anglo-Saxon England appears to be the Ismere charter of 736, London, British Library, Cotton Augustus II.3, facsimile in A. Bruckner, *Chartae Latinae Antiquiores*, III (Olten and Lausanne, 1963), no. 183, 22–3, but the practice from later copies is probably earlier, Kenneth Harrison, for example, discusses W. Birch, *Cartularium Saxonicum* (Oxford, 1885), nos. 43 and 51 dating from 675 and 680 (and others), and agrees with R. L. Poole that there is no necessity for dating practice in Anglo-Saxon charters to have been dependent on Bede: it could just as well have been associated with the Easter tables of Dionysius Exiguus: Kenneth Harrison, *The Framework of Anglo-Saxon History to A. D. 900* (Cambridge, 1976), 65–75. AD dating is not used in dating Frankish royal documents until the 870s, though in private charters it appears in the early ninth century: see Harry Bresslau,

The passing of apparently simple chronological time, therefore, comprises a whole series of other measurements, interests and symbols. All these are necessarily linked with the means by which time is calculated and measured for the co-ordination of social activity. By way of context let me first briefly describe the ways in which the days were divided and then grouped in the early middle ages. For most people, the passing of time during the day was measured in the early middle ages by the movements of the sun. Few would have had clocks or would have experienced time regulated by bells. Sunlight (i.e. daylight) was a natural determinant and could be linked with religious observance. Monastic rules further regulated the daily routine of praying, working, eating, sleeping. The *Rule of Benedict*, for example, adjusted the length of hour in relation to the amount of daylight in winter and summer.[17] Longer days yielded longer day hours. The time for prayer had also to be determined, and at night it was governed by the position of the stars.[18] Interest in time measurement led to various calculations and inventions of mechanical ways—sundials, clepsydra, clepsammia, the famous candle clock of King Alfred[19]—to record the passing of time, not all of which would yield equal hours.[20] In calculating months and years, on the other hand, the moon plays as important a role as the sun. The division of the months into the Christian week is essentially that of the Jews, defined in the first chapter of the book of Genesis; the Romans had grouped days in eight.

Conversion to Christianity, therefore, meant, first of all, adjustment to a new daily cycle, reinforced by a religious symbolism attached to Sunday to which Constantine's decree concerning Sunday observance on the *die dominica*, differentiating it clearly from the Jewish sabbath, contributed. Gregory of Tours, for example, maintained that the Sunday

---

Handbuch der Urkundenlehre (2 vols., Berlin, 1931), III, 427–8. The diplomata of Charlemagne of 783, 788 and 791 with AD dating formulae, nos. 149, 161, 169, survive in later copies and the AD formulae are thought to be later interpolations: *MGH Diplomatum Karolinorum. I, Pippini, Carlomanni, Caroli Magni Diplomata*, ed. Engelbert Mühlbacher (Munich, 1979), 202–3, 218–19, 226–8. Councils and synods, on the other hand, are dated according to the year of the Incarnation in both England and the Continent from the 740s onwards.

[17] *Rule of Benedict*, c. 8, ed. and trans. Justin McCann (1952), 48–9, and his notes 175–6.

[18] See, for example, Gregory of Tours, *De cursu stellarum*, ed. B. Krusch, *MGH Scriptores rerum Merovingicarum*, I (Hannover, 1885), 854–72, and Steven C. McCluskey, 'Gregory of Tours, Monastic Timekeeping and Early Christian Attitudes to Astronomy', *Isis*, 81 (1990), 9–22.

[19] Asser, *Vita Alfredi regis*, cc. 103, 104, ed. W. H. Stevenson, *Asser's Life of King Alfred* (Oxford, 1904; reimp. 1959), 89–91; Eng. trans. Simon Keynes and Michael Lapidge, *Alfred the Great, Asser's Life of King Alfred and Other Contemporary Sources* (Harmondsworth, 1983), 107–9.

[20] E. J. Bickerman, *Chronology of the Ancient World* (1980), Richard Sorabji, *Time, Creation and the Continuum* (1983), and David Landes, *Revolution in Time: Clocks and the Making of the Modern World* (Cambridge, MA, 1983).

of the Resurrection was the first day of the week, not the seventh.

This is the day of the resurrection of our Lord Jesus Christ, which we rightly call Sunday because of the holy rising again. In the beginning this was the first day to see the light, and it deserves to be the first to see our Lord rise from the tomb.[21]

Secondly, as is well known, Christian time is a combination of Hebrew lunar and Roman solar elements. The moveable feasts such as Easter are derived from Jewish festivals and the fixed remainder of the calendar is Roman. The associations behind these are both astronomical and historical and again have both Roman and Jewish elements; Christmas coincides with the old Roman winter solstice and the crucifixion and conception coincide with the vernal equinox. There are, of course, historical reasons for the choice of the date of Easter linked with the cycle of Jewish religious festivals. The Jewish Passover, 14th Nisan, the first month of the Hebrew religious calendar was celebrated on the first full moon after the vernal equinox. The Christians gradually fixed Easter on the Sunday following 14th Nisan (by about 120 AD) but many disputes remained; Quartodecimans, for example, continued to observe Easter on 14th Nisan regardless of what day of the week it fell, rather than Sunday. If Easter were to be a moveable feast, calendars were needed to determine the correct day. Cyclic tables like our Julian calendar were regarded as the most useful, for these combined movements of sun and moon.[22] All this is to orient time in relation to Christian anniversaries such as the crucifixion and resurrection.

So far, so familiar. But different calculations abounded in late antiquity and the early middle ages as dates and the conjunction of moon and sun were calculated according to various methods and cycles. How was anyone to ensure that Easter was celebrated each year on the correct and, above all, on the same day? The earlier solution for the pope in relation to the churches under his jurisdiction appeared to

---

[21] Gregory of Tours, *Historiae*,I, 23, ed. B. Krusch, *MGH, Scriptores rerum merovingicarum* I (Hannover, 1885), 44; Eng. trans. Lewis Thorpe, *Gregory of Tours. The History of the Franks* (Harmondsworth, 1974), 83.

[22] For lucid explanations see Kenneth Harrison, *The Framework of Anglo-Saxon History to A. D. 900* (Cambridge, 1976), and Wallis, *Reason and Reckoning*. One lunar month = 29.5306 days; one solar year = 365.2422 days; excess lunar months in a solar year .3683. To reconcile lunar and solar years the computist or calendar maker must intercalate 3 lunar months every 8 years; 4 lunar months every 11 years; 7 lunar months every 19 years; (this is the Alexandrine cycle, which is the most nearly accurate); 31 months every 84 years (a cycle of 532 years, that is, the Victorine, was also used). Even the 19-year cycle needed correction and adjustment because it came to a total of 6440.75 days, one day more than 19 Julian years = 6939.75 days. To correct it the *saltus lunae*, one lunar day was omitted at the end of the nineteenth year. This fixed lunar XIV.

be the announcement of the day of Easter in the subsequent year, much as universities or schools publish the dates of term in advance. One or two such announcements have survived, such as Pope Leo's Paschal Letter of 454 addressed to the churches of Gaul and Spain.[23] This followed the Alexandrine calculations associated with Cyril and announced the day of Easter for 455 as Sunday 24 April, to be observed for the sake of unity with the apostolic sees (Alexandria and Rome). Observing the date of Easter at the same time thus becomes a straightforward symbol of unity.

An alternative solution might be the circulation of approved tables on which Easter had been calculated well in advance, so that everyone would be able to see what the date would be. Thus Victorius of Aquitaine, the *calculator scrupulosus*, produced tables based on the nine-teenth-year Alexandrian cycle but modified, if not muddled, in such a way as to produce a different date of Easter from the Alexandrian calculations for thirteen years out of the nineteen, prompting Victorius to dub the dates the Latin and the Greek Easters and to leave the choice of which date to observe to users of his table.[24] He also related his cycle to the year of the Passion of Christ, year 1 (= *annus mundi* 5229).[25]

A further effort to get matters straight was made by Dionysius Exiguus, who composed his famous *Libellus de cyclo magno paschae* between 525 and 532 in order to cover the years 532 to 625.[26] He introduced the use of the year of the birth of Christ, rather than the year of the Passion, as his fixed point, but the main function of his work was to fix the date of Easter each year and to advocate the nineteen-year cycle for such calculations. It was Dionysius therefore who advocated the use of the Christian era. Perhaps inevitably, the Victorine and Dionysian (as well as other) methods of calculation were adopted by different regions, with the consequences that Bede, in his account of Easter observance in Northumbria and the debate at Whitby in 664, has made very familiar.[27]

---

[23] Leo the Great, Epistola 138, ed. J. P. Migne, *Patrologia Latina cursus completus* [hereafter *PL*] 54 (Paris, 1846), cols. 1101–2.

[24] Compare Columbanus, Epistola 1, ed. G. S. M. Walker, *Sancti Columbani Opera*, Scriptores Latini Hiberniae 2 (Dublin, 1970), 1–7.

[25] Victurius, ed. T. Mommsen, *Victurius Aquitanus Cursus Paschalis CCCLVII, MGH Chronica minora*, 1 (Berlin, 1892), 676–84. See also C. W. Jones, 'The Victorian and Dionysiac Paschal Tables', *Speculum*, 3 (1934), 408–21, and Bruno Krusch, 'Studien zur christlich-mittelalterlichen Chronologie', *Abhandlungen der Preußischen Akademie der Wissenschaften, phil.-hist. Klasse*, 8, 1937 (Berlin, 1938), 4–57 [hereafter, Krusch, 'Studien'].

[26] Dionysius, *Libellus de cyclo magno paschae/ Cyclus Pachalis, PL* 67, 483–508, especially col. 487 and also ed. Krusch, 'Studien', 59–87.

[27] Bede, *Historia ecclesiastica gentis anglorum*, III.25, ed. Bertram Colgrave and R. A. B. Mynors, Oxford Medieval Texts (Oxford, 1969), 295–309.

If the tables in circulation established the principles clearly enough, then a third way of ensuring the proper and simultaneous observance of Easter was to teach people how to do the necessary calculations. The skills of arithmetical computation or *computus* became an established part of the school curriculum. Thus a sense of the annual Christian cycle in relation to the movements of sun, moon and stars, to liturgy, to history (in that the nineteen-year cycles began with the year of the Incarnation) was instilled in all those receiving basic training in the schools. The *Admonitio Generalis* in 789 issued by Charlemagne enjoined that the clergy should know *computus* and that it should be taught in the schools.[28] Tracts on *computus*, comprising short astronomical and computistical discussion and tables applied to the skill in creating and understanding ecclesiastical calendars, survive in abundance. So do Easter tables, yearly calendars, lists of calculations, tables to help, verses for memorising, dialogues for school catechism and multiplication tables.[29]

Bede's *De ratione temporum* was by no means the only influential text. Bede's influence on the Franks in their dating systems and notably their calculation of the date of Easter and dating according to the Christian era has hitherto been assumed to have been direct and more or less immediate. I have argued elsewhere, however, that the Franks' interest in AD and their Easter calculations were not derived from Bede but directly from Dionysius Exiguus.[30]

As far as the Franks were concerned, the authority of Dionysius' calculations, knowledge of which they undoubtedly had, were probably reinforced by the facts that he was also associated with the authoritative collection of canon law and papal decretals known as the *Dionysiana*, and that it was the system used in Rome.[31] There is ample evidence of independent Frankish and especially Caolingian recourse to papal authority in ecclesiastical matters in the course of the later seventh and

---

[28] *Admonitio Generalis*, 789, c. 72, ed. A. Boretius, *MGH Capitularia regum francorum*, I (Hannover, 1883), 60.

[29] On all these, particularly manuscripts from Fulda and the Reichenau, see Wesley Stevens, *Cycles of Time and Scientific Learning in Medieval Europe*, Variorum Collected Studies Series (Aldershot, 1995), chapters I, VI–XI.

[30] Rosamond McKitterick, 'The Perception of Time in Late Antiquity and the Early Middle Ages', in *The Transformation of Tradition*, ed. Marco Mostert (Leiden, forthcoming).

[31] Dionysius Exiguus, ed. H. Wurm, *Studien und Text zur Dekretalsammlung des Dionysius Exiguus*, Kanonistische Studien und Texte 16 (Bonn, 1939; reprinted Amsterdam, 1964), and W. B. M. Peitz, *Dionysius Exiguus Studien* (Bonn, 1960). For the background see Rosamond McKitterick, 'Knowledge of Canon Law in the Frankish Kingdoms before 789: The Manuscript Evidence', *Journal of Theological Studies*, n.s. 36 (1985), 97–117, reprinted in Rosamond McKitterick, *Books, Scribes and Learning in the Frankish Kingdoms, 6th–9th centuries*, Variorum Collected Studies Series (Aldershot, 1994), chapter II.

first half of the eighth centuries without the use of Anglo-Saxon intermediaries.[32]

Apart from Easter tables and calendars in early eighth-century Frankish manuscripts, we need also to take into account the evidence for Frankish arithmetical reckoning and compilations which included time calculations. In about 737 a Frankish manual directed against the 'Latin' reckoning of Victorius and preferring Dionysius was compiled. It also advocates beginning the year on 1 March. It consists of thirty short chapters and was designed for teaching at some level for it is addressed to children and the laity. It is extant in only one manuscript, Berlin, Deutsche Staatsbibliothek, Phillipps 1831, fols. 138r–42r.[33] An improved version of this text was produced in about 760 in the Rhineland. It considered computing the date of Easter and arithmetical calculations, explained lunar months, the cycle of the years and seasons, and advocated the use of AD dating. Although it excerpted some chapters from Bede's *De temporum ratione*, it followed Jerome rather than Bede in calculating the date of the age of the world. In 792 this text was further extended and Archbishop Hildebold of Cologne had it copied into his manual on time in 805.[34] Other miscellaneous texts were produced at the end of the eighth century, attributed in the Patrologia to 'pseudo-Bede' though some are Frankish and one or two are now thought to be Irish.[35] In the 780s a *libellus annalis* was composed[36] which acted as the precursor of what Borst has called the 'A' version of a Carolingian Encyclopaedia on time produced in 793, possibly in Verona under the aegis of Bishop Egino, for it is from thence that its

---

[32] See, for example, Pippin's queries directed to Pope Zacharias, reported by Zacharias to Boniface in 747, ed. Michael Tangl, *Die Briefe des Heiligen Bonifatius und Lullus*, no. 77, *MGH Epistolae Selectae in usum scholarum*, 1 (Berlin, 1916), 159–61, and responded to by Zacharias, ed. W. Gundlach, *Epistolae Merowingici et Karolini aevi, MGH Epistulae*, III (Hannover, 1892), 479–87.

[33] Bruno Krusch, 'Das älteste fränkische Lehrbuch der dionysianischen Zeitrechnung', *Mélanges offerts à Emile Chatelain* (Paris, 1910), 232–42. For details on this and the other Carolingian 'encyclopaedias of time' see Arno Borst, 'Alkuin und die Enzyklopädie von 809', in *Science in Western and Eastern Civilization in Carolingian Times*, ed. Paul Leo Butzer and Dietrich Lohrmann (Basle, Boston and Berlin, 1993), 53–78 [hereafter Borst, 'Enzyklopädie'].

[34] Cologne, Dombibliothek, MS 83 II, fols. 59r–69r. Also unedited. Two copies of it from the middle of the ninth century: Karlsruhe Landesbibliothek, Aug. CLXVII fols. 6r–12r and St Gallen, Stiftsbibliothek 248, fols. 76–82. See A. Cordoliani, 'Une encyclopédie carolingienne de comput: les Sententiae in laude computi', *Bibliothèque de l'Ecole des Chartres*, 104 (1943), 237–43, and 'Les traités de comput du haut moyen âge 526–103', *Archivum latinitatis medii aevi*, 17 (1942), 51–72.

[35] *De ratione computandi*, ed. D. O Croinin and M. Walsh, Studies and Texts (Toronto, 1988). Another manuscript is in Paris, Bibliothèque Nationale, MS n.a.lat. 456, fols. 189–90v.

[36] Borst, 'Enzyklopädie', 54, credits Alcuin with this.

oldest and fullest manuscript comes. The text of this Encyclopaedia offers verbal explanations of time reckoning rather than tables. It draws on Bede's *De ratione temporum*, but does not cite him by name.[37] The 'B' version of this Encyclopaedia, compiled at Aachen in 809, included in Book II practical formulae for reckoning the existing year according to the year of the Incarnation. It is this Encyclopaedia, in its 793 and 809 versions which, in Borst's opinion, ruled European thinking about time for the next 300 years.[38]

For our purposes the Carolingian manuals and Encyclopaedia on time indicate a strong interest in the year of the Incarnation and in the reckoning of time, as well as affirmation of Dionysius' calculations on the part of the Franks and the Frankish royal court from at least 737 onwards. The insistence of Charlemagne on time reckoning and that clergy should know the *computus*, and the king's own wish to be taught computation, recorded by Einhard,[39] suggest more than arithmetical games with numbers on the part of monks of mathematical bent in isolated monasteries. It needs to be stressed, moreover, that the issue of deciding on the date for Easter to be recognised and observed, as well as the promotion of the necessary training for the making of the calculations, involves jurisdiction of central and of local government. It entails the acknowledgement of personal or party affiliation to that government and its own religious and political loyalties. It enhances the authority of those who insist on a particular observation of time. Here we see ecclesiastical, and especially monastic, learning in conjunction with Frankish political power keeping to a strict liturgical model of time and using it to exert authority over the daily lives of all Christians by a control of time in the present and organising it in the future to which the Frankish rulers were party.

Such control of Christian time in association with the court can also be observed in the organisation and recording of the past, for the *Annales regni francorum* (Royal Frankish Annals) [hereafter *ARF*] are the first to use the year of the Incarnation as the organising principle of the narrative on a yearly basis (as distinct from Bede's use of AD dating as a reference system in the *Historia ecclesiastica*). It is to the *ARF*, therefore, that I now turn.

Annals as an historical form have been generally accepted in historical

---

[37] Best manuscript, Berlin, Deutsche Staatsbibliothek, Phillipps 1831, fols. 116r–25v. See also London, British Library, Royal 13 A XI, fols. 126v–39v, and Paris, Bibliothèque Nationale lat. 4860.

[38] Borst, 'Enzyklopädie', 71–3.

[39] Discebat artem computandi: Einhard, *Vita Karoli*, c. 25, ed. O. Holder-Egger, *MGH Scriptores rerum germanicarum in usum scholarum separatim editi*, 25 (Berlin, 1911), and R. Rau, Quellen zur karolingische Reichsgeschichte i (Darmstadt, 1974), 196.

scholarship as having been developed from notes in Easter tables,[40] much as you see illustrated from a St Gallen manuscript written in the 'Hartmut period' in the second half of the ninth century, in Plate 1, where the Easter tables have brief notes added in the margin.[41] In other, later, manuscripts a page of dates was laid out, and subsequently filled in with various notes by a number of hands in an unsystematic manner.[42] The space is controlled by the layout and thus what is written is controlled as well. It would be a rather attractive irony that tables designed to set out both the rhythm for the future and chart the cyclical liturgical year should have given rise to notes about the past. Although annal entries in Easter tables (that is, 'Paschal annals') are attested to in extant manuscripts dating from the ninth century onwards, I am no longer convinced that this is how annals originally developed.[43] The first, perhaps minor, difficulty is that the manuscripts containing Easter tables with annal entries, with one exception, post-date annal manuscripts by some decades.[44] Their codicological context is usually that of canon law, *computus*, necrologies and

[40] See Bruno Krusch, 'Ueber eine Handschrift des Victorius', *Neues Archiv der Gesellschaft für ältere deutsche Geschichtskunde*, 9 (1883/4), 269–82, Reginald Lane Poole, *Chronicles and Annals. A Brief Outline of their Origin and Growth* (Oxford, 1926) [hereafter, Poole, *Chronicles and Annals*], C. W. Jones, *Saints' Lives and Early Chronicles in Early England* (Ithaca, 1947), and M. McCormick, *Les annales du haut moyen âge*, Typologie des sources du moyen âge occidental, fasc. 14 (Turnhout, 1975), especially 27. I, too, repeated this old orthodoxy in my *The Frankish Kingdoms under the Carolingians, 751–987* (London, 1983), 2–6 [hereafter, McKitterick, *Frankish Kingdoms*].

[41] St Gallen, Stiftsbibliothek 250, p. 14: *Annales S. Gallenses brevissimi, 718–889*, MGH Scriptores I (Hannover, 1826), 69.

[42] For example, the tenth-century codex Einsiedeln Stiftsbibliothek MS 356: illustrated in Poole, *Chronicles and Annals*, opposite p. 6.

[43] For firm support of the traditional view see Daibhi O Croinin, 'Early Irish Annals from Easter Tables: A Case Restated', *Peritia*, 2 (1983), 74–86, but his case is undermined by his assumption that Easter tables are copied from exemplars and take over any annal entries from the exemplars. There would, however, be no necessity for a full exemplar when compiling a new set of Easter tables and the annal entries we find against earlier dates in tables in late ninth-, tenth-and eleventh-century manuscripts may be the result of a quite different interest in relation to the historical associations of the centre in which the tables were compiled. Harrison also voices scepticism about the connection between Paschal annals and annals in *Framework*, 45.

[44] The exception is the eighth-century copy of Victurius, *Canon paschalis* from Jouarre, now in Gotha, Landesbibliothek Mbr. I.75, fols. 70–122, which has single non-historical entries in eighth-century Merovingian cursive on fols. 77v and 89v. Against the year 501 it has the note 'Gundubadus fuit in Abinione', recorded by Krusch, 'Ueber eine Handschrift der Victorius', p. 277. On the manuscript's origin see Rosamond McKitterick, 'Nuns' Scriptoria in England and Francia in the Eighth Century', *Francia*, 19/1 (1992), 1–35 at 5, reprinted in McKitterick, *Books, Scribes and Learning*, chapter VII. It should be noted in relation to the point made in note 43 above that the event singled out in the Easter tables is also described in another manuscript belonging to this same Jouarre group, namely, Paris, Bibliothèque Nationale lat. 17654, containing Gregory of Tours' *Historiae*.

St Gallen, Stiftsbibliothek 250, p. 14 (reduced). 'Paschal Annal' entries in Easter tables.

liturgy.[45] St Gallen, Stiftsbibliothek 250, is a case in point. The earliest ninth-century manuscript containing Paschal annals (Leiden, Universiteitsbliotheek MS Scaliger 28), on the other hand, does reflect a codicological association between Easter chronology and historical record.[46]

[45] See the codices listed by A. Cordoliani, 'Contribution à la littérature du comput ecclésiasticque au moyen âge', *Studi Medievali*, 3rd series, 1 (1960), 107–37, and 2 (1961), 169–73, and *idem*, 'Les traités de comput du haut moyen âge (526–1003), *Archivum Latinitatis Medii Aevi*, 17 (1942), 51–72.

[46] G. I. Lieftinck, *Manuscrits datés conservés dans les pays-bas. Catalogue paléographique des manuscrits en écriture latine portant des indications de date, I. Les manuscrits d'origine étrangère (1816–*

Generally considered to have been written at Flavigny about 816, that is, some twenty or so years after the first portion of the Royal Frankish Annals was completed, it includes Bede's *De temporum ratione* and Victurius, excerpts from various texts concerned with the calculation of Easter and chronological questions, and the text known as the *Chronicon universale* to 741 ascribed in the manuscript to Bede.[47] The Paschal annals are inserted in the margins of fols. 3–21.[48]

Secondly, and more crucially, such a designation downgrades the annal as a form of historical writing to too great an extent. The link with the year of the Incarnation which makes such an explicit association between the history of the Franks and the linear progression of Christian history should be separated from the essentially ahistorical liturgical cycle represented by Easter. Easter tables with annal entries seem to me a legitimate adaptation of the idea of annals. Annals, on the other hand, belong to the extraordinary revolution in historical writing to be observed in the Carolingian period,[49] and the sense of history so evident in a wide variety of sources,[50] coupled with the Carolingian preoccupations with time reckoning outlined above. The Frankish annals, and especially the *ARF*, explicitly linked the Frankish present to the whole course of Christian history and the life of Christ.

Such a development needs to be related to a wider change in the interaction of church and society. In many ways the early middle ages witnessed the triumph of the saints' cult as the fundamental preoccupation of society.[51] Local saints and the churches which controlled the cult of their memories increasingly became the foci of community action. There is an obvious connection between the necrologies and memorial books providing networks of association and memory over the entire Frankish realm and the writing of history.[52] The cult of the dead and a sense of history were inextricably entwined. Easter tables, necrologies and martyrologies were the texts by which the church had Christianized and controlled time and space. Chronological

---

c. 1550) (Amsterdam, 1964), 91–2 and Plates 1–3. I am very grateful to Dr A. Th. Bouwman of the Leiden Universiteitsbibliotheek for kindly answering my queries about this manuscript and sending me photographs. I am now preparing a study of Scaliger 28.

[47] Ed. G. Waitz, *MGH Scriptores*, XIII (Hannover, 1881), 1–19.

[48] *Annales Flaviniacenses et Lausonenses*, ed. G. Pertz, *MGH Scriptores*, III (Hannover, 1839), 149–52.

[49] Innes and McKitterick, 'Writing of History'.

[50] See the comments by Thomas F. X. Noble, 'Tradition and Learning in Search of Ideology', in *The Gentle Voices of Teachers. Aspects of Learning in the Carolingian Age*, ed. Richard Sullivan (Columbus, OH, 1995), 227–60.

[51] I draw in this paragraph on Innes and McKitterick, 'Writing of History'.

[52] See Karl Schmid, *Gebetsgedenken und adliges Selbstverständnis im Mittelalter: Ausgewählte Beiträge. Festgabe zu seinem 60. Geburtstag* (Sigmaringen, 1983).

correctness in the dating of church festivals gained impetus from reformers aiming at unanimity of practice.

Annals were a further, and secular, reflection of the same mentality and might be described, from one perspective, as a very literate form of timekeeping. Yet there might be thought to be no particular reason why the annals should use the Christian era dating scheme rather than any other. As a literary form their structure was determined by the annual cycle of a community; this led to a cyclical sense of time, moulded by the yearly rota of ritual. For the *ARF* in particular, however, the peripatetic rhythm of the political court was fitted *into* the liturgical cycle, with the place at which the court spent Christmas and Easter frequently recorded[53] and a year's cycle according to the year of the Incarnation established.

The extraordinary structure of the *ARF* becomes striking when seen in conjunction with the disorderly treatment of time in the so-called Continuations of the Chronicle of Fredegar completed in the second half of the eighth century. There the passing of kings (and to a lesser extent, of mayors) comprises the dating scheme, but in some chapters many years pass and in others only one. Thus thirty years pass in chapter 6. In chapter 8, Pippin II's death in 714 is recorded. He had ruled over the Franks for twenty-seven and a half years. Sometimes, as in chapter 12, we are told that a year passed. In chapter 14 the events are recounted as occurring in the course of the following year. In the chapter concerning Charles Martel's campaign in Aquitaine the chronology is most compressed. From chapter 24, however, the chapters are set down more or less on a yearly basis though inexact phrases are used, such as *eodem anno*; *Quo peracto tempore*; *His transactis sequente anno*; *post haec*; *evolutur igitur anno*. In *c.* 50, an entry relating to 768, there is the first record of where the ruler spent the Christmas period.[54] Generally a time *sequence* is clear, but the length of time between events and the duration of certain affairs are very much less than clear. It is possibly significant, moreover, that the more precise section of Fredegar in chronological terms is precisely that covered by the *ARF*.[55] The manuscript tradition of Fredegar may well play a crucial role here,

---

[53] For example, *ARF*, s.a. 771, 32.

[54] Fredegar, ed. John Michael Wallace-Hadrill, *The Fourth Book of the Chronicle of Fredegar and its Continuations* (1960), 85–6, 87, 90, 91, 24, 117–18.

[55] It has always been assumed hitherto that the Royal Frankish Annalist drew on Fredegar. It may well be that the relationship for the section covering the years 741–68 should be reversed (from a practical point of view it is easier to write a chronologically diffuse account drawn from a precise year-by-year record than vice versa) but this needs further work, especially once the new edition of Fredegar, in preparation by Roger Collins, become available. See his preliminary essay: Roger Collins, *Fredegar*, Authors of the Middle Ages. Historical and Religious Writers of the Latin West vol. IV, no. 13 (Aldershot, 1996).

given the predominance of manuscripts dating from the Carolingian period which contain this portion of Fredegar.[56]

The *ARF*, therefore, make significant comments on the context in which contemporary Frankish history is to be understood, but they are also an astonishingly under-appreciated source in terms of their content and propaganda value.[57] Attention has been largely focused hitherto, apart from the efforts to establish the text in the early years of this century, on the ostensibly fuller and more sophisticated continuations of the annals known as the *Annals of St Bertin* and *Annals of Fulda*.[58] This may be due to these texts being capable of association with particular authors and centres, whereas the identity of the author and precise place of production of the *ARF* still elude us, even if a writer associated with the royal court be accepted. Further, the *ARF* appear to be a straightforward text that can be quarried safely for facts. Appearances, however, can be deceptive.

By way of reminder, here are some practical details. In the textual discussion of the annals as a genre, the *ARF* are regarded as the most representative of the so-called major annals. Originally known to editors as the *Annales Laurissenses maiores*, their name was changed when Ranke drew attention to their 'official' nature and the Carolingian point of view they express.[59] They have been associated in consequence with the royal court and thus were produced 'when the keeping of an official record of political and public events appears to have been the responsibility of the archchaplain, or someone working for him, at the royal court'.[60] The production of the *ARF* coincides with the creation by Charlemagne of a large public court, focused on the new palace at Aachen. If there was no attempt at 'public' record-keeping before then,[61] this is possibly due to the court not being, until Charlemagne's

---

[56] Rosamond McKitterick, 'The Audience for Latin Historiography in the Early Middle Ages. Text Transmission and Manuscript Dissemination', in Scharer and Scheibelreiter, *Historiographie*, 96–114.

[57] A notable exception is Matthias Becher's comprehensive exposure of the lies woven together in the *ARF*'s account of Tassilo of Bavaria: *Eid und Herrschaft. Untersuchungen zum Herrscherethos Karls des Großen*, Vorträge und Forschungen Sonderband 39 (Sigmaringen, 1993), especially 21–77.

[58] For valuable discussions of these texts see, on the Annals of St Bertin, Janet L. Nelson, 'The Annals of St Bertin', in *Charles the Bald. Court and Kingdom*, ed. Janet L. Nelson and Margaret Gibson (2nd edn, 1990), 23–40, and also reprinted in Janet L. Nelson, *Politics and Ritual in Early Medieval Europe* (1986), 173–94, and her Introduction to her translation, *The Annals of St Bertin* (Manchester, 1991); on the Annals of Fulda see Timothy Reuter's Introduction to his translation, *The Annals of Fulda* (Manchester, 1992).

[59] L. Ranke, 'Zur Kritik fränkisch-deutscher Reichsannalen', *Abhandlungen der königlichen Akademie der Wissenschaften* (Berlin, 1854), 415–56.

[60] Innes and McKitterick, 'The Writing of History', p. 208.

[61] On the possible understanding of 'public' and 'private' in the ninth century see Matthew Innes, 'Social and Political Processes in the Carolingian Middle Rhine Valley,

later years, a public forum with a centripetal political force.[62]

The *ARF* run from 741 to 829 and begin with the death of Charles Martel. Up to 788 the annal entries, according to the current orthodoxy, supposedly drew on earlier, so-called 'minor annals' but are presenting their own view. Halphen suggested seventy years ago that these minor annals were in fact derived from the *ARF* and that the *ARF* were original rather than derivative compositions from 768.[63] This suggestion has hitherto been largely disregarded,[64] but I wish now not only to revive Halphen's whiff of heresy but expand it to embrace the entire narrative from its chronological starting point in 741. There is simply no need for them to have been derived from (an) earlier account(s), as distinct from having been deliberately created with a miscellany of material, oral and written, contributing information.[65] The traditional view of the lack of originality of the entries before 788 cannot be substantiated and rests on a contorted understanding of the original text's composition in relation to the surviving manuscripts; it should be discarded.

What is at stake is the very conception of the *ARF*'s narrative. Rather than thinking of the year entries as year-by-year jottings, they should be recognised as a skilfully constructed, highly selective portrayal of the careers of the Carolingian rulers whose fortune and success is identified with that of the Frankish people. The narrative from 741 to 793 is agreed to have been written down by one person at one go, and then continued, possibly by different people. The entries for *c.* 807–29, however, have a certain unity of tone and style[66] and those for 820–9 have been attributed to Hilduin, abbot of St Denis. Not everyone accepts the attributions of author to particular sections, largely because the dates of apparent stylistic continuity do not coincide with the known

---

c.750–c.875' (PhD thesis, University of Cambridge, 1995, and *Social Processes and the State: The Middle Rhine Valley from the Merovingians to the Ottonians* (forthcoming, Cambridge University Press).

[62] See, for example, the comments in Janet L. Nelson, 'Kingship and Royal Government', in *The New Cambridge Medieval History*, II: *700–900*, ed. Rosamond McKitterick (Cambridge, 1995), 383–430, especially 417.

[63] Louis Halphen, *Etudes critiques sur l'histoire de Charlemagne* (Paris, 1921).

[64] W. Wattenbach, W. Levison and H. Löwe, *Deutschlands Geschichtsquellen im Mittelalter. Vorzeit und Karolinger*, II (Weimar, 1953), 245–58, provide the general view and see also McKitterick, *Frankish Kingdoms*, 3–4.

[65] See the important discussion by Hartmut Hoffman, *Untersuchungen zur karolingische Annalistik*, Bonner Historische Forschungen 10 (Bonn, 1958), who also summarises the discussion up until then.

[66] I have benefited here from the comments made by Timothy Reuter in his paper, 'The Limits of Quellen-und Ideologie Kritik: The Case of the Revised Annales Regni Francorum and its Implications for Carolingian Historical Writing', at the George Macaulay Trevelyan Colloquium, 'New Perspectives on Ninth Century Francia', Cambridge 30 November 1996, and wish to thank him for his permission to cite them here.

dates of those to whom the work is usually attributed, notably, members of the royal writing office. There are, moreover, many attempts in the post-801 entries to keep alive themes addressed in the earlier texts, notably the interaction on the part of the Franks with a host of non-Franks, some more exotic than others. Further, there is extraordinary sympathy between the pre-787 and the post-787 sections; they are coherent and their emphases are markedly similar.

The manuscripts potentially provide the possibility of determining how this text might have been composed, but in fact present major problems. In fact, the Vienna copy of the Lorsch annals (Vienna, Österreichische Nationalbibliothek Cod. 515, Plate 2) is the only surviving original fragment of any Frankish annals text to give us an indication of responsibility, for here the scribe (though not necessarily the author) who entered the account for 801 is clearly different from he who wrote up 802. No original manuscript of the *ARF* has been identified. Analysis of authorship has therefore to be on stylistic and therefore inevitably somewhat subjective grounds. Dutton, for example, has a vision of the process of composition of the *ARF* as follows:

> The annalist rarely saw the events he recorded ... : instead he gathered reports of these events throughout the year and fashioned them into a single annal entry in February. He would note the date, make some comment on the weather of that winter and describe in a roughly chronological and regional progression the main event of the year. Last the annalist would place information of general interest at the end of the entry ... There was no necessary order ... He ordered disorder.[67]

This is not necessarily too fanciful a scenario for some later ninth-century annal writing, but it cannot be applied to the *ARF*, and especially not to the sections 741–93 and 793–807. These appear to have been written in two bursts and were designed to present a very particular narrative. I shall return to this point below. The purportedly original manuscript, now lost, was reported to have contained the annals to 793 by Canisius, its seventeenth-century editor, and that is what he reproduces in his text.[68] It is self-evidently incomplete, however, for in the middle of the entry for 793, the text breaks off at *multi ibidem ceciderunt devtraq; parte* ... and the editor adds *Caetera desunt*. This casts doubt on the significance of the customary 793 date surmised for this lost manuscript. Was it really first composed about then, and should

[67] Paul Edward Dutton, The *Politics of Dreaming in the Carolingian Empire* (Lincoln, NB, and London, 1994) 86–7.
[68] Heinrich Canisius, *Antiquae Lectiones*, III (Ingolstadt, 1603), 187–217; his text is based on a transcript in the Bavarian ducal library of an 'old manuscript from Lorsch'.

Vienna, Österreichische Nationalbibliothek Cod. 515, fol. 4r (reduced). Annales laureshamenses, 794–803, upper Rhine. A new scribe makes the entry for 802.

this lost manuscript really be at the top of the stemma where Kurze placed it? Further, the content of the original text is impossible now to determine, unless it be the edition of Canisius and the manuscripts in Kurze's Class B. In any case, the section 788–93 in Canisius seems to include the text of the Lorsch Annals. Even in Kurze's edition, however, differences both in relation to Canisius, and other codices, have crept in. Whatever the original author(s) may have written, later copyists and compilers felt at liberty to alter sentences, change tenses and adjectives, insert extra words and omit others.

The puzzle becomes still more complicated on examination of the classic *MGH* edition of Friedrich Kurze. It was published in 1898 and based on that of Georg Pertz in 1820.[69] It is clear that what the printed edition of 1898 represents is a composite text, in which many ninth-century scribes as well as nineteenth-century editors have played a role.

We read a text, therefore, which mirrors the process of reception and attests to an audience in the ninth century. The *ARF*'s message has to be understood not just as the clever construction it once was, but also as a collaborative piece of image making by many Frankish scribes over a number of decades. Certainly in some of the later manuscripts of the annals scribes add titles to sections as they will. This can be seen in Plate 3, Vienna, Österreichische Nationalbibliothek Cod. 473. In this manuscript the text is divided at 814, the year of the death of Charlemagne and has the title *Gesta Domni Karoli Magni et Praecellentissimi Francorum Imperatoris*. The next section, running from 814, when Louis the Pious succeeded his father, to 829, has been given the title *Gesta Hludovici Imperatoris*. Such a small change in fact alters entirely the focus of the work as well as being a telling indication of what this ninth-century scribe thought the annals were really about.[70]

The most dramatic adjustments to the text, recognised as a separate entity even in 1898,[71] are in the so-called 'E' group of manuscripts,

---

[69] *ARF*, ed. Georg Pertz, *MRH Scriptores* (Hannover, 1826).

[70] The *ARF* were continued as the Annals of St Bertin to 882 in the West Frankish kingdom and as the annals of Fulda in the East Frankish version to 887/901, though neither of these is a contemporary title. See the references in n. 58 above. It is possible that when we find references to *Gesta Francorum* in library catalogues of the ninth century, it is the *ARF* that are being described. If I am right this in itself is significant. I discuss this manuscript more fully in 'L'idéologie politique dans l'historiographie Carolingienne' in R. Le Jan, S. Lebecq, B. Judic (eds), *La royauté et les élites laïques et ecclésiastiques dans l'Europe Carolingienne (du début du XIe siècle aux environs de 920)* (Lille, 1997). English translation in Y. Hen and M. Innes (eds), *Using the past in early medieval Europe: politics, memory and identity* (Cambridge, forthcoming); (hereafter 'L'idéologie politique').

[71] Kurze printed the revised version on the recto pages of his edition. The English translation by Bernard Scholz preserved this differentiation, by printing the main addition of the Reviser in indented paragraphs in relation to the main text: B. Scholz, *Carolingian Chronicles* (Ann Arbor, 1970). Kurze lists the 'E' manuscripts, xii–xv.

Vienna, Österreichische Nationalbibliothek Cod. 473, fol. 143v (reduced). Annales regni francorum ('D' family), s.IX from St Amand. The text is divided in the manuscript at 814. The first section has the title *Gesta Domni Karoli Magni* and the second, 814–29, the title *Gesta Hludovici Imperatoris.*

where revisions were added for a number of years 741–812. These were once ascribed to Einhard but now simply remain unattributed. The Latin was made more stylish and various small amendments were introduced as well as extra information here and there which is of considerable importance. An example of this is to be found in the Vienna copy of the 'E' version of the annals for 796 (Plate 4), where I have indicated, first, the beginning of the year entry where the original *Adrianus papa obiit* etc. has been altered to: *Romae Hadriano defuncto leo pontificatum suscepit* etc. and, secondly, the addition of information about the requirement that the Roman people make their submission and swear an oath of fidelity to the king through his representatives. Further, the details added about Carloman and Pippin and their intentions on accession to power in 741 give glimpses of greater political tensions than the main text would allow, though it is arguable that the expansions serve primarily to elucidate and reinforce the text and make it more intelligible rather than altering the main thrust of the Royal Frankish annalist's message. Nevertheless, the Reviser also permits us to observe a further process of constructing the past on the foundations of a predecessor.

Thus, under the year 741, the anonymous author of the *ARF* started his account with the laconic observation that Charles, mayor of the palace died: *Carolus maior domus defunctus est*. The next entry, for 742, records how Carloman and Pippin, mayors of the palace, divided the kingdom of the Franks among themselves, and mounted a campaign against Hunald, duke of the Aquitainians. Carloman also laid Alemannia waste. In 743 both Pippin and Carloman started a war against Odilo duke of the Bavarians. Carloman advanced into Saxony and the following year Pippin and Carloman together invaded Saxony and captured Duke Theodoric. Not until 747 is a man called Grifo mentioned who required a great deal of effort on Pippin's part to subdue.[72] The annalist sets a brisk pace for his narrative. The fact that he may have been writing as many as forty years after these events may have contributed to his brevity and selectivity, though other historians before and since, such as Bede or Gregory of Tours, recounting events long before their own lifetimes, have not felt so inhibited. The 'Reviser' of these same annals, working thirty years later again, that is, around 817,[73] moreover, was moved to add to the entry for 741 at some length, not only the incidental information that Carloman and Pippin had a half brother called Grifo who disputed the succession with them, but also further detail that serves to fill in the context for the first annalist's bald account of campaigns against Bavarians, Saxons, Alemans and

[72] *ARF*, s.a. 741, 743, 747, pp. 2, 4, 6.
[73] For discussion of this date, McKitterick, 'L'idéologie politique'.

Vienna, Österreichische Nationalbibliothek Cod. 510, fol. 84r. Annales regni francorum ('E' or Revised text), s.IX[ex]. The unrevised *ARF* reads at DCCXCVI: *Adrianus papa obiit, et Leo mox ut in locum eius successit, misit legatos cum muneribus ad regem.* The additional sentence mentions the submission of the Roman people and their oath of fidelity.

others. It is the Reviser who asserts that from quelling Grifo's bid for a share of the kingdom in 741 onwards, Carloman and Pippin applied themselves to restoring order in the kingdom and to recovering the provinces which had fallen away *from the Franks* after their father's death. It is the Reviser who not only alerts us to the degree to which the original annalist constructed a very particular version of the Frankish past, but also allows us to observe the reception and augmentation of that construction during the reigns of Pippin's son and grandson, Charlemagne and Louis the Pious. Many other insertions add circumstantial details of Charlemagne's campaigns, with the names of his generals and his opponents, especially in the expeditions against the Saxons, the Avars and the Byzantines in Benevento.

By the time the revisions were made, however, it appears to have been possible to acknowledge, and thus to locate in the past, opposition to Carolingian rule. In 768, for example, when Pippin III had died, his kingdom was divided between his two sons, Charles (Charlemagne) and Carloman. Three years later, Carloman died and Charlemagne was left as sole ruler. The original version of the annals mentions that Charles and Carloman were raised to the kingship. In 769 Charlemagne, the 'glorious lord king Charles (*gloriosus domnus Carolulus rex*)', went on campaign in Aquitaine and joined his brother at Duasdives. From there Carloman suddenly returned to Francia (*inde Carlomannus se revertendo Franciam item arripiens*). Carloman is mentioned again in 770 as meeting his mother Bertrada. In 771 the annalist noted laconically that Carloman died at the villa of Samoussy and that his wife with a few Franks departed for Italy.[74]

The Reviser, on the other hand, provides a long account of the invasion of and campaign in Aquitaine, and that Carloman refused to assist his brother by the evil counsel of his *proceres*. The next year the dowager Queen Bertrada's visit is extended to a journey to Italy 'in the interest of peace'. In 771 the Reviser adds the gloss that the king 'bore patiently' with the departure of Carloman's wife and retinue for Italy 'though it was needless'.[75]

The Reviser is still a staunch admirer of Charlemagne. Indeed, if anything, the additions serve to make Carloman's doings murkier and more treacherous. The portrayal of blamelessness on Charlemagne's part nevertheless conveys something of his ruthlessness as well. So too, the accounts of further opposition, notably the revolt of Charlemagne's eldest, but officially illegitimate, son Pippin the Hunchback in 792, and the conspiracy among the 'eastern Franks' in 785 led by Count Hardrad are recorded as past aberrations in the Franks' loyalty to their ruler. In

[74] *ARF*, s.a. 768, 769, 770, 771, pp. 26, 28, 30, 32.
[75] *Ibid.*, s.a. 768, 770, 771, pp. 27, 29, 31, 33.

the entry for 817, moreover, the annalist responsible for this section noted that the leaders of the rebellion of Bernard of Italy included Reginhar, son of Count Meginhar, whose maternal grandfather Hardrad once conspired against Charles. He thereby links this passage with the Reviser's note for 785 and acknowledges a tradition of disloyalty and opposition to the ruler within a particular family.[76] He can now afford to take a high moral stance and use it to highlight legitimate power.

The moral indignation conveyed by the Reviser when noting opposition; the bold way he emphasises Charlemagne's difficulties with the treachery of and lack of co-operation from his brother, his son and some of his leading magnates seem to me of a piece with the interpretation offered for the revolt of Louis the Pious's nephew Bernard against Louis. That is, the indication that close members of the family had rebelled against the head of the family before, and were quite clearly in the wrong, provides a context of vindication in which to understand not only the revolts but the way Charlemagne and Louis dealt with them. There is such distinct coherence between the revised version and this later portion, 808–20 of the annals in tone and style, that it may well be to the author of this section that we may attribute the revised 'E' version of the Royal Frankish Annals. The revised version and these later portions represent a skilful augmentation of memory and a masterly enhancement of the righteousness of the Carolingian rulers. Read in this context the 'revised annals' enhance further the legitimacy of the Carolingian rulers and Louis's succession, as well as the *imperium*, that is, rule, of the Franks over many peoples.

In judging the effectiveness of the emphases and views propounded in the Royal Frankish Annals and their dissemination, on the other hand, the manuscript evidence is of course crucial and unambiguous. It is in fact the most complex of the manuscript traditions of any work of Carolingian historiography. Five different groups among the thirty-nine surviving *ARF* manuscripts, fragments or reports and transcripts of others once extant were differentiated by F. Kurze in 1895; no one has yet improved on his work, though he himself did not explore the implications of his groupings nor of the individual representatives within them.[77]

The 'A' and 'D' groups have only a handful of surviving representatives and some are lost, notably, as mentioned earlier, the original 'A' codex, possibly from Lorsch. Members of the 'D' group were copied

[76] *Ibid.*, s.a. 785, p. 71, and McKitterick, *Frankish Kingdoms*, 135.
[77] *ARF*, viii–xix.

in centres from Worms on the Rhine to Altaich on the Danube near Passau, roughly speaking western and eastern Germany. The 'B' group manuscripts only go as far as 813 and may all stem from a common exemplar. The 'C' group, from the west Frankish kingdom and with one representative (St Petersburg Saltykov-Schedrin Library F.O.IV.4) that was based on a codex compiled for King Charles the Bald himself,[78] continues to 829, but is divided into two different families: one in which the annals were appended by the scribes to copies of the earlier histories known as the *Liber Historiae Francorum* and the Continuations of Fredegar, and the other where they were later continued by Prudentius of Troyes and Hincmar of Rheims and form the text now known as the Annals of St Bertin. It is at present the most highly regarded by modern historians, but this appears to be only because it includes St Omer, Bibliothèque Municipale MS 705, that is, the main manuscript of the Annals of St Bertin. That is to say, the status of one group has been highlighted at the expense of another for possibly inappropriate reasons. More importantly the assessment of the *ARF* has apparently been made hitherto with the reflection of hindsight from the later text, not the earlier, with the consequence that its own achievement in writing history and strongly influential interpretation has been overshadowed. The 'E' version, as I have already mentioned, is that containing the revised version and appears to be a version circulating from the Rhineland eastwards. The greater majority of these manuscripts date to the ninth century; two or three are from the eleventh and twelfth century. The version of Frankish history propounded by the annals is nevertheless incorporated in some form into the histories written in the twelfth century and later and thereby extended their influence throughout the middle ages.

The codicological context of the annals is also of significance for they were rarely transmitted on their own. The annals are implicated in the transmission of Fredegar's Continuations (class D and E manuscripts) the *Liber Historiae Francorum* and the Lorsch annals ('B' group).[79] Further, the *ARF* are often found in conjunction with the *Vita Karoli* of Einhard, the Astronomer's Life of Louis the Pious and Thegan's Life of Louis the Pious. In other words, the *ARF* form the base text of a large number of composite Frankish history books each of which were compiled to serve a particular author's or compiler's purpose in relation to whatever audience, or audiences, that author or compiler had in mind. Important associations could thus be made by juxta-

---

[78] Rosamond McKitterick, 'Charles the Bald (823–877) and his Library; the Patronage of Learning', *English Historical Review*, 95 (1980), 28–47; reprinted in McKitterick, *Frankish Kings and Culture*, chapter V.

[79] See Collins, *Fredegar*, 119–31.

position. The origin and provenance of these Frankish history books, moreover, point to dissemination of the *ARF* throughout the Frankish realm, east and west, from St Bertin to Altaich. Despite additions or omissions, and rearrangements or attachments to other historical texts which enable one to differentiate between the different groups, the text of the common elements remains remarkably stable. Many writers, scribes and manuscript compilers were familiar with the *ARF*. If is to be identified with the *Gesta francorum* mentioned in the ninth-century library catalogues I referred to above, we can posit still further circulation and reproduction of this text. Given that some of the surviving manuscripts and library catalogues have lay ownership and secular associations, the *ARF* reached a remarkably wide audience throughout the Frankish kingdoms. Further, it is conceivable that this dissemination was directed initially and deliberately from the court. In the face of the loss of the original manuscript, nothing can be proven, but two factors can be taken into account. First, if the original annal manuscript described by Canisius did indeed come from Lorsch, the strong connections between the early Carolingian court and Lorsch render a link with the court production of copies of an 'official' history a possibility.[80] Secondly, an analogy may be drawn between the possible dissemination of a particular officially approved history and the production and promotion of other officially approved and promoted versions of texts such as the Gospels, the Dionysio-Hadriana collection of canon law, the Homiliary of Paul the Deacon, the Hadrianum Sacramentary[81] and, from Louis the Pious's reign, law books.[82]

The wide dissemination is undoubtedly a consequence of the powerful story the text contains. There is the rhythmic insistence on the year of our Lord to which I have already referred. This, together with the record of where the court spent Easter and Christmas reinforces the narrative's Christian framework. The fact that God is presented as being on the side of the Franks further enhances their supremacy and legitimacy.

Secondly, there is the complete absence of the Merovingian rulers in the section before 751. The military campaigns are led by the

---

[80] Bernhard Bischoff, *Lorsch im Spiegel seiner Handschriften*, Münchener Beiträge zur Mediävistik und Renaissance-Forschung, Beiheft (Munich, 1974), 54–7.

[81] See Rosamond McKitterick, 'Royal Patronage of Culture in the Frankish Kingdoms under the Carolingians: Motives and Consequences', in *Committenti e produzione artistico-letteraria nell'alto medioevo occidentale*, Settimane di Studio del Centro Italiano de Studi sull'alto Medioevo 39 (Spoleto, 1992), 93–129, reprinted in McKitterick, *Frankish Kings and Culture*, chapter VII. Also, Rosamond McKitterick, 'Unity and Diversity in the Carolingian Church', in *Unity and Diversity in the Church*, ed. Robert Swanson, Studies in Church History 32 (Oxford, 1996), 59–82.

[82] Rosamond McKitterick, 'Zur Herstellung von Kapitularien: Die Arbeit des *leges* Skriptoriums', *Mitteilungen des Instituts für Österreichische Geschichtsforschung*, 101 (1993), 3–16.

Carolingian mayors of the palace and the mayors are supreme in all non-military matters as well.

Thirdly, and most prominently, there is the stress on Franks. As one reads it becomes something close to overkill. Pippin, Carloman and Charlemagne do everything in concert with, with the consent of, with the support of, the Franks. Pippin goes on campaign with the Frankish army in 747 (*cum exercitu francorum*). In 751 he is elected *secundum morem Francorum et elevatus a Francis in regno in Suessionis civitate*. In 755 Pippin with the *Franks* is the victor against the Lombards in Italy and returns to *Francia* (*Pippinus rex cum Francis victor extitit*). Pippin consults the Franks, he holds assemblies with the Franks. (In 757 Pippin held an assembly *in compendio cum Francis* and again in 760 *consilium fecit cum Francis*.) In 774 the Lombards came and submitted to the glorious lord King Charles and the Franks; in 775 it is the Franks who are led against the Saxons by Charlemagne. Peoples, territories and cities are conquered and placed under Frankish rule.

Such stress on the Franks as a *gens* (a people) is unprecedented either in Merovingian or in other eighth-century narrative sources. For the *Liber Historiae Francorum* the term 'Franks' refers quite clearly to the Neustrians, that is, those living in the area in western France between the Seine and the Loire. In 'Fredegar' it is less clear to whom the author is referring when he mentions Franks in the narrative, but he does distinguish *Franci* from Austrasians and it is only in the latter part of the account that it is possible to understand Francia as the entire region north of the Loire across to the Rhine, peopled by the Franks. One might suppose that this indicates that it is the general view by the middle of the eighth century that all those ruled by the Carolingians are Franks. On this reading the Royal Frankish Annalist is reflecting some degree of consensus by the time he is writing. On the other hand, the manuscripts in which the Continuations of Fredegar are copied are ninth-century Carolingian versions which may have been adapted in the light of an understanding, propagated by the Royal Frankish Annalist, of the word Franks as pertaining to all those, whether Neustrian or Austrasian, under Carolingian rule. The Royal Frankish Annalist, therefore, created a far more comprehensive idea of Frankish identity than had ever been used before and a notion of the *gens Francorum* specifically associated with the Carolingian mayors and kings.[83]

[83] This is in contrast to the Anglo-Saxons who lack the emphasis on a particular family: see Sarah Foot, 'The Making of Angelcynn: English Identity before the Norman Conquest', *TRHS*, 6th series (1996), 25–49. On questions of identity see Walter Pohl's excellent paper, 'Tradition, Ethnogenese und literarische Gestaltung: eine Zwischenbilanz', in *Ethnogenese und Überlieferung. Angewandte Methoden der Frühmittelalterforschung*, ed. K. Brunner and B. Merta (Vienna and Munich, 1994), 9–26.

It is significant in this respect that the text builds up a strong sense of the Franks in opposition to other people. When one reads the *ARF* for expansion and consolidation of the Frankish realm, it is easy to focus on conquest rather than the clever way the author is describing how the Franks systematically, so it seems, set out to swallow up all other *gentes* (peoples) who in due course become appendages to the Franks. From 741 when, according to the reviser of the annals, Carloman and Pippin set out to recover the areas lost to the Franks after Charles Martel's death, there is a battery of reiterations of Pippin and Charles and the Franks in opposition to Aquitani, Lombards, Bavarians, Saxons, Bretons etc.; throughout the whole text I have counted thirty-seven different peoples with whom the Franks collectively, plus their ruler, have dealings. The greater majority of these dealings are as opponents of the Franks and duly conquered, defeated or brought into submission to them. We find them subsequently added to the list of those going with the Franks somewhere to beat up someone else.

If one reads steadily the *ARF*'s account to 807, taking in 800 on the way, becoming an emperor of the Romans is simply the term used to denote becoming the ruler of the Romans or one ruler over many subject peoples: the latter is the standard sense of *imperium* in the middle ages and it is certainly how both Bede and Alcuin use it. Thus the coronation of Charlemagne as emperor in 800 in the *ARF* can be read as just one further instance of another people, the *Romani*, brought under Charlemagne and Frankish rule. It is soon said and passed over. Less space is in fact accorded the *Romani* than the *Aquitani*, the *Baiuuuarii* and above all the *Saxones*, the *Wascones*, the *Wilzi* and the *Brittani*. Rather, it is the incorporation of all these peoples into an all-encompassing Frankish *gens* that the *ARF* really wishes to stress.[84]

The Royal Frankish Annals forge a Frankish identity by constant reiteration and triumphal narrative. The ruler and the Franks are the achievers and together create the great realm. Consolidated in an historical and Christian framework, this is the message passed on to their contemporaries and to posterity. The insistence on precise chronology is a deliberate device to enhance a very determined expression of the Franks' identity and cultural affiliations. Self-image is as important as perceived image. Whether or not the history constructed by the Royal Frankish Annalists for the Franks bore any relation to reality is to some degree irrelevant, for what has concerned me in this paper is the

---

[84] Hraban Maur takes up this theme in his *Liber de Oblatione Puerorum*, where he insists on the *gens francorum* as the legitimate succession of other imperial gentes, *PL* 107, col. 432.

construction of a past, its coherence and consistency, and the degree to which such a construction constitutes the formation of the collective memory of the newly formed Frankish people under Carolingian rule. Although many different categories of text could yield an understanding of the Franks and their sense of history, I have deliberately focused here on one highly influential historical narrative because of the very particular message it conveys. The Royal Frankish Annalists in fact constructed so powerful an image of their society and its events, and evoked such a convincing sense of identity, that it is their version that has been remembered, and believed, ever since.[85]

[85] Preliminary versions of different parts of this paper were presented to the Workshop, 'Tracking down the Franks' in King's College London, Denys Hay Seminar of the University of Edinburgh and the conference for Dutch graduate students in Medieval Studies at Driebergen, organised by the University of Utrecht, in February and March, 1996. I am particularly grateful to my audiences on these occasions, and to the Fellows of the Royal Historical Society assembled in Leeds in May for their lively discussion and suggestions. I wish also to thank Mayke de Jong most warmly for her critical reading and valuable suggestions for the final version of this paper.

ENGLAND, BRITAIN AND THE AUDIT OF WAR
The Prothero Lecture
By Kenneth O. Morgan

READ 2 JULY 1996

THE award of the Booker Prize for 1995 to Pat Barker's *Ghost Road* did more than pay tribute to the latest powerful novel in the author's 'Regeneration Cycle'.[1] It also emphasised once again how much the historical and cultural consciousness of twentieth-century Britain is dominated by images of war. With the obvious exception of Northern Ireland, Great Britain has been an unusually peaceful and stable country in a century marked by revolution and upheaval. Yet our national experience has been shaped, almost obsessed, by two world wars in a way true of few, if any, other countries. Memories of 1914 and 1939 tower over us like Lutyens's massive monument at Thiepval. The war leaders, David Lloyd George and Winston Churchill, are commonly thought of as our two greatest prime ministers in modern times (though another, more recent, prime minister, victorious in the Falklands, still has her champions). Armistice day, Remembrance Sunday and the wearing of poppies retain their potency as all-powerful national symbols of sacrifice. The British Legion remains an influential pressure group. The eightieth anniversary of the battle of the Somme in July 1996 emphasised anew the enduring impact of the tragedies of the first world war. More generally, the fiftieth anniversaries of VE Day and VJ Day the previous year were nationwide ceremonies of remembrance for the sacrifices of the second. Almost every episode in current history, especially where Europe is involved, is commonly linked with memories of earlier conflict. Even the 1996 crisis in Anglo-German relations, such as it was, arising from 'mad cow disease' evoked comparison with 1939. The *Independent* satirically evoked Paul Nash's famous sketch, 'Over the Top'. The *Guardian* pondered whether the rifts over possible European Monetary Union or creeping federalism should be linked with national preservation or national purgation, whether with Neville Chamberlain in 1939 or Rupert Brooke in 1914.[2]

However, the received impression of the two world wars shows fundamental differences. The first world war is, irredeemably it seems,

[1] Pat Barker, *Regeneration* (1991); *The Eye in the Door* (1993); *The Ghost Road* (1995).
[2] *Independent*, 23 May 1996; Martin Kettle in *Guardian*, 23 May 1996.

associated with tragedy and disaster, with the mass slaughter of the trenches during the war, and cynical betrayal by the 'hard-faced men' in the aftermath of the peace. It is seen not just as slaughter, but as senseless slaughter, conceived in dishonour. The colossal human sacrifice of the war is generally linked with bitter recollection of the total failure to achieve that 'land fit for heroes' in the years that followed. The first world war, indeed, has generated a good deal of historical literature along these themes, notably in the fascinating divergence between Paul Fussell and Jay Winter as to the most appropriate forms of popular commemoration and mourning, whether traditional artistic techniques were sufficient in themselves or a new 'modernist' language needed to tell the brutal truths about total war.[3] A distinguished range of recent literature has explored the potential of both approaches, most notably perhaps in Sebastian Faulks's remarkable novel *Birdsong*, which deals with the social and cultural legacy of the battle of the Somme. Other writers have explored the devaluation of language that occurs when poets, historians or other remembrancers attempt to describe the unspeakable.[4]

The second world war, by contrast, is almost universally seen as a good war. It has been projected not just as the defeat of the tyrant, Hitler, but as a war for social justice, when a people's war was followed, in Britain at least, by a people's peace. The most celebrated treatment of this theme, perhaps, is the moving finale of Alan Taylor's *English History, 1914–1945*:

> Traditional values lost much of their force. Other values took their place. Imperial greatness was on the way out; the welfare state was on the way in. The British empire declined; the condition of the people improved. Few now sang 'Land of Hope and Glory'. Few even sang 'England Arise'. England had risen all the same.[5]

The contrast between the two wars is enshrined, for ever it seems, in popular legend and cultural imagery. The martial objectives of 1914 are contrasted with the human civilising rationale of 1939. There is an immense gulf between the bitter satire of Joan Littlewood's *Oh, What a Lovely War!* and the affectionate household knockabout of the long-running television series, *Dad's Army*.

It may well be that this kind of contrast is the right one to make. Perhaps the first world war is irredeemably dreadful and the second incontestably beneficial, and nothing more need be said. But historians

---

[3] Paul Fussell, *The Great War and Modern Memory* 1975); Jay Winter, *Sites of Memory, Sites of Mourning. The Great War in European Cultural History* (Cambridge, 1995).

[4] e.g. Geoff Dyer, *The Missing of the Somme* (1996 edn).

[5] A. J. P. Taylor, *English History, 1914–1945* (Oxford, 1965), 600.

ought surely to examine these two fundamental experiences, to re-evaluate the evidence, and see whether the contrast between them is really so stark. Certainly books that challenge the conventional wisdom are to be welcomed, including particularly Corelli Barnett's *Audit of War*.[6] I reject several of its conclusions but I applaud its capacity to provoke debate. For that reason, therefore, I flagrantly appropriate his title and hope that the author will condone my doing so as a contribution to an important ongoing debate.

The heroic appeal of the first world war was already seriously tarnished by the time that Lloyd George, Clemenceau and Woodrow Wilson were putting their signatures to the Treaty of Versailles in July 1919. Anti-war critics like Ramsay MacDonald and the members of the Union of Democratic Control were attaining new respectability. Criticism of the 'system of Versailles' began to mount. War demagogues like Pemberton Billing and Horatio Bottomley were on their way to oblivion, in Bottomley's case to conviction to seven years of penal servitude. Thereafter there was a growing reaction against what had happened to the nation, especially its lost generation of slaughtered manhood, between 1914 and 1918. The horror of the trenches became the dominant cultural image. The literature, both poetry and prose, of the post-war years was almost wholly anti-war. It is epitomised by Philip Sassoon, whose encounters with the army psychologist, W. H. R. Rivers, provide the core of Pat Barker's *Regeneration* almost eighty years on.

Even the government itself was hesitant about how to respond to the conflict. From the Armistice onwards, ministers' crises of conscience became public knowledge. There was a significant debate in Lloyd George's Cabinet in 1919 over the design and message of Lutyens's cenotaph. Ministers agreed that triumphalism of a traditional militaristic kind should be abandoned. The memorial should not be situated in Parliament Square as a flamboyant public statement but rather in Whitehall as a working street. The emphasis should be not so much on 'the glorious dead' *en masse* but on the finality and uniqueness of individual suffering. It should offer a personalised message, emphasising the fragility of each individual, not an impersonal statement like the grave of the 'unknown soldier'. This, indeed, was very much the view of Edwin Lutyens himself. He would be designing, he told Lloyd George, an empty tomb, 'a cenotaph not a catafalque'. His eventual, powerful monument was stark and simple with the war imagery stripped away. It was a triumph of understatement.[7]

[6] C. Barnett, *The Audit of War: The Illusion and Reality of Britain as a Great Nation* (new paperback edn, 1996).
[7] Allen Greenberg, 'Lutyens' Cenotaph', *Journal of the Society of Architectural Historians*,

A somewhat similar process occurred in music. The stirring martial themes of the war years gave way to more gentle compositions. The folk melodies of Vaughan Williams and Delius were much in vogue. Edward Elgar was almost reinvented. He became after the war less the composer of the strident tones of *Pomp and Circumstance*, which somewhat lost popularity. It was a reflective Elgar, the composer of the restrained and autumnal cello concerto (1919), who was now admired, not as the celebrant of imperial conquest but as the voice of the Malvern hills, an eternal England, pastoral and humane. In much the same way in politics, the Midlands ironmaster, Stanley Baldwin, was to turn himself into the ruminating 'Farmer Stan' of Strube's cartoons, the admirer of the rustic novel, *Precious Bane*, Mary Webb's Shropshire idyll.

Leaders of the forces in the war soon became popular scapegoats. The first world war threw up no military heroes with the possible exception of General Allenby whose mobile campaign against the Turks in Palestine had necessarily avoided the static slaughter of the western front. Field Marshal Haig withdrew to Bemyside from public life, in contrast to the enduring eminence of Marshals Foch or Pétain in France or Hindenburg who rose to be president of Germany. The political leaders of the war also suffered eclipse. Lloyd George, for all his record of partial achievement as a peacetime premier in 1919–22, was a casualty of total war, overtaken by anti-war critics like Ramsay MacDonald and destined to remain out of power for the remaining twenty-three years of his life. Winston Churchill was another victim, tarred with the failures of Gallipoli for which he largely received the blame. His political recovery began in 1924 when he re-emerged as a Conservative chancellor whose financial policy focused in some measure on severely cutting back expenditure on armaments. But not until the unexpected advent of a supreme national emergency in 1939 were his career and reputation salvaged. The new political leaders after 1922 represented a reaction against the war ethos and free-wheeling individuals like Lloyd George and Churchill. They were led by Baldwin, the apostle of 'peace in our time' at home and abroad, MacDonald whose brave new world rhetoric symbolised the post-war outlook, and, not least, Neville Chamberlain, sacked in 1917 by Lloyd George after mishandling national service and who was to appear for most of the thirties as the new giant of British political life.

On the left, the Great War was identified with capitalism, with profiteering and betrayal, J. B. Priestley captured this mood in his radio broadcasts in July 1940:

58, 1 (March 1989), 5–21; Christopher Hussey, *The Life Sir Edwin Lutyens* (1984 edn), 391–5.

I'll tell you what we did for young men and their young wives at the end of the last war. We did nothing—except let them take their chance in a world in which every gangster and trickster and stupid insensitive fool or rogue was let loose to do his damnedest. After the cheering and the flag-waving were over, and all the medals were given out, somehow the young heroes disappeared, but after a year or two there were a lot of shabby young-oldish men who didn't seem to be lucky in the scramble for easy jobs and quick profits, and so tried to sell us second-hand cars or office supplies we didn't want, or even trailed round the suburbs asking to be allowed to demonstrate the latest vacuum cleaner.[8]

There was a constant repetition of the betrayal of the returning warriors with their dreams of a land fit for heroes. Keynes told the world that the root causes lay in the unwholesome 'coupon' election of December 1918 which, he wrongly claimed, was dominated by jingoism and chauvinism. Soon, the British labour movement and many radicals besides were to link the triumphalism of the war with mass unemployment, with the deception of the miners over the Sankey report which called for nationalisation of the mines, with the undermining of the Triple Alliance at the time of 'Black Friday' and with the reactionary social cuts of the Geddes Axe.

If the left condemned the war for its links with capitalism, the right conversely associated it with socialism, with the controls of a war economy, with undermining the party system and the conventions of the constitutional order in general. Hence the peculiarly reassuring appeal of Baldwin's style of normalcy and 'safety first', as against the adventurism of men like Lloyd George, Churchill and Lord Birkenhead. An entire generation of war leadership was ridiculed or reviled. Liddell Hart condemned the generals and the admirals, John Maynard Keynes attacked the politicians, the Left Book Club denounced the industrialists and their allies, the newspaper proprietors, in a collective mood of Never Again.

Interestingly, one other country also illustrated this degree of revulsion against the war, another victorious power, namely the United States. By the thirties, anger against the 'merchants of death' who had supposedly dragged Americans into a European war, a feeling at first largely confined to German-Americans and left-wing radicals like Fighting Bob La Follette, was widespread.[9] It was fanned by the isolationism of the time, and popular hostility to the supposed 'merchants of death' voiced by the Nye Committee in 1935. For businessmen,

---

[8] J. B. Priestley, *Postscripts* 1940), 42; cf. Sian Nicholas, ' "Sly Demagogues" and Wartime Radio: J. B. Priestley and the BBC', *20th Century British History*, 6, 3 (1995), esp. 254–61.
[9] Cf. John A. Thompson, *Reformers and War* (Cambridge, 1987).

the war meant the disruption of markets with war debts left unpaid by perfidious Europeans. For liberals, it brought prohibition, the 'red scare', attacks on immigrants both through restrictive racial quotas and through the attack of the judiciary on harmless foreigners like Sacco and Vanzetti. The war, victorious though it was, created no military hero in the United States, no new Grant or Robert E. Lee. Ironically, perhaps the only heroic figure popularly acclaimed after 1918 was a civilian, Herbert Hoover, director of the humanitarian relief programme to feed a starving continent, a rare hero in Keynes's *Economic Consequences*, although his reputation did not long survive.

Now no one can dispute the human tragedy and mass destruction that the first world war brought for Britain and other combatants, their centrality in the sorry catalogue of the crimes and follies of mankind. However it should also be noted that the war years did offer Britain a mood of change and new opportunities for reform which over-simplified later accounts have tended to obscure. The much-reviled Lloyd George coalition government did have several positive achievements both during and after the war years.[10] The social agenda of the pre-war New Liberalism was given a new impetus. There were Christopher Addison's Housing Act to make housing a social service for the first time, H. A. L. Fisher's comprehensive Education Act, a newly created Ministry of Health under Addison, a minimum wage and relatively generous extension of the system of unemployment insurance. There were random social landmarks as varied as the Whitley Councils, the University Grants Committee and the Forestry Commission with the first vague beginnings of a public concern with the environment. It was not revolutionary, but the Independent Labour Party were ruefully to acknowledge that four years of war had achieved more for the social objectives of Keir Hardie than had decades of peace. And, of course, women saw in the war the first signs of civil liberation, not only in women over thirty being granted the franchise for the first time but also in new employment opportunities in the teaching and other professions.

There were also some broader national landmarks which should be recorded, in economic, foreign and imperial policy. In all of them, new approaches were at least attempted if not carried through. In economic and industrial affairs. Lloyd George's managerial style in wartime suggested a new way forward. A less adversarial system of industrial relations was proposed, for all the attention rightly focused on the massive nationwide strikes of the years 1919–21. The corporate approach foreshadowed by the Whitley councils in the public services, seemed to

---

[10] See Kenneth O. Morgan, *Consensus and Disunity. The Lloyd George Coalition Government, 1918–1922* (Oxford, 1979), 8off.

reach its climax with the National Industrial Conference convened in the spring of 1919, along with the creation of a national rather than a piecemeal system of wage bargaining.[11]

It led to very little, of course. Most of the gains were wiped out in the turbulent strike-torn summer of 1919, while the government's policy of decontrol, and deflationary policies intended as a precursor to the return to the gold standard led to major stoppages in the mines, amongst railway and other transport workers, and in many other industries. Even the police went on strike in 1919 with much resultant violence and loss of life in Merseyside. The armed forces were freely used to coerce the workers and a nationwide strike-bearing apparatus set up under the Emergency Powers Act. The National Industrial Conference proved to be a total failure: it was noted that, in any case, the Triple Alliance unions had stayed away from it from the outset.

On the other hand, not everything was lost. There was much restructuring on both sides of industry that resulted. Major employers like Sir Allan Smith built on wartime corporatism to form the National Council of Employers' Organisation which largely superseded the FBI and claimed to speak for industrial employers as a whole. On the trade union side, the General Council of the TUC came into being in 1921, with new claims for authority shown in its meetings with Lloyd George over the problem of unemployment at Gairloch in October 1921.

The impression of unrelieved industrial chaos between 1918 and 1926 is actually distinctly misleading. It applied mainly in the coalmining industry in 1919–21, then as later truly a special case with its own distinctive problems in relation to productivity, costs and overseas markets. After 1922 the TUC looked back to a post-war phase under Lloyd George's aegis which saw, if hardly beer and sandwiches at No. 10, at least more access to government and more effective dialogue with the employers. Stanley Baldwin, to some degree, recreated that mood in the later 1920s. Certainly by then, despite the General Strike in 1926, the character of British industrial relations could be seen as more orderly and less confrontational than before the war.

International policy also saw a potential change of direction. It is often forgotten how commanding Britain's position was in world affairs after the Armistice, especially with the USA isolationist and choosing to stay on the sidelines. In this new climate, Lloyd George, the most powerful of the peacemakers to survive beyond Versailles, attempted to forge a new, more vigorous form of European, perhaps world, leadership for Britain, in a fashion unique since the end of the

[11] For the Conference, see Rodney Lowe, 'The Failure of Consensus in Britain: The National Industrial Conference, 1919–21', *Historical Journal*, 21, 3 (September 1978), 649ff. More generally, Keith Middlemas, *Politics in Industrial Society* (London, 1979), 137ff.

Napoleonic wars. He led the way to restoring both Germany and the Soviet Union, the two pariah states, to the comity of nations. He also adapted British foreign policy (with the reluctant acquiescence of his foreign secretary, Curzon) to the needs of industrial and commercial policy: one important landmark was the Trade Treaty with the Soviet Union in 1921 and its *de facto* recognition. It is worth recalling that Lloyd George after 1918 was the first British prime minister to have to confront the facts of industrial decline and to remodel policy accordingly.

In terms of international security and stability, a possible moment of breakthrough came in December 1921–January 1922. There was the prospect of the remarkable novelty of a British fifty-year treaty guarantee for the eastern frontier of France against future possible German invasion alongside a moderate settlement of German post-war reparations. It applied only to western Europe; beyond Germany's eastern boundaries, Lloyd George told Briand that 'populations in that quarter of Europe were unstable and excitable'. It was, however, a major step for British foreign policy which had since 1812 avoided the 'continental commitment', and was visualised as the precursor to a European economic settlement at Genoa. The meeting of Lloyd George and Briand at Cannes in January 1922 would, it was hoped, lay the groundwork for a treaty, despite disputes on French submarine construction and other details. Briand was warned by Ribot, 'Ah, Briand, vous êtes déjà allé à Canossa. Prenez garde que vous n'alliez pas à Cannes aussi!'[12] In fact, as is well known, the Lloyd George–Briand partnership was disastrously undermined when a political crisis in Paris resulted from the fateful comic golf match on the links at Cannes. Briand fell from power and was replaced by the intransigent anti-German Lorrainer, Raymond Poincaré. Genoa came to nothing, undermined by the Rapallo treaty between the Soviet Union and the German foreign minister, Walter Rathenau, himself shortly to be assassinated. Nevertheless, there had been a fleeting moment when British foreign policy could just possibly have been given a new direction. What journalists nowadays choose to call a defining moment might have perished on the Cannes golf links in January 1922.

Thereafter, a powerful reaction followed against post-war foreign policy, a conviction that there should be no foreign entanglements. Lloyd George's active foreign policy was popularly associated with threats of war. It is indeed true that he fell from office following a

---

[12] Conversation between Lloyd George and Briand, London, 21 December 1921, Rohan Butler and J. P. T. Butler, eds., *Documents on British Foreign Policy, 1919–1939*, First Series, XV (London, HMSO, 1967), 786; conversation between Lloyd George and Briand, Cannes, 4 January 1922, W. N. Medlicott, Douglas Dakin and M. E. Lambert, eds., *ibid*, XIX (London, HMSO, 1974), 7.

belligerent phase of policy in the eastern Mediterranean in support of Greece and a confrontation with the Turks at Chanak. But his government had been crumbling since Cannes. Chanak was an uncharacteristic, if politically fatal, episode in foreign policy. What resulted, however, was something much broader, a reaction against an active foreign policy in general. Herein lay the roots of appeasement in its various forms. Much of the responsibility, in fact, lies in one powerful, brilliantly written book, J. M. Keynes's, *Economic Consequences of the Peace*. A best-seller from the start, it proved to be an immensely damaging book. It was not really a work of economics at all, but a personal polemic reinforced by his private attachment to Germany (and perhaps illustrated by his curious homosexual attachment to the German delegate at Paris, Dr Melchior).[13] Keynes was in large measure responsible for the mood of revulsion against the 'system of Versailles', a treaty whose imperfections he exaggerated.

Thereafter, there followed a phase of greater isolation in British international policy. Bonar Law captured the new mood as early as October 1922 during the Chanak crisis when he warned of the dangers of Britain's acting as 'policeman of the world'.[14] Appeasement, initially in passive form, then more dynamically under Neville Chamberlain in 1937, drove British policy henceforth. Ironically, the first great appeaser was none other than Lloyd George himself. His Fontainebleau memorandum of March 1919, during the Paris peace conference, in which he, Smuts and others warned of the dangers of a stern treatment of Germany over frontiers and reparations, was an early document in the history of appeasement. He helped to undermine his own policy, unwittingly at first, more culpably with his visit to Hitler in Berchestesgaden in 1936. An ineffective British response to the dictators was the partial outcome.

Finally, in imperial policy, there was again a prospect of a new direction after 1918. During the war, the empire was to reach its greatest extent. An Imperial War Cabinet met in Downing Street and General Smuts joined the British government. After 1919 Churchill as colonial secretary massively built up the British domain in the Middle East through the mandate system, like a second Alexander the Great. Yet the war also brought a clear sense too of the perceived limits to imperial power. This was shown most graphically in events in Ireland. After a very dark period, the 'troubles' of the war with the IRA, the Free State

[13] Robert Skidelsky, *John Maynard Keynes: Hopes Betrayed, 1883–1920* (1983), 360–1. It is unfortunate that the author's analysis of *The Economic Consequences of the Peace*, particularly its financial arguments, is relatively brief. Keynes added to the impact of his book with his *Essays in Biography* (1933) including a celebrated and inaccurate study of Lloyd George, withheld from the *Economic Consequences*.

[14] Bonar Law, letter in *Times*, 7 October 1922.

Treaty was signed by Lloyd George with Arthur Griffith and Michael Collins, acting on behalf of Sinn Fein. On the basis of partition, the least of the possible evils, peace was brought to Ireland for the first time since the Act of Union. The Free State Treaty, in contrast to the Unionist rhetoric over home rule before 1914 was now seen as heralding neither the break-up of the United Kingdom nor the fragmentation of the empire. It was viewed rather as a measured, specific act of decolonisation. The cause of the small rump of southern Unionists was swept aside for the greater good. And, until the civil rights movement fifty years later, it worked.

What the war years showed with extreme clarity was that the empire was not cohesive. In the crisis of Chanak, only distant New Zealand was prepared to support the mother country in its possible fight with the Turks. The Imperial War Cabinet was a very short-term phenomenon. The post-war period was in fact a phase of moderation and partial devolution in imperial policy, even though such a conclusion could hardly be gleaned by recent film spectaculars on Mahatma Gandhi and Michael Collins. There was a major extension of self-government in Egypt, and more strikingly in India. The Montagu–Chelmsford reforms pointed India for the first time in the direction of effective home rule on a provincial basis, comprehending Hindu, Muslim and Sikh. The disgraced General Dyer of Amritsar fame was sent packing, for all the protests of the Diehards. There was indeed a supreme irony that during the twenties, Lutyens's and Baker's imperial edifices were rising up on the slopes of Raisina at New Delhi. Georges Clemenceau saw them in the later twenties and observed 'it will be the grandest ruin of them all'.[15] An early visitor who came to tea with the viceroy, Halifax, in his new government house in 1931 was to be the Congress leader, Mahatma Gandhi, already perhaps contemplating his inheritance.

In assessing the consequences of the first world war, and its potential for change, there is another important aspect to consider. It should be noted that there were at least five wars that took place in 1914–18, an English war, a Scottish war, a Welsh war, an Irish war and, quite distinct, an Ulster war. The first world war, like much else in modern British history was an exercise in pluralism and should be considered as such.

The different experience of Ireland, north and south, is obvious and needs no repetition here. In Scotland, there did appear to be a major transformation at work after 1918 which might differentiate it from England. Its epicentre was Red Clydeside, the twenty-one seats out of

---

[15] Robert Grant Irving, *Indian Summer. Lutyens, Baker and Imperial Delhi* (New Haven and London, 1981), 355.

twenty-eight in Clydeside won by Labour, almost wholly ILP, members in November 1922. It was symbolised by Davy Kirkwood addressing the crowds at Glasgow station as the Labour members set forth to Westminster, tribunes of proletarian revolt. 'When we come back this station and this railway will belong to the people!' But Red Clydeside was not altogether what it appeared to be. It was the product of some adventitious factors, notably the switch of allegiance of Irish voters in Glasgow following the Irish Treaty. In fact, the socialist upsurge was largely confined to the Glasgow area. It was riven here by sectarian conflict between the ILP and mainstream Labour. The later years of Jimmy Maxton, beloved permanent rebel, marginalised author of the 'Living Wage', illustrated the extent of the failure. John Maclean died young, a charismatic but essentially parochial rebel. He died young in 1923, his dream of a Scottish workers' republic a hopeless chimera.[16]

In Wales, by contrast, the war years did suggest that wider changes were in train. The Welsh nation and its Liberal nonconformist champions had seemed central to the winning of the war. There was from December 1916 a Welsh prime minister, surrounded in Downing Street by a Welsh Mafia headed by the famous Welsh-speaking 'microbe' and 'fluid person', Thomas Jones of Rhymney.[17] It was also a war claimed to be fought on behalf of Welsh values: Lloyd George told a massed audience of London Welshmen at the Queen's Hall in London on 19 September 1914 that it was a war fought on behalf of 'the little five-foot-five nations', Serbia, Montenegro, Belgium—and no doubt Wales.[18] Even the most famous popular song of the war, 'Keep the Home Fires Burning', was written by the youthful Welshman, Ivor Novello, hitherto best known as the son of Clara Novello Davies, celebrated conductor of the Royal Welsh Ladies Choir. The aspirations of Liberal Wales now appeared to be fulfilled; in 1920 even the age-old aspiration of the disestablishment of the church of England in Wales was achieved.

The war appeared to confirm the hegemony in Wales of the middle-class Liberal ascendancy that had dominated the nation since the 'great election' of 1868 first saw the erosion of the rule of the Anglican landowner.[19]. But in fact it saw major transformations that were to propel that ascendancy to its early demise. Its legacy was disestablishment—but not only of the Welsh church but of the gentry, and much of the whole

[16] There is a vivid account of the departure from Glasgow station in Emanuel Shinwell, *Conflict without Malice* 1955), 76–7. Shinwell, member for Linlithgow, was not a Glasgow member himself. For Maxton, see Gordon Brown, *Maxton* (Edinburgh, 1986), and David Howell, *A Lost Left* (Manchester, 1986), for John Maclean.

[17] See E. L. Ellis, *T.J.: The Life of Dr Thomas Jones C.H.* (Cardiff, 1992).

[18] This is printed in David Lloyd George, *From Terror to Triumph* (1915), 1–15.

[19] On this, see Kenneth O. Morgan, *Wales in British Politics, 1868–1922* (3rd edn, Cardiff, 1980).

panoply of pre-war society, Liberal as well as Tory. The chapels, triumphalist in blessing the war as a righteous crusade for the good, their ministers preaching in the pulpit in full military uniform, were supreme amongst war casualties. A new socialist upsurge had been anticipated during the pre-war industrial turbulence, the era of Taff Vale and Tonypandy. Now after 1918 the Central Labour College, with its Marxist ideology, was to produce a new leadership elite, young workers like Jim Griffiths, Morgan Phillips, Ness Edwards, Lewis Jones and above all Aneurin Bevan of Tredegar, who were to challenge and displace the old Liberal elite and the values of *Cymru Fydd*.[20]

More than in Scotland, then, the war was to generate a period of sweeping change in Wales. It produced a new nationalism, with the foundation of Plaid Cymru, the Welsh Nationalist Party, in 1925 under the presidency of a war veteran, the Liverpool Welshman, Saunders Lewis. It also saw a new internationalism through David Davies and his enthusiasm for the League of Nations Union, symbolised by his Woodrow Wilson chair of International Politics at Aberystwyth. At a different remove, the return of a Christian Pacifist as member for the University of Wales in 1924 was a reaction against wartime Liberalism of a more startling kind. It suggested the growing disillusion and radicalising of the liberal intelligentsia.[21] Wales, and perhaps Scotland, was less a prey to the post-war Baldwinian mood of 'normalcy'.

It is often claimed that the first world war was essentially integrative in identifying Wales and Scotland more completely than ever before with the United Kingdom. In many ways the precise reverse is true. It marked a regionalisation of cultures, which led in the inter-war years to something of a regionalisation of protest. Much of the turbulence of industrial relations from 1919 onwards focused on Scotland and Wales, in Clydeside and the Welsh coalfield in particular.[22] It was they also who experienced the most savage of responses from the authorities, notably from Captain Lionel Lindsay, a veteran of Sir Garnet Wolseley's regime in Egypt who became a long-serving chief constable of Glamorgan. The Scots and the Welsh were to infiltrate English political culture too in the thirties, in such previously quiescent places as Coventry and Oxford. Professor Rees Davies's recent statement on the importance of pluralism in analysing the culture of medieval Britain is capable of application to a far more modern period also.[23]

[20] The only book on the College is W. W. Craik, *The Central Labour College* (London, 1964).

[21] Kenneth O. Morgan, *Modern Wales: Politics, Places and People* (Cardiff, 1995), 102ff.

[22] See Jane Morgan, *Conflict and Order. The Police and Labour Disputes in England and Wales, 1900–1939* (Oxford, 1987).

[23] Professor Rees Davies's inaugural lecture, University of Oxford, delivered 29 February 1995.

The second world war has from the first always been vastly more popular. It evokes an image not of betrayal but of solidarity, of 'pulling through together' as the Ministry of Information posters put it. Artistic representations of the war emphasised the ideal of a classless unity, as in Henry Moore's sketches of citizens huddling together for mutual protection in the London underground during the blitz. There has been an abiding sense of a communal ideal, of social citizenship. The dominant intellectual figure is that of William Beveridge, truly another People's William, with the generous comprehensive ideal embodied in his famous 1942 report on Social Insurance. The divided nation of the mass unemployment in 'depressed areas' alongside consumer affluence in the southern suburbs, would be banished. The process of the evacuation of schoolchildren from English cities was commonly (if mistakenly) believed to have eroded the class divide and brought the people to a closer understanding. Unlike 1914–18, the writers and artists and musicians of the time were almost wholly sympathetic, as is shown in the wartime work of Henry Moore, Paul Nash, John Piper or William Walton. Benjamin Britten and Michael Tippett, both conscientious objectors, are distinct exceptions. Tippett, indeed, whose oratorio *A Child of our Time* (1941) had a strongly political thrust, actually went to prison, but he was a very rare phenomenon. Cyril Connolly's *Horizon* was a vehicle for literary criticism not for political or social protest.[24] Amongst the population at large, Churchill enjoyed an unambiguous role as the warrior hero. After Alamein, everyone endorsed his leadership from the Communists to Colonel Blimp. And the war was won, conclusively, in the last major victory for British arms. Montgomery was for a time hailed as a new Wellington or Marlborough.

Despite Churchill, however, the main impact of the war seemed to be on the British left. This time it truly was a people's war, even though Mass Observation surveys suggested that the people took some time to recognise this fact about themselves. George Orwell united patriotism with social revolution in *The Lion and the Unicorn*: his evocation of Englishness was appropriated by a Conservative prime minister, John Major, fifty years on. Harold Laski went further in *The Revolution of our Time* in suggesting the revolutionary potential of the conflict.[25] A clear left-wing critique of society emerged. There might have been something more, a genuine radical revolutionary moment as indicated in lightning strikes in the Welsh valleys or perhaps the mystique of Nye Bevan in 1942–3.

But mainstream Labour skilfully appropriated the war images for itself. Labour's democratic socialism was constitutional, familiar and

[24] Paul Fussell, *Wartime* (Oxford, 1989), 209ff.
[25] Isaac Kramnick and Barry Sheerman, *Harold Laski. A Life on the Left* (1993), 467ff.

reassuring, a paean to neighbourliness, not a threat to private savings or ideas of public morality. Labour ministers like Bevin, Dalton and Morrison impinged just as much on the national consciousness just as much as did Churchill. After 1945 an elderly government, most of whom remembered 1918 with much clarity, concentrated on avoiding the mistakes made after the previous war; they focused on social reform, the mixed economy and 'fair shares'. There was concern in 1946 when Bevan seemed to be building insufficient 'homes for heroes'. The images of the war dominated Labour thinking down, perhaps, to the leadership of Michael Foot, author of *The Guilty Men* in 1940, in the election of 1983. Mrs Thatcher's counter-revolution was directed largely at processes and ideas generated essentially by the war and its 'debilitating consensus' of high taxes and state control.

The war leaders of 1939–45 were almost universally popular and remained so. Again there is a parallel with the United States, in the abiding popularity of wartime leaders of heroes from Eisenhower and Marshall through to John F. Kennedy and George Bush. In 1952 there was a prospect of Eisenhower being enlisted as presidential candidate by either main party. It was instructive, though, that another wartime hero, Bob Dole, was reluctant to proclaim his own military achievements in the 1996 presidential election because it drew attention to his age. An era was ending here, too.

The war evoked above all traditional images—a sense of pastoral Englishness, the peace of the countryside, the non-military and neigh-bourly aspects of British (or, more narrowly, English) life. No one embodied them more perfectly than the post-war Labour premier, Clement Attlee, with his love of cricket and the *Times* crossword, and his personal devotion to Haileybury school. Small wonder that Anthony Howard has called his regime the most complete restoration of tra-ditional values in British history since the return of Charles II in 1660.[26] Public and civic institutions recovered their old popularity after the depression years—the monarchy (its sheen restored after the mishaps of Edward VIII), 'the mother of parliaments', the armed services, even civil servants with their classical degrees from Oxford, the 'gentlemen in Whitehall' whom the socialist Douglas Jay assured his pre-and post-war readers genuinely did know better.[27]

The second world war marked a national climacteric. Down to the 1980s two generations of British political leaders, from Churchill to Callaghan, were dominated by the memories of the wartime experience.

[26] Anthony Howard, 'We are the Masters Now', in *The Age of Austerity*, ed. Michael Sissons and Philip French (new edn, Oxford, 1986), 19.

[27] Douglas Jay, *The Socialist Case* (2nd edn, 1947), 258. To be fair, the author was applying this dictum specifically to education and health.

On the right, of course, Churchill himself returned to office in 1951 and, despite failing health, remained premier for four more years. Macmillan, Eden and Heath were all in different ways heavily influenced by wartime experience (the former, of course, had been a courageous soldier in the first world war as well). Conversely R. A. Butler remained suspect in many Tory circles as a man of Munich, in 1957 and in 1963 (even though in the latter case he was defeated by Alec Douglas-Home, once Chamberlain's ministerial aide when he met Hitler in 1938). On the British left, the impress of wartime experiences was even clearer. Their leaders had been intimately involved in service at the highest level, as wartime planners (Gaitskell, Jay, Wilson), as members of the armed services (Callaghan, Healey, Jenkins) or as opinion formers (Foot). A new intellectual aristocracy had come into being—Noel Annan's 'donnish dominion' of the liberal-socialist intelligentsia.

Where the first world war aroused a need for change, the second world war generated a massive nostalgia. There was for decades a cult of Churchill as war hero, and rapt audiences for the biographies of Martin Gilbert and others. Films would replay the old themes—*The Wooden Horse*, *Dambusters*, *The Bridge over the River Kwai* and countless others down to the mid-1980s. On television, there were huge audiences for the whimsical Home Guard portrayed in *Dad's Army*, the Changi women prisoners in *Tenko* and the grotesque parody of all wartime foreigners in *'Allo, 'Allo*. After 1918 the British had turned back to pre-war stereotypes, the cult of 'business as usual', the centrality of the gold standard, even in the cause of reform. After 1945, they turned not to the pre-war years, linked with mass unemployment and the diplomacy of appeasement, but to the heady experience of 1939–45. One notable aspect is that the second world war produced its own stereotypes of women as did the first. But in 1939–45 they were all individual women— in fiction, Greer Garson's Mrs Miniver, in real life the Queen Mother, a heroine of the blitz, Myra Hess playing on indefatigably at the National Gallery, or the all-time forces' sweetheart, Vera Lynn. By contrast, 1914–18 produced only Nurse Cavell, the eternal martyred symbol of womanhood in general.[28]

Like the first world war, the second had many wrong lessons attached to it. After 1918 there had been perhaps too indiscriminate a sense of revulsion; after 1945 there was perhaps too much euphoria, with damaging consequences for our national experience.

First it should be noted that, for all the successes of the wartime production drive and the attempts of Cripps and others to promote

---

[28] On the other hand, Harold L. Smith, in Smith, ed., *War and Social Change. British Society in the Second World War* (Manchester, 1988), 208ff, has argued persuasively that the status of women in general was not enhanced by the war years.

industrial efficiency after 1945, the economy was not modernised as a result of the wartime experience. In particular, after 1951 the failure to re-equip the economy as other European nations were doing was deeply damaging. In 1950 a quarter of the world trade in manufacturing came from British factories; by 1964 the figure had slumped to 14 per cent. The British growth rate in the fifties was only 58 per cent of the OECD average.[29] The reason for this did not lie in the frittering away of precious resources in building the New Jerusalem, as has sometimes been alleged. In many ways, the welfare state and post-war regional policies to promote full employment had salutary economic consequences, eventually emulated by other more successful economies overseas. Nor can the limited and moderate programme of nationalisation carried out reasonably be seen as a fundamental cause of industrial failure. Gas, electricity, civil aviation, cable and wireless were all commercial successes. And it would be hard indeed to argue that the progress of the coal mines suffered from the removal of the private coalowners, many of whom should have been removed for incompetence and a few perhaps prosecuted for criminal negligence in their flagrant ignoring of safety regulations that cost so many lives at Gresford and elsewhere.[30]

Rather was it a case that inadequate attention was paid to modernisation, to strategies of investment, to the training of managers or the reskilling of labour (here the limited pre-war apprentice system was favoured by both employers and unions). Employers were consistently obstructive towards government initiatives such as Cripps's Development Councils, and of course the bulk of the economy was still in private hands. On all sides there were illusions about the British economy because the war had been won and because of the export boom between 1948 and 1955 when such potential rivals as West Germany were still in the process of recovery. The emphasis remained on production rather than innovation, on what Dr Tomlinson has called 'present output rather than future competitiveness'.[31] Inadequate advantage was taken of the advent of Marshall Aid and there was undue attachment to the sterling area. By international standards, rates of domestic productivity were low. They remained low in 1963 when

---

[29] Data in Roger Middleton, *Government versus the Market* (1996).

[30] For the neglect of safety regulations, see Barry Supple, *The History of the British Coal Industry*, vol. IV, 1913–46 (Oxford, 1987), 426ff. In the Gresford, Wrexham, coal disaster in September 1934, 265 miners (including boys) were killed in an explosion. Despite clear evidence of flagrant negligence by the managers, the outcome was that in 1937 there were fines of £15 imposed on each of four charges, and £20 each on four other charges.

[31] Jim Tomlinson, 'Mr Attlee's Supply-Side Socialism', *Economic History Review*, 46, 1 (1993), 1–22. For a fuller treatment, see the same author's *Democratic Socialism and Economic Policy. The Attlee Years, 1945–1951* (Cambridge, 1996), 68ff.

Harold Wilson made his later, perhaps excessively derided, speech to party conference about science and the 'white heat' of a new technology. It was an attempt to break out of a low-growth, low-productivity cycle but it came too late and was inadequately conceived when it came.

The Festival of Britain in 1951 sought to stimulate innovation in industry and technology, and in design. But Gerald Barry's successful attempt to make the Festival a 'national autobiography'[32] led it to become a celebration of traditions, and to a nostalgic view of the national identity. There was little enough evidence of wartime radicalism. More generally, illusions prevailed about industrial relations in Britain, based on war years in which 'we all pulled through together'. In practice, Britain's industrial system was deeply adversarial, and this was not seriously challenged until the abortive Bullock report of 1976 under the Callaghan administration attempted to introduce something similar to the co-determination of the Germans which Helmut Schmidt tried to promote with his fellow social democrat, the British prime minister. That also failed amidst disputes between union leaders and the CBI.[33]

In constitutional matters, also, the second world war proved disappointing. There had been widespread criticism of the British constitution after the crisis of 1931. Left-wing condemnation of legislative corruption came from Harold Laski and from the Guilty Men school. On the moderate right, Harold Macmillan and others called for an industrial parliament which would be far more appropriate for industrial investment and planning than the Westminster model. But winning the war ended serious constitutional debate for forty years. Mrs Thatcher in her 1988 Bruges speech was to hail 'Big Ben chiming out for liberty' and thereby to oppose systemic innovation. The first world war had in fact seen much dynamism in both theory and practice. Lloyd George's Garden Suburb of private advisers included innovative writers on the constitution such as Leo Amery and Professor Adams. There were radical new practices in the War Cabinet and its secretariat.[34] But after 1945 Attlee suppressed talk of constitutional change, whether the Lords, the civil service or local government. In practice what little reform there has been has mostly come under the Conservatives, including life peers and the remodelling of local government for the first time since 1888.

The war in fact reinforced a mood of constitutional conservatism. The ABCA current affairs classes in the army are sometimes

---

[32] Fred Leventhal, ' "A Tonic to the Nation": The Festival of Britain, 1951', *Albion*, 27, 3 (Fall 1995), 449–50.

[33] I cover this episode in some detail in my forthcoming official biography of Lord Callaghan (Oxford, 1997), pp. 560–2. I am indebted to Lord Callaghan, HE Helmut Schmidt, Lord Murray of Epping Forest and Mr Jack Jones for first-hand information.

[34] See especially John Turner, *Lloyd George's Secretariat* (Cambridge, 1980).

represented as cauldrons of political argument, a new version of the Putney Debates.[35] In fact, this is much exaggerated. The ABCA literature hailed 'the mother of parliaments' and referred to John Lilburne and the Levellers as a citizen army of proto-backbenchers in a democratic House of Commons, almost the 1922 Committee under arms. It was the patriotism not the radicalism of Freeborn John and his comrades that was emphasised. The effect of the second world war was to underline the glories of an unwritten constitution and conceptions of national sovereignty rooted. Burke-like, in history, instinct and prescription. Small wonder that Attlee and his socialist colleagues refused to tamper with it, even in gerrymandered Northern Ireland.

International policy was another area where the second world war might be thought to have had harmful effects on subsequent British history. Foreign policy might well have been too timid after 1918, or at least after 1922. After 1945 it was surely too ambitious. Britain took pride in its role as one of the 'big three' at Potsdam, and in its intimate relationship to the United States in the Bevin era. The idea of the supposed 'special relationship' reached its high point in the period when Oliver Franks was ambassador to Washington in 1948–52 and when Britain could press its claim, as Franks somewhat curiously put it, to be standing outside and ahead of 'the queue of European powers'.[36] Churchill laid much emphasis on the wartime alliance when pressing for a 'summit conference' with the Russians in 1953, but his old comrade President Eisenhower did not respond warmly.[37]

What the war did for Britain, therefore, was to kindle illusions about its great power role and thereby to indulge in a massive over-extension of its resources around the world—what Corelli Barnett rightly calls 'global overstretch'. Dissenting voices like that of Attlee in 1945 were swept aside by the Chiefs of Staff.[38] In any case, the strong attachment to the role of Commonwealth leadership felt by Labour and Conservative governments alike encouraged a worldwide outlook. There was also heavy pressure from the United States for Britain, in receipt of massive

---

[35] An interesting work is S. P. MacKenzie, *Politics and Military Morale* (Oxford, 1992). For the non-radicalizing effect of ABCA classes, see J. A. Crang, 'Politics on Parade: Army Education and the 1945 General Election', *History*, 81, 262 (April 1996), esp. 224–6. For some perceptive comments on the second world war and ideas of 'heritage', see Raphael Samuel, *Theatres of Memory* (1994), 208.

[36] This phrase appears in Franks to Attlee, 15 July 1950 (PRO, PREM 8/1405). See also Alex Danchev, *Oliver Franks, Founding Father* (Oxford, 1993), 109ff.

[37] Churchill to Eisenhower, 21 April 1953, Eisenhower to Churchill, 5 May 1953 (PRO, PREM 11/421).

[38] See Corelli Barnett, *The Lost Victory. British Dreams, British Realities, 1945–1950* (1995), 70–102. Attlee's views appear in PRO, CAB 129/1, 1 September 1945, and CAB 131/2, 13 March 1946.

assistance under the Marshall Aid programme, to retain its strategic presence in the Middle East and South-East Asia. As late as 1966 Harold Wilson was pressed hard in Washington to retain the expensive British naval base in Singapore. For their part, British governments, whether under Attlee or Churchill, viewed a role on the world stage as a posthumous response to Munich, appeasement and pre-war 'pacifism' (of which Labour in particular was deeply conscious). This led to an inflated and unaffordable defence posture from 1945 until the belated withdrawal from bases east of Suez in the later 1960s. National service was expensively maintained to hold on to imperial outposts from Belize to Hong Kong. An unduly ambitious rearmament programme was embarked upon in 1951, relatively more costly than that of the United States, the result of Gaitskell's political attachment to the Americans overcoming the accurate economic criticisms put forward (contrary to many later accounts) by Aneurin Bevan.[39]

More serious still, a long-term independent nuclear weapons programme was begun in 1946, in large measure for prestige reasons and to retain Britain's symbolic role at the top negotiating table. It continued, through Polaris and Chevaline, down to the adoption of Trident D5 missiles under Mrs Thatcher. Ernest Bevin had observed in 1946 that, if there was an atomic bomb in the world, 'We ought to have a bloody Union Jack flying on top of it.'[40] It was a major cause of long-term economic weakness, a failure to recognise the diminution of British power long before 1939, and a constitutional aberration since from 1946 onwards all discussions of nuclear weaponry were carefully concealed from Cabinet and parliament.

This leads to the final aspect of the damaging consequences of the war, namely the abiding intense suspicion of 'Europe', however defined. Wartime memories were repeatedly used to reinforce the British sense of isolation from the continent. Much was made of memories of Dunkirk (getting out of foreign entanglements in the most direct way) and 'standing alone' during the Battle of Britain while feeble foreigners capitulated or collaborated in the face of Hitler's *Wehrmacht*. It bred a patriotism of an intensely English kind variously illustrated by Eliot's 'East Coker' and (especially) 'Little Gidding', John Piper's watercolours of decaying parish churches, or the war art of Paul Nash, fiercely realistic in its portrayal of the muddy misery of the trenches in the first world war, but in the second a hymn to the mystical beauty of the English countryside, which combat aircraft manoeuvring overhead almost seemed to embellish. On a popular level, this Englishness showed

---

[39] For a fuller analysis of the dispute between Gaitskell and Bevan, see Kenneth O. Morgan, *Labour in Power, 1945–1951* (Oxford, 1984), 441ff.

[40] Peter Hennessy, *Never Again* (1992), 268.

itself in a sentimental attachment to the 'white cliffs of Dover' extolled by Dame Vera Lynn.

In this climate of opinion, moves towards European integration, as opposed to specific functional co-operation in the Western Union, were seldom taken seriously by British governments. In 1950 the Labour government refused to join the Schuman Plan for a coal and steel community; Morrison reported that 'the Durham miners won't wear it'.[41] Churchill and Eden were no more positive. There were efforts to undermine the Messina conference and almost a kind of contempt for the Treaty of Rome at its inception amongst British diplomats, as wrong over Europe in 1955–7 as they had been in 1938.[42] The eventual entry into the EEC in 1973 was a reluctant move taken from a defensive posture. The British remained a Euro-sceptic nation. Anti-German prejudice remained widespread on the British right, right down to the outcry over beef exports in 1996 and assaults on the reputation of Beethoven, composer of the EU's *Ode to Joy*. The result was that, with the special relationship with the US increasingly marginal and probably killed off by Nixon and Heath, and the Commonwealth fragmenting with decolonisation, the war helped a process by which British foreign policy was left rudderless for a generation. There remains force in Dean Acheson's much criticised observation in 1962 that Britain had lost an empire and failed to find a role. Governmental and popular attitudes to Europe illustrate his point.

The second world war, then, helped shape a novel kind of English nationalism. How was this replicated elsewhere in the United Kingdom? Wales, as has been seen, took something of a distinctive course after 1918. This was notably less true after 1945. There was indeed a remarkable lack of attention to the events of war by Welsh poets and other writers. Alun Llywelyn Williams's volume *Cerddi* (Songs) is a rare exception.[43] The Welsh-language cultural world was embarrassed by the pre-war anti-Semitism and neo-fascism of Saunders Lewis, the president of Plaid Cymru, who declared his personal neutrality in 1939. The by-election in the University of Wales constituency in 1943 revealed a powerful division in the Welsh-speaking community, and especially so in the ranks of the intellectuals identified with the distinguished literary periodical, *Y Llenor*.[44]

---

[41] Bernard Donoughue and G. W. Jones, *Herbert Morrison. Portrait of a Politician* (1973), 481.

[42] e.g. Sir Roger Makins (UK ambassador in Washington) to members of US State Department, 21–2 December 1955 (PRO, FO317/115999), M 1017/14, in the British government, Peter Thorneycroft applied the term 'fool's paradise' to the Messina conference and Macmillan spoke scornfully of 'seismic eruptions' in Sicily.

[43] Elwyn Evans, *Alun Llywelyn-Williams* (Cardiff, 1991), 37ff.

[44] D. Hywel Davies, *The Welsh Nationalist Party, 1922–1945* (Cardiff, 1983), 237ff. Lewis

In Scotland, also, many writers largely ignored what they perhaps felt was largely an English war. Edwin Muir's 'Scotland 1941' focuses on the seventeenth century rather than the twentieth.[45] Culturally, the second world war seems largely to have passed the Welsh and Scots by. The quintessential images of the war, and of what the country felt it was defending, were essentially timeless English concepts. Eliot's later Quartets were one product of them, Orwell and Priestley's social populism were others. For all that, the war ended with the integrative process much advanced, with the Labour Party's ascendancy in Wales and Scotland confirmed and those nations the more inextricably bound up in the centralist processes of the United Kingdom.

It could be that, as far as Scotland and Wales are concerned, the second world war might represent a lost opportunity. There was, for instance, the remarkable work of Tom Johnston at the Scottish Office in 1941–5.[46] By all accounts, he used the alleged political threat from the Scottish Nationalists (who actually won a by-election at Motherwell in 1945) to force through the greatest phase of internal change Scotland had known since the Act of Union in 1707. The Council of State and Council of Industry established in Edinburgh implied a dramatic expansion of internal self-government. However, Johnston's premature retirement in 1945 meant that it could not be followed through, and unionism prevailed. In Wales, there was almost nothing by way of devolution. Suggestions to this effect from James Griffiths on the Welsh Council of Reconstruction led nowhere. Ideas of devolution, political as well as industrial, did not emerge seriously until the report of the Kilbrandon commission in 1973. Probably the sense of national identity was not sharpened by the war in Scotland and Wales as it was after 1918. Only in very recent times, with the idea of a 'Europe of nations' current in Scotland and (to a lesser degree) in Wales in the 1990s was there some prospect of change of outlook.[47]

The conclusion, then, seems to be that both world wars have been somewhat misrepresented in their effects on British history. There was actually some sense of renewal after 1918. A new kind of middle-class radicalism, powerful in the planning enthusiasms of the thirties, was released. Conversely, the effect of 1945 was to confirm traditional values and received images. The radical impulse of the war years was in many ways stifled.

---

was defeated by Professor W.J. Gruffydd, a former member of Plaid Cymru, standing as a Liberal.

[45] Angus Calder, *The Myth of the Blitz* (1991), 73–4.

[46] Christopher Harvie, 'Labour in Scotland during the Second World War', *Historical Journal*, 26, 4 (December 1983), especially 929–34; and Graham Walker, *Thomas Johnston* (Manchester, 1988), 151ff.

[47] See Christopher Harvie, *The Rise of Regional Europe* (1993).

Of course, the second world war had many far more positive consequences, too. It helped foster the welfare state, full employment and a more realistic view of empire. The stability of Britain after 1945, and indeed since 1918, has been almost unique in twentieth-century Europe. The threat of foreign invasion and internal economic disaster have both been successfully confronted. We have lapsed neither into Bonapartism nor anarchy.

Yet in many ways the wrong conclusions appear to have been drawn from both world conflicts. The reasons for this are diverse and complicated. However (if it is not the wrong note to strike in a Prothero lecture!) it could be argued that historians themselves have much to answer for. We have had after each war far too much emphasis on 'the lessons of history' and misconceived lessons at that. The history of the first world war was hijacked in the 1920s by the critics, by the Union of Democratic Control, by Keynes and Norman Angell and the critics of the left. They led the search for secret treaties and clandestine diplomacy, and the roots of what Lowes Dickinson called 'the international anarchy'. As Alan Taylor memorably recalled, the dissenters had taken over and proclaimed the conventional post-war wisdom.[48] Conversely, after 1945 there was excessive triumphalism and consensual celebration, epitomised by Trevelyan's praise of the eternal virtues of the yeoman in his wartime *English Social History* and by the writings of Arthur Bryant, his pre-war anti-Semitism and support for Franco conveniently set aside.[49] And of course no historian had more impact than the wartime titan himself, Winston Churchill.[50] When A. J. P. Taylor tried to present an alternative, if provocative, scenario in his *Origins of the Second World war*, he was (initially) hissed off the stage as an irresponsible gadfly or fellow-traveller.

But in each case, fortunately, things have improved. Here, too, historians have led the way. The first world war also led to the founding of the Institute of International Affairs, later Chatham House. H. W. V. Temperley's impeccably edited volumes on the History of the Peace Conference were an early product. Today we have the seriousness now attached to contemporary history, and the works of historians like Donald Watt and Alastair Parker which have laid down new standards of scholarship for the study of the

---

[48] A. J. P. Taylor, *The Troublemakers* (1957), 178, citing works by Bertrand Russell, Lowes Dickinson, G. P. Gooch and H. N. Brailsford, all members of the Union of Democratic Control during the war.

[49] See Andrew Roberts, 'Patriotism: The Last Refuge of Sir Arthur Bryant', in *Eminent Churchillians* (1993), 287ff.

[50] See the excellent collective volume, Robert Blake and Wm Roger Louis, eds., *Churchill* (Oxford, 1993).

1930s.[51] It is possible, therefore, to end on a more hopeful note, appropriate perhaps for this occasion. Historians may now be using their skills to help us fight free from the old stereotypes. Perhaps as the fiftieth anniversary of VE and VJ are safely behind us, it may be that for the British people the war is finally over. No longer need we designate the past half century as 'post-war Britain'. Perhaps we have at last come to terms with victory as other nations have come to terms with defeat. The British have long prided themselves, and with justice, on a war record of liberating other, less fortunate, peoples. Perhaps they can now turn finally to liberating themselves.

[51] D. C. Watt, *How War Came* (1989); R. A. C. Parker, *Chamberlain and Appeasement. British Policy and the Coming of the Second World War* (1993).

AGAINST 'ENGLISHNESS':
ENGLISH CULTURE AND THE LIMITS TO RURAL
NOSTALGIA, 1850–1940*

By Peter Mandler

READ 25 OCTOBER 1996

OVER the last fifteen years, a substantial literature has welled up, practically from nowhere, purporting to anatomise 'Englishness'. 'Englishness', this literature suggests, is not a true estimate of national character, an enduring national essence, but rather a historical construct that was developed towards the end of the nineteenth century by the 'dominant classes' in British society in order to tame or thwart the tendencies of their day towards modernism, urbanism and democracy that might otherwise have overwhelmed elite culture. These aspirations for social control determined the lineaments of the new 'Englishness'. Nostalgic, deferential and rural, 'Englishness' identified the squire-archical village of Southern or 'Deep' England as the template on which the national character had been formed and thus the ideal towards which it must inevitably return. Purveyed by the 'dominant classes' to the wider culture by means of a potent array of educational and political instruments—ranging from the magazine *Country Life* to the folk-song fad to the National Trust to Stanley Baldwin's radio broadcasts—'Englishness' reversed the modernising thrust of the Industrial Revolution and has condemned late twentieth-century Britain to economic decline, cultural stagnation and social division.

The diagnosis of a rural-nostalgic 'Englishness' as the taproot of Britain's twentieth-century trajectory is of relatively recent vintage. Traditional ideas of the English national character refer to an appetite for hierarchy, but also to a pragmatism, puritanism and utilitarianism that are aligned with (rather than hostile to) urbanism and economic growth. In the 1950s and 60s, these older characterisations were expanded to take into account the rise of Labour and the welfare state, which if anything cast the English as more naturally urban and egalitarian. As recently as 1982, Jan Marsh, in her subtle survey of the

---

*For help in clarifying my arguments, and especially with the international comparisons, I owe much to discussions with Sheryl Kroen, Mark Mazower, Susan Pedersen and Aron Rodrigue, and to comments from the audience when I presented an earlier version of this paper to the Society in October 1996.

pastoral strain in Victorian culture, *Back to the Land*, concluded that 'the anti-industrial manifestations described here ... soon fell into obscurity, overtaken in the twentieth century by political and economic events of far greater significance'.

Yet in a closing rhetorical flourish Marsh did detect some legacy of late Victorian pastoralism in a dilute popular antipathy to urban life surviving under the surface of those more important political and economic transformations.[1] And it was, of course, Martin Wiener's *English Culture and the Decline of the Industrial Spirit 1850–1950*[2] published at about the same time, that first and most influentially reversed Marsh's priorities, taking the political and economic transformations of the twentieth century as ephemeral and the pastoralism of the late nineteenth century as foundational to modern British life. Wiener's book nicely caught the journalistic mood of the post-consensus dispensation. It was hailed by *enragés* both of the Right and of the Left, who shared his dislike of the limp-wristed liberal Establishment, while differing on whether it needed refreshment by capitalist or proletarian vigour. Ignored by most political historians, who prefer not to conceptualise at such an elevated level, Wiener's thesis has been taken up enthusiastically by the cultural studies field, which has recast it as 'Englishness'— notably in the volume of that title edited by Robert Colls and Philip Dodd, and since then in a flood of monographs and textbooks. In this cultural studies avatar, 'Englishness' has become a thesis not only about economic decline but also about anti-modernism in culture and conservatism in society and politics.[3] In this form, it has metastasised into a wide variety of fields, as the most compact account of modern English culture available that can be slotted into virtually any argument about modern England to give it a 'cultural' dimension.[4]

In this paper my aim is to challenge the description of the culture

---

[1] Jan Marsh, *Back to the Land: The Pastoral Impulse in England, from 1880 to 1914* (1982), 245–8.

[2] (Cambridge, 1981).

[3] To cite only the more conspicuous book-length studies: Robert Colls and Philip Dodd, eds., *Englishness: Politics and Culture 1880–1920* (1986); Christopher Shaw and Malcolm Chase, eds., *The Imagined Past: History and Nostalgia* (Manchester, 1989); Stephen Daniels, *Fields of Vision: Landscape Imagery and National Identity in England and the United States* (Cambridge, 1993); Georgina Boyes, *The Imagined Village: Culture, Ideology and the English Folk Revival* (Manchester, 1993); Michael Bunce, *The Countryside Ideal: Anglo-American Images of Landscape* (1994); John Taylor, *A Dream of England: Landscape, Photography and the Tourist's Imagination* (Manchester, 1994); Judy Giles and Tim Middleton, eds., *Writing Englishness 1900–1950* (1995).

[4] Their number is legion, but two recent examples of intelligent books gratuitously incorporating the 'Englishness' thesis are Mike Savage and Andrew Miles, *The Remaking of the British Working Class 1840–1940* (1994), 87–8; Mrinalini Sinha, *Colonial Masculinity: The 'Manly Englishman' and the 'Effeminate Bengali' in the Late Nineteenth Century* (Manchester, 1995), 71, 183.

shared by Wiener and the 'Englishness' literature. Wiener's argument
that 'Englishness' was a source of economic decline has already been
widely disputed (most ably, by W. D. Rubinstein), but the usual approach
of these arguments is to challenge the alleged effect—economic
decline—and to leave untouched the alleged cultural causes.[5] This has
left the field free for the inflation of 'Englishness' into a general
description of English culture and a general explanation for an ever-
widening array of non-economic effects. I wish to go to the root of the
matter, to ask what it means to say that a culture is 'backward' or 'anti-
modern' and to test whether English culture of the late nineteenth and
early twentieth centuries merits that description. I will start by questioning whether national cultures absorbed in their rural past are
necessarily 'backward' or 'anti-modern', suggesting that across Europe
the historical impulse and modernisation often went hand in hand in
the nineteenth century, causing little cognitive dissonance. Then I will
consider the body of nostalgic texts and images that are usually cited
as evidence of mounting 'Englishness' between 1880 and 1914, seeking
to fix them in their proper place, demonstrating their limits, and
arguing that a nostalgic interest in the countryside actually had less
place in England than elsewhere in Europe. Finally, I will carry the
argument into the inter-war period, when, I will suggest, England did
become a kind of 'post-urban' culture, but not in the backward-looking
way so often assumed and, still, less tempted by true rural nostalgia
than other European cultures.

I

Historians of Continental Europe are more comfortable than British
historians with the idea that rapid modernisation and myths about the
national past go hand in hand. They tend to assume, as we do not,
that both elites and public in, say, France or Germany turned to stories
about an essential national character enduring through the ages in
order to warrant the rapid political, social and economic changes of
the nineteenth century.[6] In contrast, I would argue, the English political

[5] For criticisms of the cultural explanation for British economic 'decline', see Bruce
Collins and Keith Robbins, eds., *British Culture and Economic Decline* (1990); W. D. Rubinstein,
Capitalism, Culture and Decline in Britain, 1750–1990 (1993); David Edgerton, *Science, Technology
and the British Industrial 'Decline', 1870–1970* (Cambridge, 1996).

[6] See, e.g., Pierre Nora, ed., *Les lieux de mémoire* (7 vols., Paris, 1984–92), esp. vols. II,
III; Nicholas Green, *The Spectacle of Nature: Landscape and Bourgeois Culture in Nineteenth-
Century France* (Manchester, 1990); Celia Applegate, *A Nation of Provincials: The German Idea
of Heimat* (Berkeley, 1990); Françoise Choay, *L'allégorie du patrimoine* (Paris, 1992). But the
latter still adopts, on slender evidence, the conventional view that England has a nostalgic
rather than (as in France) a progressive feeling for the past.

elite—which was not newly minted in the nineteenth century, not the creature of revolution—did not feel the need to authorise itself by an appeal to history and was, in fact, by European standards peculiarly uninterested in its own national past. History, as we know, remained virtually unstudied at the ancient universities until late in the nineteenth century. The history that *was* read by elite Britons tended to be either non-national (that is, ancient Greek and Roman history) or the bland story of evolving political institutions over at most the past two centuries, as in the work of Hallam or—not *that* much more ambitious—Macaulay. Foreign visitors to England were amazed at how much history remained intact in the elite world—ancient institutions preserved, country houses studded with art and portraits—but also at how thoughtless the English ruling class was about its heritage—philistine about art, careless about preservation, adapting constantly and pragmatically to changing times.[7]

Below the elite level, however, the English experience up to the middle of the nineteenth century was very much an experience of revolutionary change: in patterns of work and residence, in the degree of urbanisation and (most relevant for our present purposes) in the degree of cultural literacy. Even those who are sceptical about the first of these (the industrial) would be hard pressed to deny the urban and cultural revolutions. Whereas in the mid-eighteenth century, England and Wales were no more urbanised than most European countries, by the mid-nineteenth century they had soared over the 50 per cent level while all other European countries except Belgium remained below 30 per cent.[8] The cultural nation grew even more rapidly. Although behind some Continental countries in the provision of *public* facilities—free libraries, primary schools, higher education—England's highly urbanised and commercialised culture had spread printed text and images to an unusually large proportion of the population by 1850. Cheap novels sold in parts, steel engravings, penny weeklies, Sunday newspapers reached millions. All of the leading authorities on mass culture in mid-nineteenth-century England speak of a 'transformation' which did not, of course, wipe out the old rural culture of oral tradition, chapbooks and broadsides but which certainly overlaid it with a whole range of novel forms and themes.[9]

[7] E.g. Ralph Waldo Emerson, *English Traits* (Boston, 1857), 188–90; Henry James, 'In Warwickshire', 1st pub. 1877, repr. in *English Hours* (1960), 136–7.

[8] See the useful comparative discussion in Paul M. Hohenberg and Lynn Hollen Lees, *The Making of Urban Europe 1000–1950* (1985), 217–26.

[9] E.g. Richard Altick, *The English Common Reader* (1957); Louis James, *Fiction for the Working Man* (1963); Patricia Anderson, *The Printed Image and the Transformation of Popular Culture, 1790–1860* (Oxford, 1991). Unfortunately, cultural changes of this kind are rarely discussed in comparative perspective; but see Stephen Bann, *The Clothing of Clio: A Study of the Representation of History in Nineteenth-Century Britain and France* (Cambridge, 1984),

Among those novel themes was, as with Continental peoples experiencing change, an intense interest in national history, providing a pedigree not in this case for a new ruling class but for a newly cultured populace. Popular interest in English history greatly outstripped elite interest and focused on different objects: not so much on the recent development of political institutions, more on the vernacular literature and folk customs of an older Merrie England, seen as the wellspring of modern mass culture.[10] It is this popular appetite for English history that explains the extraordinary cult of Walter Scott—in the mid-nineteenth century, much stronger in popular than in elite circles—and the great popularity of Harrison Ainsworth, especially noted for his romances of Tudor times. In early Victorian popular culture, unlike elite culture, English history was inescapable. Imitations of the Scott and Ainsworth style infested the widest-circulating magazines, prints and novels of the day. As Olive Anderson has shown, the same old-English historical preoccupations dominated popular political discussion at the time of the Crimean war, while historical references in Parliament were limited to rather colourless evocations of the ancient world and eighteenth-century diplomacy.[11]

To recapitulate the argument so far: around 1850, English culture was both unlike and like that of other European peoples in its relationships to national history. Its political elite was unusually heedless of the past. Unlike Continental elites, it had no conscious project of national mobilisation through history. Underneath the elite, however, English mass culture was—like its Continental equivalents—developing a historical consciousness of its own, but without national leadership. Non-elite English culture in 1850 looked backward as it looked forward—the Janus-face which Martin Wiener finds exceptional, but which I think was a pan-European phenomenon.

II

This constellation of forces, this relationship to the national past, began to shift towards the end of the nineteenth century. Unlike Wiener and the 'Englishness' claque, I would argue that the primary shift is *away*

---

showing parallels at least with France that should give believers in 'English exceptionalism' some pause.

[10] I provide evidence for these assertions in ' "In the Olden Time": Romantic History and English National Identity, 1820–1850', *A Union of Multiple Identities?*, ed. Laurence Brockliss and David Eastwood (Manchester, 1997), and *The Fall and Rise of the Stately Home* (1997), chs. 1–2.

[11] Olive Anderson, 'The Political Uses of History in Mid Nineteenth-Century England', *Past and Present*, 36 (1967), 87–105.

from an absorption in the national past among most sections of the cultural nation, while the shift *towards* a swooning nostalgia for the rural past takes place only among a small, articulate but not necessarily influential *avant-garde* (or, rather, a *derrière-garde*).

In the second half of the nineteenth century, urbanisation and the extension of the cultural nation continued in England, chronologically and quantitatively ahead of the rest of Europe. Most important for present purposes was the completion of the urbanisation process. As a result of the agricultural depression and a renewed burst of endogenous growth in the towns, Britain as a whole had by 1900 reached its present-day level of around 80 per cent of the population living in urban areas, a level that even Germany reached only in the 1960s. By this point, well over a century after rural-to-urban migration had begun to take off, the urban condition was accepted as permanent and normal. On the Continent, migration to the towns was still circular and temporary; many migrants kept their rural ties and returned at appropriate seasonal or life-cycle points to peasant communities. In England, migration was predominantly between towns.[12] The more tentative nature of urban life on the Continent was also reflected in the urban fabric: there were more likely to be smallholdings and market gardens within city limits; Britain had only the pale substitute of the allotments movement. Urban workers on the Continent, if they had the option, were more likely to holiday in or retire to the country; urban workers in Britain developed the unique institution of the commercial seaside holiday, the leisure city by the sea.[13] Like all peoples displaced from the countryside in the modern period—like European peasants in the nineteenth century or Latin American peasants in the twentieth—English urbanites kept alive a folk myth of the rural home, the return to the land, but it is hard to escape the conclusion that in England that myth was dimmer, more ethereal, and getting dimmer still with every generation.[14]

A nation that had come to terms with its urbanity had less need to justify its condition, less need of the origin-myth of Merrie England that the culture industry had peddled so successfully in the early nineteenth century. History was at a discount. Late Victorian urban

---

[12] Hohenberg and Lees, *Urban Europe*, 254–5.

[13] Lutz Holzner, 'The Role of History and Tradition in the Urban Geography of West Germany', *Annals of the Association of American Geographers*, 60 (1970), 315–39.

[14] Avner Offer makes the point that the late Victorian attempt to create a 'property-owning democracy' in Britain, analogous to the peasant democracies of France and Germany, had inevitably to take an urban form. While he also devotes a chapter to elite pastoralism, he concludes, 'The urban worker was not converted by the romantic impulse of Liberalism.' *Property and Politics, 1870–1914* (Oxford, 1981), 148–50, 349. Like Marsh's *Back to the Land*, Offer's book reflects the more balanced view of pastoralism's place in British culture prevailing before the impact of Wiener.

culture was more populist, commercial and present-minded. The development of photography, the instantaneous communication made possible first by the telegraph and later by the telephone, and the concomitant development of a brisker, shorter, newsier style in the mass media helped to form an audience much more internationalist in its tastes, more 'up-to-the-minute'. Jose Harris has spoken of 'the unique dominance of the present time' in this period.[15] Insofar as English history retained an appeal, it was no longer in the mass but in a niche market. Thus Scott and Ainsworth became ghettoised as romances for the middle-class adolescent. History in general became less a part of the fabric of national life and more something you learned in school (and there it became less English and more imperial—the populist themes of Merrie England were superseded by homilies on the manly exploits of Drake, Raleigh, Wellington and Nelson).[16]

Similar trends affected all national cultures in Europe, though on the Continent they came slower and later. What really distinguished the English experience is that de-historicising trends went unchecked by state or elite action. The educational system was not harnessed to transmit a sense of national history to the mass of the people in the way that it was in France or Germany; history was not even a compulsory school subject until 1900. Nor did the state legislate for historic preservation and conservation; the British had fewer powers in this area than any other western European state, both at local and central levels. This was partly due to the English tradition of *laissez-faire*, especially in cultural matters. But because of the English elite's prevailing lack of interest in national history, the default of government was not met by private action. There was no English equivalent to the *Heimatschutz* movement in Germany.[17] In England, the local antiquarian societies that had sprung up in the 1830s and 40s throughout Europe remained inward-looking and specialised, whereas elsewhere they inter-penetrated with local elites, becoming important provincial institutions like the German *Verschönerungsvereine* (civic beautification societies) or the French *sociétés savantes* (provincial academies in which antiquarian interests were central).[18]

[15] Jose Harris, *Private Lives, Public Spirit: A Social History of Britain 1870–1914* (Oxford, 1993), 33.

[16] Valerie E. Chancellor, *History for their Masters: Opinion in the English History Textbook, 1800–1914* (Bath, 1970), 70–5.

[17] Stefan Muthesius, 'The Origins of the German Conservation Movement', in *Planning for Conservation*, ed. Roger Kain (1981), 47; see also Christian F. Otto, 'Modern Environment and Historical Continuity: The Heimatschutz Discourse in Germany', *Art Journal*, 43 (1983), 148–57, and Applegate, *Nation of Provincials*.

[18] Even in France, where centralising tendencies are sometimes alleged to have killed off such provincial initiatives, the latter were spurs to rather than overwhelmed by state action; see G. Baldwin Brown, *The Care of Ancient Monuments* (Cambridge, 1905), 74–9,

Nor, despite the unusual predominance of landowners in the British political elite, did that elite take steps to slow the final exodus of the rural population. In their prematurely urbanised polity, English landowners had long since seen the wisdom of abandoning special claims for the countryside, positioning themselves as a professional governing class in tune with modern, urban life. The rural population was too small to wield any political power on its own. There was consequently hardly any political constituency in England for agricultural protection, almost uniquely in Europe, and this further accelerated agricultural contraction and rural depopulation.

Writers on 'Englishness' have been much impressed by the supposed strength of the 'back to the land' movement in late Victorian England, but in comparison to the Continent the English movement looks puny and narrow. Across Europe, urbanisation triggered ruling-class concerns about the degeneration of the national stock, the effacement of a virtuous and healthy peasantry by urban troglodytes.[19] The result on the Continent was the fixing of peasant concerns at the centre of national policy, particularly tariffs aimed at protecting agriculture but also social policies to shore up village life. Most notoriously, what Stanley Hoffman called 'the stalemate society' was established in France after 1878, an alliance between peasantry and peasant-oriented bourgeoisie which slowed economic growth and preserved a traditional social hierarchy.[20] Similar protective policies were adopted in Germany and Italy, while in Denmark, the Netherlands and Belgium the peasantry was preserved not by protection but by rapid adaptation and modernisation.[21]

In England, by contrast, the peasantry had been effaced long ago; there was no opportunity of modernising it and there was to be no serious attempt to re-establish it. Even on the romantic wing of the Liberal party, where the idealisation of the peasant reached its apogee, there was a widespread feeling that the best feasible outcome was the restoration not of a peasantry but of peasant values in the city. Charles

---

and Françoise Bercé, 'Arcisse de Caumont et Les Sociétés Savantes', in *Les lieux*, ed. Nora, III, 533–67.

[19] For comparative studies of 'degeneration', showing it to be a pan-European phenomenon, see Andrew Lees, *Cities Perceived: Urban Society in European and American Thought, 1820–1940* (Manchester, 1985), ch. 6; Daniel Pick, *Faces of Degeneration: A European Disorder, c. 1848–c.1918* (Cambridge, 1989).

[20] Stanley Hoffmann, 'Paradoxes of the French Political Community', in Hoffman *et al.*, *In Search of France* (Cambridge, MA, 1963), esp. 3–8. This line of thinking has been extended recently into a full-blown cultural indictment of the Third Republic remarkably similar to the 'Englishness' diagnosis: see Herman Lebovics, *True France: The Wars over Cultural Identity, 1900–1945* (1992).

[21] This comparison was made as early as 1935 by the agricultural expert Sir Daniel Hall in his Rede Lecture, *The Pace of Progress* (Cambridge, 1935), esp. 12, 21–34.

Masterman, who while in opposition advocated a total reconstruction of the land on the basis of 'some form of yeoman or peasant proprietorship', as in France or Denmark, in government accepted the death of that dream and turned his attention to a spiritual revival among urban folk. '[I]n the crumbling and decay of English rural life,' he wrote in 1909,

> and the vanishing of that 'yeoman' class which in Scotland provides a continuous breeding ground of great men, it would seem that it is from the suburban and professional people we must more and more demand a supply of men and women of capacity and energy adequate to the work of the world.

No Continental politician who claimed to represent the peasant would dare accept so far 'the crumbling and decay of rural life'.[22]

As Masterman appreciated, the peculiar emptiness of the English countryside, in addition to depriving it of political muscle, also posed difficulties to those who would idealise it aesthetically. Continental landscape still looked and felt like the national home, but English landscape was obviously the creation and possession of a small elite. 'The beauty of continental landscape', Masterman observed,

> is the beauty of 'peasants' country': the beauty that is provided by security and close cultivation, excited wherever the peasant is assured that he will reap what he has sown. The beauty of English landscape is the beauty of 'landlords' country'—the open woods, the large grass fields and wide hedges, the ample demesnes, which signify a country given up less to industry than to opulence and dignified ease. The one is a park: the other, a source of food supply and the breeding-place of men. The typical English countryside is that of great avenues leading to residences which lack no comfort, broad parks, stretches of private land, sparsely cultivated, but convenient for hunting, shooting, and a kind of stately splendour. The typical continental countryside is that of tiny white-washed or wooden broad-eaved cottages, freely scattered over a region of fruit and flowers and close-tilled coveted land, which, in fact, is one large garden.[23]

While, as we know today, the empty, park-like English landscape can be readily appropriated by an urban population seeking exercise and recreation, it was not any longer seen as a 'national home', at least

[22] Cf. C. F. G. Masterman, 'The English City', in *England: A Nation*, ed. Lucian Oldershaw (1904), 64–6, and *The Condition of England* (1909), 82–3.

[23] Masterman, *Condition of England*, 201–2. Illustrations of just such contemporary idealisations of 'peasants' country' on the Continent can be found in François Cachin, 'Le paysage du peintre', in *Les lieux*, ed. Nora, II, 463–5, 475–6.

not by the great mass of the people. For all these reasons, I think that at the turn of the century the countryside was in England, more than elsewhere in Europe, losing its utility as a symbol of national identity.

III

Who then *were* the authors and audience of the rural-nostalgic vision before the first world war? For, of course, I do not mean to deny the existence of this vision; what I dispute is the grand claim made for it by the 'Englishness' literature. Rural nostalgia, we are told, was deeply embedded in the 'dominant classes', the 'shapers of middle-and upper-class opinion', across the political spectrum. Consequently, these ideas became the 'dominant English cultural ideal', slowing economic growth, halting urbanisation, preserving the countryside, taming commercial culture with a conservative 'national' version. Against this, I have suggested that the dominant classes were those who conformed with or facilitated rapid urbanisation, the collapse of the countryside, the commercialisation of the culture. The ideologues of 'Englishness' were, rather, those who fulminated against the dominant classes and propagandised for an 'Englishness' that they felt was practically near extinction. Distinct from the true dominant classes, they have their own sociology and chronology.

We can trace their origins to the 1870s and 80s. Already in those decades there was a consciousness among the more aesthetically and historically minded of professional men that a vicious combination of democratisation and ruling-class abdication was threatening to strip England of its art and learning. Matthew Arnold denounced both aristocratic Barbarians and bourgeois Philistines and, as Raymond Williams argued, practically invented the idea of 'culture' as an antidote to be administered by a clerisy of people like himself. In the same spirit and at the same time, John Ruskin proselytised for a humbler posture towards the national past than had been common among a utilitarian ruling class. In these years there was still some optimism about the chances of diffusing 'sweetness and light' amongst the dominant classes, especially among the Philistines of the middle class. In the early Arts and Crafts movement, in the Queen Anne movement in architecture, in Tennysonian poetic circles and, latterly, the aesthetic movement proper, artistic men felt that they were winning some independence from the landed establishment by means of professional middle-class patronage and that therefore their influence was both purer and better diffused. While in retrospect some of these movements have been interpreted as evidence of the gentrification of the bourgeoisie, at the time they were more likely to be considered bourgeois rebellions against the stolid barbarians of the aristocracy. On the whole, their exponents tended to be Liberals and viewed their acculturating mission as liberating and progressive. Nor was their point of view particularly rural; some artists and architects had begun to migrate into the countryside— there were colonies in Surrey, Kent and the Cotswolds by the 1880s— but their marketplace was still primarily urban, and the Queen Anne style, for example, was purposely designed as a fresh, modern style for town architecture.[24]

However, the progressive, optimistic spirit of the aesthetic movement suffered profound reversals in the 1890s. A surprising consensus developed among aesthetic people in that decade that the spread of 'sweetness and light' was not keeping pace with modernisation, but was, rather, being swamped by it. For Hermann Muthesius, German cultural attaché and happy denizen of Bohemian Kensington, the 90s saw an unmistakable ebbing of artistic creativity; thereafter, the Arts and Crafts styles that he so admired in late Victorian London would flourish more happily in his native Berlin.[25] To the Tory aesthete George Wyndham, the 90s marked the beginning of the end of cultural development: 'there are now no movements: only stagnation. We live in a phase of indolent mediocrity. I remember the seventies and eighties and declare that this is Autumn; but an Autumn of more mist than usual and no mellow fruit.'[26]

Such pessimism was not just artistic paranoia. While a shift in cultural mood is notoriously difficult to pinpoint, there were ominous signs evident to everyone in the 90s. After a period when avant-garde art had been modish in High Society, fashionable opinion turned against it in the mid-90s. The travails of Oscar Wilde were symptom as well as cause. The eclipse of political Liberalism between 1886 and 1906 deprived the aesthetically minded of a solid centre. Among a wider bourgeois public, interest in art also declined: attendance at the Royal Academy shows fell from a peak in 1879, the *Times* began to reduce its coverage, and no artist after the 1890s came to fill the space in public life once occupied by Millais and Leighton.[27] The romanticism evident

[24] Raymond Williams, *Culture and Society, 1780–1950* (1958), esp. chs. 6–7. See also T. W. Heyck, *The Transformation of Intellectual Life in Victorian England* (1982), chs. 7–8, for a view largely uninfluenced by Wiener but which (against the grain of the general argument) throws him in at the last minute (p. 227).

[25] Hermann Muthesius, *The English House* (1904–5), ed. Dennis Sharp (Oxford, 1987), 27–30.

[26] Wyndham to his mother, 9 Sept. 1907: J. W. Mackail and Guy Wyndham, *Life and Letters of George Wyndham* (2 vols., 1925), II, 580–1.

[27] Paula Gillett, *The Victorian Painter's World* (Gloucester, 1990), 17, 68, 192–4; Janet Oppenheim Minihan, *The Nationalization of Culture* (1977), 164–7.

in literature in the 1870s and 80s gave way to realism and 'smartness', that modern quality so abhorred by the aesthete; it was in 1901 that the quintessentially smart author Elinor Glyn made fashionable the epithet 'boring' for use by philistines to squelch everything tasteful.[28]

The result of this swing in public mood was a fragmentation of the artistic community. Many chose to swim with the tide, like the architect Reginald Blomfield who abandoned his former Arts and Crafts loyalties for a grander, more manly style suited (he said) to an imperial, commercial and unaesthetic nation.[29] For others, however, the only honest reaction was a bitter recoil, a furious retreat especially from the British Establishment which, artists felt, had first toyed with, then spurned them. Some retreated into a purer aestheticism, a fantasy world without any social moorings. Others retreated, literally, into the country. Among both the romantic Tory followers of W. E. Henley and the romantic socialist followers of William Morris, the country acquired a talismanic significance as everything that contemporary, urban England was not but yet might be. Of course, this polar opposition required a sleight of hand, as the real countryside of the present— depopulated, plantation-like, increasingly subject to speculative develop- ment—was not suited to a rural idyll. Morris's ideal was of the old English countryside of the fifteenth century, and it is significant that he had to penetrate into what was then a remote bit of Oxfordshire to find it—an 'out of the way corner', as he described Kelmscott, where 'people built Gothic till the beginning or middle of last century'.[30] Thereafter the Cotswolds, atypical countryside without great estates but with plenty of small manor houses, became a favourite place of refuge for the marginalised aesthete; famously, C. R. Ashbee decamped with his Guild of Handicraft to Chipping Campden in 1902. Most of the central Arts and Crafts bodies in London dissolved within the next few years. But it was not necessary to make a physical break in order to settle, metaphorically, in the country, and this is what increasing numbers of writers and artists did around the turn of the century.

The mutual estrangement of the 'dominant classes' and *some* of their aesthetic auxiliaries helps, I think, to explain the special passion for rural nostalgia among the latter in this period. There were still of course important non-nostalgic responses to the English countryside: the turn of the century was a period of enhanced concern about urban overcrowding, rural depopulation and the maldistribution of land ownership. But the nostalgic literature which is associated with 'English-

---

[28] In her novel, *The Visits of Elizabeth*.

[29] Reginald Blomfield, *A Short History of Renaissance Architecture in England 1500–1800* (1900), 298–303.

[30] E. P. Thompson, *William Morris: Romantic to Revolutionary* (New York, 1976), 173–4.

ness' does not address these themes. It is less concerned with solving present-day social problems than with hymning a lost Eden, characterised by decent squires, honest craftsmanship and organic community, and its social commentary focuses interestingly on the betrayal of this Eden by the modern-minded absentee landowner.

Let me illustrate this point by reference to two works often cited in the 'Englishness' scholarship. The Poet Laureate Alfred Austin published *Haunts of Ancient Peace* in 1902; taking its title from Tennyson's 'Palace of Art'—'an English home ... a haunt of ancient Peace'—the book comprises a travelogue in search of Old England, its heroine sick of paper-mills, tubular bridges, motor-cars, model farms, elementary schools and the like, craving instead 'the urbanity of the Past ... washing-days, home-made jams, lavender bags, recitation of Gray's *Elegy*, and morning and evening prayers'. Penetrating beyond the 'corrugated iron farm-sheds and barbed wire' of the modern countryside, she and her poet-companion find their paradise in the cottage homes, the irregular fields, the ecclesiastical ruins of the back country. What is striking about Austin's *Haunts*, however, is that it devotes nearly as much space to partisan condemnation of present-day enemies as it does to evocations of timeless Englishness, thus disrupting the eirenic impact of the latter. One of the first 'haunts' the travellers encounter, remembered by the poet as formerly the home of 'a gentleman, a scholar, a statesman, a patriot', has degenerated under his heir into

> a hell of modern revelry. Book-makers, women it would be a libel on Athens and Alcibiades to speak of as Aspasias, and music-hall buffoons, were then its chief visitors, and Bridge, with high stakes, its principal diversion. Its tenant is periodically summoned for driving his Motor Cars beyond the pace permitted by the law, and this is the least heinous of his offences ... one must be content to say, '*Guarda, e passa*' [i.e. beware, pass it by].

Shortly thereafter they meet a painter in a ruined abbey, who joins the poet in a tirade against the English insensitivity to art. The tour closes with a poem attacking Gladstone for faddishness and insensitivity to the past, and a final diatribe against 'the babel of utterances called Public Opinion, but which is in reality the opinion of no one who is independent, competent, and sincere'. The only member of the governing classes singled out for praise in the entire book is the chatelaine of a modest Elizabethan manor house, portrayed presiding over the annual meeting of the Red-and-White Rose Society (ostensibly nonpartisan but immediately recognisable as the Primrose League of the preceding generation). Far from conveying a message of national unity behind timeless national symbols, the effect—especially to contemporaries—is of an alienated and rather dated romantic Tory with a bee in his bonnet about the abdication of the landowning class.[31]

Very similar messages in a more coded form appeared in a now-famous fantasy published a few years later. Its author was a Bank of England official who in his younger days had gone through a Ruskin–Morris phase, contributed both to *The Yellow Book* and to Henley's *National Observer*, and flirted with the simple life and paganism. As his biographer tells us, he grew increasingly depressed by public indifference to all these things, withdrew into a 'country of the mind' as a 'refuge from actuality', and then took a sharp turn into anti-democratic misanthropy when shot at random by a deranged Socialist rampaging through the Bank in November 1903. Kenneth Grahame published *The Wind in the Willows* five years later. Set in stretches of the Thames that Grahame knew well, the story was a paean to the countryside of his youth destroyed by the railway and the motor car and, most recently, by the Liberal electoral victory of 1906. As in Austin's *Haunts*, the essential contrast is between the old kind of squire—Rat, Mole, Badger, Otter—and the new—Toad of Toad Hall (patterned to some degree on the mountebank Horatio Bottomley). Toad's seduction by the motor car admits to Toad Hall the stoats and weasels of the modern democracy. Though the story ends happily, the old squires kicking out the cowardly mob and saving Toad from himself, Grahame himself admitted that the outcome was contrived and deliberately fantastical—a vision of what ought to be rather than what was. 'Of course Toad never really reformed; he was by nature incapable of it', Grahame wrote to a private correspondent in 1908. 'But the subject is a painful one to pursue.'[32]

Works like these were protests against the spirit of the age and against the dominant classes. They were not uncontroversial appeals to a consensual 'Englishness' but were rather angry and fiercely partisan, immediately recognisable to contemporary readers as bearing a specific aesthetic and political charge. Certainly they came from all political camps—this is a point insisted upon by the 'Englishness' school, as if testimony to the ubiquity of these ideas—but in all cases they came from tiny romantic minorities in those camps, railing against their philistine masters.[33] I have chosen two romantic Tory texts, but the political bias was if anything clearer in romantic Liberal and especially

---

[31] Alfred Austin, *Haunts of Ancient Peace* (1902), quotes at 19–21, 64–6, 142; Austin is cited as typical or influential by Wiener, *English Culture*, 45, 49–50, a point then picked up by Wiener's imitators, e.g. Bunce, *Countryside Ideal*, 53; Peter Brooker and Peter Widdowson, 'A Literature for England', in *Englishness*, ed. Colls and Dodd, 126, 128. Twice in Colls and Dodd the *Quarterly Review*'s praise for Austin as 'a concrete individual Englishman' is cited as evidence of his populist credentials.

[32] I owe this analysis to Peter Green, *Kenneth Grahame* (1959), 240–8.

[33] For the significance attached to the fact that rural nostalgia could be found 'across the political spectrum', see Wiener, *English Culture*, 42, 46; Boyes, *Imagined Village*, 86 n.4.

Socialist writing. In all cases, the animus is aimed not only at political enemies but also at 'false friends'—as we have seen, in Austin and Grahame's romantic Tory version, against the kind of landowner who dominated the modern Tory party.

I do not mean to suggest that such books had no audience, only that that audience was select, well-bounded, self-consciously anti-establishment, certainly not very close to the centres of social and political power. It is, of course, possible that a modern society perfectly at ease with itself might still for various reasons entertain ruralist fantasies—to write itself a pedigree, as the mid-Victorians did, or to satisfy safely urges repressed in the cause of modernisation—a possibility not really considered by the 'Englishness' school. But I would argue that many of the texts cited by this school were too conspicuously alienated even for this innocent purpose.

Stronger limits still apply to those associations and pressure groups that sought to do more than simply fantasise about the lost countryside, but tried to re-enact or preserve it. A well-rounded assessment of English culture in this period would not put anywhere near its centre phenomena such as the folk-song revival or the staging of maypole dances in a few dozen villages; such things reflect the values of some *bien-pensant* Bohemians and would-be squires, but nothing like the British Establishment or even the average upper-middle-class family. Hardly any contemporaries would have recognised them as emblematic of the 'national culture', as claimed by the 'Englishness' literature.[34] Nor, despite vigorous attempts to write a whiggish history of the present-day heritage industry, was much attention paid to the preservation of the history and beauty of the old English countryside. Wiener calls the Society for the Protection of Ancient Buildings (SPAB) a 'national institution' by 1920, but if so it was a very small and ineffectual national institution.[35] While moderately successful among the artists and architects who comprised its tiny membership—capable, for instance, of affecting ideas about the techniques of restoration—SPAB was totally incapable of influencing the ideas of the wider public. It was indeed almost invisible even to the educated. Its membership had soared to the dizzying height of 443 by 1910. When government appointed a Royal Commission on Historical Monuments in 1908, it deliberately excluded the SPAB's chief spokesman as a 'faddist' and an 'extremist'.[36]

---

[34] For such claims, see Boyes, *Imagined Village*, 27–36, 63–5; Bunce, *Countryside Ideal*, 13–14, 32–3. Dodd, 'Englishness and National Culture', makes similar claims for even less significant phenomena, such as the Edwardian campaign for a National Theatre which was (should it have to be pointed out?) a dismal failure.

[35] Wiener, *English Culture*, 68.

[36] C. R. Peers to Lord Beauchamp, 23 Nov. 1912: Public Record Office, WORK 14/2270.

The National Trust, whatever its triumphalist histories might say, suffered a similar fate before the war. It had even fewer members than the SPAB in 1910, mostly the same cast of artists and architects, with a few philanthropic landlords thrown in. It was also distrusted by government as wet and faddish, and by most landlords as a threat to private property. So, too, were the early advocates of town and country planning and of nature reserves.[37] All of these groups were rejected not solely on the grounds of *laissez-faire*, but also because countryside preservation was widely perceived both by the Establishment and by the electorate as too precious and static an approach for a great progressive nation like Britain. This helps to explain the often-noted (but never resolved) paradox that ideas about historic preservation, nature conservation and countryside planning originated in England, but were implemented far more widely on the Continent.[38] The fact is that before the first world war, English culture as a whole was aggressively urban and materialist, and the rural-nostalgic vision of 'Englishness' remained the province of impassioned and highly articulate but fairly marginal artistic groups.

IV

Let me conclude with some reflections on whether or how far this balance of forces shifted in the inter-war period. It is in the inter-war period that, the 'Englishness' literature claims, the rural-nostalgic vision accumulating in elite culture was successfully diffused to a wider, mainly suburban audience. Stanley Baldwin's famous speech of May 1924—'To me, England is the country, and the country is England' (and then it goes on about scythes, and ploughs, and corncrakes)—is taken to symbolise a national consensus against industrialism, urbanism and Bolshevism, in favour of the easy life, the countryside and deference to one's betters. I agree that popular interest in the countryside grew tremendously in these years, but I would want to characterise that interest as unrelated to pre-war romanticism and, in fact, not very nostalgic. Fortunately, scholarly work on the inter-war period has been awakening to the intense modernity of this period, including its interest in the countryside, but this work has

---

[37] Karl Ditt, 'Nature Conservation in England and Germany 1900–70: Forerunner of Environmental Protection?', *Contemporary European History*, 5 (1996), 1–28, notes the early failure of nature conservation in England as compared to Germany.

[38] E.g. Stephen Tschudi Madsen, *Restoration and Anti-Restoration* (Oslo, 1976), 98, 102–3; Choay, *L'allégorie du patrimoine*, 114; Ditt, 'Nature Conservation', 4. This particularly puzzles Continental writers today, who have been told that the English are a highly history-conscious people but who can see the far more palpable signs of this consciousness closer to home.

not yet been properly applied to questioning the narrative of 'Englishness', which is what I want to do here.[39]

England after 1918 became the world's first post-urban country; that is, its population growth slowed dramatically and its cities stopped growing intensively. Reflecting rising living standards and prevailing inner-city congestion, cities began to decentralise, flowing out into the countryside in waves of privately owned suburban homes. This movement might be interpreted as something peculiarly English—the horror of the inner city, the passion for the private detached house in a rural setting—but it is in fact the pattern since followed by most crowded western countries (and many uncrowded ones, such as the United States, Australia and Canada). Nor do I think suburbanisation should necessarily be seen as a capitulation to rural values. Its immediate effect was to bring the city into the country, rather than the country to the city. The suburb was always recognisable as part of an urban system. It helped form the world's first conurbation, stretching from Liverpool to London.[40] It was nothing like an English village. A great deal too much has been made of bits of half-timbering plastered onto 30s semis, while plainer facts about the inter-war suburb are ignored: it had no landowners (that was one of its selling points to home owners); its central institution was not the church, but the cinema (in all of London suburbia, fewer than two dozen new churches were built, while more than fifty cinemas were built in Middlesex alone);[41] its economic lifeline was the urban transport system and urban white-collar employment.

In all these ways, suburbia was post-urban rather than ruralist or anti-urban. 'Post-urban' also describes the inter-war interest in rural leisure. The English had before the first world war been rather retrograde in their lack of appreciation for the leisure potential of the countryside. Urban workers holidayed in urban colonies at the seaside. Much to the displeasure of rural romantics, the ruling elite had preferred Continental resorts and foreign wilderness (such as Switzerland) to the native variety. As seaside capacity became strained, policymakers began to argue for the promotion of inland holidays. Suburbanites moving out of city centres were susceptible to this appeal. The central European

---

[39] Alison Light, *Forever England: Femininity, Literature and Conservatism between the Wars* (1991), marks something of a breakthrough. But I want to pay tribute also to two earlier articles that rejected the simple-minded diagnosis of nostalgia: John Lowerson, 'Battles for the Countryside', in *Class, Culture and Social Change: A New View of the 1930s*, ed. Frank Gloversmith (Brighton, 1980), 258–80; Alex Potts, ' "Constable Country" between the Wars', in *Patriotism: The Making and Unmaking of British National Identity, III: National Fictions*, ed. Raphael Samuel (1989), 160–86.

[40] Peter Hall *et al., The Containment of Urban England* (2 vols., 1973), I, 59–62. It is interesting that, pre-Wiener, Peter Hall's view was that interwar suburanisation was the 'modern' development, whereas the postwar containment was driven by elite nostalgia.

[41] Alan A. Jackson, *Semi-Detached London* (Didcot, 1991), 96, 142.

fashions for hiking and hostelling caught on, complete with the Continental uniform of khaki shirt and trousers or shorts, Basque beret and short socks. Having caught up with the Continentals, the English then forged ahead with motor tourism—like suburbanisation, a post-urban trend subsequently imitated elsewhere.[42]

It is important to note that contemporaries did not see suburbanisation and the boom in rural leisure as fostering a more reverential attitude to the countryside, but quite the reverse. The kind of person who wrote or read the pre-war Arcadian literature was appalled by the invasion of the townsman: that is not what they had meant at all. As Cyril Joad, supposedly the rambler's champion, complained in 1937, 'the townsman let loose upon the country is from the point of view of utility a liability, and from that of amenity a blight'.[43] Joad and his preservationist confrères undoubtedly saw the suburbanite and the motorist as importing city life into the country rather than vice versa. Accordingly they attempted to erect a new set of preservationist ramparts, alongside the flimsy barriers previously set up by the SPAB and the National Trust. More draconian ideas about green belts to throttle the suburb, strict planning controls to preserve agriculture and scenery in the countryside, and the appointment of landowners as 'trustees' for the public good were floated by new bodies such as the Council for the Preservation of Rural England.

But the further proliferation of preservationist ideas among intellectuals like Joad should not, any more than in the earlier period, blind us to their almost complete invisibility outside those circles. Landowners, for instance, showed no interest at all in taking on the job of 'trustees' for public amenity; those who were not eagerly selling their acres to tenant-farmers or suburban developers were getting on with their traditional business of commercial agriculture. When the National Trust approached landowners in the mid-30s about developing a trusteeship scheme, the scheme was rebuffed as pretentious nonsense at best, socialist at worst.[44] It is revealing that Joad, like Austin and Grahame, blamed landowners as much as the plebs for neglecting the countryside. 'To hit balls with pieces of wood', he sneered,

---

[42] Some of this is captured in Frank Trentmann, 'Civilisation and its Discontents: English Neo-Romanticism and the Transformation of Anti-Modernism in Twentieth-Century Western Culture', *Journal of Contemporary History*, 29 (1994), 583–625, though the author still leans excessively towards an 'anti-modern' interpretation of the outdoor movement. Similar conclusions could be reached about the pervasiveness on the Continent of other ruralist fashions, falsely supposed to be particularly English, such as angling or amateur landscape painting.

[43] C. E. M. Joad, 'The People's Claim', in *Britain and the Beast*, ed. Clough Williams-Ellis (1937), 71–2.

[44] Mandler, *Fall and Rise*, 295–308.

or to kick them with leather boots, or more frequently to watch over people hitting or kicking them; to kill birds and animals; to amble slowly over glazed floors to the strains of negroid music; to lunch in London and dine in Paris—these for the governing-class Westerner constitute the pursuits of the good life.[45]

Landowners did not wish to be trustees for the public, and the public did not want the countryside to be held in trust for them, either. Popular countryside literature of the inter-war years was not interested in the rural idyll as portrayed in the romantic pre-war literature. While appreciative of scenic beauty and its recreational potential, the mass audience was distinctly hostile to the traditional rural social fabric which was thought unpleasantly feudal and anachronistic; the idea was not to preserve the countryside, but to break it up and/or put it to good use. As before the war, the great British public all but ignored the activities of the National Trust, and of new bodies like the CPRE.[46] When they did notice preservationism, they thought it backward and elitist. The BBC rejected C. R. Ashbee's call for a preservationist campaign on radio in the early 30s on precisely those grounds. Its broadcasting on the countryside in the 30s was carefully pitched to accommodate mass leisure and materialist aspirations, anxious, as the Director of Talks said in 1935, 'about the BBC appearing to moralise and to be grandmotherly'.[47]

Nor did government respond positively to preservationist efforts. One speech by Stanley Baldwin evoking the sounds of scythes and corncrakes—more often quoted in the 1980s than in the 1920s[48]—does not signify a policy. The most recent study of agricultural policy in this period discounts the influence both of romantic ruralists making the case for the yeoman farmer and of the 'few surviving adherents of the "squirearchical principle"'. While Baldwin certainly nursed some ruralist fantasies himself, he was very isolated in the Tory ranks and by 1929 his views had been effectively steamrollered by Neville Chamberlain's policy of planned shrinkage and quasi-corporatist modernisation,

---

[45] Joad, 'People's Claim', 66–7.

[46] Mandler, *Fall and Rise*, 227–41.

[47] J. R. Rose-Troup, Director of Talks, to W. E. G. Murray, Assistant Controller, 25 Nov. 1935: BBC Written Archives Centre, R51/425.

[48] Citations of Baldwin's speech abound: e.g. Bill Schwarz, 'The Language of Constitutionalism: Baldwinite Conservatism', in *Formations of Nation and People* (1984), 14–16; Patrick Wright, *On Living in an Old Country* (1985), 82; Alun Howkins, 'The Discovery of Rural England', in *Englishness*, ed. Colls and Dodd, 82; Paul Street, 'Painting Deepest England', in *Imagined Past*, ed. Shaw and Chase, 68–9; Paul Rich, 'A Question of Life and Death to England: Patriotism and the British Intellectuals, c. 1886–1945', *New Community*, 15 (1988–9), 501; Bunce, *Countryside Ideal*, 34–5; Trentmann, 'Civilisation', 585.

ultimately backed by the landed interest.[49] In the planning sphere, British controls remained among the weakest in Europe, the 1932 Town & Country Planning Act contributing something to urban planning but nothing to urban containment or rural planning.[50] The head of the Office of Works mourned in 1927 that Britain had fewer provisions to preserve historic buildings 'than any other country in Europe, with the exception of the Balkan States and Turkey'.[51] Even in the 1930s, when the CPRE made an effort to harmonise its preservationist proposals with urban interests (by seeking compromise on electrification plans, for instance, or shifting the balance between agriculture and leisure uses), it was still regarded by most politicians and civil servants as a gang of cranks beneath notice. On the one occasion, in 1937, when government was obliged to consider seriously 'the adequacy of planning powers to preserve the countryside', it reminded the preservation lobby sternly that

> it is necessary to remember that the countryside is not the preserve of the wealthy and leisured classes. The country rightly prides itself on the fact that since the War there has been an unparalleled building development, a development which every Government has done its utmost to stimulate, and whose effect has been to create new and better social conditions for a very large number of persons.[52]

This populist, *laissez-faire*, pro-growth policy remained the mainspring of government's approach to the countryside at least until 1945 (after which Labour tried to add an element of planning for rural design and leisure) and in some respects practically to the present day.

If indeed we ask when culture and politics *did* began to show signs of idealising and fossilising the old English countryside, we must approach perilously close to the present day. Undoubtedly during the second world war there were more evocations of a timeless Englishness, often linked to the countryside, than previously; but this feature of wartime generally (it was evident in the first world war as well) was eclipsed in peace when, as Raphael Samuel has argued recently, historicising notions of Englishness once again took a back seat to the

[49] Andrew Fenton Cooper, *British Agricultural Policy, 1912–36: A Study in Conservative Politics* (Manchester, 1989), esp. 1–4, 64–71, 94.

[50] John Sheail, *Rural Conservation in Inter-War Britain* (Oxford, 1981), is an important book, but ultimately fails in my view to rehabilitate the 1932 Act; cf. Peter Mandler, 'Politics and the English Landscape since the First World War', *Huntington Library Quarterly*, 55 (1992), 459–76.

[51] Sir Lionel Earle to First Commissioner of Works, 12 Jan. 1927: Public Record Office, WORK 14/2312.

[52] Memorandum, 'Preservation of the Countryside', prepared (probably by Evelyn Sharp) for the Town & Country Advisory Committee meeting of 12 Nov. 1937: Public Record Office, HLG 52/709.

technological, the timely and the up-to-the-minute.[53] While rural tourism continued to develop in the post-war years, accelerated by an influx of Americans in the 1960s, this phenomenon was not perceived at the time as unusual or unhealthy for a developing modern economy or society. There was a spurt of politically motivated warnings against Britain's anachronistic governing structures in the early 60s, but these soon yielded to Harold Wilson's 'white heat of the technological revolution' and the prevailing image of Britain at home and abroad was one of swinging, not sinking.[54] As late as 1970, a writer complaining that '[school]children read about the demoralising effects of the large city ... the farmer plowing along in the setting sun with his horse-pulled handplow is the glorified alternative' was referring not to English but to German children.[55]

The widespread sense that England was entering a phase of terminal decline, that this might have cultural as well as economic origins and that an overplus of love for the countryside might be fundamentally at fault is not really evident until the 1970s.[56] As all of Europe entered a phase of slow growth, environmental consciousness and concern for national heritage, England probably experienced this reversal more profoundly than most, having been for so long casual and neglectful about its environment and history. The 'Englishness' scholarship, it seems to me, is part of this sudden change of heart; that is, it reflects more than most historical writing the agenda of the present rather than the story of the past. There was, after all, no English analogue to the French feeling for *la France profonde* in the nineteenth or most of the twentieth centuries, just as there was no English equivalent to the *Heimatschutz* movement. The very locution 'Deep England', hastily translated from the French by the cultural studies industry ostensibly to describe a historically rooted concept, and the idea of a Department of National Heritage, also a rough approximation of a French institution, are both products not of the late nineteenth but of the late twentieth century. *Guarda, e passa.*

---

[53] Raphael Samuel, *Theatres of Memory* (1994), 51–9.

[54] Jim Tomlinson, 'Inventing "Decline": The Falling Behind of the British Economy in the Postwar Years', *Economic History Review*, 49 (1996), 731–57, charts the emergence of notions of economic decline in the 1950s and 60s, but with the cultural analysis still largely absent. Even the awareness of relative economic decline was, Tomlinson points out, masked by high absolute living standards.

[55] Holzner, 'Role of History and Tradition', 331.

[56] It would be interesting to trace the rise of the cultural analysis of decline more closely; in an appendix to *English Culture* (167–70), Wiener notes the preponderance of economic analyses but also cites evidence of a culturalist backlash in works dating (though he does not point to this fact) from the early 1970s.

THE CROMWELLIAN DECADE: AUTHORITY AND CONSENT

By C. S. L. Davies

READ 27 MARCH 1996 AT THE INSTITUTE OF HISTORICAL RESEARCH LONDON

The 1530s always remained classic Elton territory, in spite of later and fruitful excursions into the Cecilian world and beyond. [1] How distinctive were the thirties? Are we still justified in talking about a 'Revolution'? In a historical climate which puts the accent on continuities, such talk has become unfashionable. Productive reform was characteristic of the Wolsey ministry, of the reigns of Henry VII and of Edward IV, and perhaps had its origin with Margaret of Anjou's regime.[2] Equally historians are now very aware of the gap between aspiration and reality, the sheer difficulty of effecting real change, and especially in such areas as religious practice. They are also aware of how un-revolutionary in many respects were the succeeding years; of how many of the initiatives of the thirties were not followed up in the later years of Henry VIII or even in the otherwise revolutionary reign of Edward VI; above all of the Elizabethan regime with its avoidance whenever possible of confrontation and its attempts to recreate many of the ancient continuities. The thirties did represent a watershed in very many areas, did introduce changes which would be difficult if not necessarily impossible to reverse. But to try to make the thirties the fulcrum around which English history revolves is to invite refutation and the probability that the degree of real change will be underestimated as a result. Where, for instance, *Tudor Revolution in Government* deals with the particular it remains a remarkable work: inevitably sharpened by subsequent research, but none the less pointing in the right direction on changes in the financial departments, and above all in the evolution of a formal Privy Council. [3] Where it falls down is in its attempt to chart a spurious and procrustean 'medieval–modern' divide, differentiating 'informal' or 'household' from 'bureaucratic' types of administration, and so making the Cromwellian reforms the most important changes

---

[1] I am grateful to Dr G. W. Bernard, Mr John D. Cooper, Dr S. J. Gunn, Mr David Rundle, Dr Tim Thornton and Dr John Watts for valuable comments.

[2] See, e.g., David Starkey, 'Which Age of Reform?', in *Revolution Reassessed*, ed. Christopher Coleman and David Starkey (Oxford, 1986), 13–27.

[3] *Revolution Reassessed*, ed. Coleman and Starkey, seems, for the moment at least, to have silenced discussion on the 'administrative revolution'.

in the machinery of government between the Norman Conquest and the reign of Victoria.

In other respects, of course, most notably in the position of the church, the 1530s undeniably constitute a watershed in a long-term perspective. The claim for the distinctiveness of the decade must come from the ambitious nature of the changes which were attempted, and from their sheer number. But even more striking is the way in which the changes were justified by invoking a particular concept of the English polity in the preambles to statutes; that of a self-sufficient, organic 'commonwealth' of England. Perhaps Geoffrey Elton's most notable achievement was to have established that point. In doing so he raised crucial questions of authority and consent, maintaining consistently, even if with varying emphasis, that what was established was 'constitutional or limited monarchy', a government which 'insisted on testing all powers, including its own, against the law, this being regarded as independent of executive action and in practice treated as such'.[4]

I would suggest that the Henrician regime, so often seen as marching purposefully forward to build a 'strong' state, was one very conscious of its own weaknesses as it was driven by the king's predelictions and desires into increasingly dangerous waters. Much of its characteristic activity was in fact defensive. The 'high' doctrines of sovereignty, majesty and so on were, in a sense, bluster. Henry's ministers, advisers, confidants were engaged in one sense in trying to contain the manifestations of the royal will, in seeking to control it, or at least to divert it into harmless channels; but,in the end, having to facilitate its operation and make the best of the situation. That seems to be obviously true of Henry's early years, of the attempts by ministers inherited from his father to moderate his militaristic impulse. It is also true of the forties, notably in the duke of Norfolk's despairing messages to his son to stop feeding Henry's machismo by performing deeds of derring-do at Boulogne; 'for what [Norfolk] and the rest of the Council worketh in, for the surrender of Boulogne and the concluding of a peace, in six days, you, with your letters set back in six hours, such importance be your letters in the king's opinion at this time'.[5] The king's will is of the essence in the 'divorce' issue. But recent research has, if anything, made more acute the problem Elton tackled in 'King or Minister?', that of hesitation, reluctance to proceed, even when it seemed the way forward was already well mapped. Ideas existed in profusion, arguments about the invalidity of papal dispensations to marry a deceased brother's widow, about English jurisdictional self-sufficiency, were well marshalled

---

[4] *Tudors* (1955), 168; 'Political Creed', *Studies* 2, 235; *Studies* 3, 434 (review of Joel Hurstfield, *Freedom, Corruption, and Government*).

[5] *Letters and Papers of Henry VIII* [hereafter *LP*], XX, pt II, no.738.

by the autumn of 1530.[6] And yet Henry held back when a consultative group of lawyers and clerics gave a majority view that Parliament could not authorise the archbishop of Canterbury to rule authoritatively on the marriage.[7] It was another two years before Cromwell could get to work drafting the Act in Restraint of Appeals, and Anne Boleyn begin to be officially recognised as a future queen, after the 'Submission of the Clergy', More's resignation as chancellor, the peace treaty with France and the fortuitous death of Archbishop Warham. Uncertainty, fear of the consequences, seem to be the keynotes, until impatience and a conjunction of favourable events produced action.

Officially inspired pamphlets expounded a vision of an English commonwealth, united as never before under a ruler surpassing his predecessors in all kingly qualities, and so uniquely equipped to attain virtue, justice and prosperity.[8] Cromwell himself noted that 'except that the people perceive themselves by reason of the said alteration, to be in better ease than they were before', they would not accept the new dispensation.[9] Ostentatious concern for a new order may indicate a government unsure of itself, anxious, not necessarily to win popularity (as Wolsey had discovered, attacking enclosures was liable to bring down the wrath of the influential), but to establish its legitimacy as the upholder of social justice, the epitome of Christian kingship. It is perhaps significant in this connection that Richard III's Parliament produced a reform programme; and similarly that the government of Charles I was to pursue a policy of social justice. I am not suggesting that the establishment of legitimacy was the only motive for 'good government'. But the elaborate justifications expressed in preambles to statutes, the concern to relate the particular to the general principles of the common good, suggest a particular concern for 'public opinion'; in part, perhaps, to facilitate enforcement, but in part, too, to popularise the idea of an organic community, of a 'common wealth'. The 1533 act 'to destroy choughs, crows and rooks' may be taken as a slightly absurd example, with its solemn assertion that 'innumerable number of rooks and crows and choughs do daily breed and increase throughout this realm, which rooks, crows and choughs do yearly destroy devour

[6] Graham Nicholson, 'The Act of Appeals and the English Reformation', in *Law and Government under the Tudors: Essays Presented to Sir Geoffrey Elton on his Retirement*, ed. Claire Cross, David Loades and J.J. Scarisbrick (Cambridge, 1988), 19–30; Virginia Murphy, 'The Literature and Propaganda of Henry VIII's First Divorce', in *The Reign of Henry VIII*, ed. Diarmaid MacCulloch (1995), 135–58.

[7] *Calendar of State Papers, Spanish* [hereafter *CSP Span.*], *1529–30*, no. 460, p. 758.

[8] See the pamphleteers, preachers and memorialists discussed in *Policy and Police*, cap. 4, and *Reform and Renewal*, cap. 3.

[9] 'Anon. MS on the King's Marriage', in *Records of the Reformation*, ed. Nicholas Pocock (2 vols., Oxford, 1870), II, 487–9, discussed in *Policy and Police*, 183.

and consume a wonderful and marvellous great quantity of corn and grain of all kinds ... to the great prejudice, damage, and undoing of the great number of all the tillers, husbands, and sowers of the earth ... ', going on to organise parish drives against these vermin, arranging for the proper upkeep of crow nets, and the compulsory payment of rewards by occupiers of land to those who present dead birds at the rate of six for a penny.[10] The frontispiece to the Great Bible of 1539, in which a huge Henry VIII distributes the word of God to grateful subjects, carefully arranged in due social order, is perhaps a special example of the same propaganda point.[11]

The frontispiece stresses the benefit to subjects of the new dispensation. The danger, obviously, was that subjects would think that unacceptable upheaval was being imposed on them merely to satisfy the king's personal convenience. The promised benefits could take different forms, according to the predelictions of the moment. In 1530, for instance, Henry emphasised to the papal nuncio his determination to extirpate heresy;[12] and this theme was to surface again with the Six Articles Act and the subsequent burnings. Alternatively (or, perhaps, as another aspect of the same policy), the accent might be on reform of abuses, notably the inappropriate use of images, or on the better administration of the church, in the sense of campaigns against pluralism, or for the provision of new bishoprics. The act for the creation of the new bishoprics, passed at the same time as that confirming the surrender of the greater monasteries, trumpeted a major programme for reform in its preamble, which Henry himself wrote; contrasting the 'slothful and ungodly life' of the religious with the 'better use' to which their assets could be put, 'whereby God's word might the better be set forth, children brought up in learning, clerks nourished in the universities, old servants decayed to have livings, almshouses for poor folk to be sustained in, Readers of Greek, Hebrew, and Latin to have good stipend, daily alms to be ministered, mending of high ways, exhibition for ministers of the church'.[13] Radical change carried with it the promise of a better tomorrow. The general intrusiveness of the Henrician state, the act, for instance, making 'buggery committed with mankind or beast' a capital offence, the provision in the Six Articles act for priests keeping wives to be hanged, and for those keeping concubines to be imprisoned and to be hanged for the second offence, with identical

---

[10] 24 Hen. VIII c.10 in *Statutes of the Realm*, [hereafter *SR*], ed. A. Luders *et al.*, (11 vols., 1810–28), III, 425–6.

[11] See Philip Hughes, *The Reformation in England* (rev. edn, 3 vols. in one, 1963), II, plate 2; it is intriguing that the whole society, including laywomen, is shown speaking Latin (if only 'vivat rex'), except for a solitary 'God save the king' by the lowest placed layman.

[12] *CSP Span., 1529–30*, no. 460, p. 761.

[13] 31 Hen. VIII c. 9, *SR*, III, 728; J.J. Scarisbrick, *Henry VIII* (1968), 513.

penalties for the women, the first witchcraft statute in 1542, go even further and indicate a determination, apparently by the king himself, to establish a tight, controlled, political community not a little reminiscent of Utopia.[14] The same might be said of schemes of public works financed by graduated taxation, or of attempts to control the price of cuts of meat.[15] Much of this legislation was so ambitious, so patently unenforceable that I am tempted to believe that proclaiming godly intentions in rotund phrases was an end in itself; appealing, perhaps, to Henry's self-image as the much-misunderstood King David; 'his delight is in the law of the Lord; and in his law doth he meditate day and night'.[16] Whatever the motive, the declared aim of creating a positively godly, harmonious, participatory, society was a striking feature of the thirties.

Legislation, I am suggesting, is a branch of public relations; though not only that. Sydney Anglo wrote in 1969 that Anne Boleyn's coronation represented 'both a beginning and an end in the history of Early Tudor public spectacle ... He had now to turn his attention from the display and glitter, which had marked ... his earlier years ... The pageanteer, court reveller, and scenic artist were succeeded as purveyors of royal propaganda by the political pamphleteer, preacher, and public executioner.'[17] That verdict needs modification.[18] There was certainly no decline in magnificence as such; the *History of the King's Works* shows work on palaces at a peak in the thirties[19]; we need only remind ourselves of Holbein's great dynastic portrait of Henry VII and Elizabeth of York, and Henry VIII and Jane Seymour at Whitehall. When necessary Henry could put on a show. When Stephen Gardiner went on embassy to the emperor in 1540, he took an entourage of 150,

---

[14] 25 Hen. VIII c. 6; 31 Hen. VIII c. 14, ss. 5 and 20; 33 Hen. VIII c. 8 (*SR*, III, 441, 739–43, 837). For Henry's probable interest in the first two measures, see *Reform and Renewal*, 148, and MacCulloch, 'Henry VIII and the Reform of the Church', in *The Reign of Henry VIII*, ed. MacCulloch,159–80, at 178. Henry Brinklow complained that the Six Articles were unprecedently draconian, 'for the pope never made the marriage of priests to be death'; *The Complaynt of Roderyck Mors*, ed. J. Meadows Cowper, Early English Text Soc., extra ser., 22 (1874), 57.

[15] *Reform and Renewal*, 122–3 (St German made the initial proposal for public works; see J. A. Guy, *Christopher St German on Chancery and Statute*, Selden Soc., suppl. series, 6 (1985), 127–35); R. W. Heinze, *The Proclamations of the Tudor Kings* (Cambridge, 1976), 112–16.

[16] Pamela Tudor-Craig, 'Henry VIII and King David', in *Early Tudor England: Proceedings of the 1987 Harlaxton Symposium*, ed. Daniel Williams (Woodbridge, 1989), 183–205, esp. 197; the quotation is from the first psalm.

[17] Sydney Anglo, *Spectacle, Pageantry, and Early Tudor Policy*, (Oxford, 1969), 261.

[18] See the revision of Anglo's views generally in his *Images of Tudor Kingship* (1992), esp. 109–12.

[19] H. M. Colvin and John Summerson, 'The King's Houses, 1485–1660', in *The History of the King's Works*, ed. Colvin (6 vols., 1963–82), IV, 1–364, at 5–7.

each with gold chains.[20] Any decline in tourneying was probably due to Henry's age, especially after his accident in January 1536.[21] Nevertheless an additional note creeps in in the thirties. To magnificence and to the dispensing of justice is added an attempt to persuade subjects that they formed an active part of a purposefully orientated society. A leading minister who held the posts of lord privy seal and the king's vice-regent in ecclesiastical affairs was perhaps more appropriate to the new era than one who would flaunt the pomp of cardinal, legate and lord chancellor.

'Common Wealth', as David Starkey has shown, had been a political catch-phrase since 1450; and, of course, the concept of the 'common good' is a good deal older than that.[22] But what is remarkable is how consistently, in the thirties, the organic concept is invoked in justification of policy. By contrast, in Wolsey's time there was a strong air of *de haut en bas*; the accent was on the majesty of the state, of the 'enormities' committed by offenders to the derogation of that majesty.[23] In the legislation of the 1523 Parliament some public acts carry a brief explanation in terms of the public good; others plunge straight in without preamble.[24] The whole question of the language in which legislation is framed could repay much closer investigation. But for the moment I would suggest that the elaboration of the justificatory preamble, the quasi-automatic reference to the health of the body politic, the accent on that body rather than on its head, does seem new—whether, as Geoffrey Elton maintained, due to the political vision of Thomas Cromwell, or to the enormity of the programme being undertaken and the need to drag as many subjects as possible on board.[25]

Popular participation meant, of course, an emphasis on Parliament as the means through which that participation was expressed. The thirties, as Elton insisted, were distinguished in their emphasis on parliamentary sovereignty, or at least parliamentary omnicompetence; the assertion that supreme political authority in England lay in king-in-parliament, in a sense, in the nation incorporated, that there could be no appeal against its decisions to any earthly body. At the same

[20] Glyn Redworth, *In Defence of the Church Catholic: The Life of Stephen Gardiner* (Oxford, 1990), 141.
[21] Scarisbrick, *Henry VIII*, 485.
[22] Starkey, 'Which Age of Reform?'.
[23] Peter Gwyn, *The King's Cardinal* (1990), 116, and J. A. Guy, *The Cardinal's Court* (Hassocks, 1977), 30, 37, 120 for Wolsey's Star Chamber orations.
[24] *SR*, III, 206–81; compare 14 & 15 Hen. VIII caps. 1 and 2, *SR*, III, 206–9.
[25] Elton came close to accepting this; 'Cromwell treated Parliament as the only instrument available, and usable despite the difficulties involved, for the carrying out of a major reform programme'; 'Redivus', *Studies* 3, 386.

time the boundary between the secular and the religious sphere was shifted massively in favour of the former. Of course, the invocation of Parliament was in part a propaganda device, to justify what might seem a weak case both to foreign rulers (including the pope) and to potentially sceptical subjects. As St German's championing of parliamentary sovereignty suggests, the concept had its roots deep in the world of the Inns of Court.[26] Legal opinion was by no means united. In 1506 a majority of the judges held that an act of parliament could not make the king a parson, or even, in one opinion, extinguish the obligation to pay tithe. In 1527 John More, Thomas's father, held that a statute could not alter the custom of gavelkind.[27] However, as Norman Doe has shown, the trend among pre-Reformation judges was towards the positivistic interpretation of statute; holding that a statute was valid in itself, rather than being open to challenge on the grounds of its not being consonant with natural law.[28] In that sense, the deployment of parliamentary authority in the thirties was a natural extension of an existing trend, although by earlier standards breathtaking in its claims on what had been unequivocally spiritual domain.

The invocation of Parliament did not necessarily mean an emphasis on the popular will, however much Henry VIII was happy to use parliamentary consent to justify his proceedings. As Elton himself indicated, and as John Guy has since demonstrated more systematically, the Reformation statutes were ambiguous as between 'descending' and 'ascending' theories of authority: of authority given by God to rulers and recognised by Parliament; and of authority derived from and conferred by the people knit together in a body politic.[29] Strict logic took second place to expediency. Elton drew attention to the preamble to the Six Articles act. The king as supreme head, mindful of the need for doctrinal unity, had commanded Parliament and Convocation to

[26] Guy, St German, 24–5.

[27] The Reports of Sir John Spelman, ed. J. H. Baker, 2 vols., Selden Soc., 93–4 (1977–8 for 1976–7), II, introduction, 44, 65; pace Parliament, 34–5, the case is 1506 (21 Hen. VII), not 1529; see Les reportes del cases Edw. V–Hen. VIII (1679; repr. 1981), Hilary 21 Hen. VII, pl. 1.

[28] Norman Doe, Fundamental Authority in Late Medieval English Law (Cambridge, 1990). Doe also considers judge-made law, but the positivistic case seems strongest in the case of statute, and there seems no case of sixteenth-century judges disallowing statute; 57–9, 79.

[29] 'Lex', in Studies 4, 37–57, esp. 41–3; John Guy, 'The Henrician Age', in The Varieties of British Political Thought, 1500–1800, ed. J. G. A. Pocock (Cambridge, 1993), 13–46, and 'The Rhetoric of Counsel in Early Modern England', in Tudor Political Culture, ed. Dale Hoak, (Cambridge, 1995), 292–310. Cf. also Shelley Lockwood, 'Marsilius of Padua and the Case for the Royal Ecclesiastical Supremacy', supra, 6th ser., I, (1991), 89–119, for William Marshall's adaptation of Marsilio not only to replace popular sovereignty by parliamentary authority, but to diminish restraints on the prince.

consider the problem, had personally propounded the articles agreed by the clergy in Parliament, where it was in turn discussed; the results were agreed by the 'consent of the king's highness', the 'assent' of the lords spiritual and temporal, and of the 'learned clergy' in Convocation, and the 'consent' of the Commons.[30] (This seems to put king and Commons on a higher plane than everybody else, but that was not, I take it, intended.) This really does seem to be snatching at every conceivable vestige of authority, no doubt because the crown was engaged in an unprecedented and logically dubious action, namely ruling on the correct interpretation of contested Christian doctrine.[31]

The need to invoke as much authority as possible for the Reformation changes did produce some surprisingly populist statements; even if few went quite as far as John Morris, receiver of Syon, inveigled into professing that the Holy Ghost was present in Parliament.[32] Elton drew attention to the 1534 act abolishing Peter's Pence, with its potentially radical statement about laws which 'the people of this your realm have taken at their free liberty by their own consent to be used amongst them', though qualified 'as by the suffrance of your grace and your progenitors'.[33] Stephen Gardiner's *De Vera Obedientia* is in large part a disquisition on the scriptural doctrine of obedience due by subjects to God-created kings. Yet there comes through a strong emphasis on the parliamentary recognition of Henry's supreme headship, even though it is quickly qualified by the assertion that such recognition was only necessary 'to remove that deceit [the papal claim] from the eyes of the vulgar'.[34] Gardiner goes further by claiming that every individual has

[30] 'Lex', *Studies* 4, 46; the act (its title, revealingly, 'An act abolishing diversity in opinions'), 31 Hen. VIII c.14, see *Constitution* (1982), 399–401, or *SR*, III, 739–43. Cf. the circular of 1535 which invokes the law of God, Scripture, 'due consultation and deliberate advisement and consent' of 'all other our nobles and commons temporal assembled in our high court of parliament, and by authority of the same', for the abolition of papal power and the 'grant' of the supreme headship; adding the subsequent 'recognition' of the king's new style by bishops and clergy, in convocation and by their individual oaths; *Tudor Royal Proclamations*, ed. P. L. Hughes and J. F. Larkin (3 vols., New Haven, CT, 1964–9), I, no. 158.

[31] For political thinkers urging apparently incompatible positions in support of the same argument, see Antony Black, 'Political Languages in Later Medieval Europe', and Diana Perry, 'Paradisis de Puteo – a Fifteenth-Century Civilian's concept of Papal Sovereignty', in *Church and Sovereignty: Essays in Honour of Michael Wilks*, ed. Diana Wood, Studies in Church History, Subsidia, 9 (Oxford, 1991), 313–28 and 369–92.

[32] *Reform and Renewal*, 67. Strictly Morris conceded only that 'the Holy Ghost is as verily present' at the making of an act of parliament 'as ever it was at any General Council', possibly an equivocation.

[33] 'Lex', *Studies* 4, 47–8; 25 Hen. VIII c. 21, *SR*, III, 464–71, at 464.

[34] *Obedience in Church and State: Three Political Tracts by Stephen Gardiner*, ed. Pierre Janelle (Cambridge, 1930), 90, 92. The tendentious English translation of Mary's reign went further in talking of the title 'granted' by Parliament, 91; and cf. 'Lex', *Studies* 4, 47, quoting *Obedience*, 115.

fully agreed to Henry's title: 'omnes plane constantissimo consensu in hoc convenerunt', the learned, and the unlearned both men and women, 'docti pariter, atque indocti tum viri tum feminae'.[35] I take it that he is referring here not to parliamentary enactment but to the oath to be sworn 'by all subjects' under the 1534 Succession Act. He had himself raised with Cromwell the question as to whether the oath should be tendered to women.[36]

The Succession oath underlines the isssues of forced consent. On the one hand it committed the individual not merely to observe the law, but to positive approval of the entire legislation of the Reformation Parliament; on the other, refusal incurred the penalties of misprision of treason (imprisonment and forfeiture of goods); in Elton's words, this 'was really something new—the first employment, though certainly not the last, of a spiritual instrument of commitment as a political test'.[37] A regime which demands a show of unanimous consent is more coercive than one which merely imposes its will from above; in that the former is attempting to extract a much greater commitment.[38] The Reformation Parliament had objected to the invidious use of oaths by the church courts in heresy trials; it was now imposing the dilemma faced by suspected heretics on the nation at large.

The Succession oath is a specific case of the general question of parliamentary consent, the alleged binding of all the people by their own will. In a real sense, the notion that the entire nation partook of deliberation in Parliament and could be held to have willed everything done there was an obvious fiction, albeit a necessary one.[39] Parliament was plainly subject to a good deal of pressure, while the very theory of the representation of Englishmen and Englishwomen was potentially open to criticism, not merely in terms of Thomas Smith's 'fourth sort of men which do not rule' or in the absence of effective choice in most

[35] *Obedience*, 156.

[36] *Letters of Stephen Gardiner*, ed. J. A. Muller, (Cambridge, 1933) , no. 42, pp. 56–7.

[37] *Policy and Police*, 222–4; Hughes, *Reformation*, I, 270 for a convenient printing of the oath as set out in *Lords Journal*, I, 82. The oath-taker was sworn 'to your cunning, wit, and uttermost of your power, without guile, fraud or other undue means ... [to] keep, maintain and defend this Act ... and all other Acts and Statutes made since the beginning of this present parliament'. Elton's implied analogy with the Test Acts surely fails, in that the latter were voluntary in the sense of being imposed on aspirants to offices, not on all subjects.

[38] J. L. Talmon, *The Origins of Totalitarian Democracy* (1952).

[39] The legal fiction seems to have begun as a device to prevent a plea of ignorance of a statute; see Chief Justice Thorpe in 1366, cited 'Representation', *Studies* 2, 36. It soon became a claim that all Englishmen (and Englishwomen?) had personally willed a statute; Doe, *Fundamental Authority*, 8, 16–18, 39. Interestingly 25 Hen. VIII c. 27 (*SR*, III, 483–4), deposing the Italian bishops of Salisbury and Worcester, excused the king for having appointed them because of his ignorance of existing law.

constituencies, but also in terms of the unequal representation of different parts of the country. It was also potentially damaging to parliamentary authority that parliaments found themselves contradicting what previous parliaments had held to be unalterable and undeniable truths; in matters of doctrine, or in successive adjustments of the succession laws. Sir Edward Coke, citing *Doctor and Student*, solemnly opined that it was unthinkable that a statute made with the authority of the whole realm 'will recite a thing against the truth'.[40] Humbug is no doubt a necessary ingredient of any functioning political system; those gravely enunciated statements which everybody makes a show of accepting as profound truths while they are self-evident nonsense.

However, even dubious political doctrine can generate its own logical progression. The rhetoric of popular consent through Parliament worked towards the extension of representation to areas hitherto exempt. The Reformation statutes were initially imposed on Wales, Cheshire and Durham, Man, Calais, the Channel Islands and Ireland by fiat of the Westminster Parliament, as territories dependent on the English crown. Calais and Wales were both granted representation in the English Parliament in 1536; in the case of Calais this involved, too, its transfer from Henry's kingdom of France to his kingdom of England.[41] There was an abortive attempt to recruit representatives from the Channel Islands in 1541.[42] Logic, however, had its limits. Durham was left out in the cold; and Cheshire was only given representation in 1543 as a result of a petition by the inhabitants deploring their 'disherisons, losses and damages' as a result of their being subjected to (non-religious) legislation in which they had no part.[43]

Ireland provides an interesting study of the interaction of 'descending' and 'ascending' theories in this respect. 'This land of Ireland' was held to

---

[40] *Fourth Part of the Institutes of the Laws of England* (1681 edn), cap. 74, p. 343; cf. St. German, *Doctor and Student*, ed. T. F. T. Plucknett and J. L. Barton, Selden Soc., 91 (1974), 300. The question at issue concerned tithe and therefore the law of God.

[41] *The House of Commons, 1509–1558*, ed. S. T. Bindoff, History of Parliament Trust, 3 vols. (1982), I, 264, 284. The Calais act refers to the town as 'one of the most principal treasures belonging to his Realm of England'. For an attempted refutation of the statement that Tournai was represented at Westminster in 1514 (*ibid.*, I, 285) and for a discussion of the status of Calais, see C. S. L. Davies, 'Tournai and the English Crown, 1513–9', *Historical Journal*, 40 (1997).

[42] *House of Commons*, I, 283–4.

[43] Durham was granted representation in 1673, *pace* the uncharacteristic error in 'Representation', *Studies* 2, 42, 51. Robert Cecil was unaware in 1597 that it was not represented; Mark A. Kishlansky, *Parliamentary Selection: Social and Political Choice in Early Modern England* (Cambridge, 1986), 23. For Cheshire see 34 & 35 Hen. VIII c. 13 (*SR*, III, 911) , discussed by Tim Thornton, 'Political Society in Early Tudor Cheshire, 1480–1560' (DPhil thesis, Oxford University, 1993), 152–4.

be 'depending and belonging' to the imperial crown of England; English legislation on the succession and on the headship were therefore applicable to Ireland. Nevertheless Henry ordered in 1534 the calling of an Irish Parliament to enact parallel legislation; and, after the suppression of the Kildare rebellion, the Parliament met in 1536–7. As Brendan Bradshaw has shown, the original intention seems to have been little more than to register the English acts. Such elements of 'consent' as appear in the Irish acts, the notion of a body politic envisaging itself in its spiritual capacity as 'Hibernica Ecclesia', were not in the original form of the statutes as drafted at Westminster, but were inserted by the administration in Dublin. Even so, clerical consent was not forthcoming; a further act was necessary declaring that the clerical proctors, hitherto in effect a third house, had never been actual 'members' of the Irish Parliament but were merely 'counsellors and assistants' much like the convocation within the realm of England.[44] Quite clearly, the notion of 'consent', even among the English inhabitants of Ireland, was spurious. Nevertheless, the rhetoric of Reformation helped fashion the policy suggested by Bishop Staples in 1537 and carried out in 1541–2: of Henry as 'king of Ireland', with the implication of a theoretical unity of the whole island, the reinvention of Irish chiefs as English-style peers, and the eventual broadening of the area represented in parliament to embrace the island as a whole.[45] In the event Irish turmoil and English politics meant the abandonment of the 'softly-softly' approach of 1541–2. The Irish Parliament did not meet again until 1557. The Edwardian religious legislation was imposed on Ireland, as were the Marian counter-measures even before the 1557 Parliament belatedly reversed the Henrician legislation. In 1560 an Irish Parliament passed acts of Supremacy and Uniformity on the English model. Interestingly, the same Parliament abolished capitular elections of royal nominees to bishoprics, as 'in very deed no elections', but merely 'colours, shadows, or pretences of election'; an observation which would have been equally relevant in England.[46] In Ireland, certainly, the rhetoric of Reformation, the need for apparent consent, was far from the dominant consideration. Nevertheless, as an irritant, as a statement of best political practice, rhetoric had its effect, and did help to transform the Irish Parliament, whatever its weaknesses, into a legislative body with claims, at least, to determine the direction of policy.

The doctrine of consent is reflected in the reactions of the Pilgrimage

---

[44] Brendan Bradshaw, *The Irish Constitutional Revolution of the Sixteenth Century* (Cambridge, 1979), 145–6, 157–8; Steven G. Ellis, *Tudor Ireland* (1985), 131–2, 193–5. For the Irish legislation, see *Statutes at Large: Ireland* (20 vols., Dublin, 1786–1801), I, 66–174.

[45] Bradshaw, *Revolution*, 156–7, 193–4, 232–3, 264; Ellis, *Ireland*, 134–41. Henry insisted on re-enacting the kingship act to eliminate any trace of a 'grant' of the title.

[46] *Statutes at Large: Ireland*, I, 252–73, 275–304; quotation at 300. Cf. Ellis, *Tudor Ireland*, 210–11, 236.

of Grace. The rebel use of oaths to bind together their force may well be a reflection of, and reaction to, the mass swearing to the succession two years before, and the more explicitly anti-papal oath or declaration imposed on the clergy since.[47] The consistent use of 'common wealth' language by the Pilgrims may reflect parliamentary language. Above all the Pilgrims took seriously the claim that Parliament represented the nation, in their challenge to the credentials of the Westminster Parliament on that basis; their demand for a parliament to be held at York, for more seats for the north, and for a reduction in the number of 'king's servants' among MPs. This may have been due to the influence of lawyers like Robert Aske himself, and above all Sir Thomas Tempest, who seems to have first raised the issue. But it also, presumably, reflects the degree the issue of consent had been central to official propaganda during 1534–6.[48]

The doctrine of popular consent expressed through Parliament was to become a staple of parliamentary and legal discourse.[49] What is interesting, however, is how little it seems to have entered into the wider popular consciousness at the time, how much less pervasive it was in practice than the 'descending' theory of authority. Henry in his answer to the Lincolnshire rebels hardly includes them in the 'common wealth'; 'the rude commons of one shire, and that one of the most brute and beastly of the whole realm'. In the next paragraph he argues that the 'suppression of religious houses and monasteries' was 'granted us by all the nobles, spiritual and temporal, of this our realm, and by all the commons of the same by Act of Parliament'.[50] The personal nature of Henry's concept of kingship, the 'granted us', is interesting. Henry's reply to the Yorkshire rebels, drawn up in his own hand, lacks any reference to consent; Henry is the 'Supreme Head here in Earth' of 'our own church', which 'is a thing which nothing pertaineth to any of you our commons'.[51] When he comes to 'the laws of the commonwealth' Henry can only think of the 'many wholesome, commodious and beneficial acts made for the common wealth' in his own time, so many more than

---

[47] M. H. Dodds and Ruth Dodds, *The Pilgrimage of Grace 1536–7 and the Exeter Conspiracy 1538* (2 vols., Cambridge, 1915), I, 182; M. L. Bush, ' "Up for the Commonweal": The Significance of Tax Grievances in the English Rebellions of 1536', *English Historical Review*, 106 (1991), 299–318.

[48] Dodds, *Pilgrimage*, I, 357–61; Michael Bush, *The Pilgrimage of Grace* (Manchester, 1996), 167–8.

[49] Patrick Collinson, 'The Monarchical Republic of Queen Elizabeth I', *Bull. of the John Rylands Library*, 69 (1986–7), 394–424.

[50] Dodds, *Pilgrimage*, I, 136–8, at 136.

[51] Hughes, *Reformation*, I, 338, compares Henry's 'our own church' with Gardiner's invocation, 'cum summo populi consensu, suaeque [my italics] ecclesiae iudicio', *Obedience*, 86.

by his predecessors; rather, like the word of God in the Bible frontispiece, laws are handed down from on high by a beneficient king. Henry's disingenuous account of how many more nobles there were in his council in 1536 than in 1509 concludes with the brusque reminder 'we would ye knew that it appertaineth nothing to any of our subjects to appoint us our Council'. In the final sentence Henry gets the language of commonwealth subtly wrong. 'Thus I, as your head, pray for you my members, that God might light you ... to knowledge and declare yourselves our true subjects henceforth.'[52]

There are several examples of the same paternalist tendency when Henry takes up the pen. In 1539 he amended a draft proclamation issuing provisional directions pending the introduction of the Six Articles. Henry altered the reference to the proclamation being authorised by Parliament, to the more general statement that Parliament had given its authorization to the king to act (admittedly with the advice of the council).[53] And, famously, Henry drafted alterations to the coronation oath to remove apparent constraints upon the king, swearing to uphold laws and customs '*not prejudicial to his crown or imperial jurisdiction*' and which 'the nobles and people have made and chosen *with his consent*'.[54] Henry's use of language is consistently egotistic; he envisages the crown in highly personal terms, with the accent on his powers, rights, duties (to God), Henry as well-meaning in principle, anxious to do good to 'his' people, but all very much in terms of his benevolence. Equally, the language used of Henry by others is dangerously personal, magnifying Henry's own supposed qualities rather than the institutional majesty of the office. Speaker Rich in 1536 compared Henry to Solomon (for prudence and justice), Samson (strength and fortitude) and Absalom (body and beauty); a little later Henry became 'the sun [which] dispels evil vapours'.[55] Audley in 1542 held that God had 'anointed [Henry] with the oil of sapience, above his fellows, above the rest of the kings in the earth, and above all his progenitors', and went on to talk of Henry's 'perfect knowledge of the Word of God', his 'exact understanding of the art military' and 'politic knowledge'.[56]

[52] Dodds, *Pilgrimage*, I, 275–8; John Guy, in Guy and Alastair Fox, *Reassessing the Henrician Age* (Oxford, 1986), 145, also characterises Henry's answer as 'disingenuous'.

[53] *Proclamations*, I, no. 191. The authority quoted by Henry is obscure. The editors believe it may anticipate the Proclamations Act which was introduced in the immediately subsequent Parliament, on the grounds that the Supremacy Act makes no mention of the council, 285 n.1. Perhaps this is another example of Henry reaching for justification regardless of legal nicety.

[54] Tudor-Craig, 'Henry VIII and King David', 199, for convenient edition of the revised oath; 187, for dating.

[55] Stanford E. Lehmberg, *The Later Parliaments of Henry VIII, 1536–1547* (Cambridge, 1977), 16, 36.

[56] *Ibid.*, 141. Cf. also Sir Robert Wingfield's telling Henry that he had been ordained

True, in his speech on Ferrer's case in 1543 Henry produced classic commonwealth language; 'we be informed by our judges that we at no time stand so highly in our estate royal as in time of Parliament, wherein we as head and you as members are conjoined and knit together into one body politic', so that the least offence to an MP 'is to be judged as done against our person and the whole court of Parliament'.[57] But that statement, made I suggest for public effect, needs to be set against the evidence of Henry's own comments in his more unguarded moments, and the language of flattery with which he was habitually surrounded.

Official replies to rebels made in fact surprisingly little use of the argument from popular consent. The only reference to Parliament in Cranmer's reply to the western rebels in 1549 was in relation to their demand for the reintroduction of the act of Six Articles. Cranmer noted that that act was so much 'against the truth, and common judgements both of divines and lawyers, that if the king's majesty himself had not come personally into the parliament house, those laws had never passed'; the act had only been applied with any vigour for one year, and that in any case the present laws, 'which be and ever have been the laws of all other countries also' were superior to 'new laws which never were but in this realm only, and were here in force not fully thirteen months'.[58] This line of argument must have raised a wry smile from the ghost of Thomas More. There seems to have been a similar reluctance to use the popular consent argument by such writers as Cheke, Morison and Nichols.[59]

Indeed contemporary observers seem to have been pretty matter-of-fact about Parliament. Parliament is mentioned in Wriothesley's chronicle; acts are passed, but the sense is always of an external authority, the normal means of voting taxes or enacting legislation, with no hint of change brought about by the will of the nation.[60] Edward Hall, himself an MP, is fuller and more interesting. He gives

---

since before the Creation to restore the principles of Christianity; *LP*, XIV, pt I, no. 368. I owe this reference to Dr Bernard.

[57] Lehmberg, *Later Parliaments*, 170.

[58] *English Historical Documents, 1485–1558*, ed. C. H. Williams (1967), 361–86, at 367.

[59] John Cheke, *The Hurt of Sedicion* (1549); Richard Morison, *Apomaxis Calumnarium Convitiorumque* (1537–8), *An Exhortation* ... (1539), *An Inuective* ... (1539), and above all, *A Lamentation* ... , and *Remedy for Sedition*, both 1536, and conveniently available in *Humanist Scholarship and Public Order*, ed. D. S. Berkowitz (Washington, 1984); Nichols, in *Troubles connected with the Prayer-Book of 1549*, ed. Nicholas Pocock, Camden Ser., new ser., 37 (1884), 141–93, at 169. This last was ascribed by Pocock to Udall, but see G. Scheurweghs in *British Museum Quarterly*, 8 (1933–4), 24–5; I owe this reference to John D. Cooper. For Nichols, see Robert Whiting, *The Blind Devotion of the People* (Cambridge, 1989), *passim*.

[60] *Wriothesley's Chronicle*, ed. W. D. Hamilton, 2 vols., Camden Soc., new ser., 11 & 20 (1875 and 1877), I, 26, 102–3, II, 9–10.

a strong impression of the ability of the Commons to make trouble, but generally deplores such activities, contrasting 'froward persons' with 'the wiser sort', fearful that the former will provoke the king. His own speech in favour of the Six Articles seems to have been motivated by prudence of this sort. He explains the 1529 release of the king from his obligation to repay the forced loans of 1522–3 as due to the number of king's servants in the Commons and their 'labouring' of other MPs. As an insider, Hall is very aware of the diversity of members and the operations of particular interest groups; there is little sense of commonwealth, little use of 'organic' language except in quotations from royal speeches.[61] The only commentator to pay the doctrine of parliamentary consent the compliment of challenging it seems to have been Henry Brinklow, smarting from the passing of the Six Articles.[62]

A thorough examination of the language used about Parliament, outside the special contexts of statute and legal text, would be illuminating. My impression is that the rhetoric of the Reformation statutes had in practice a rather limited impact on the country at large. Parliament was routinely invoked as part of the 'common authority' of the realm. The more thorough-going point, that it represented the will of the English people, was also mentioned, but, perhaps because of its implausibility, much less frequently.[63] Not until the seventeenth century was it taken sufficiently to heart to generate debate about the meaning of representation or the rationale of the franchise.[64]

The Cromwellian decade was very much *sui generis*. The failure to provide a successor to Cromwell as vice-gerent in spirituals (for reasons not explained) helps make the point. While the vice-gerency represented very forcefully, even brutally, lay domination over the clergy, it also provided the institutional unity which the Church of England otherwise lacked, and for which the High Commissions were to be eventually a poor substitute.[65] A continued vice-gerency, with a modernised canon

---

[61] Edward Hall, *The Union of the Two Noble and Illustre Famelies of Lancastre and Yorke* (1809), 767, 774–5, 785, 828, 864–5; Lehmberg, *Later Parliaments*, 73.

[62] Brinklow, *Roderyck Mors*, 57.

[63] William Thomas's able defence of Henry's actions invokes parliamentary authority and its supposed free speech, but not popular consent; *The Pilgrim*, ed. J.A. Froude (1861). Thomas Starkey, *Exhortation to Unitie and Obedience*, (?1535–6), talks of the people's acceptance of the abolition of papal power 'by the high providence of our most noble prince, and by common authority here in our nation', presumably Parliament, but without specifically advancing the theory of popular consent through Parliament, fol. 43v.

[64] While they disagree on timing, both Derek Hirst, *The Representative of the People?* (Cambridge, 1975), and Kishlansky, *Parliamentary Selection*, see this as a seventeenth-century development.

[65] R. H. Helmholz, *Roman Canon Law in Reformation England* (Cambridge, 1990), cap. 2, 28–54; F. D. Logan, 'Thomas Cromwell and the Vice-Gerency in Spirituals', *Eng. Hist.*

law, might have made a reality of that dual-structured state, of separate lay and clerical spheres united only in the person of the monarch of which, in certain moods, Elizabeth I and Charles I dreamed.[66] That in turn would open up the fundamental question raised in the debate on the Petition of Right, of whether the common law (including both customary and statutory elements) was the fundamental English law; or whether it was just one of a number of possible co-existing jurisdictions, including ecclesiastical, civil and martial law, giving the royal prerogative considerable room for manoeuvre.[67]

The programme of the thirties was cut short, and in many ways cut back. This is obviously true in a variety of details; for instance, the abandonment of wildly impractical economic policies, such as the attempt to control the price of meat by statute.[68] Neither the more authoritarian aspects of policy, nor the organic, commonwealth spirit invoked in parliamentary preambles was allowed full scope. It is also worth stressing a more fundamental point: the sense that an activist 'revolutionary' political programme was in itself at odds with a profoundly conservative social system. This lies at the heart of the 'revisionist' critique of religious policy. But it has more general application, and was well expressed in a recent paper by Joe Slavin, with its emphasis on the 'deeply laid social bases of Tudor political life': 'concrete personal rights, social duties, and local political obligations' all 'tied closely to irrational traditions of kinship, property systems, customary law and other matters not easily contained within conceptual formulas, and ... rooted in belief systems—especially religious beliefs' which contrasted with the programme of dramatic change by legislative fiat.[69] In the event the crown's success in driving a wedge between clergy and laity in the Reformation Parliament, in conjunction with the relative lightness of the tax burden on the laity in the thirties, helped make these disconcerting changes acceptable. How different the outcome might have been is shown by the feelings expressed in the Pilgrimage of Grace that the very fabric of material and spiritual life was threatened by a

---

Rev., 103 (1988), 658–67; Diarmid MacCulloch, *Thomas Cranmer* (New Haven and London, 1996), 122–3, 129–30, 133–5, 165–6, 184, 272.

[66] Claire Cross, *The Royal Supremacy in the Elizabethan Church* (1969), 35–6; John Guy, 'The 1590's: The Second Reign of Elizabeth I?', in *The Reign of Elizabeth I*, ed. Guy (Cambridge, 1995), 1–19, at 11–13; Conrad Russell, *The Fall of the British Monarchies, 1637–1642* (Oxford, 1991), 39–40; cf. 'Redivivus', *Studies* 3, 385.

[67] J. G. A. Pocock, *The Ancient Constitution and the Feudal Law: A Reissue with Retrospect* (Cambridge, 1987), 289–94.

[68] Heinze, *Proclamations*, 113–16; there were attempts as late as 1551–2 to settle meat prices by proclamation (240–2), but apparently none under Mary or Elizabeth.

[69] A. J. Slavin, 'The Tudor State, Reformation, and Understanding Change through the Looking Glass', in *Political Thought and the Tudor Commonwealth*, ed. Paul A. Fideler and T. F. Mayer (1992), 223–53, quotation at 224.

predatory crown, following the relatively modest tax voted in 1534.[70]

Interestingly, Geoffrey Elton recognised in one of his later papers the extent to which rapid change in itself militated against traditional liberties; 'the law-generated liberties of Englishmen could last only while the law was regarded in what I have called the medieval manner, as an independent component within the social and political structure of the state; the sixteenth century, which used the law of Parliament to remake the state, temporarily weakened the hold of this doctrine'.[71] Whatever else, the Cromwellian decade was an adventurous, innovative, period. We can certainly find roots in the late medieval kingdom of state control of the church, of the invocation of national community and of the doctrine of parliamentary sovereignty. But these ideas were applied and developed in the 1530s in a way which justifies Elton's use of 'revolution', even if much of the revolution was aborted. Nevertheless real 'consent' was problematic, even in Parliament. It is difficult to find anything more than grudging acceptance or acquiescence in the country at large. The regime was authoritarian; and the language in which politics were described, except when authors were in legalistic mode, bears out that point.

Sir Thomas Smith distinguished three sorts of tyrant. The first 'by force commeth to the monarchy against the will of the people'; the second 'breaketh laws already made at his pleasure, maketh other without the advice of the people'; the third 'regardeth not the wealth of his people, but the advancement of himself, his faction, and kindred'. 'These definitions do contain three differences: the obtaining of the authority, the manner of administration thereof, and the but or mark whereunto it doth tend and shoot.'[72] Formally the Henrician regime was not a tyranny by any of these criteria. Henry's claim to the throne was not seriously disputed. He professed himself at all times concerned for the 'wealth of his people'. Laws were enacted through Parliament, and Parliament, it was claimed, represented the corporate identity of the people. Trials were conducted according to 'due process'. To that extent the claim that this was a 'constitutional monarchy' is justified. But it is necessary to look at the underlying reality. There can be little doubt that policy was conducted largely according to Henry's wishes, that those wishes were increasingly determined by mood-swings and that policy thereby depended on the outcome of a struggle by rival factions to activate one or other of the bundles of contradictory royal prejudices.[73] The fall of Cromwell is a

[70] Bush, *Pilgrimage*, 408–14; Roger Schofield, 'Taxation and the Political Limits of the Tudor State', in *Law and Government*, 227–55.

[71] 'Human Rights and the Liberties of Englishmen', *Studies* 4, 58–76, at 74.

[72] Sir Thomas Smith, *De Republica Anglorum*, ed. Mary Dewar (Cambridge, 1982), 53.

[73] 'Faction' has become a term of art. I share the multi-dimensional view of Tudor politics expounded by Steven Gunn, 'The Structure of Politics in Early Tudor England',

classic example of this process, as is the way in which the religious future of the country came to hang on the outcome of attempts to turn Henry against his current queen.[74] Henry's tendency to confound his wishes and the national good and to depict himself as the misunderstood servant of God merely exacerbated the personal nature of his rule.

Equally, constitutional forms were respected precisely because the responsiveness of courts and parliaments to royal pressure made them valuable instruments in the implementation of policy.[75] Again, for this reason, 'constitutional monarchy' means a good deal less than Elton implied. It is interesting that he came to measure Parliament's con-, tribution in terms of its 'constructive' role in the framing of legislation, and to scorn any 'critical' stance taken by MPs.[76] Similarly, he argued that the extension of the doctrine of treason was justified in order to bring treason trials more firmly into due process; in effect, by so broadening the definition of treason as to make it unnecessary for the crown to 'construct' a dubious case in order to bring it within the terms of the 1352 act.[77] Even if this special pleading were accepted, it would be undercut by the wholesale extension of attainder procedures in the thirties which made a mockery of any legal process and showed parliament to be the instrument of the royal will.[78] Professor Hurstfield's argument that due process is not incompatible with tyranny is surely correct.[79] It is impossible to abstract Henry VIII from the Henrician regime, to consider the mechanism of government without considering its purpose; and it is difficult not to see Henry's instincts as basically tyrannical. Curiously, with all Geoffrey Elton's contempt for Henry's

supra, 6th ser., V (1995), 59–90; i.e. I do not believe that Henry must necessarily be classified as either puppet or puppeteer, but rather that the relationships between king and his entourage were multi-dimensional and varied according to circumstances.

[74] 'Decline and Fall', *Studies* I, 189–230; it would be redundant to list the works of Lacey Baldwin Smith, J.J. Scarisbrick, E. W. Ives and David Starkey.

[75] Cf. Eric Ives, *The Common Lawyers of Pre-Reformation England* (Cambridge, 1983), 244–5; 'there was not the antithesis between "Tudor Despotism" and the rule of law and king-in-parliament which has sometimes been supposed; rather the royal will operated through due legal process and the "High Court of Parliament" ... The Tudor courts rendered the power of the crown legitimate.' I am grateful to Dr John Watts for reminding me of this passage. Elton himself could write that the Tudor monarchs, 'content with the reality of great political power, ... *never bothered* [my italics] to clothe it in a formal doctrine of absolutism'; *Constitution* (1982), 14. Since I accept that the forms of traditional government were respected, discussion of the allegedly despotic aims behind the Proclamations Act is not necessary here.

[76] *Parliament*, 22–4, 346–7, 378–9.

[77] *Policy and Police*, cap. 6, esp. 288–9.

[78] S. E. Lehmberg, 'Parliamentary Attainder in the Reign of Henry VIII', *Historical Journal*, 18 (1975), 675–702.

[79] Joel Hurstfield, 'Was there a Tudor Despotism after all?', *supra*, 5th ser., XVII (1967), 83–108; repr. in Hurstfield, *Freedom, Corruption and Government in Elizabethan England* (Cambridge, MA, 1973), 23–49.

personality, or perhaps because of that contempt, Henry features in his work primarily as a major irritant, likely (nowhere more obviously than in the fall of Cromwell) to upset the serious business of state-building. But Henry can hardly be relegated to the sidelines. The Cromwellian decade served to magnify, not to limit, his power. The 'consent' of his subjects was a means to that end.

PLACE AND PUBLIC FINANCE

By R. W. Hoyle

READ 27 MARCH 1996 AT THE INSTITUTE OF HISTORICAL RESEARCH LONDON

READING over Elton's work afresh now, sadly, there will be no more, prompts a series of reflections. It is a great body of writing both in quality and quantity: but it is extremely narrow. Elton wrote about a remarkably short time range to which he repeatedly returned. He had little patience with Wolsey, no great interest in the history of the 1540s or 1550s and his excursion into the history of Elizabeth's earlier parliaments was not one which evidently brought him much pleasure. His first book established the reputation of Thomas Cromwell: one of his last pieces of writing considered how much or how little his view of Cromwell had changed, and the very last piece to be published was a defence of Cromwell from modern claims of corruption.[1] It is hard to think of another major historian who has made so good a living from so short a temporal span. It is also striking how little of Elton's output is actually about politics: he was essentially a student of institutions and even ideas rather than of the interaction of men. His later interest in the law seems almost a rejection of politics.

There is, however, another defining absence in Elton's work which is for my purposes more significant. I think that I was aware of it over a long period, but it crystallized on reading a comment made by Professor Patrick Collinson in his Bindoff Lecture: 'Sir Geoffrey Elton had good English mud on his boots when cultivating the potatoes in his Cambridge garden, but not otherwise. He had no time (literally) for the countryside and almost never went there.'[2]

The observation I wish to make is not that Elton was not Hoskins, a historian with an equally distinguished and individual position and who did (notoriously) advise the historian to get mud on his boots, but rather that Elton was indifferent to place.[3] Politics, political institutions for Elton are not spatially rooted. They do not happen in a particular

---

[1] *Tudor Revolution: Thomas Cromwell (1991)*; 'How corrupt was Thomas Cromwell?', *Historical Journal* [hereafter *HJ*], 36 (1993).

[2] P. Collinson, *Tudor England Revisited* (Queen Mary and Westfield College, University of London, sixth annual Bindoff lecture, 1995), 22. I am grateful to Dr Steve Hindle for telling me of this and Professor Collinson for kindly sending me a copy. And I remain happy to be counted amongst Professor Collinson's friends (p. 3).

[3] When I remarked on this to my student Nigel Morgan, he immediately made the comparison with another, slightly older, emigree, Nikolaus Pevsner. Quite.

place. It is not simply that the corridors of power are not located in space, but that there is the assumption that what went on outside those corridors was an irrelevance to policy making and administration. One might go so far as to say that the issues on which Elton's work on the 1530s has been most revised most are issues of place. *Where* did Henrician politics happen; *where* did the privy council meet; *where* were the royal reserves held?

Unusually, perhaps less so for his generation than for those which followed, Elton never followed his subjects, not even Thomas Cromwell, into local society. There is no study by Elton akin to Collinson on Cranbrook.[4] It was Mary Robertson and not Elton who wrote about both Cromwell's estate building and the way in which he attempted to manage particular counties.[5]

On one of the few occasions when Elton did trespass into county society, one felt that his touch was far from sure. It seemed when Elton's essay on the Pilgrimage of Grace first appeared in 1978 that his grasp of the workings of local society was pretty slight. His analysis was mechanical and those below the status of gentry were automatons, capable of being led but never an independent force in their own right. (Elton wrote that he thought that Penry Williams made too much of disturbances in his *Tudor Regime* perhaps because he, Elton, saw disorder amongst the lower orders as being essentially directed by the gentry.[6] This point of view comes over very strongly in the Pilgrimage paper.) In a sense there is a disjunction between the rich culture of grudging and complaint discovered by Elton in *Policy and Police*, in which ordinary people show their appetite for political gossip (and their willingness to comment on what they heard), and his rejection of their capacity for independent political action as outlined in the Pilgrimage article.

The rejection of the local is perhaps most marked in *The English*. I am divided between regarding this as a rather slight pot-boiling study and a summation of his guiding beliefs.[7] *The English* starts not with an account of England as a geographical area, the southern part of one of two islands on the north-west edge of Europe, nor with comments on the orthodox divide between lowland and highland, North and South, English and

[4]P. Collinson, 'Cranbrook and the Fletchers: Popular and Unpopular Religion in the Kentish Weald', in *Reformation Principle and Practice*, ed. P. N. Brooks (1980).

[5]M. L. Robertson, 'Profit and Purpose in the Development of Thomas Cromwell's Landed Estates', *Journal of British Studies*, 29 (1990); ' "The Art of the Possible": Thomas Cromwell's Management of West Country Government', *HJ*, 32 (1989), and the debate, H. M. Speight, 'The Politics of Good Governance: Thomas Cromwell and the Government of the Southwest of England', and Robertson, 'A Reply to Helen Speight', *HJ*, 37 (1994).

[6]'Pilgrimage of Grace', *Studies* 3 (36); *English*, 120 n. 9.

[7]In another paper at the conference, Lewis Elton held that *The English* was one of Elton's most personal and heartfelt books so we must treat it seriously.

Celtic, but with the expansion of Wessex in 927. Throughout this book, Elton writes without reference to place: there is no shifting between the local and the national with the local illustrating the larger theme, nor any recognition of local characteristics, peculiarities or rivalries, even those between North and South. The much reproduced map of the medieval village of Boarstall in Buckinghamshire appears to illustrate the section on post-Black Death conditions in the countryside, but neither Boarstall nor any where else is discussed in the text and Boarstall itself is not flattered with an index entry.[8] The Eltonian approach is akin to that adopted by a generation of modern Economic Historians. The subject was England or France, the unit of account for which statistical sources survived. Within that unit, local variations in experience were at best uninteresting and at worst irrelevant.

This analogy brings me to Economic History and so step closer towards public finance. The breach between Elton and Economic History was well known at the time: it is part of his legacy that the breach, for early modernists, yet has to be healed. Elton published two shorter notes in *Economic History Review* early in his career and occasionally reviewed for them. The break between Elton's type of history and that which the *Review* espoused in the 1970s and 1980s is perhaps best illustrated by the fact that *Revolution Reassessed*, the patricidal volume edited by Coleman and Starkey, never received a mention in the *Review* where *The Tudor Revolution in Government* was treated at length. Indeed, I can find only one Elton student who has published in *Economic History Review* in the past twenty-five years. The alienation from, or perhaps increasing disinterest in, Economic History may also be illustrated by the failure of *Reform and Reformation* to contain the introductory surveys of economy and society which were otherwise obligatory to that series: and this compares with *England under the Tudors* which did start out with such a survey. And yet much of, say, *Reform and Renewal* is Economic History according to any broad church definition at which one might arrive. Again, the Eltonian concern with institutions and policy is very similar to that of some modern economic historians whose natural home is the files of the Treasury or the spending departments. What Elton would surely have deplored is those economic historians who, on the basis of a few widely scattered and suspect statistics of uncertain quality, can arrive at conclusions about such questions as agricultural or labour productivity by means which most us cannot follow.

There can be little doubt that Elton, in his writings at least, was not much interested in public finance in either the sense of the getting and

---

[8] Indeed, the illustrations are never referred to in the text: but they are of place and so quite alien to the approach of the text. Elton, in short, wrote an unillustrated book. The publishers' picture searcher did the rest, as indeed he acknowledges in the foreword.

spending of the state's income, or in the sense of the role of the state in the economy. His forte was the history of institutions and administration, many of which had financial responsibilities. We would probably recognise that on some important issues he was mistaken and his work has been justly revised. There was no revolution in government in the 1530s: government was, and remained much more medieval and personal than Elton ever allowed. In particular he underestimated the political and fiscal importance of the household. The revenue courts of the 1530s were of little long-term importance, although some of their working methods were incorporated into the refurbished Exchequer in 1552–4, and even the revenue courts were more personal and less bureaucratic in their management than might once have been allowed. I, for one, cannot accept the later Eltonian claim that there was a revolution in taxation in the 1530s.[9] Whether the notion of the peacetime subsidy is finally accepted or judged to be erroneous, there is a revealing point to be made about the quite distinct approaches which Elton and I have taken to the issue. For Elton, the issues concern constitutional precedent. His natural sources are the preambles to the statutes, the declarations whereby government made the nation aware of its intentions. For Elton the questions are about the establishment of new precedent and the refurbishment of old, where for me they are much more about money, receipts and expenditures; and politics. The difference in emphasis is extremely important.

The total achievement of Elton and his students, David Starkey, Christopher Coleman and J. D. Alsop amongst others, is that we now understand, with greater clarity than was ever possible before, how the administrative systems before, during and after the 1530s worked. That is that we know a great deal about the channels down which the crown's money passed, but we still know relatively little about how much money, about its sources or expenditure. Of course, in revealing to us where the king's reserves were held and in whose custody, Starkey in particular has shown the way in which no balance sheet can be made; for the records do not survive.[10] Hence the debate about the degree to which the attack on the church in 1531–2 was driven by immediate financial need will never be resolved with certainty.[11] The

---

[9] 'Taxation', *Studies* 3, which was followed by a critique by Dr Harriss and further articles by Dr Alsop and Dr Harriss. R. W. Hoyle 'Crown, Parliament and Taxation in Sixteenth-Century England', *English Historical Review* [hereafter *EHR*], 109 (1994), is merely the latest (and doubtless not the last).

[10] D. Starkey, 'Court and Government', in *Revolution Reassessed. Revisions in the History of Tudor Government and Administration*, ed. C. Coleman and D. Starkey (1986), 37–46.

[11] J. Guy, 'Henry VIII and the Praemunire Manoeuvres of 1530–1', *EHR*, 97 (1982); G. W. Bernard, 'The Pardon of the Clergy Reconsidered', *Journal of Ecclesiastical History*, 37 (1986).

irony, as Elton himself pointed out, is that throughout Henry's reign the Exchequer was keeping full records which survive perfectly but was receiving only the residual crown income, whilst the institutions which mattered, notably the privy purse, were keeping only slight records which for the most part are lost.[12] That said, there has been a disinterest until recently in working out even in round terms how much was received and how much was spent, and in the light of that knowledge, pondering the role which crown finance played in the determination of policy.

Every generation though reinvents History, and it is a pleasure to report that the work of reinvention is going on apace. There is firstly the work of the European Science Foundation on the 'Origins of the modern state in Europe', the first volume of which has recently appeared.[13] O'Brien and Hunt have outlined the 'rise of a fiscal state in England' over the long period 1485–1815.[14] Amongst English early modernists a great deal of work is in progress which is decidely un-Eltonian in its approach. It is concerned with money, often with the payment of money, often unwillingly, by the taxpayer in the counties and the difficulty which the crown and its local servants found in raising that money from taxpayers who, not unreasonably, preferred it to stay in their pockets. Gunn has now published a general account of crown finance in the early sixteenth century whilst I have offered a series of estimates of the cost of war in the reign of Henry VIII together with some comments on how war was funded.[15] For the later sixteenth and early seventeenth centuries, I and others have described the declining fortunes of the crown lands and Dr Braddick has outlined the practical workings of taxation at the local level.[16] Dr Bernard has published an account of the Amicable Grant which spans foreign policy, government policy and the implementation of that ultimately abortive attempt to raise money.[17] Dr Bush has added a whole dimension to our understanding of taxation by suggesting that it could be violently resisted.[18] And there is the assumption that corporate poverty was a significant factor in determining policy. It was a theme of the *Estates of the English Crown, 1558–1640*. It is very marked in Dr Adams's recent

[12] Elton, *England, 1200–1640* (1969), 50.
[13] R. Bonney, ed., *Economic Systems and State Finance* (1995).
[14] P. K. Brien and P. A. Hunt, 'The Rise of a Fiscal State in England, 1485–1815', *Historical Research*, 66 (1993).
[15] S. J. Gunn, *Early Tudor Government, 1485–1558* (1995), ch. 3; R. W. Hoyle, 'War and Public Finance', in *The Reign of Henry VIII*, ed. D. MacCulloch (1995).
[16] R. W. Hoyle, ed., *The Estates of the English Crown, 1558–1640* (1992); M. J. Braddick, *Parliamentary Taxation in Seventeenth-Century England* (1994).
[17] G. W. Bernard, *War, Taxation and Rebellion in Early Modern England. Henry VIII, Wolsey and the Amicable Grant of 1525* (1986).
[18] M. L. Bush, 'Tax Reform and Rebellion in Early Modern England', *History*, 76 (1991).

account of patronage in the reign of Elizabeth.[19] But there are still large areas of which we are ignorant. There are, for instance, no modern studies of the the crown lands in the reign of Henry VIII or the customs in the sixteenth century generally. Even though Professor Russell admits 'The Poverty of the Crown' to be amongst the causes of the English Civil War, the modern study of the financial history of the early Stuarts has hardly begun.[20]

For these, and for too many other matters, one is still obliged to turn to F. C. Dietz's two volumes first published in 1921 and 1932.[21] Dietz represents the alternative economic and empirical tradition of writing about public finance. Dietz is often criticised for error, for looking at the wrong documents, for relying too much on contemporary digests. All this is doubtless true. But it would be remiss not to reflect on the magnitude of his achievement, all the more so for an American historian who spent relatively little time in the English archives. The aim for the next generation must surely be to prepare a new Dietz, a new study of public finance between 1500 and 1640.

This raises the question of what such a book would look like. I would suggest that it would be the work of a group of individuals rather than the lone scholar, itself a rejection of an Eltonian approach to history writing. Secondly, it would contain a mass of tabulated data. The advent of cheap and portable computing power makes it possible to reaudit the surviving accounts at least selectively and so achieve an understanding of the dynamics of public finance which was beyond the reach of contemporaries—or, indeed, Elton's generation.

What of content? First, it would be much less about institutions and much more about the individuals who formulated policy. Indeed, one of the matters that will have to be explained is a negative: why in the first half of the sixteenth century financial institutions could be created and dismembered with some ease, but the situation as it existed in 1558 remained substantially the *status quo* until 1640.[22] The institutions are merely the pipes and vessels through which the crown's finances flowed.

---

[19] S. Adams, 'The Patronage of the Crown in Elizabethan Politics: The 1590s in Perspective', in *The reign of Elizabeth I. Court and Culture in the Last Decade*, ed. J. Guy (1995).

[20] C. Russell, *The Causes of the English Civil War* (1990), ch. 7, but see the accounts in R. Cust, *The Forced Loan and English Politics, 1626–1628* (1987), K. Sharpe, *The Personal Rule of Charles I* (1992), ch. 3, and M. C. Fissel, *The Bishops' Wars. Charles I's Campaigns against Scotland, 1638–1640* (1994).

[21] F. C. Dietz, *English Government Finance, 1485–1558*, University of Illinois, Studies in the Social Sciences, ix (1920) and *English Public Finance, 1558–1641* (1932), both reprinted as *English Public Finance, 1485–1641* (2 vols., 1964).

[22] This is not merely a matter which affects the financial organs of government. Who, in 1537, would have supposed that the Councils in the North and Wales would survive until after 1640?

A thorough understanding of their procedures and records is vital: but the key to public finance lies elsewhere.

Secondly, a new account must pay much more attention to the cost of Ireland to the Exchequer. It is a relatively simple matter to use the materials presented by Dietz and the full tabulation of Exchequer transfers to Ireland compiled by Dr Sheehan to calculate, in rough and ready terms, what Ireland cost the Exchequer. The figures are presented in summary form in table 1.[23] Over the reign of Elizabeth, so far as can be ascertained, 8 per cent of the receipts of the Exchequer were directly transfered to the Irish Treasurer for War. In 1599 and 1600, at the height of the conquest of Ulster, the figure was around 30 per cent in years when the Exchequer was awash with taxation and land sale revenues. Overall, there were eight years when 20 per cent or more of the Exchequer's income was transferred. Put another way, Ireland cost nearly twice as much as the income from land sales; it cost approximately three-quarters of the sum raised by lay taxation. Overall, 45 per cent of the income raised by sales of land and lay and clerical taxation was spent on the Irish wars.

Thirdly, the revised Dietz must contain an account of how government did—or did not—cope with inflation. As inflation seems to hold the key to many characteristics of late sixteenth-century government, it is with the consequences of inflation for public finance that the rest of this paper is concerned.[24] There has long been an appreciation of the slow rise in prices produced by the rising demand for agricultural produce in the sixteenth century and the increased circulation of precious metals within Europe following upon the discovery of the Americas. Sixteenth-century historians have been aware, since the later 1960s, of the severity of monetary debasement in the middle and later 1540s. The basic consequence of debasement is that it roughly halved all fixed incomes within less than a decade. Of course those who traded in current prices, for instance merchants or farmers, could outride the dangers of this relatively readily. Likewise those who held bullion. For landowners it was a disaster. Inflation undermined all landed wealth. Landlords needed to claw back their real income. At the moment it appears that there was probably a generation's delay before they learnt how to do so. One way was to raise fines on customary lands or, even better, convert customary tenancies into leaseholds. Another was to increase rentals through sponsoring the enclosure of common and so

[23] F. C. Dietz, 'The Exchequer in Elizabeth's reign', *Smith College Studies in History*, 8 (2) (1923), 80–90; A. Sheehan, 'Irish Revenues and English Subventions, 1559–1622', in *Proc. Royal Irish Academy*, 90C(2) (1990).
[24] The fullest account of the consequences (as opposed to the causes) of inflation is D. M. Palliser, *The Age of Elizabeth. England under the Later Tudors, 1547–1603* (2nd edn, 1992), 173–86.

Table One   The income of the Elizabethan Exchequer and the cost of Ireland compared

	Exchequer receipts	Land sales	Lay taxation	Clerical subsides	Clerical benevolence	Extra-ordinary income	Ordinary income	Exchequer payments to Ireland	Payments as % of total receipts	Payments as % of extra-ordinary income
1559–63	1,627,333	374,104	285,228	32,822		692,154	935,180	54,938	3.3	7.8
1564–68	985,129	43,272	221,990	23,938		254,822	730,307	129,872	13.2	51.0
1569–73	996,439	9,293	210,412	33,695		253,400	742,039	104,903	10.5	41.4
1574–78	993,301	8,021	170,363	16,208		194,592	738,709	115,815	12.4	59.5
1579–83	1,082,559	685	165,816	29,171		195,672	886,887	226,583	20.9	115.8
1584–88	1,299,431	3,691	232,130	37,128	5,305	278,254	1,021,186	198,840	15.3	71.5
1589–93	1,850,821	127,941	381,141	49,180	9,749	568,011	1,282,811	106,248	5.7	18.7
1594–98	2,136,558	3,799	470,533	76,703		551,035	1,585,523	304,771	14.3	55.3
1599–1603	2,464,428	367,701	341,551	71,597		780,849	1,683,579	448,816	18.2	57.5
TOTAL										
1559–1603	13,435,999	938,507	2,479,164	370,442	15,054	3,768,789	9,606,221	1,689,886	7.95	44.8

Notes

1. The table summarizes a larger table calculated on an annual basis. All values are sterling and were entered to the nearest pound. The table is provided for illustrative purposes only: as the following notes suggest, the figures are neither exact nor accurate to the last pound.

2. For some years Dietz gives no or only partial figures. For 1561 he provides only a gross total of receipts. The figures for 1559–63 are therefore for the four years 1559–60 and 1562–3. Likewise there are no figures for 1574: 1574–88 is actually 1575–8 (four years).

3. Dietz only gives receipts at the Exchequer. On three occasions (the land sale commissions of 1561, 1563 and 1589), the proceeds of sales were held by a Treasurer appointed for that purpose. Their receipts, taken from Dietz, *English Public Finance 1558–1603*, pp. 19, 63–4, have been added to Exchequer receipts as follows: 1559–63, £176,643, 1589–93, £126,305. The figure for land sales in the reign of Elizabeth which I gave in *The Estates of the English Crown 1558–1640*, table 1.2, £816,439, is £122,068 less than the figure in this table. The method of calculation is quite different and the major disparity seems to lie in the figures for the first quinquennium. I am at a loss to know why.

4. The method employed to calculate the table was to take Dietz's figure for total receipts (column 1), to extract from his tables the values for land sales (col. 2), lay taxation (col. 3), clerical subsidies (col. 4) and clerical benevolences (col. 5) which were then summed to form the figure for extraordinary income (col. 6). This was then subtracted from the receipts to produce 'ordinary income' (col. 7). Exchequer payments were taken from Sheehan.

5. Forced loans are regarded as being fiscally neutral in the medium term and, for simplicity's sake, are disregarded.

Source: based on figures provided by F. C. Dietz, 'The Exchequer in Elizabeth's Reign', *Smith College Studies in History*, 8 (2), (1923), 80–9 (columns 1–7), and Anthony Sheehan, 'Irish Revenues and English Subventions, 1559–1622', *Proc. Royal Irish Academy*, 90C(2) (1990), table 2 (i). Further, relatively minor payments itemized in Sheehan's tables (ii) and (iii) are not included.

extend the cultivated area. In order to bring either of these to pass, it was necessary to develop a new range of management techniques which necessitated the making of accurate measurements and valuations of land. The development of estate surveying in England is not simply about the transfer of techniques from military to civilian uses: it is, most importantly, a delayed response to the undermining of landed income.[25] The surveyor, represented most obviously by the self-advertising John Norden, was the company doctor and management consultant of the late sixteenth and early seventeenth centuries. From the point of view of the economic historian, there is nothing at all surprising about a crisis in landed fortunes in the later sixteenth century.

Both Elton's generation and those succeeding have been slow to integrate the experience of debasement into their view of the sixteenth century. The Phelps Brown–Hopkins index of 1956 had drawn the outline graph of price movements. Kerridge, earlier in the decade, had shown the upward in trend in rents on a number of estates in the sixteenth century.[26] But when Stone contributed a new introduction to Tawney's *Agrarian Problem in the Sixteenth Century* in 1967 (just at the moment when Challis was publishing his early work), he saw the new awareness of 'demographic growth as a destabilising factor' as altering Tawney's conclusions and went on to state that 'Demographic growth outpacing agricultural output pushed up the price of food and fuel far beyond those for industrial goods or wages.' 'The rise in prices [was] caused mostly by demographic pressure but aided by the influx of bullion and by monetary inflation.'[27] Hoskins's *The Age of Plunder* (1976), a work deeply hostile to Henry VIII, makes scant reference to debasement even though he would have enjoyed arguing that not even the currency was safe from Henry's rapacity. Elton himself, writing in the mid-1970s, appreciated the background increase in prices but was quick to seise upon the deleterious effects of debasement upon prices and exports. He recognised clearly enough that 'from this time it became unwise to depend on any sort of fixed income, whether wages, salaries or rents'. (He also saw the rise in prices as stimulating capitalist

[25] As indeed Stone recognised in 1967, 'Introduction', xv. For the most recent account of the origins of estate surveying, P. D. A. Harvey, 'English Estate Maps, their Early History and their Use as Historical Evidence', in *Rural Images. Estate Maps in the Old World and the New*, ed. D. Buisseret (1996).

[26] E. W. J. Kerridge, 'The Movement of Rent, 1540–1640', *Economic History Review*, 2nd ser., 6 (1953).

[27] L. Stone, 'Introduction to the Torchbook Edition', in R. H. Tawney, *The Agrarian Problem in the Sixteenth Century* (1912; repr. 1967), xi. When Stone considered the problem of government insolvency in his *The Causes of the English Revolution, 1529–1642* (1972), 60–2, he made no reference to inflation, stressing instead the failure to retain the monastic lands.

activity and social mobility but this is by the way.)[28] What Elton did not do was appreciate the consequences of inflation on public finance: it does not appear in his list of the legacies of the fag end of Henry's reign, nor does Elton appear to discuss it anywhere else.[29]

Elton's warning of the dangers of living on fixed income applied to the crown more than anyone else. The Doctor in *The Discourse of the Common Weal* realised this in 1549: the King would be squeezed between the declining value of his incomes and the need to buy munitions abroad in current prices.[30] The crown was slow to respond to the problems which inflation made for its landed estates. There was no attempt to increase rents when leases came up for renewal and in this important respect, the Courts of Augmentations and the Exchequer compare very poorly with the Duchy of Lancaster in the reign of Henry VII. Surveyors, in the sense of individuals who measured and valued lands, were employed on the estates from after 1598, but too late. Of course, the declining number of monastic pensions and annuities, responsibility for whose payment the crown had accepted at the Dissolution, did make for an upward increase in income received at the Exchequer;[31] but this misses the crucial point that the Elizabethan Privy Council had no answer to the problem of inflation as such and was frequently hostile to those who, through oppression, bullying and sharp practice, did see the need to increase income.[32]

The only area in which the crown undertook a revision of its income was customs. The issuing of the new Book of Rates in 1558 needs no further discussion (though one might notice that this remained in force for forty-six years). The *Valor Ecclesiasticus* was never revised to take account of post-inflationary clerical incomes: the incomes finally assigned to Queen Anne's Bounty in 1704 were in 1535 prices. Worse still, the government completely lost its grip on those areas of its income which should have adjusted automatically with the level of prices. That the valuations of land in Inquisitions Post Mortem remain fixed at pre-1543 prices in the short term may reasonably be explained by the general short-term inflexibility in rents. When the same price scale continued to be used in the early seventeenth century, then we may suspect fraud—or custom. By Charles I's reign the Court of Wards

---

[28] *Reform and Reformation*, 315.

[29] *Ibid.*, 316.

[30] *The Discourse of the Common Weal of England*, ed., E. Lamont (1893), pp. 34–5. Amongst modern writers, Palliser, in *The Age of Elizabeth*, sees Smith's fears for the crown as 'vindicated', 176.

[31] Hoyle, 'Introduction', to Hoyle, *Estates of the English Crown*, 12–13, 35.

[32] See, for instance, S. E. Kershaw, 'Power and Duty in the Elizabethan Aristocracy: George, Earl of Shrewsbury, the Glossopdale Dispute and the Council', in *The Tudor Nobility*, ed. G. W. Bernard, (1992).

automatically assumed that all estate valuations returned to it were described at a tenth of their true value.[33] Subsidy valuations on goods (but not lands) should have adjusted in line with inflation—they were a proportion of the assessed value—but they did not, and in the absence of any sanction against fraud, both the inquisitions and the subsidy became an increasing travesty as the century progressed.

Any new Dietz then needs to be informed by the notion that Henry VIII's debasement (which accelerated an underlying inflation) was a defining moment in the sixteenth century. It completely knocked the bottom out of landed incomes and provided a challenge to landowners which most declined to accept for a generation and the crown for rather longer. The penalty for not addressing inflation was, quite simply, the corporate poverty of the later sixteenth century. This can be seen, for instance, in the management of the household. Whilst the financial history of the Elizabethan household remains to be written, it is clear that the salaries of servants went unamended and forced them to supplement their salaries by embezzlement. Sir James Croft wrote that as the queen would not raise the wages of her servants, they were 'driven out of necessity to make spoil of as much as they can embezzle'.[34] On the other hand, if the costs of the household as an employer could to some degree be controlled, its charges as a purchaser of foodstuffs, manufactured products and services inevitably rose. The Elizabethan instinct, or rather the Burghleian instinct, was to control the problem of rising costs in the household by a policy of extreme economy. As early as 1563 an enquiry into rising expenditures was under way. In 1577 after a series of progresses of great duration, Burghley drew up regulations to reduce costs by avoiding waste. The aim was to keep the budget within £40,000 per annum. Burghley went so far as to propose that the progress be abandoned for a saving of £2,000 per annum. In fact a digest of earlier accounts prepared for Burghley showed that Edward VI's household expenses varied between £46,500 and £65,953 and Mary's from £47,552 to £75,044. Elizabeth's own charges had reached £59,881 in one year, but this was an extreme, and Burghley's cost cutting must surely illustrate the degree to which the Elizabethan court was impoverished by trying to exist with a budget which would have been tight by the prices of the 1540s.[35]

The failure may also be seen in the crown's increasing inability to

[33] Russell, *Causes of the English Civil War*, 173.

[34] Dietz, *English Public Finance 1558–1640*, 418. Dr Adams thinks that only the yeoman of the Guard and the Stable staff received increases; S. Adams, ' "Eliza enthroned"? The Court and its Politics', in *The Reign of Elizabeth I*, ed. C. Haigh (1984), 55.

[35] M. Cole, 'The Royal Travel. Elizabethan Progresses and their Role in Government' (PhD thesis, University of Virginia, 1985), 126–8, and the helpful comments in Adams, ' "Eliza Enthroned"?', 56–9.

offer a reasonable level of reward to its servants and the increasingly bizarre forms which its gifts and grants took. These finally came to be more a licence to exploit the nation through monopolies or to compound with individuals through grants in reversion rather than gifts which had an immediate cash value to the grantee or cost to the crown.[36] On the other hand, the forms that these concessions took often had the effect of inviting individuals to modernise aspects of the crown's affairs whilst allowing the crown to keep its distance from unpopular initiatives. This can be seen in the way in which crown lands might be exchanged at low valuations, their rents and fines raised and then the same lands reconveyed to the crown.[37] The farming of customs may be seen in a similar light. The customary and corrupt practices of the existing customs officials were eradicated by bringing in new officials responsible to farmers whose own self-interest was linked to their financial success.[38] Of course, the costs of modernization in terms of time and the employment of professionals was probably large and the whole process distasteful to those who wished to be seen to be whiter than white. And consequently, much of the profit stuck to those willing to court unpopularity by bullying or evicting tenants or keeping a more watchful eye over trade. Likewise, there was a tolerance of petty corruption amongst the crown's officers: private negotiation for favours and access, the raking off of a percentage of every transaction (seen most clearly in the dealings of the Court of Wards with suitors) was the necessary price of an inability to adjust income and salaries in line with inflation.

It might also be suggested that the poverty of government was an important factor in determining the character and shape of mid-sixteenth-century Irish history. However little agreement there is amongst Irish historians, there is a consensus that the English government's policy towards Ireland was driven by parsimony. One observer of Irish affairs estimated that the English had spent £1.3m on Ireland between 1534 and 1572 upon which Canny comments that 'all in England were worried at the enormous and increasing expense and experimented with different policies in the hope that these would reduce the cost of Ireland to the English Crown' whilst Dr Brady refers to 'the basic desideratum of all Tudor governments in their dealings with Ireland: that of defending England's interests in the island in the cheapest possible manner'.[39] An account of sixteenth-century Irish

---

[36] Adams, 'The Patronage of the Crown in Elizabethan politics'.

[37] D. L. Thomas, 'The Elizabethan Crown Lands, their Purposes and Problems', in *Estates of the English Crown*, ed. Hoyle, 80–1.

[38] Dietz, *English Public Finance 1558–1640*, ch. 14.

[39] Nicholas Canny, *The Elizabethan Conquest of Ireland. A Pattern Established, 1565–1576* (1976), 32; Ciaran Brady, *The Chief Governors. The Rise and Fall of Reform Government in Tudor Ireland, 1536–1588* (1994), 16.

history seen through the eyes of the English Exchequer has, however, still to be written. It is clear enough though that the programmes which incoming lord deputies negotiated with Elizabeth were, in effect, fixed cost contracts for the delivery of Irish government. During the process of negotiation, proposals might be trimmed. A plan in 1568 to establish fourteen garrisons in Ulster eventually emerged as a plan for three (which were never built). Where there was a competition for the lord deputyship as in 1574–5, the contenders might undercut each other to try and secure the office.[40] And the vain hope of saving money encouraged a flirtation with joint-stock company colonization in the early 1570s.[41]

Having committed themselves to governing within a fixed budget (albeit relying on supplies of specie which might not arrive on time[42]) successive lord deputies were forced either to run up debts because of the inadequacy of their subventions, to establish instruments of government which were self-financing or to place an increasing part of the costs of government on the inhabitants of the Pale. Here it is noticeable that lord deputies repeatedly used the one means to raise income from which domestic Elizabethan government recoiled: they exploited the prerogative. The 'Cess' was purveyance and much more: it developed quickly after mid-century into a general obligation to victual and billet the military establishment of the Pale. Cessing grew with the increased number of troops stationed in Ireland from the 1560s: but it also altered from being an occasional levy to a continuous imposition. The burden of the cess and doubts about its legality forced the community of the Pale into first opposition and then rebellion.[43]

Any yet at the same time as the Elizabethan government was trying to avoid living beyond its means by economies, the Exchequer was running a surplus which had reached £270,000 by mid-1585. This, though impressive, was marginal to government spending, forming only 4.5 per cent of all income in the first twenty-seven years of the reign. The surplus was only achieved by intermittent land sales and the raising of subsidies. (Here it might be noticed that taxation, lay and clerical, formed 20 per cent of all income in 1558–85 and land sales 7.2 per cent or rather more than the accumulated surplus.) Although Mildmay could offer a self-satisfied account of the state of the crown's finances to Parliament in 1576, it remains the case that Elizabeth did not ride out the consequences of inflation even with economies in spending

[40] Canny, *Conquest of Ireland*, 63–4, 76; Brady, *Chief Governors*, 144–6.

[41] Canny, *Elizabethan Conquest*, ch. 4 esp. 86–8.

[42] Brady, *Chief Governors*, 233

[43] For the Cess, the fullest account is Brady, *Chief Governors*, ch. 6. Brady's 'Conservative Subversives: The Community of the Pale and the Dublin Administration, 1556–86', in *Radicals, Rebels and Establishments*, ed. P.J. Corish (1985), remains useful.

without land sales and taxation. Moreover, the policy of economy was self-defeating and stored up horrors for the future. If the inadequacy of the funding for Ireland led to the undermining of the English interest in Ireland and a major revolt, then we might reasonably suppose that the policy of economy did not, in the long term, deliver economies. Likewise the whole approach of Elizabethan government to finance persuaded the English that they could have their government and foreign policy on the cheap. It was a view from which the early Stuarts failed to wean the English: the Civil War may reasonably be seen as a belated exercise in public education as to what government and especially war really cost.

The central issue for late sixteenth-century government was how to return the real income of the crown to its value pre-debasement. It failed to do so, perhaps never tried to do so. The problem could be resolved by raising rents and taxes to new, more realistic values or, alternatively, the establishment of new forms of taxation. The last was not attempted within England although there may be more to be said about the enlargement of purveyance which may, in a small sense, mirror the cess. The raising of rents was problematic given the contractural obligations which bound the crown, in common with all landowners, to their tenants. The subsidy presented other problems.[44] In essence the valuations for the subsidy continued to be made in pre-debasement prices. The crown's answer to this was to increase the rate at which the subsidy was levied: in response the individual valuations tumbled and the crown tried to rescue something by asking for 'repeater' subsidies. There was no attempt to make assessments reflect post-inflation values. After 1563, as the result of a move in the House of Commons, the subsidy valuations were not even made on oath. In 1576, in his address to the commons on the subject of the queen's finances, Mildmay admitted that the 'taxation of subsidies' was 'favourable', 'whereby far less cometh to Her Majesty's coffers than by the law is granted, a matter now drawn to be so usual as is hard to be reformed'.[45]

The performance of the subsidy under Elizabeth was lamentable compared to that of the early sixteenth century. In the 1520s in particular, the subsidy was levied with great thoroughness. The four subsidies granted in 1523, of which the last two were levied only on richer taxpayers, brought in £155,518. The four granted in 1601 raised in the order of £290,000 or an increase of 86 per cent: but the price of foodstuffs had more than trebled between the 1520s and the first

---

[44] For these, see Braddick, *Parliamentary Taxation*, ch. 2, and a forthcoming paper of mine, 'Political Society and the Failure of the Subsidy in Tudor England'.

[45] *Proceedings in the Parliaments of Elizabeth I*, ed. T. E. Hartley, I (1981), p. 443.

decade of the seventeenth century.[46] In Norfolk, the first two subsidies granted in 1523 generated £7,740: the four granted in 1601 £10,426 or only a third more.[47] As Dr Braddick has argued, the failure of the subsidy placed a new emphasis on that reliable old dog, the fifteenth.[48]

It may be helpful to compare the income received from the subsidy and land sales in the difficult conditions of the 1590s and the first years of the new century. In the nine years 1595–1603 sales produced £388,028 and the subsidy £561,190 or 70 per cent more.[49] That is to say that a doubling of the income from the subsidy would have more than obviated the need to sell lands. This would probably have implied more than doubling the number of taxpayers given that a majority of the relatively wealthy were already taxed and those householders who were omitted were of middling or smaller wealth. Hence to raise the yield of the subsidy to this degree would have required an enormous administrative effort and the breaking of those locally understood systems of rotation (where individuals appeared only occasionally) and 'bearing' (where those named in the subsidy spread their assessment over others unnamed). On the other hand, it is clear that only a minority of the householders paid the subsidy in any one year and far fewer than paid the fifteenth, poor rates or other locally administered taxes.[50] There was certainly no shortage of individuals who could reasonably appear in the subsidy.

A historian of France might extrapolate from the conventional wisdom current there: that the crown lost a struggle with the landowners for peasant rent.[51] Such an explanation fails to fit the chronology of decline. Rather it is instructive to compare the approach of the two Henrys with that of Elizabeth. Following on Dr Bush's work, we now appreciate that taxation prompted more disorder before 1536 (arguably the last great taxation revolt) than we appreciated. The two Henrys were prepared to risk disorder to secure taxation, perhaps most extremely in

[46] For the income from the 1523 subsidy, Hoyle, 'War and Public Finance', the figure being taken from Dr R. S. Schofield's unpublished thesis. The only available figures for the value of Elizabethan subsidies derive ultimately from a Jacobean compilation which gives consolidated figures for the subsidies and fifteenths granted statute by statute, Public Record Office, SP14/37 no. 38. The figures given here deduct the fifteenth at a rate of £29,000. Palliser, *The Age of Elizabeth*, table 5.2 after Phelps Brown and Hopkins.

[47] 1524–5, figures taken from J. Sheail, 'The Regional Distribution of Wealth in England as Indicated in the 1524/5 Lay Subsidy Returns' (PhD thesis, University of London, 1967), those for 1601 calculated from Braddick, *Parliamentary Taxation*, app. 3.

[48] Braddick, *Parliamentary Taxation*, 62.

[49] Figures calculated from Dietz, 'The Exchequer in Elizabeth's Reign', 87–9.

[50] I will offer examples in Hoyle, 'Political Society and the Failure of the Subsidy in Tudor England'.

[51] See for instance the analysis of J. B. Collins, *Fiscal Limits of Absolutism. Direct Taxation in Early Seventeenth-Century France* (1988), 200–13.

Henry VIII's desperate attempt to raise money in 1525. Public opinion was mobilised through information about the king's needs being disseminated through the subsidy preamble: in 1525 the chosen instrument was the royal briefing transmitted through personal interviews held in the shires.[52] The role of the nobility or the Gentlemen of the Privy Chamber in the assessing of taxation remains unexplored, but when the marquess of Dorset is found dealing wth Coventry over the forced loan in 1523, we may suspect that they had some supervisory role and were charged to represent the royal interest. Likewise Wolsey appears to have dealt direct with the City of London.[53] And, in 1525 at least, the earls of Norfolk and Suffolk were prepared to put on a show of force to encourage payment.[54] The early Tudors were plainly not deterred by minor risings and footdragging: their successors apparently were. The sequence of revolts between 1536 and 1570 offered the lesson to those who lived through them that the loyalty of the population at large to the government could not be relied upon. There was therefore a need to tread carefully in placing impositions upon them least disorder resulted. Again, Sir Thomas Smith's Doctor was the first to articulate the need for caution: 'and yet that way of gathering treasure is not always the most safe for the prince's surety: for we see many times the profits of such subsidies spent in appeasing of the people who are moved to sedition partly by occasion of the same'.[55] In 1586, Sir Francis Walsingham urged Sir John Perrot not to introduce a more efficient system of taxation in Ireland 'least it should breed a general discontent throughout the whole realm [of Ireland] as it hath often times fallen out here in this realm that like charges laid upon our people bred very dangerous tumults'.[56] In 1598 Burghley urged that a peace with Spain was preferable to continued heavy taxation because of the danger of rebellion.[57] And additional similar musings could be offered. The early Tudors recognised that the co-operation of the lower orders could not be relied upon: they needed to be manipulated, cajoled and persuaded not only by the gentry but by central government itself working through the gentry. Before 1547 there was a willingness to chance all to win all: after 1558 nothing was ventured and nothing gained.

[52] For the use of subsidy preambles, Hoyle, 'Crown, Parliament and Taxation', 1179–80, 1187–96; for the royal briefing, G. W. Bernard and R. W. Hoyle, 'The Instructions for the Levying of the Amicable Grant, March 1525', *Historical Research*, 67 (1994), 193–4, and local interviews, Bernard, *War, Taxation and Rebellion*, 76–8.

[53] C. Phythian-Adams, *Desolation of a City. Coventry and the Urban Crisis of the Late Middle Ages* (1979), 62; Hall, *Chronicle*, p. 645.

[54] Bernard, *War, Taxation and Rebellion*, 76–83.

[55] *Discourse*, ed. Lamont, 35.

[56] *CSPD Ireland, 1586–8*, 35.

[57] W. Camden, *A History of the Most Renowned and Victorious Princess Elizabeth* (1675 edn), p. 555.

What we see under Elizabeth is a rejection of the type of high pressure techniques of expropriation employed in early seventeenth-century France. Taxation was not backed by threat or actual force. The subsidy was self-regulating with townships contributing no more than their individual taxpayers were willing or able to pay. In contrast, the French practice was to levy centrally decided quotas. The English system may have served to keep yields low; but this essentially voluntary (if not consensual) approach also meant that the costs of collection were minimal and little was siphoned off into the hands of local officeholders. By comparison, French troops sent to enforce collection often took what they collected in their own costs and wages.[58] But there is also little sign that the Elizabethans employed the methods of public education used by Henry VIII—whether the subsidy preambles or the local briefings in which the king's needs were outlined to doubtless reluctant taxpayers. It may be that a protracted phoney war with Spain and a grumbling civil war in Ireland (if so the subjugation may be called) were not flags to which the English would rally.[59] And there are some examples from later in the century of the subsidy commissioners taking the side of the taxpayer against the privy council.[60] Part of the difficulty might be that the crown had allowed the affinity described by Professor Guy for the 1520s to atrophy, part that only a limited range of the nobility and gentry had contact with an inward looking and attenuated court which offered little in the way of reward.[61] Hence the Elizabethan regime was decidely a low pressure one. It made as little effort to peer into men's accounts and pocketbooks as it did into their hearts and consciences over religion. And possibly for the same reason: was it considered too dangerous for a regime riddled with insecurities and which, because of the problem of the succession, probably never felt that its perpetuation was guaranteed? It was also tempted by the easy option of making up the shortfall by selling lands.[62] In the process of doing so it lost control (in a fiscal sense) over town and countryside.[63] Fiscal information about individuals had been

[58] See the examples cited by Collins, *Fiscal Limits of Absolutism*, 203.

[59] For a discussion of the educative value of the preambles, Hoyle, 'Crown, Parliament and Taxation'.

[60] I intend to discuss this in the forthcoming paper, 'Political Society and the Failure of the Subsidy in Tudor England'.

[61] John Guy, 'Thomas Wolsey, Thomas Cromwell and the Reform of Henrician Government', in *Reign of Henry VIII*, ed. MacCulloch, 53–7; Adams, ' "Eliza Enthroned"?', esp. 68–71.

[62] Although the significance of this should not be over stressed. Land sales from the reign amounted to only 27 per cent of income from taxation making the point that even a failing taxation system could produce much more for the crown than a resort to capital sales.

[63] That is that power flowed back to the parish or village community. For this approach,

obtained by the Exchequer only in 1522 and then by guile. The subsidy stature of 1523 had laid down that lists of taxpayers were to be supplied and, with some misunderstanding of the requirement (or footdragging), this was done. The subsidy lists supplied subsequently formed the basis of demands for prerogative taxes and loans.[64] This was information which Elizabeth no longer possessed in anything akin to an accurate form. She could not demand broadly based forced loans (as in 1522–3 or 1544) or benevolences (as in 1545) because she no longer knew who to ask or for how much. Likewise fraud and underassessment became endemic in the surveys made for the Court of Wards and perhaps also in the customs. Income suffered; but there was no determination to reverse the situation.

Inflation undermined income. Government largely created but had no response to the devaluation of its revenue. The inability of the crown to secure accurate returns of its entitlements from its own officers precluded it from clawing back its losses from inflation. Its failure to discipline them allowed its income to atrophy yet further, a process seen with greatest clarity in the decline of the subsidy. And in some areas at least, the failure of income coloured the character of public policy. This is a whole dimension of public finance which has no part in the Eltonian scheme which is, after all, concerned with the institutions of finance rather than the finance itself. At some point within a revised Dietz, questions will have to be asked about not only the purpose of government, but the personalities of government. The shift must be from manuscripts to money, from auditors to authority. It must recognise that central government, and such organs of government as the Exchequer, monitored the public finance of the kingdom but did relatively little to control it. Rather, success or failure lay in the hands of subsidymen, customs officials, escheators and their juries, a whole range of individuals in the counties who had to be persuaded, cajoled or coerced into parting with their money. In this way, the study of public finance is also the study of place. Public Finance is not something which happens in Westminster. It is not merely the study of the central institutions of deposit or account: it is equally importantly the study of all those individuals, local officers, reluctant taxpayers and smuggling merchants, whose payments, individually unimportant, collectively formed the crown's income. Elton's forte lay in the period when sheer force of personality seems to have been able to mobilise all these individuals. Outside a limited period government seems neither to have

---

see C. Dyer, 'Taxation and Communities in Late Medieval England', in *Progress and Problems in Medieval England*, ed. R. Britnell and J. Hatcher (1996). I am grateful to Prof. Dyer for sending me a copy of his paper.

[64] Hoyle, 'Crown, Parliament and Taxation', 1178–9.

persuaded, cajoled nor coerced enough: it progressively and knowingly institutionalised practices which amounted to fraud. These are new vistas to be explored for, as Elton himself wrote, 'One thing that I certainly suspected I have found to be entirely true: far more history than is written remains to be written. We are still a long way from the evening of our labours.'[65] Amen to that.

---

[65] His concluding remarks to the preface of *England, 1200–1640* (1968).

THE PARLIAMENT OF ENGLAND
By Pauline Croft

READ 27 MARCH 1996 AT THE INSTITUTE OF HISTORICAL RESEARCH LONDON

REREADING the thousands of words that Geoffrey Elton penned on English parliamentary history has been a fascinating and a humbling experience. The analytical power, the mastery of sources, the clarity of argument compel unstinting admiration. Although he generously acknowledged the contributions made by friends and students, he was the paramount revisionist of early modern parliamentary history.

The assault on established views began remarkably early. The two most often cited articles, 'Parliament', and the Neale lecture, 'Functions', were published in 1974 and 1979 respectively.[1] Yet already in the 1960s, he had begun to sketch out the agenda for new research and fresh thinking in both the sixteenth and the seventeenth centuries. By 1971, his later views had all been outlined, most vigorously in his survey, 'Studying the History of Parliament'. Elton acknowledged that in medieval England parliament had experienced 'a unique political and social development', but he warned against 'a very partial view of the nature of the institution'. Parliamentary history had 'traditionally been treated as though all that mattered was the ambition of elected representatives to limit the power of the executive'. This essentially eighteenth-century approach was particularly seductive for American scholars since it mirrored the deliberate design of their own representative institutions. By contrast the Westminster parliament must be seen in the sixteenth century not as a check on action, but a participator, the creator of legislation. The extensive use of diaries and letters, which highlighted dramatic incidents or recorded only those issues of interest to the writer, led to distortion. The value of parliament, to the monarch and to the realm, arose from its legislative work. Yet the bills and acts which constituted the essence of parliamentary activity had largely been ignored. Elton urged a systematic investigation of their planning and passage, the task which he later set himself in *The Parliament of England*. Only then would it become clear that the normal atmosphere of sessions was co-operative, not conflictive. Debate was important in both houses, of course, but what mattered more was the outcome, the efficient processing of bills. 'Legislation' he magisterially

---

[1] *Studies* 3 (33:1) and (35).

opined, 'always represents the co-operation, however obtained, of all those present ... unresolved conflict becomes a sign of genuine failure on the part of all those concerned.'[2]

The new perspective, emphasizing productive outcomes, would require not biographies of members of the Lords or the Commons, nor more editions of debates, but studies of management and political competence. Administrative questions were more fruitful than constitutional ones. Those who got business done, and the ways they did it, should command our attention, not the orators or spoilers. 'With luck', he wrote, 'we may even be able to expose for the illusion it is the conviction that only opposition entitles a man to respect.' This sideswipe foreshadowed his later attack on Peter Wentworth as a grossly overestimated figure, totally unrepresentative of opinion in the lower house—or at least, as I once heard Geoffrey ebulliently say, about as representative as Dennis Skinner.[3]

Elton also pointed in 1971 to the importance not just of legislation in general but of private bills and acts in particular. The way in which parliament was used by individuals and interests to arrange their own affairs was almost totally neglected by historians, although the quantity of work and time involved, the financial outlays entailed, and the complex processes developed for the purpose, all indicated the significance of private bill matters in every session. To many families and interest groups, parliament offered a permanent solution to their more intractable problems. Disputes over land, over dowries, over titles, over corporate privileges and local improvements like town paving bills or fen drainage, ended up seeking a resolution by way of private bill. Here, Elton suggested, 'lie unsuspected reasons for the endurance of the institution through all sorts of political troubles'.[4]

Throughout his early work Elton emphasized that sixteenth-century England was a deferential society linked by shared attitudes to social status. So Sir John Neale's habit of largely ignoring the upper house and equating parliament with the Commons was a cardinal error. The Lords must be reinstated as an essential component of the parliamentary trinity. Their distinction of birth brought them closer to the sovereign than ordinary mortals, and their influence in the localities remained vital for political stability; perhaps most importantly, the Lords enjoyed a notable share of the legislative initiative. Elton consistently campaigned to put them centre stage, deriding those for whom 'the Lords stood in the wings and made their rare appearances as a body—rather like the chorus in *Iolanthe*'. Any whiggish preconceptions about the rise of the

---

[2] 'Studying the History of Parliament', *Studies* 2, 3–4, 7, 8–9.
[3] *Ibid.*, 9. 'Functions', *Studies* 3 (35), 159.
[4] 'Studying', 11.

Commons to supremacy in the sixteenth century must be set aside. Especially after Burghley's elevation in 1571, the upper house, Elton argued, was probably the more important, exercising conciliar control over the lower.[5]

These central points—the value of a parliament as a working instrument of government, the crucial importance of legislation both public and private, the need to pay attention to management, the role of the Lords and above all the warning not to focus our attention exclusively on political conflict—all now seem so self-evident as to be anodyne. That is an index of the success of the Eltonian revolution in Tudor studies over the last thirty-odd years. At the time, his views were often ill-received, and were attacked in 1971 by Professor Jack Hexter. Elton used the opportunity to restate his case, in an unusually light-hearted piece with appropriate quotations from Thomas Cromwell, who had clearly dealt with a fair number of Hexters in his time. Elton rebuked those historians who habitually treated the disputacious reigns of the early Stuarts as typical, while welcoming the efforts of Hexter's own Center for Parliamentary History at Yale to provide editions of debates illuminating the breakdown of consensus. 'I am right glad ye are in the place ye are in and will do what shall lie in me to aid you in your office', Cromwell–Elton assured his antagonist.[6] Once again, however, he pointed to the importance of parliamentary legislation and the pragmatism of members who saw that there was work to be done rather than debating triumphs to be scored. He remarked that although the parliaments of the early Stuarts had been endlessly discussed, the business activity and organization of those famous sessions remained to be studied.[7] Private acts were still ignored, as Hexter himself had done in asserting that Charles I's first parliament passed only seven statutes.[8] To contemporaries like the judges in 1623, ruling on the status of the Addled Parliament, a non-legislating assembly did not even deserve the title, an interpretation formally endorsed by Coke in his *Institutes*. Both the session of 1614 and its successor in 1621, which passed only two subsidy bills, should be seen as novelties and anomalies, for a high degree of ultimate co-operation was 'the prevalent behaviour of centuries'. It was only when that flow of statutes ceased that the whole function and purpose of parliaments was rendered problematical.[9]

---

[5] 'Functions', *Studies* 3 (35), 157, 162, 170.

[6] 'Studying: B, A Reply', 15.

[7] At last the work is being done. The pioneering thesis by Dr Christopher Kyle, supervised by Professor Michael Graves, '*Lex Loquens*: Legislation in the Parliament of 1624' (PhD thesis, University of Auckland, 1994), shows exactly what is needed for each parliament.

[8] Only seven were printed, a very different matter. 'Studying', *Studies* 2, 17.

[9] *Ibid.*, 14, 16.

Virtually all of Elton's points have become, if not a new orthodoxy—still to emerge for the early seventeenth century—then essential parts of our interpretative repertoire. Clearly he was the prime revisionist for Stuart parliaments, as well as for Tudor ones, in the sense of setting a new agenda for a generation of researchers. Already in 1965, Elton had made an early foray into the Stuart period with 'A High Road to Civil War?'. A classic phrase was immediately added to our historical vocabulary. Elton defended the Tudor achievement, insisting that the political inheritance handed over in 1603 was entirely viable. The 1604 Apology of the Commons, probably more than any other single document, had persuaded historians of the inevitability of conflict. For S. R. Gardiner, 'To understand the Apology is to understand the causes of the success of the English revolution.' Elton proposed a very different interpretation; the Apology expressed a minority opinion rejected by the House at the time as too extreme. The notion, stemming from Gardiner, that the Commons was a coherent body which preserved its unity for eighty-four years, starting in 1604, he regarded as a 'mystical concept', for Elton a term of the utmost disapproval. Memorably, he exposed the fallacy of much earlier writing on the Jacobean period, by skewering 'the quite real if very curious belief that somehow only James I ever had problems'. In 1604, effective co-operation between the king and his parliament was still perfectly possible, *provided* that the Tudor skills of sessional planning and day-to-day management were deployed. It was their absence that caused the frictions of 1604, not the shadow of a far-off civil war. All that was needed for the continuance of good government was a degree of 'tactful and sensible adjustment'.[10]

Again in 1965, Elton addressed the early Stuart period in a review published in an Italian journal which has received rather less attention than it deserved. Once more he attacked the belief that the Commons were hostile to the crown and intent on putting forward their own programme. He warned that any assumption of the inexorable coming of civil war would distort an appreciation of the real context, which still exhibited far more signs of agreement than hostility. Not least, Elton anticipated by thirty years the currently fashionable view that the real problem was largely the inability of Charles I and his ministers to operate any political system effectively. He also pointed to the continuity of a very similar parliamentary system right up to the early nineteenth century, thereby anticipating more recent arguments for an English *ancien régime*.[11] For a succinct statement of the revisionist case as it was to develop over the next twenty-five years, that review would be hard to beat.

[10] 'High Road', *Studies* 2 (28), 166, 170, 181–2.
[11] 'Stuart Century', *Studies* 2, 155–63.

Regrettably, in one major area Elton has not been followed. With his cosmopolitan background, he was profoundly aware of the need for a European dimension in the study of English institutions. His substantial survey of 1969, 'The Body of the Whole Realm', on the development of representation from the fourteenth to the sixteenth centuries, was enriched by an incisive set of comparisons. Elton recognised the key fact, that as a result of the creation of borough seats, the House of Commons was a much larger house, not only proportionately to population but also absolutely, than the representative assemblies of France and Spain. By 1500 the English parliament was far and away the largest representative body in existence in Europe, and its great size significantly affected English ideas of representation.

Elton also pointed to the early and continuous efficiency of the English parliament, active and business-like by the fourteenth century with its machinery for the settlement of petitions. Although its French name suggested a talk-shop, it emerged more importantly as a means of achieving positive action on behalf of whoever could run it. In part this was due to the role of the Lords. There was nothing exceptional in either their composition or function; the aristocratic upper houses of England, France, the Iberian peninsula and Italy were very similar. What was distinctive, wrote Elton shrewdly, 'was the degree of precision, the thoroughness of systematic organisation, which the control of the Crown created'. By the fifteenth century, the English aristocracy, uniquely in Europe, was defined as a parliamentary peerage.[12]

Elton also emphasized that much of the value of a parliament derived from the fact that the members of the lower house came with *plena potestas*, ensuring that their agreement meant that the monarch could rely on agreement in the nation at large, at least in the sense that an agreement could be imposed without undue force. Unless a parliament could bind everyone, it was hardly worth the trouble of calling such a large gathering. 'Every Englishman is intended to be there present either in person or by procuration and attorney.' That had been true for two hundred years before Sir Thomas Smith produced the classic formulation in *De Republica Anglorum*. Such high representative status was not enjoyed elsewhere. The Burgundian estates could do little without referring back to their constituents. The delegates of the Cortes of Castile, much to the irritation of Charles V and his successors, spoke only for the great cities, not the whole realm, and their authority was commensurately lessened.[13] In these apparently minor but cumulatively major differences resided the practical value to English monarchs of calling a parliament.

---

[12] 'Representation', *Studies* 2 (22), 38–9.
[13] *Ibid.*, 47–8. 'Parliament', *Studies* 3 (33:1), 6.

In a key revisionist insight, Elton also noted that troublesome and negative assemblies which offered little or nothing to rulers were elsewhere falling into disuse during the early sixteenth century. The continental model, often with a highly developed organisation like the Cortes of Aragon, had frequently been specifically designed to shackle kings.[14] When monarchs began to find these assemblies more trouble than they were worth, and when the funding they voted was less and less worth collecting, then they were increasingly ignored. In the early sixteenth century, there were signs that at Westminster, too, the negative and troublesome elements were beginning to outweigh the useful. The early Henrician parliaments of 1515 and 1523 might have fitted the continental pattern of increasing obsolescence all too well, especially if Wolsey, an incompetent parliamentary manager, had remained in power. To Elton, what ensured the survival of the English parliament at this dangerous juncture was Henry VIII's divorce. The crisis removed Wolsey, at the same time forcing the king and his new advisers to look to a parliamentary programme as the only means at hand to offer a solution.[15]

The importance of the Reformation parliament had never been in doubt, although Elton was novel in setting the sterile and ill-tempered 1520s in a European context and pointing to the risks of obstructionism. However, the value of parliament to the crown in the 1530s, Elton argued, itself depended on an earlier and often overlooked development, whose significance again depended on making the continental comparison. The key was the removal after 1340 of any real ecclesiastical estate on the European model, that is to say, meeting separately and with a veto. The bishops and abbots remained in parliament, but as individual members of the upper house sitting as replaceable tenants in chief. Ecclesiastical matters were mostly dealt with by the Convocation, meeting alongside a parliament but no part of it. Whatever the survival of estates theory and vocabulary, culminating in the debate on the Nineteen Propositions, the clerical estate in the English parliament had diverged from its continental equivalents long before the Reformation.[16] Without that earlier bifurcation, Henry VIII and even the master-planner Thomas Cromwell might not have found a parliament adaptable to their ends.

These crackling pages show Elton at the height of his formidable powers. Like a brilliant lighthouse beam, he swept across the European landscape, highlighting comparisons from France, Spain and the low countries; he illuminated unexpected features and scattered rays of light

---

[14] 'Representation', *Studies* 2 (22), 48.

[15] *Ibid.*, 52.

[16] *Ibid.*, 23, 35, 38. For a further discussion of estates theory, *Parliament*, 17–22.

on the additional work that was needed. These remarkable explorations are, to me, among the most stimulating parts of his whole vast œuvre. Elton later reinforced these points by emphasizing the increasing sense of isolation felt by the Elizabethan Commons, proud of their parliamentary inheritance. In 1571 Sir Humphrey Gilbert warned of the extent of royal powers in France, Denmark and Portugal, 'where as the Crowne became more free soe are all the subjects thereby rather made slaves'. An anonymous speaker urged a House of Commons composed of knowledgeable local men, since countries without a proper lower house all suffered grave consequences, from the monarchies of Castile and Portugal, who 'in makeinge of lawes use theire owne absolute discretions', or Denmark who consulted only the nobility 'and nothinge of his comons', or the Italian city-states reduced to shadows of their former selves; not to mention the other end of the spectrum, what he rather vaguely called 'the monstrous governments of the common people in some part of Germany'.[17] These sentiments, often indicating a wide knowledge of European developments, suggest that Elton was right when he insisted that already by 1619, when the first assembly of the colony of Virginia met, it was imitating an institution regarded as having experienced a unique course of development. Englishmen in the Americas immediately assumed that they would need their own local version of parliament; by contrast Spanish settlers saw no need for a Cortes, nor Frenchmen for an estates-general.[18] But we can only establish the accurate parameters of that view of English development by distinguishing between what is commonplace and what is remarkable about parliament. Sadly, Elton's interest in comparative parliamentary history was to prove so avant-garde that he had virtually no successors, and the standard works available to him now desperately need updating.[19] As long as we lack any substantial, sophisticated study of the English parliament in a European context, a whole dimension is absent from our understanding.

There can be no doubt that Elton had made an astonishing impact on both Tudor and Stuart parliamentary history in the 1960s and 1970s. His later work provoked a more mixed reaction, even significant disquiet. *The Parliament of England 1559–1581*, a systematic exposition of the bills and acts of the seven earlier Elizabethan sessions, produced

---

[17] *Parliament*, 228. *Proceedings in the Parliament of Elizabeth 1*, ed. T. E. Hartley, vol. I, 1558–81 (Leicester, 1981), 224–5, 228.

[18] 'Representation', *Studies* 2 (22), 19.

[19] G. Griffiths, *Representative Government in Western Europe in the Sixteenth Century* (Oxford, 1968), and A. R. Myers, *Parliaments and Estates in Europe to 1789* (1975). Conrad Russell has made two brief but sparkling contributions: 'Wars and Estates in England, France and Spain, c.1580–c.1640', and 'The Catholic Wind', in *Unrevolutionary England 1603–1642* (1990).

social, economic and political history of the highest value.[20] The meticulous examination of both failed and successful legislation revealed the immensely complex interweaving of centre and locality, and underscored the limited powers of Elizabethan government in a multiplicity of areas, not least law reform. Social historians agree that statutes are a bad guide to what actually happened at the local level, but the assumption is still made that they probably constitute 'a useful barometer of what governments and parliaments thought desirable'.[21] In future, anyone tempted to generalize too confidently about that barometer must start by mastering Elton's probing analysis of just who, exactly, thought just what, exactly, was desirable. Sometimes it was the privy council, sometimes a mere handful of individuals with very limited ends in mind. The key point was that, before anything could be said, the most careful tracing of the emergence of these measures was necessary.

On bills to help the poor and to prevent criminal vagrancy, for example, Elton detailed the role of private initiative preceding privy council action. Although the latters predominated they could not always secure their ends. Conversely, although Speaker Williams in his address in 1563 urged the interests of schools and universities, the subsequent promotion of education in the session came from private, usually local, initiatives. The privy councillors were not behind his initial plea and ignored the interests of the man they put in the Speaker's chair.[22] In another definitive revision, Elton dissected the 1563 statute of Artificers to demonstrate that, *pace* Bindoff, it was in fact the conflation of two government bills, though modified in its passage through both Houses.[23]

The immensely laborious tabulation of all bills and acts so far known, proved that in each parliamentary session an enormous amount of time was spent on trade and shipping, farming, assorted manufacturing processes and more private concerns such as restitution in blood, naturalization, estate acts and local bills for paving or drainage. Here was the daily bread and butter of Westminster, justifying Elton's assertion that to concentrate exclusively on the great debates was to ignore most of what actually took up the time. 'It is not, I think, generally known how much was dealt with in parliament', he had

---

[20] Elton confined himself to the first part of the region leaving the later sessions to his research student David Dean. Dr Dean's book *Law Making and Society in Late Elizabethan England* (Cambridge, 1996) was published just as this article was going to press. I am greatly indebted to him for letting me see an earlier typescript and for many illuminating discussions of his findings.

[21] D. M. Palliser, *The Age of Elizabeth: A Social and Economic History of England* (2nd edn., 1993), 145.

[22] *Parliament*, 273–4.

[23] *Ibid.*, 267.

written in 1979.[24] Now he had demonstrated it beyond dispute.

The sheer range and variety of legislation also underscored the practical value of a parliament as a genuine focus of national interests. 'We have not yet fully grasped how widely spread the interest in promoting legislation could be', Elton commented, reinforcing his view that parliament was an instrument for stability, not contention, since Tudor society could respond flexibly to its problems. He touched also on the role of parliament in sounding out or forming public opinion. Since most sessions were overwhelmed by far more bills than could possibly have been passed, how serious were their promoters? Money was involved, particularly in putting forward a private bill, but also time and effort. In a vivid image, Elton described many bills as 'experimental balloons', representing 'no more than an expression of a potential concern and a search for possible support'.[25] Recently, historians focusing on the question of public opinion in early modern England have canvassed a variety of expressions including the theatre, scurrilous libels, newsletters and entries of current news in diaries.[26] We should now add the 'experimental balloons', with their ideas both sensible and cranky about what needed doing in Elizabethan England. Parliament, called by the crown for its own purposes, was also a national sounding-board, 'a means available to all sorts of Englishmen for the pursuit of their own ends'.[27]

As a guide to legislative effort *The Parliament of England* will remain both definitive and invaluable; but it was shot through with some worrying assumptions and assertions. It was only to be expected that Elton would repeat his conviction that parliament was a highly sophisticated instrument for the making of law. Unfortunately it increasingly appeared to be all that parliament was about, that nothing else really counted. Pym's comment, made in different circumstances, that 'bills are the end of a parliament', was taken as 'an admirable and memorable definition'.[28] The obsession with legislation seemed to be the consequence of following to the letter a frequently repeated Eltonian diktat. Since the 1960s, he had insisted that historians must concentrate on the records generated by parliament itself, the Journals of the Lords and the Commons—the clerks' record rather than the members'—and, above all, the original bills and acts. Even the diaries, letters and other

[24] 'Functions', *Studies* 3 (35), 63, 179.

[25] *Parliament*, 106.

[26] For a general survey, P. Croft, 'Libels, Popular Literacy and Public Opinion in Early Modern England', *Historical Research*, 68 (1995), 266–85, and for the wider context, David Underdown, *A Freeborn People: Politics and the Nation in Seventeenth-Century England* (Oxford, 1996).

[27] *Parliament*, 106.

[28] *Ibid.*, 25.

commentaries of members themselves were largely irrelevant since they were external records. Why historians should deprive themselves of external records was never made clear. More seriously, a moment's reflection will reveal the danger of judging any institution merely by its own paperwork. If the records of the original Globe theatre survived, we should presumably find that its chief functions were providing wages for actors and collecting entrance-money from patrons. There would be few mentions of Shakespeare's plays, since the descriptions of performances were drawn up by irrelevant outsiders who came to view them. There is no need to labour the point. An exclusive concentration on internal records is likely to prove deeply misleading when assessing the functions of any complex multi-layer institution.

The problems of confining the history of parliament to what can be deduced from its own archive do not end there. Famously in 1971 Elton expressed the hope that historians would at last discover the road to the House of Lords Record Office.[29] Studying the materials available in the Victoria Tower—he should have mentioned the lift, not the road—further convinced him that the real role of parliament was essentially, in effect exclusively, legislative. All the official sources, Elton wrote in 1986, 'overwhelmingly testify to the concept of Parliament as a law-producing machinery'; 'rolls, print and Original Acts constitute the archival production of the whole parliament'.[30] Yet the researcher in the House of Lords Record Office finds out immediately that in 1834 a great fire swept the Palace of Westminster, which destroyed the majority of the domestic records of the House of Commons. The survival of the Lords records was due in part to the efforts of a clerk who threw many hundreds of random bundles out of the blazing building into Old Palace Yard. Exactly what was lost is impossible to say. In the seventeenth century, for example, the Commons clerk still possessed '11 bags of papers of Queen Elizabeth' and in the early nineteenth century the clerks several times complained of ancient papers which crowded the presses in the corridors.[31] These must be presumed burned. Nor was the fire the sole cause of the damage. Major manuscripts, including the originals of the Commons Journals for 1584 to 1601, and some of the volumes of the Lords Journals had disappeared earlier.[32] Elton was perfectly aware both of the earlier losses, and of the 1834 fire, but he rarely reflected on the problem and tended to come up with some eccentric conclusions.[33] Here is a repository that has

[29] 'Studying', *Studies* 2, 9.

[30] *Parliament*, 6, 9.

[31] Maurice F. Bond, *Guide to the Records of Parliament* (1971), 3. *Parliament*, 9–10.

[32] Bond, *Guide*, 28, 207.

[33] For example, he doubted that the very few paper bills remaining could represent the fragments of a far greater archive, on the grounds that 'more survive after 1584, which

suffered grievously. To equate what must in part be a group of chance survivals with 'the archival production of the whole parliament', and then to define the very nature of the institution by those survivals, seems highly unwise.

This blindness was all the odder since Elton had written brilliantly on the incomplete early journals of the Lords. In a masterly example of the technical historian's art, he made clear what could, and could not, be said in the present state of knowledge. He emphasized that materials frequently disappeared in the sixteenth century because it was not fully established that the clerk of the parliaments should hand papers on to his successor. He also pointed to the extraordinary fragment describing a debate in the Lords in 1449, on supplies for the war in France. Nothing resembling that semi-official minute of an upper house debate survives until 1610, itself an enormous gap.[34] Elton berated Neale for ignoring the Lords, but in *The Parliament of England* he made no allowance for the silence created by these and other losses in the records. The disappearance of so much material relating to debates should caution against assertions that the making of legislation was the whole end of a parliament and that by implication debate was unimportant.

Even more regrettably, Elton's treatment of parliament as over-whelmingly a legislative machine fell all too easily into the subtle but disastrous distortion of equating one bill with another, a mistake he did not make earlier. On a simple headcount, the majority of the acts of the Reformation Parliament relate to social and economic matters, but he never allowed a purely quantitive approach to overshadow Thomas Cromwell's great statutes. Elton's discussion of the act in restraint of appeals pointed to its powerful and striking preamble, which took up half the initial draft. A propaganda statement of novel political ideas, the preamble was a prerequisite of Cromwell's strategy, at least as important as the actual legislation.[35] Such a radical statute could not be lumped together with the act reforming the government of Calais, or the innumerable local measures on economic regulation.

Years later, a growing disinclination to discriminate between measures of greater or lesser significance was presumably the reason why Elton in his Neale lecture made sweeping assertions, now endlessly parroted in undergraduate essays, that parliament was not called for political

suggests a similar disproportion before the fire'. *Parliament*, 9. Can this really mean that he assumed that the fire carefully burned only a percentage of each missing class of record?

[34] 'The Early Journals of the House of Lords', *English Historical Review*, 352 (1974), 481–512. *Proceedings in Parliament 1610, I: The House of Lords*, ed. Elizabeth Read Foster (New Haven and London, 1966), xxv–xxvi.

[35] 'Evolution', *Studies* 2 (24), 86–8, 90–1.

reasons, nor was it thought of as a political assembly.[36] The argument depends on a bizarre polarisation. By insisting that 'bills and acts of all kinds, not political issues, were the business of parliament', Elton created a dichotomy which implied that bills and acts had nothing to do with political issues; that somehow they were all uncontentious and neutral measures. Counter-arguments are almost embarrassingly obvious. Few statutes could be more political than the acts of 1534, 1536, 1544, 1553, 1559 and 1585, all of which clarified the succession to the throne, the single most contentious issue of high politics throughout the Tudor century. On the succession, the brief treatment by Elton barely touches on the passions and the fears that emerge so vividly in the 1563 petitions of both the Lords and the Commons, both insisting that the queen's purpose in summoning them, so soon after her attack of near-fatal smallpox in 1562, must be for a settlement of the succession. The Lords were particularly forceful. Elizabeth must use 'the aptnes and opportunity of the time, by reason of this parliament, whereby both such advise, consideration and consent as is requisite in so great and weighty a cause, may be better had and used now then at any other time when no parliament is'. Consultation, followed by a political decision embodied in statute, was the point of the session.[37] The suggestion that somehow Elizabethan legislation can be divorced from politics is unsustainable in the context of polarized sessions such as 1563.

Elton's treatment of the 1572 session, called most probably at the insistence of the privy council against the wishes of the queen, was equally unbalanced. To him it merely proved that parliament was an instrument of privy council propaganda, an arena in which the monarch was pressured, but to no avail. 'This degree of powerlessness, this dependence on sources of power outside itself had always been the truth about the Parliament as a participant in national politics ... it had neither power nor politics: it had no function apart from the granting of supply and the making of laws both general and private.' These conclusions about 1572 presumably lie behind the statement that he had come to doubt if parliament ever really mattered at all, except as a stage sometimes used by the real contenders over government and policy. The queen emerges unscathed and triumphant, and the political ferment over the duke of Norfolk and the queen of Scots is dismissed as 'clamour'.[38] Yet 1572 saw an extraordinary outpouring of Marian resistance theory. The bishops' position papers, the writings of Digges and Dannet on the possibility of choosing a new monarch if Elizabeth

---

[36] 'Functions', *Studies* 3 (35), 159.
[37] Hartley, *Proceedings*, I, 59.
[38] *Parliament*, ix, 376–7.

should fail to protect Protestantism, the arguments pressed by Thomas Norton and Speaker Bell of the validity of self-defence against a potential usurper: all prove that parliamentary debates could articulate the deepest fears and angers of the political nation.[39] Elton emphasized the short-term royal victory without evaluating the longer-term impact. There is hardly a mention of the execution of Norfolk, to which the queen was driven in mid-session, and none of the fact that a dissolution proved to be the only despairing way of stopping the flow of impassioned rhetoric. Parliament and the privy council were thwarted, but it is impossible to divorce the debates of 1572 from the bloody outcome at Fotheringay in 1587. Any appreciation of the role of political opinion in steering the queen down paths she did not want to take must put parliamentary pressure at the forefront. Elton had been the champion of the flexible and responsive Tudor state, which he envisaged as a polity deeply conscious of the restraints of the law and dependent on the co-operation of its political elite. In his account of 1572 there is an extraordinary reversal of roles; he turned without noticing it into a believer in the hitherto-despised Tudor despotism.

Exactly the same points must be made as regards Elizabethan bills and acts on religion, on which Elton declined to provide a full discussion on the grounds that they had been extensively covered elsewhere.[40] The omission allowed him to ignore their immense political freight. In 1563, for example, the act extending the oath of supremacy more widely aimed to restrict public office and most professional occupations to Protestants; a highly political matter, since England in 1563 was by no means a fully Protestantized nation. In 1584 the act against Jesuits and seminary priests turned every Englishman ordained under the authority of Rome since 1559 into a traitor. Treachery is by definition a matter of politics. It is difficult to see Elton's cursory and often impatient discussion of religious matters, such as the 1571 bill to confirm the Thirty-Nine articles, as anything other than a strategy of evasion. Nothing could make these examples of legislation fit his assertion that Elizabethan parliaments were essentially non-political.[41]

The sheer volume of legislation revealed by his researches led Elton to praise what he called 'the thoroughly skilled and businesslike way' in which a parliament fulfilled its law-making role.[42] This was not

---

[39] Gerald Bowler, ' "An Axe or An Acte": The Parliament of 1572 and Resistance Theory in Early Elizabethan England', *Canadian Journal of History*, 19 (1984), 349–59.

[40] *Parliament*, 198.

[41] Hence the refusal to accept the key distinction between doctrine and discipline which lies at the heart of the debate on the bill to confirm the Thirty-Nine Articles. *Parliament*, 210–14. I owe this point to Conrad Russell in *Times Higher Educational Supplement*, 9 Jan. 1987, 16.

[42] *Parliament*, ix.

untrue, but his exclusive focus ignored some very different contemporary attitudes. Elton's enthusiasm was not shared by Lord Keeper Bacon for one. In 1563, Bacon told the Commons, 'I would advise you to make your laws as playne and as few as may be, for many be burdenous and doubtful to understand. And secondly, to make them as brief as the matter will suffer. And thirdly, that you proceed to the great and weighty matters first and th'other of smaller importance after.'[43] In 1571, Bacon acknowledged the importance of establishing or dissolving laws as a prime cause of the assembly of members at Westminster, but he put equal emphasis on the need to examine the 'want and superfluitie of lawes ... whether there be too many lawes for anything, which breedeth so many doubtes that the subject sometime is to seeke howe to observe them and the counsellor howe to give advise concerning them'.[44] This perception of the excess of laws, and ill-made laws at that, forms an important counterbalance to Elton's account. Many members of the Commons viewed their efforts with similar scepticism. Mr Dalton in 1584 was unimpressed by a proposed bill on fraudulent conveyances; 'here we go about to remedy a mischief with an inconvenience'.[45] These attitudes do not chime with the efficient machine depicted by Elton.

Enthusiasm for legislation was often muted for other reasons. One issue on which there was no consensus was agriculture. A speaker in 1585 pointed out that successive bills on tillage had been greatly subject to the vagaries of economic opinion. The house should be cautious of rushing to a legislative endorsement of what might prove a short-lived fashion; after all, 'what an alteration we have had in hats.'[46] Even ultimately successful bills often aroused controversy and had failed in earlier sessions. The bill protecting young pheasants and partridges was not followed in 1571, fell victim to prolonged disagreement between the two houses in 1576, but shot through in 1581. Such idiosyncratic histories suggest the random attention-span of members of parliament rather than their efficiency.[47]

Likewise the government was often very far from seeing parliament as a body with a supremely legislative function. The privy council put its best efforts into reminding the political elite assembled at Westminster that an active local magistracy was more useful than the drafting of superfluous bills. To the privy council, members must be urged to observe and enforce the laws and thereby set an example to their

---

[43] Hartley, *Proceedings*, I, 78–9.
[44] *Ibid.*, 183.
[45] Hartley, *Proceedings in the Parliaments of Elizabeth 1*, vol. II, 1584–9 (Leicester, 1995), 106.
[46] Hartley, *Proceedings*, II, 62.
[47] *Parliament*, 235. Hartley, *Proceedings*, II, 106.

neighbours. In creating this sense of obligation, debate played a key role. In 1559 Elizabeth conveyed her commendation of the wisdom and diligence of the Commons in considering the great and weighty causes of the parliament. She trusted, meaningfully, that since they had all fully debated, so they would humbly obey the laws made and passed.[48] Members were strongly admonished against being, in the lord keeper's word, 'drones', too slothful to attend any court, sessions or assizes unless their own private interests were involved. The need to set a law-abiding and diligent example back home was one to which government spokesmen returned again and again. However much legislation was produced at Westminster, it would remain a dead letter unless it was enforced in the country. Those who came up to a parliament must also be active law-enforcers on their return to their localities.

The biographies complied by the History of Parliament Trust comprehensively demonstrate the dual role of members of the Commons. Of course it is possible to find the occasional Wodehousian 'drone', but the overwhelming impression is of men who were indispensable in the counties. A career like that of Sir Robert Wroth, veteran of nine parliaments and at the end of the reign the only surviving Marian exile still in the Commons, makes the point perfectly. JP for both Middlesex and Essex for twenty-five years each; commissioner for gaol delivery, repeatedly commissioner in both Middlesex and Essex for the subsidy, commissioner for musters, captain of the militia, sheriff, commissioner of sewers, commissioner of oyer and terminer, commissioner repeatedly for treason trials—Parry, Babington and lesser lights such as O'Cullen and Thomas; Wroth as an old man went on to serve James I as commissioner for both the Union and the examination of the Gunpowder plotters. This roll-call of strenuous activity leaves out the lesser offices which probably gave him particular pleasure, such as his riding forestership of Waltham Forest and his commissionership of home counties swans.[49] Constructive dialogue between the privy council and stalwarts like Sir Robert Wroth was the very essence of an Elizabethan parliament, at least as important as legislation and arguably in the long term far more so. Yet it is precisely this sense of dialogue between the regime and its supporters that is missing from Elton's last book.

The problem was that the book was essentially a dialogue with the dead: with Sir John Neale.[50] Intent on demolishing Neale's thesis of a rising House of Commons led into opposition by a group of ardent

---

[48] Hartley, *Proceedings*, I, 47.

[49] *The History of Parliament. The House of Commons 1558–1603*, P. W. Hasler (3 vols., 1981), III, 658–63. Additional information from The History of Parliament Trust.

[50] As pointed out by the late Dr Jennifer Loach, *Times Literary Supplement*, 5 June 1987, 602. I wish to acknowledge the many enjoyable discussions on the issues addressed in this paper which I shared with Dr Loach.

puritans, Elton ended by depicting instead a depoliticised assembly of faceless men, fitting together the nuts and bolts of legislation. The importance of discussion, the involvement in great issues, the need to win hearts and minds, had all been fully present in his earlier work, but by 1986 his bitter historiographical dispute with the shade of Neale had led Elton to sideline the whole dimension of political dialogue.[51]

Nowhere is this more misleading than in the account of the raising of supply. Convinced that by the end of the 1530s the Tudor state was accustoming its subjects to accept ordinary peacetime taxation, Elton now depicted subsidy bills and their attendant debates as 'pure routine'.[52] It is true that Elizabeth was never refused supply, even in the desperate 1590s which Elton excluded from his purview. However, if we follow government spokesmen for the subsidy, there emerges, not pure routine, but a remarkable commitment to parliamentary dialogue. Lord Keeper Bacon in 1563 described the need for supply for 'defence against the forreyne enemye abroade and his confederates' as the last and greatest cause of the parliament. He gave a full account of the problems that the queen had found at her accession, 'her realm in a ragged and torne state'. He outlined her policy in 1559–60 towards Scotland, supporting its Protestant reformation, and later her support of French Protestants with the Le Havre expedition. He pointed to Elizabeth's personal frugality, her willingness to sell crown lands and her avoidance of 'superfluous and sumptuous buildeings of delighte'. His place required of him 'the declaracion of the proceedinges', though he was sure of their willingness to give.[53] In 1566, the succession crisis became entangled with the subsidy, but in 1571 the same themes were set out again. Bacon noted the inestimable benefits of more than a decade of peace, interrupted only by 'the rageinge Romaniste rebelles', the northern rising of 1569. The need for supply arose from the extraordinary charges necessitated by the suppression of that rebellion, the 'continual growing expenses of Ireland' and the additional costs of escorting merchant shipping whilst England was still locked in the trade embargo with Spain and the low countries.[54] In 1576 Sir Walter Mildmay took

[51] For example, 'Stuart Century', *Studies* 2, 159. 'Parliament was part of the king's government, called to assist him by making grants and laws, but also designed to keep the crown in touch with opinion and an accepted occasion for complaint and protest.'

[52] *Parliament*, 168. For the most recent contribution to the discussion, R. W. Hoyle, 'Crown, Parliament and Taxation in Sixteenth Century England', *English Historical Review*, 19 (1994), 1174–98. Dr Hoyle persuasively reaffirms the intimate relationship of parliamentary taxation and the needs of war in the government's requests for supply throughout the century. He notes however that Elizabethan preambles tended to lose their educative function compared to those of Henry VIII, although the full case continued to be made in the Commons.

[53] Hartley, *Proceedings*, I, 84–5.

[54] *Ibid.*, 185–7.

over, beginning again in 1559 with the delivery from popery but pointing to the benefits of the sure peace now enjoyed with Scotland, 'which in tymes past was found always very tickle'. Supply was still needed for prudent self-defence, in case 'the tayle of thoes stormes which are so bitter and so boystrous in other countryes may reach us also before they be ended'. Already the revolt of the Netherlands was concerning the privy council. In 1581 Mildmay gave a detailed account of the affairs of Ireland since the excommunication of Elizabeth in 1570. He described the revolt of the earl of Desmond, the projected invasion of Stukeley financed by Pope Gregory XIII, and the landing at Smerwick in 1579, where very fortunately 'the Italians and Spaniardes were ... pull'd out by the eares ... and cutt in peeces'. Behind all these conspiracies lay 'the implacable malice of the pope and his confederates', aimed at England, 'the only sovereign monarchy that most doth maynteyne and countenance religion'.[55]

All these speeches must be seen as sustained efforts at the dissemination of information, explanations of high policy, and vindications of the rightness of actions taken earlier. Tacitly they accepted the need to account for previous moneys collected and spent, emphasising always the queen's cost-consciousness and her generosity in giving her own income for the defence of the realm. The time and effort put into this process of dialogue and openness paid off; the Elizabethan regime survived the war years and carried its subjects with it through dark times, as government spokesmen continued patiently to outline the current situation and its dangers. In the light of these speeches, it is impossible to regard the obtaining of supply simply as a matter of conciliar management that by 1581 had become routine. Central to the role and importance of the English parliament, back to the fourteenth century, was its ability to raise taxes with minimum friction and maximum national harmony. Once again the overemphasis on the legislative machine drained away from Elton's account the equally vital dimension of debate. The government of Elizabeth did not make that mistake; it was well aware that full explanations and demonstrations of fiscal responsibility were essential to the funding and survival of the state. In that interplay of dialogue and response lay the crucial political function of a parliament.

Reviewing his labours after completing his book, Elton announced that he was exceptionally relieved to be done with the parliaments of Elizabeth.[56] It is hard to avoid the conclusion that he had imposed most of the tedium on himself, by allowing his earlier breadth of vision to narrow. Yet even in the lopsided treatment of its subject, *The*

---

[55] *Ibid.*, 441–2, 504.
[56] *Parliament*, ix.

Parliament of England circled again around the great issues that had always fascinated him, even as he roared out his disagreements. Elton was never interested in fashionable trivia. The preface also contains his epitaph, one to which all historians must aspire. 'It has always been my conviction', he wrote, 'that all learned works on history constitute staging posts on the road to further knowledge'. No one planted more staging-posts in unknown territory than Geoffrey Elton. He moved Tudor and Stuart parliamentary history onward, into radically different areas of discussion. We all remain permanently in his debt.

THOMAS CROMWELL'S DOCTRINE OF
PARLIAMENTARY SOVEREIGNTY

By Conrad Russell

READ 27 MARCH 1996 AT THE INSTITUTE OF HISTORICAL RESEARCH LONDON

IN attending a conference on 'The Eltonian Legacy', most of us are here to pay tribute to a teacher or a patron. I am here for the no less heartfelt, but rather trickier, task of paying tribute to a much-missed sparring partner. My first encounter with Geoffrey Elton was at long range, through his review of *The Crisis of Parliaments*, which I can now describe, recollecting it in tranquillity, as my first encounter with Test Match bowling. It was a bit like taking guard in one's first Test to find oneself facing Curtly Ambrose. Like many such encounters, it gave rise to a firm, but always competitive, friendship.

That review started one of those long debates by letter, like an endless exchange of legal pleadings, with which most of Geoffrey's friends became familiar. It was the first of many such exchanges, in the course of which he produced many memorable lines. My favourite was his reply when I asked whether he had any evidence on when Henry and Anne first went to bed together, and he replied: 'We won't know this till we meet Henry and Anne in the next world, and even than I'm not sure I'd believe them.' That first round abundantly confirmed what one elder colleague told me early in the correspondence: 'Whatever anyone says about Geoffrey, he does want to get at the truth.'

He had no liking for humbug, and would not have taken kindly a tribute which attempted to pretend to a degree of agreement which did not exist. I pay tribute to him, in the way he would have wished, by the fact that, forty years almost to the day after I first encountered his work, I am still thinking about it and being goaded into new ideas by it. That is, I think, the tribute which he would have wanted.

In dealing with Thomas Cromwell's doctrine of Parliamentary sovereignty, we begin with a clear agreement on the actual content of the ideas we are discussing. They are the ideas he set out in his article on 'The Political Creed of Thomas Cromwell', in *TRHS* (1956).[1] A sovereign power can do whatever it likes. As Robert Cecil, following his father, said in 1610, 'I know not what an Act of Parliament may not do.'[2] As

---

[1] 'Political Creed', *Studies* 2 (31), 215–35.
[2] Elizabeth Read Foster, *Proceedings in Parliament 1610* (2 vols., New Haven, 1966) [hereafter Foster, *Proceedings*], I, 66.

his father had said, it could make a man a woman (though we must gloss this by saying it is true in law but not in biology). As John Selden said in 1628, by an Act of Parliament 'it might be made death to rise before nine a clock'—and I wish it had been.[3] Because an Act of Parliament could do what it liked, it could not bind its successors. It excluded the jurisdiction of any foreign authority. Because Parliament represented the body of the whole realm, the King in Parliament, as James Whitelocke insisted in 1610, could control the King out of Parliament.[4] A sovereign power had no room for liberties, where its writ did not run. As Laurence Hyde said in 1607, the Welsh 'never were united, until by H.8 they were discharged of all such regallities, and made even as wee, thereby participating all privileges and advantages with us, and are since as good subjects as any of us'.[5]

All these quotations illustrate ideas which were part of Cromwell's doctrine of Parliamentary sovereignty, and all of them illustrate the enduring mark which those ideas have left in the legal and political thinking of England. That far, Geoffrey and I are, and have always been, in entire agreement. Where we begin to diverge is in how we place these ideas in the development of English history as a whole.

I have come to the conclusion, after prolonged thought, that the difference between us was never historical: it was philosophical. When preparing this paper, every time I have fastened on a piece of evidence which I thought upheld my views where they were most distinctive from his, I found he had been there before me. I recall no case where I have so consistently had this experience since I used to challenge Sir Frank Stenton when I was an undergraduate. In both cases, I think the experience marks the fact that we are doing business with one of the great masters of our craft. The capacity for recording the evidence which does not appear to fit our case is one of the great skills of our profession, and in Geoffrey Elton's work it is clearly manifest.

In these cases, disagreement is quickly driven on to the philosophical level, and in this case, it is where it belongs. When Geoffrey Elton used the words 'modern' and 'mediaeval', he spoke as a realist: when I use them, I speak as a nominalist. When he said that the 1530s 'mark quite definitely the end of the mediaeval constitution and the beginning of the modern',[6] he thought he was making an objective and verifiable

---

[3] 'Hayward Townshend's Journals', ed. A. F. Pollard and Marjorie Blatcher, *Bulletin of the Institute of Historical Research, 12* (1934–5), 17, but see also 17n for the suggestion that the 'woman' in the quotation may not be what she seems. Conrad Russell, *Parliaments and English Politics 1621–1629* (Oxford, 1979) [hereafter Russell, *Parliaments 1621–1629*], 352.

[4] *Parliamentary Debates in 1610*, ed. S. R. Gardiner, Camden Soc. 1st series, lxxxi (1862), 103.

[5] *The Parliamentary Diary of Robert Bowyer*, ed. D. H. Willson (Minneapolis, 1931), 244.

[6] Geoffrey Elton, *England under the Tudors* (1st edn, 1955) [hereafter Elton, *Tudors*], 168.

statement. He believed that, in a realist sense, there was an objective division between mediaeval and modern history, and he thought he had found it. I think that any such division is a historian's version of the Holy Grail, and if I speak about 'modern' and 'mediaeval' history, I am making a statement about where the twentieth century (but not necessarily the twenty-first) finds it convenient to divide its exam papers.

It is because he believed this objective distinction was there to be found that he thought he had found it in the 1530s, and that Cronmwell's doctrine of Parliamentary sovereignty was part of it. When he described the victory of Cromwell over what he called in one of his letters 'the complex of beliefs embodied in More', he thought he was describing a permanent and irreversible shift. I think he was describing a heavy and rather bumpy dip in the movement of a seesaw which has been going up and down at least since the reign of Edward I, and is still doing so today. Cromwell may have shifted the centre of gravity of this seesaw to his advantage, but he did not stop it tilting. I can see more anticipations of Cromwell, and more survivals of More, than he could. Where we both see these things, I give them more importance than he did, because he saw the anticipations as leading up to, and the survivals as leading down from, a watershed. If I give them more weight than he did, it is because I see no watershed, and therefore cannot take any evidence as evidence on where I should place it. In that context, the struggle between Cromwell's ideas and More's looks like only one round, even if a big one, in a cyclical struggle whose issue, if any, is still in the future.

He said that in the 1530s judges 'began to obey statute in a way they had never done before'.[7] It is now possible to test this assertion against Norman Doe's book on *Fundamental Authority in Late Mediaeval English Law*. Norman Doe sees a contest among fourteenth- and fifteenth-century judges between the natural law and the positivist views of law, between a view which saw law as rooted in morality, and expressing a body of eternal principles, and a view which saw law as made by a law-maker, whose will, right or wrong, was law until it was repealed. He says that 'in the late mediaeval period the tension was beginning, with considerable regularity, to be resolved in favour of the positivist thesis'. He concludes that 'the modern notion of sovereignty is clearly implicit in the incipient mediaeval positivist thesis'.[8] In 1460, when Parliament looked at the previous year's legislation passed in the

---

For a fuller statement of this philosophical position, see Geoffrey Elton, *The Tudor Revoluton in Government: Administrative Change in the Reign of Henry VIII* (Cambridge, 1953), 1–9.

[7] Elton, *Tudors*, 169.

[8] Norman Doe, *Fundamental Authority in Late Mediaeval English Law* (Cambridge, 1990) [hereafter Doe, *Fundamental Authority*], 174, 178.

Parliament of Devils, they found it 'against all good faith and conscience' and that it had been passed in a Parliament 'without due and free elections', yet they did not declare it void: they repealed it in the normal way. In 1443, Justice Paston had to judge on a statute whose effects were agreed to be mischievous, but said 'yet this will be held for law until it be repealed and annulled'.[9] This judgement is exactly on all fours with the judgement in the case of the Bude and Torrington Railway in 1871, which, until the judgement of the court of appeal in the case of Bate v. Chief Adjudication Officer, was the last appearance of any claim to fundamental law before the English courts.[10]

There was nothing new, either, about claims to override papal jurisdiction. In the reign of Edward I, Pope Boniface VIII, in the bull *Clericis Laicos*, forbade the clergy to pay royal taxes. Edward, in a gesture Henry VIII would surely have understood, responded by threatening to outlaw all the clergy. Boniface climbed down in a bull entitled *Etsi de Statu*.[11] The first statute of *Praemunire*, in 1353, threatened the same penalty of outlawry against those who took cases out of the realm whose cognizance belonged to the king's courts. When Chief Justice Thorpe ruled that the bishop of Chichester was bound by this statute even though it had not been sufficiently promulgated, because 'the law holds that every person has knowledge of it, for the Parliament represents the body of all the realm', we are in a world in which Thomas Cromwell would surely have been at home.[12] In the Standish Case of 1515, Henry dismissed a papal attempt to condemn an Act of Parliament restricting benefit of clergy on the ground that 'kings of England have never had any superior but God alone'. As usual, Geoffrey Elton used the evidence first. It was he, not I, who commented: 'Henry now knew from his judges that the law declared such reliance on Rome punishable by imprisonment at pleasure and forfeiture of goods.'[13]

This was surely all Henry needed to know before passing the Act in Restraint of Appeals, and I have never been able to understand why Geoffrey Elton thought that the block to using a statute to override papal jurisdiction between 1530 and 1532 was that Henry did not know he had the option. He said that in 1530, 'if there was a way Parliament could help him, Henry had not yet thought of it'.[14] This explanation

[9] *Ibid.*, 57, 58.
[10] *Law Reports 6 Common Pleas Division* (1871); J. W. Gough, *Fundamental Law in English History* (Oxford, 1955), 203–6.
[11] F. M. Powicke, *The Thirteenth Century* (Oxford, 1953), 674–8.
[12] *Select Documents of English Constitutional History 1307—1485*, ed. S. B. Chrimes and A. L. Brown (Edinburgh, 1961), 80–1. Doe, *Fundamental Authority*, 39.
[13] Elton, *Tudors*, 107.
[14] Geoffrey Elton, *Reform and Reformation: England 1509–1558* (1977), 131.

for the period of marking time between the end of the Blackfriars Legatine Court and the Act in Restraint of Appeals has always seemed to me repugnant to the evidence. Whatever was holding Henry back, it is hard to believe it was that he did not know he could pass an Act in Restraint of Appeals. After all, the restraint of appeals had been exactly the subject matter of the first statute of *Praemunire*. It was Geoffrey Elton himself who pointed out what brought that period of hesitation to an end: he wrote: 'The death of Warham in August 1532 opened the road to a settlement of the issue at home, by whoever should succeed at Canterbury.'[15] It is that insight which is crucial. Whatever powers Henry might enjoy, there was no point in passing a statute allowing him to apply for an English divorce, only to find that the archbishop of Canterbury refused to grant it. That would have made Henry look quite exceptionally foolish. What Henry was waiting for was not the idea: it was the opportunity.

The passing of the Act in Restraint of Appeals, and even of the Act of Supremacy and the Acts of Succession after it, did not mean that kings of England necessarily lived sovereignly ever after. Belief that the power of statute was restricted by a higher law continued, and was many times expressed during the early seventeenth century. As among fifteenth-century judges, it was a minority view, and perhaps the view of a rather smaller minority than it had been in the fifteenth century. Geoffrey Elton proved conclusively that the Commons did not write the *Apology of the Commons*, but someone did write it, and that someone said that kings of England had no power to alter religion, 'which God defend should be in the power of any mortal man whatsoever'.[16] As far as this passage is concerned, that someone may have been Nicholas Fuller, who said in 1602 that 'an Act of Parliament against the law of God directly is void'.[17] Fuller regarded the Mosaic law as a fundamental law enforceable in the courts, and would quote the Book of Deuteronomy in much the same illustrative way a modern barrister might quote the European Convention of Human Rights. His ideas were certainly nearer those of More than those of Cromwell. Tate, speaking in the Parliament of 1601, on the bill for charitable uses, 'said ... there could be no law, which was contrary to the Great Charter of England' and claimed the bill infringed Magna Carta in the point of challenge to jurors. In the case of Day v. Savage, in 1614, it was held that 'an Act of Parliament made against natural equity, as to make a man judge in his own case, is void in itself: so *jura naturae sunt immutabilia*, and they are *leges legum*'. This judgement, especially in its invocation of the law

---

[15] *Ibid.*, 175.
[16] J. R. Tanner, *Constitutional Documents of the Reign of James I* (Cambridge, 1960), 226.
[17] William Noy, *Reports* (1656), 180.

of nature, comes from a mental world which is closer to More than to Cromwell.[18]

By the 1630s, it was the king's partisans who were pleading fundamental law against Acts of Parliament. The most commonly known version of this is that of Chief Justice Finch, that Ship Money, like feudal tenures, was so inherent that no Act of Parliament could take it away.[19] What is perhaps more remarkable is how much of this case was conceded by Justice Croke in court. He said: 'If a statute were, that the king should not defend the kingdom, it were void, being against law and reason.'[20] It was not only Chief Justice Coke who was capable of talking of statutes being against law and reason. For all the talk of Parliamentary sovereignty, the awkward point remained that the basic principles of the common law, and especially the principles of natural justice on which Coke relied in *Bonham's Case*, were not derived from any Act of Parliament: they were older than Parliaments, and their authority was not Parliamentary. Edward Nicholas, in 1641, objected to Bedford's plan to revive the Great Contract, on the ground that 'the Lords and Commons in Parliament cannot assent to any thing that tends to the disherison of ye k and his crowne, to wh. they are sworne'.[21]

Perhaps the issue where the rival approaches to law show most clearly is that of the succession. That, even more than the overriding of papal jurisdiction, is the issue which touches ultimate authority, since it lays down in whom ultimate authority shall be vested. Whatever governs the law of succession is the ultimate seat of authority. Here, the victory of the ideal of Parliamentary sovereignty was, in the short term, complete. Henry VIII's authority for leaving the Crown by will was that of an Act of Parliament. In 1571, Parliament went so far as to affirm that it was treason to deny that an Act of Parliament could determine the succession.[22] The drafters of that Act were prudent to word it to be in force only during the queen's life. Had they done otherwise, they would have tarred King James I and all who recognised him with the brush of treason. James could not succeed under Henry VIII's will, since it had given priority to the Grey line over the Stuart line. It was therefore necessary for James to deny the crucial Cromwellian principle that an Act of Parliament could determine the

---

[18] Hayward Townshend, *Historical Collections* (1680), 259. *The Reports of Sir Henry Hobart* (1724), 87.

[19] *State Trials*, ed. William Cobbett and T. B. Howell (23 vols., 1783–1820), iii, 1235.

[20] *Ibid.*, 1160.

[21] Public Record Office State Papers [hereafter SP], 16/487/35. Conrad Russell, *The Fall of the British Monarchies* (Oxford, 1991), 253.

[22] Geoffrey Elton, *The Tudor Constitution: Documents and Commentary* (1st edn, Cambridge, 1960), 75.

succession. His Act of Recognition contains no enacting clause: it enacts nothing. It *recognises* the king's title by 'inherent birthright', 'being bounden thereunto by the lawes of God and man'.[23] Sir Edwin Sandys, one of the members of Parliament who had read his Elton, recognised the change which was being pushed through, and wickedly observed: 'this House hath translated the Crown fron one line to another, which it could not do'.[24]

This change in the doctrine of succession was forced on James by political necessity, rather than by any theoretical imperative. Yet it merely exacerbated the problem caused by Cromwellian doctrine to the Union of the Crowns after 1603. The national sovereignty of England had caused no problem so long as England was alone. Yet if, as James believed, he ruled over a kingdom of Britain of which England was only a part, the national sovereignty of England could be nothing but an obstacle to the orderly government of Britain. Sandys, with impeccable Cromwellian logic, observed that 'a kingdom is indivisible, and may not contain several kingdoms'. He pointed out that it was impossible to make law for the kingdom of Britain, because it did not have a sovereign power: 'England and Scotland severally can not sett a lawe to the whole, nor jointly because they are not one Parliament till they are really united'. A Parliament which was the embodiment of English national sovereignty could not accept being degraded to the status of provincial estates, nor could it easily accept union with Scotland while preserving its national sovereignty unless by annexing Scotland as it had annexed Wales. The doctrine of national sovereignty in England has been out of date ever since March 1603. As Sir Edwin Sandys put it, 'no state in the plural number'.[25]

This problem hit James most urgently over the succession. Since England and Scotland had two different laws of succession, and since he had insisted that Acts of Parliament could not change the law of succession, unless he could create a single kingdom of Britain, there was no way he could align the laws of succession. Sir John Holles, reporting Bacon's report to the Commons of 25 April 1604, said their problem was 'the mortality of the king's offspring, which though the king shall by these Parliaments of England and Scotland ty both the kingdomes to the line of the Kings of England; yet it is certain that the subject is beyond the power of a Parliament: examples heertofore Henry the 8 and other his progenitors'.[26] Some rapid rewriting of

---

[23] *Statutes of the Realm, 1 Jac.1 c.1.* See SP 14/21/52 for a Catholic reminder to James that he had no title under Henry VIII's will.

[24] *Commons' Journals* [hereafter *CJ*], I, 178, 951.

[25] SP 14/7/63. *CJ*, I, 951.

[26] *CJ*, I, 184. *Letters of John Holles*, ed. P. R. Seddon, Thoroton Soc. xxxi (3 vols., 1975), III, 522.

history was in progress. Coke records that the project for the union of laws 'could not be done but by the authoritie of the Parliament in either kingdome'. Since Coke also maintained that 'the king cannot change the natural law of a nation', it was hard to see how a union could be brought about.[27] Even James's proposal for a change of name, to Great Britain, was an insult to Cromwell's notions of national sovereignty. Coke tells us that in 1604 the judges 'unanimously resolved (I being then Attorney General, and present) that Anglia had lawes, and Scotia had lawes, but this new erected kingdome of Britannia should have no lawes'. As one member of Parliament put it: 'being English we cannot be Britaines'.[28] It was the national sovereignty of England which was the obstacle to its union with Scotland. Thomas Cromwell had done his work too well.

There is a further question which Thomas Cromwell never solved. This is the problem of the relative authority of statute and common law. This problem was briefly raised by Coke in *Bonham's Case*, and was introduced into debate in the seventeenth century, but it has not become an urgent issue until the 1990s, when it has been forced into prominence by the debates around the principle of judicial review. It has been for centuries, as Sir Edward Coke discovered, an Achilles heel in Parliament's claims to sovereignty that it cannot show how or when it acquired the powers it so proudly claims. It can show no title to them. 'Sundry divers old authentic histories and chronicles' are not enough to confer a title to power. Parliament, like everyone else, must at some time face the question: 'by what authority doest thou these things?' This was the gap at which Coke slipped in the doctrine of the ancient constitution, which was probably intended first and foremost to prevent Parliament from enacting a union with Scotland. Where Coke backed off, Mr Justice Laws, writing last year in *Public Law*, has gone ahead. He argues, in tones closer to More than to Cromwell, that 'the doctrine of Parliamentary sovereignty cannot be vouched by Parliamentary legislation; a higher-order law confers it, and must of necessity limit it'. He argues that 'the notion of sovereignty is logically prior to the Acts of Parliament themselves'. He relies on a quotation from Sir William Wade to the effect that 'it is always for the courts, in the last resort, to say what is a valid Act of Parliament'. To any Tudorist, this must be irresistibly reminiscent of More's objection to the sovereignty of Scripture, on the ground that it was for the church to say what was valid Scripture. More wheels than one are here coming

[27] Sir Edward Coke, *Fourth Institute* (1648), 347. SP 14/26/64.
[28] Coke, *Fourth Institute*, 347. Bodleian MS Tanner, 75, fol. 24. Geoffrey Elton came very near admitting this point himself: 'English National Self-Consciousness and the Parliament in the Sixteenth Century', *Studies* 4 (51), 134.

full circle.[29] A seventeenth-century writer would have known what to call a Parliamentary sovereignty conferred by Act of Parliament: he would have called it conquest.

Lord Justice Woolf and Mr Justice Laws are thus freed to argue what, historically, must be the case, that the basic principles of the common law are not derived from Parliamentary sovereignty, but are independent of it. Glanville and Bracton, whoever they may have been, did not derive their basic ideas of law from the actions of a sovereign Parliament. This enables Mr Justice Laws to argue that the principles of natural justice, which are 'the substantive principles of judicial review are judge-made, owing neither their content nor their authority as law to the legislature'.[30] In a passage which would have greatly amused Geoffrey Elton, Sir John Laws reproves me for being excessively hidebound by the doctrine of Parliamentary sovereignty. The courts, of course, are no more able to show the origins of their powers than Parliament is, but if the contest is in terms of antiquity, the claim of the courts must be superior. Lord Justice Woolf does not go so far: he relies on a claim to equality. He asks for 'a proper recognition of both the pillars of the rule of law and the equal responsibility that Parliament and the courts are under to respect the other's burdens'. He claims that 'both Parliament and the courts derive their authority from the rule of law so both are subject to it'.[31] The innuendo of the argument is that were Parliament to attack judicial review, 'which in its origin is as ancient as the common law', it might risk attacking the principles from which its own *vires* are derived, and so undermining its own legitimacy, much like the Parliament which executed the king who had summoned it. He quotes a case of 1969, when Parliament set up a commission which 'shall not be called in question in any court of law', and the provision was struck down in the courts. He suggests that if Parliament were to abolish the power of judicial review, the courts should not 'accept that the legislation means what it says'.[32]

The challenge has come sooner than Lord Justice Woolf perhaps expected. It has come in the case of Bate v. Chief Adjudication Officer. That case arises from a clause in an Act of Parliament instructing the judges to judge as if past judgements had not been made. The Court of Appeal has construed this as an instruction to judge contrary to law. In the words of Lord Justice Millett, 'it does not purport to change the law, but rather to rewrite history'.[33] If that is what Parliament intended,

[29] Sir John Laws, 'Law and Democracy', *Public Law* (1995), 87, 86.
[30] *Ibid.*, 80, 91n.
[31] Lord Woolf of Barnes, '*Droit Public*-English Style', *Public Law* (1995), 68.
[32] *Ibid.*, 68, 69, 67.
[33] Court of Appeal, 30 November 1994, Official Transcript.

is it within the legitimate scope of Parliamentary sovereignty? If the answer is 'yes', Parliamentary sovereignty means something more dictatorial than Thomas Cromwell in his wildest dreams ever envisaged: it is a Frankenstein monster which has broken loose. If the answer is 'no', Sir Thomas More is back in contention again, and the courts will again recognise a doctrine of fundamental law. Such questions recall Sir Thomas Wentworth's remark in the Parliament of 1628: 'I trust that no question shall ever stir whether the King be above the law or the law be above the King.'[34] It is possible that the House of Lords, whose judgement was given by Lord Slynn of Hadley on 16 May 1996, shared Wentworth's views. Lord Slynn succeeded in resolving this case by resolving it on an issue which raised no question of the limits of Parliamentary sovereignty. The genie was safely put back in the bottle.

The genie did not remain there for long. On 13 November 1996, the Court of Appeal gave a judgement requiring the home secretary to give reasons for refusing citizenship to Mohammed and Ali Fayed, notwithstanding the provisions of Section 44(2) of the British Nationality Act 1981. That section provided that the secretary of state 'shall not be required to assign any reason for the grant or refusal of any application under this Act', and that 'the decision of the Secretary of State ... shall not be subject to appeal to, or review in, any court'. Is a judgement reached in the face of these very robust words another *Bonham's Case*?

It is necessary to discuss this issue with extreme caution, since the case is at present *sub judice* before the House of Lords, which is likely to have given judgement before these words appear in print. However, I hope it is in order to look at what Lord Woolf has actually said. Like *Bonham's Case* itself, this judgement is not a direct challenge to the principle of Parliamentary sovereignty. It is an attempt to discover the intention of the legislature. Lord Woolf relied on the idea of fairness which is implicit in the principles of natural justice, but he emphatically did not say that Parliament, in its sovereign power, is not entitled to act unfairly and against the principles of natural justice. He said that Parliament had not said in express words that it intended to do so. In his words, 'the suggestion that notice need not be given although this would be unfair involves attributing to Parliament an intention that it has not expressly stated that a Minister should be able to act unfairly in deciding that a person lawfully in this country should be refused citisenship without the courts being able to do anything about it'.[35]

The intention of Parliament, like the intention of the man on the Clapham omnibus, must be deduced from basic principles, as well as

[34] Russell, *Parliaments 1621–1629*, 354–5.
[35] *R. v. Secretary of State for the Home Department, ex parte Mohammed Fayed*, 13 November 1996, p.19 of transcript.

from express words. If the man on the Clapham omnibus exclaims: 'I'll ------- kill you!' he will not necessarily be presumed to have threatened murder. If, on the other hand, he accompanies the offensive words by drawing a knife, he risks being presumed to intend the natural consequence of his acts. Similarly, according to Plowden, the words are only the 'image' of the statute: 'the life of the statute rests in the minds of the expositors of the words, that is the makers of the statutes'. Plowden said that 'the sages of the law have qualified the rigor of the word according to reason', but also that they 'have ever been guided by the intent of the legislature'.[36] The only way these principles can be made compatible is if the intention of Parliament is presumed to be in accord with the basic principles of the common law. This, in fact, is the assumption behind *Bonham's Case*, and the basic assumption behind judicial review. According to Professor Thorne, 'prior to the sixteenth century in England there was no difficulty in disregarding an enactment which, though reasonable and practicable in general, led to injustice in a particular instance'. Professor Thorne recognised that this became a less common approach with clearer ideas of Parliamentary sovereignty in the sixteenth century, but it did not disappear: it merely needed 'more elaborate justification'.[37] It is wholly in line with this tradition that Lord Woolf observed, when faced with the claim that the statute gave the home secretary the power to act unfairly: 'I cannot accept that this can possibly be the position. It is wholly inconsistent with the principles of administrative law to which I have referred.'

Whether this approach to the exercise of power by Parliament is ultimately upheld or not, it is interestingly in line with some of the ways in which the courts used to treat the arbitrary exercise of power by the king. There is a Year Book case of 2 Henry VII, often quoted in the seventeenth-century courts, in which the king commanded a subject to kill a man who had not been condemned. This was found to be murder in the man who obeyed the king's command.[38] The principle of presuming an intention in line with the basic principles of the common law has a very long history.

There is no immediate prospect of a judicial return to the principles of Sir Thomas More, which were in any case very far indeed from being the clear practice of the courts before 1530. However, the judicial approach to the task of discovering Parliament's intention rests, and has rested since Plowden's day, on principles very much more complex than Thomas Cromwell would have wished. Indeed, the more politically unchecked Parliament becomes in its exercise of power, the more

[36] Samuel E. Thorne, *Essays in Legal History* (1985), 11, 160.
[37] *Ibid.*, 177–8.
[38] Foster, *Proceedings*, II, 154.

vigorous the courts become in strictly construing its intention. In this way, the seesaw between the natural law and positivist views of law is still in motion. As nature abhors a vacuum, a seesaw abhors an equilibrium, and whatever the resolution of the current case, it is likely that the seesaw will remain in motion. If Thomas Cromwell introduced a revolution, it was only in the astronomical sense: we are on the way back to where we started.

POLITICS

By Simon Adams

READ 28 MARCH 1996 AT THE INSTITUTE OF HISTORICAL RESEARCH LONDON

THE legacy of Sir Geoffrey Elton to the study of Tudor politics can only be described as paradoxical. For all his reputation as a doyen of what has been termed the Cambridge school of high political history, studies of politics comprise but a small section of his *œuvre*. He never wrote a substantial account of an episode in high politics in the manner of Maurice Cowling or J. C. D. Clark.[1] If one excludes his textbooks, political subjects are treated primarily in his essays.[2] Even these, though, are not numerous. The section 'Tudor Politics' in *Studies* 1 contains eleven essays and papers. Four are reviews, two are introductions to reprinted biographies, two are essays on Thomas More and two are the famous studies of Henry VII and Henry VIII ('Rapacity and Remorse' and 'King or Minister?'), which are essentially analyses of personality. Only one article, the early 'Decline and Fall', deals with a specific political episode. For a man whose doubts about biography as an exercise are well known, there is a striking amount of biographical material here. Elton's real contribution is to be found in his later essays. *Studies* 3 contains the 'Points of Contact' trilogy, 'Pilgrimage of Grace' and 'Arthur Hall'. 'Hall', 'Piscatorial Politics' in *Studies* 4 and the final section of *Parliament of England* form a distinct corpus of Elizabethan political studies.

In the very attempt to categorize his works in this fashion we encounter a further paradox, the difficulty of establishing precisely what Elton was writing about. This difficulty may be attributed in large part to his celebrated, even notorious, combatativeness, for in almost every one of his major works there are actually two subjects: the announced one and the sub-text, which is invariably a tilt at his target of the moment. In the Elizabethan studies the attack on Sir John Neale is open and explicit. In others no names are mentioned, but those under attack are not difficult to identify.[3] To some extent these sub-texts give

---

[1] E.g. Maurice Cowling, *The Impact of Hitler* (Cambridge, 1975), or J. C. D. Clark, *The Dynamics of Change* (Cambridge, 1982).

[2] The textbooks, specifically *Tudors*, *Reformation* and *Reform and Renewal*, will not be discussed here in any detail. It could be argued that omitting them weights the scales unfairly, but ultimately they are works of synthesis.

[3] For examples, see pp. 250–1, 253 below.

his works a dated air; his sparring with eminences of the past, A. F. Pollard for example, seems of limited relevance now.[4]

Elton's two commentaries on history, *Practice* and *Political History*, are also of significance here. They were written nearly thirty years ago when he had reached a plateau of eminence. While they do not appear to have been written as a pair, retrospectively they very much read as one. Both share a strikingly defensive tone. One aspect of this defensiveness has a definite period flavour: the alarm with which he reacted to the putative student rebellion of the late 1960s.[5] More important, though possibly not unrelated, was the defensiveness over his subject. 'A good many people', he wrote in *Political History*, 'think of political history as a very old-fashioned way of looking at the past, even as a boring form of study and as not very civilised.'[6] 'Pilgrimage of Grace' begins in a similar fashion: 'Few scholars these days like to be called political or constitutional historians: it is widely held that those have ceased to be useful occupations.'[7] His unhappiness over the rise of sociology and social history permeates *Practice*.[8] Although he was determined to go down fighting (and take a few opponents with him), a distinct fatalism can be detected in both books. A decade later he referred to *Political History* 'as the one of my books which practically nobody seems to have read ... No doubt the book justifies the neglect, but I confess to an affection for this runt of the litter.'[9]

Yet these books do constitute a very real legacy in the form of his now famous emphasis on the mastery of the archive and its technical problems. It may be claimed that this is not particularly novel, yet nowhere else in recent historiographical literature is it so clearly and elegantly described. There is also a curiously prophetic note: the almost passing reference at the end of *Political History* to the 'new narrative'.[10] It might legitimately be asked how much narrative history Elton himself had written; he admitted in *Political History* that 'I tried with limited success to write such narrative in my *Reformation Europe* ... but I may add that I remain ambitious to do more of this sort of thing, and do it better.'[11] Nine years later, however, Lawrence Stone detected 'evidence of an undercurrent which is sucking many prominent "new historians"'

---

[4] See, for example, p. 251 below, and *Maitland*, 63, as well as his assessment of Pollard in the introduction to the reprint of *Wolsey*, *Studies* 1 (6), 110–15.

[5] E.g. *Political History*, 129, 150–1.

[6] *Ibid.*, 4.

[7] *Studies* 3 (36), 183.

[8] See especially 35ff.

[9] 'Pilgrimage of Grace', *Studies* 3, 184 n. 1.

[10] *Political History*, 178–9.

[11] *Ibid.*, 179.

back again into some form of narrative'.[12] There is no reference in this article to *Political History*, but towards the end Elton is described as urging on 'the new British school of young antiquarian empiricists'.[13] It is not my purpose here to discuss Elton's role in any revival of political history over the past twenty years, nor to speculate on the potential influence of this 'antiquarian empiricism' on the future of the subject. Suffice it to say that *Political History* initiated Elton's own venture into specifically political history. As he observed in 'Pilgrimage of Grace', it was 'the editor of this volume, who encouraged me to reinforce my assertions by a practical demonstration'.[14]

Elton's emphasis on the mastery of the archive raises one final paradox. It is probably not coincidental that he cut his teeth, as it were, on administrative history. Here the archives are by their nature straightforward, and if the technical problems they pose are frequently demanding, they are also obvious. Although his command of the broad range of British historical literature both past and contemporary was formidable, he only mastered two archives: the Cromwell papers and other records of the central administration for Henry VIII's reign, and what he defined, somewhat idiosyncratically, as the archive for the parliaments of 1559 to 1581.[15] He never worked in foreign, diplomatic, local, ecclesiastical or manorial archives. His one excursion into local history, 'Piscatorial Politics', was based, as he acknowledged, on the research of David Dean.[16] He could make some quite basic mistakes when commenting on Elizabethan archival sources. I have referred to two elsewhere, and a possibly more significant one will be mentioned below.[17]

The works relevant to this theme can therefore be reduced to three roughly chronological groups: those relating to Thomas Cromwell, what can be termed the 'middle period' essays and the Elizabethan

---

[12] Lawrence Stone, 'The Revival of Narrative', *Past and Present*, 85 (1979), 3–24, see p. 3.

[13] *Ibid.*, 20.

[14] *Studies* 3, p. 184 n. 1. The reference is to Barbara Malament, editor of *After the Reformation: Essays in Honor of J. H. Hexter* (Manchester, 1980), in which the essay first appeared.

[15] His command of the literature is best displayed in *Political History* and *Practice*, but see also his archival survey *England, 1200–1640* (1969), in the series 'The Sources of History', of which he was general editor.

[16] *Studies* 4 (57), see p. 119 n. 32.

[17] The reference to the 'disastrous disappearance of Leicester's papers' in 'Court', *Studies* 3 (33:3), 53, is noted in S. Adams, 'The Papers of Robert Dudley, Earl of Leicester. I', *Archives*, 20 (1992), 63. Elton was surprised to find Welsh Elizabethan parliamentary papers in the MSS of the duke of Northumberland ('Wales in Parliament', *Studies* 4, 98). For the explanation of their presence there, see my review of *Studies* 4, *History*, 79 (1994), 137. The third example is found on p. 253 below.

parliamentary studies. Certain postulates and problems first encountered in the books on Cromwell dominate the *œuvre* as whole. The middle period essays—the 'Points of Contact' series and 'Pilgrimage of Grace'— are the slightest in volume, but perhaps the most influential. This is not simply because they are the most specifically political, but also because they outline the broader interpretation of Tudor politics that informs the Elizabethan studies.

The Thomas Cromwell books form a discrete group not least because he himself brought his work on that subject formally to an end in *Reform and Renewal*, where he announced that 'this is to be my last engagement with Thomas Cromwell'.[18] It is not my purpose here to speculate as to why he never wrote or even contemplated a biography of Cromwell, but it does mean that an Eltonian overview of Cromwell's career is lacking and his place in Henrician politics remains to some extent undefined.[19] One has only to turn to the more recent work on Cromwell by David Starkey, Susan Brigden and Mary Robertson to see what is missing.[20] Moreover, looking at the three Cromwell books, *Tudor Revolution, Policy and Police* and *Reform and Renewal*, in this context, it is the sub-texts that are the most revealing. The formal subject of *Tudor Revolution* needs no description here, but the sub-text is clear: it is a sophisticated revival of the old 'new monarchies' thesis. Indeed, Elton was quite explicit about this: 'Talk of a "new monarchy" in the sixteenth century has become a little unfashionable of late ... But in some ways the reaction has gone too far; as regards political and social structure, the sixteenth century produced something quite new in England.'[21] In the introduction he was equally explicit in defining his subject as the transition from medieval to modern: 'Where it mattered most a change had occurred which entitles us to speak of a revolution from the medieval to the modern state.'[22] On the surface, *Policy and Police* is perhaps the classic example of the Eltonian method: there is a discrete archive, a discrete subject, 'the enforcement of the Reformation', and a detailed analysis of methods and procedures. Yet *Policy and Police* is really an attack on the 'Tudor despotism'. For reasons of his own, he deliberately ignored Joel Hurstfield's essay on the subject,

---

[18] *Reform and Renewal*, vii.

[19] 'Redivivus', *Studies* 3 (46), is the nearest approach to an overview.

[20] David Starkey, *The Reign of Henry VIII: Personalities and Politics* (1985). Susan Brigden, 'Thomas Cromwell and the "Brethren"', in *Law and Government under the Tudors*, ed. Claire Cross *et al.* (Cambridge, 1988), 31–49. M. L. Robertson, 'Profit and Purpose in the Development of Thomas Cromwell's Landed Estates', *Journal of British Studies* [hereafter *JBS*] (1990), 317–46.

[21] *Tudor Revolution*, 425–6.

[22] *Ibid.*, 8.

which he had criticized two years earlier in *Political History*.[23] Instead, he posed the rhetorical question 'was there a reign of terror?', and then attacked Pollard and H. A. L. Fisher for claiming that there had been no significant resistance to the break with Rome.[24] *Reform and Renewal* is basically an attack on the existence and influence of the Edwardian Commonwealthmen, a favourite theme to which he returned in a later essay.[25] It is difficult not to see R. H. Tawney as the target here.

Are these studies in Tudor politics? *Tudor Revolution* is so explicitly concerned with administration that it is tempting to say that politics were deliberately excluded. However, Eton was fully aware not only that the thrust of his argument was that the Cromwellian Revolution separated government from the court and administration from politics, but also that this might be too radical a step. He manoeuvred himself out of this potential trap by a not altogether successful compromise: 'The political life of the country centred on the court, but administration rested in the hands of agencies divorced from the household, though often in those of men not strange to court life, and the household concerned itself only with its specialised tasks.'[26]

The problems created by the 'administrative' approach are also encountered in *Policy and Police*. The conclusion of the chapter on 'Police' includes a comment on Cromwell's dependence on the co-operation of individuals over whom he had no direct control: 'he depended in the last resort on the willingness, prejudices and private ends of men over whom he had no hold except what general adjurations and warnings could add to general loyalty and the desire to stand well with the fountain of patronage'.[27] This would appear to be an admission that the patronage of the crown played a major role in the enforcement of the Reformation. We might legitimately ask for more on this important subject. However, there is no entry to patronage in the index, and my (admittedly brief) skimming of the text has turned up only one further reference. In the introduction to the chapter in which he discusses how Cromwell kept in touch with the various parts of the realm, Elton notes:

It needs to be stressed that the matters that here interest us were in life mingled with a great many other necessary occupations: foreign policy ... [etc.] and especially the laborious details of patronage on

[23] *Political History*, 56.

[24] *Policy and Police*, 2, 4.

[25] 'Commonwealth-Men', *Studies* 3 (38).

[26] *Tudor Revolution*, 373. In the later review 'Tudor Government', *Historical Journal* [hereafter *HJ*], 31 (1988), 428, he was more categorial: 'Now the book on the Tudor revolution was not about politics; as its subtitle explained, it was about administration.'

[27] *Policy and Police*, 382.

the effective use of which Cromwell in great part depended for his power and survival.[28]

This is a substantial concession. Yet nowhere in this book does Elton discuss patronage.[29] A major aspect of the story—the carrot as against the stick—has simply been omitted.

The near antithesis between policy and politics found in both *Tudor Revolution* and *Policy and Police* is if anything more explicit in *Reform and Renewal*. This is a study in the formulation of policy, but policy very narrowly defined and—in its emphasis on social and economic concerns—almost anachronistically modern. The 'policy' was formulated in very intellectual terms—to all intents and purposes it was a political programme—and it was the work primarily of Cromwell and a few intimates. Here again there is a revealing aside: 'Cromwell's connection with the City of London ... needs more study than I can give it here.'[30] It is not unfair to suggest that in any study of the formulation of economic or commercial policy this connection ought to be crucial.

Yet it was the very programmatic nature of Cromwell's ministry that Elton regarded as the measure of his greatness, as he states more or less openly in 'Redivivus', and the distinction between 'the business of government' and politics, so explicit in the Cromwell books, is never absent from the later political studies.[31] As a result, the important and influential middle period essays also have their problematic side. The strength of these essays is found in their emphasis on the political importance of the centre, an important and timely corrective to the provincialism and localism so prevalent in 1960s, and also to the negative role played by the court and the central government in the various 'general crisis' theories.[32] The three 'Points of Contact' essays address a single rather idiosyncratic theme, was there something in the central institutions under the Tudors that served a representative function responsible for stability in the sixteenth century, which then

---

[28] *Ibid.*, 164.

[29] Nor anywhere else for that matter.

[30] *Reform and Renewal*, 65.

[31] E.g. 'Cromwell worked in ways that became almost schematical', and 'the subjection of the Church was only part of Cromwell's great political programme', 'Redivivus', *Studies* 3, 380–1. The programmatic emphasis can also be found in the work of members of Elton's school, e.g. Brendan Bradshaw, *The Irish Constitutional Revolution of the Sixteenth Century* (Cambridge, 1979).

[32] The classic description of the parasitical 'Renaissance Court' is to be found in H. R. Trevor-Roper, 'The General Crisis of the Seventeenth Century', in *Crisis in Europe 1560–1600*, ed. Trevor Aston (1965), esp. 68–78. The pervasive influence of 1960s provincialism can easily be seen in the first edition (1968) of Anthony Fletcher's very successful textbook *Tudor Rebellions*.

broke down in the seventeenth? The assumption that this representative function would be served by institutions rather than by less formal means is typically Eltonian. The initial essay on parliament is straight-forward enough except for rather odd argument at the end that membership in the House of Commons might have been a first stage in political advancement. To support this case Elton made a series of comparisons of dates of entry into parliament with dates of appointment to the council. But nowhere does he supply positive evidence that the latter was a consequence of the former. This would appear to be a flagrant example of *post hoc ergo propter hoc*, and Elton certainly appreci-ated the danger, but his disclaimer verges on the disingenuous: 'I am not prepared to say that membership of the House had become a necessary prerequisite for elevation to the Privy Council, but it looks very much as though it had become a very useful first step.'[33]

'Council' poses the very interesting paradox that if a large council served a representative function, a small one was clearly more efficient. Yet the issue of absolute size may be irrelevant, given the general agreement that within the councils of Henry VII, Henry VIII (excluding the periods of Wolsey and Cromwell) and Elizabeth I, a clear 'inner ring' operated.[34] 'Court' is both the most adventurous of the series and the most vulnerable. The vulnerability is clearly evident in one of the best-known passages in the essay: 'We need no more reveries on accession tilts and symbolism, no more pretty pictures of gallants and galliards; could we instead have painful studies of Acatry and Pantry, of vicechamberlains and ladies of the Privy Chamber.'[35] Beneath the rhetorical antithesis is of course the old Etonian distinction between business and frivolity. The side-swipes at Francis Yates, Roy Strong and Sidney Angelo are in the classic mould. Yet anyone who has ever worked on the Elizabethan court knows that the archives of the court and household departments are thin on the ground at best.[36] Nor, assuming that it were possible, is there any evidence to suggest that a detailed study of the Acatry would enhance our knowledge of Eliza-bethan politics in any substantial respect. However, the most influential aspect of this essay was undoubtedly its discussion of factional politics, especially the argument that the court was where 'the battle of politics' was fought out. Here Elton found the distinction between Tudor and early Stuart politics. Under the Stuarts, 'conflict was forced out of court

---

[33] 'Parliament', *Studies* 3 (33:1), 20.
[34] Elton used the term himself to describe the councils of Henry VII and early Henry VIII, see *Tudor Revolution*, 34–5, and *Constitution* (1982), p. 90. The Elizabethan inner ring is discussed in Adams, 'Eliza Enthroned? The Court and its Politics', in *The Reign of Elizabeth I*, ed. Christopher Haigh (1984), 63, 65.
[35] 'Court', *Studies* 3, 53.
[36] See Adams, 'Eliza Enthroned?', 56–9.

into a public arena; but this was new'. Under the 'Tudors, the court maintained its centrality: 'the factions in the Country linked to members of the Court; Court faction spread its net over the shires'.[37]

This argument informs all his subsequent work on Tudor politics, beginning with 'Pilgrimage of Grace'. 'Pilgrimage of Grace' is an undoubted triumph. Without entering into the long historiography of this complex episode, the immediate background is worth noting. As well as 1960s localism, recent debate on the subject had been very much influenced by A. G. Dickens's essay 'Secular and Religious Motivation in the Pilgrimage of Grace'.[38] This was itself a controversial work, both in Dickens's pursuit of a popular Protestantism in the North of England and in his attempt to portray the Pilgrimage as something other than a revolt of northern Catholicism. Elton's essay was not definitive, and he probably would not have claimed that it was. But it did restore a political dimension to the Pilgrimage and brought to the fore the issue of the politics of faction.[39]

The conclusion of the essay is, however, curiously qualified: 'On this occasion a court faction transferred its power base to the country, a step most unusual in the sixteenth century. It had to do so because it had lost all hope of victory by conventional means.'[40] The implication that this was a rare phenomenon poses wider questions that Elton never addressed. The factional interpretation of the events of 1536 was first advanced in Eric Ives's article, 'Faction at the Court of Henry VIII: The Fall of Anne Boleyn', which was followed by an unpublished paper by David Starkey.[41] Yet the description of the faction behind the Pilgrimage as the 'Aragonese Faction' appears to have been of Elton's coining. Ives refers simply to the conservative faction, while Starkey in his later published work refers to both the conservative and the Aragonese faction.[42] Elton had in fact employed the term Aragonese on two earlier occasions.[43]

The difficulty with the argument that the Pilgrimage was the work

[37] 'Court', *Studies* 3, 56.

[38] *Studies in Church History*, 4 (1967), 39–64.

[39] A dramatic illustration of the effect of Elton's reappraisal of the Pilgrimage can be found in the comparison of the relevant section (pp. 17–39) of the third edition of Fletcher's *Tudor Rebellions* (1983) with the first two.

[40] 'Pilgrimage of Grace', *Studies* 3 (36), 211.

[41] E. W. Ives, 'Faction at the Court of Henry VIII. The Fall of Anne Boleyn', *History*, 57 (1972), 169–88. Starkey's general line of argument can be found in the relevant chapters of *Reign of Henry VIII*. Reference is made to both in 'Court' and 'Pilgrimage of Grace', *Studies* 3, 51 n. 87, and 210 n. 71.

[42] Ives, 'Faction', 182. Starkey, *Reign of Henry VIII*, 118, and *idem*, (ed.) *The English Court from the Wars of the Roses to the Civil War* (1987), 110–11.

[43] 'Court', *Studies* 3, 50, and *Reform and Reformation*, 267. 'Pilgrimage of Grace' may well have been written by the time they were published.

of the Aragonese faction lies in the fact that the main evidence for the discontents of those identified as members of the faction prior to 1536 comes from Eustache Chapuys's reports of his conversations with Lords Darcy and Hussey in 1534 and 1535. In these conversations Hussey held Henry VIII personally responsible for the break from Rome; therefore, if he was plotting anything he was plotting deposition.[44] If this was the case, then the Pilgrimage was not the result of one court faction seeking to oust another. The deposition of Henry VIII does not, of course, feature in any of the Pilgrims' public statements. Why it did not is one of the major mysteries of the whole affair. The localist interpretation actually explains its absence better, but if the Pilgrimage is to be linked to an Aragonese conspiracy then a different explanation is necessary.[45] However not only does Elton fail to address the issue of deposition, but he is quite vague about what precisely the conspirators expected to achieve and how they intended to go about it. At one point he refers simply to the conspirators 'plotting violence as their only hope'.[46] Later on he states: 'in the main the northern risings represent the effort of a defeated court faction to create a power base in the country for the purpose of achieving a political victory at court'.[47] Neither what would constitute such a political victory nor how this 'power base' would achieve it are explained.

'Pilgrimage of Grace' was Elton's last major contribution to Henrician politics. Several years after it was published a serious challenge to the 'Tudor Revolution' was mounted in the form of David Starkey's reappraisal of court politics, which only received widespread attention in the 1980s.[48] The reasons why a serious Starkey–Elton debate never got beyond the exchange in *The Historical Journal* in 1987–8 do not need rehearsal here, but its absence has left a number of questions unresolved.[49] Elton had, however, moved on into his final great project,

---

[44] The main reports of the conversations are found in Chapuys's despatches of 30 September 1534, 23 March 1535 and 11 July 1535, *Letters, Despatches and State Papers, Relating to the Negotiations between England and Spain*, V, pt 1 [1534–5] (1886), 608–11, 470–1, 512. It might be argued that deposition is not mentioned explicitly, but the references to Charles V declaring war on Henry VIII and executing a bull of excommunication can mean little else. In his account of the plotting (*Studies* 3, 209–10), Elton employed the summary of the despatch of 30 Sept. 1534 in *Letters and Papers, Foreign and Domestic, Henry VIII*, VII (1883), art. 1206.

[45] The fall of Anne Boleyn in the interval may have altered the situation. There is a hint of such an argument in 'Pilgrimage of Grace', *Studies* 3, 210.

[46] *Ibid.*, 209.

[47] *Ibid.*, 212.

[48] The reappraisal is to be found in *Reign of Henry VIII, English Court*, and explicitly in Christopher Coleman and David Starkey, ed., *Revolution Reassessed* (Oxford, 1986).

[49] The public exchange was limited to Elton's reviews of *Revolution Reassessed* and *English Court*, 'A New Age of Reform?' and 'Tudor Government', and Starkey's reply, 'Tudor Government: The Facts?', *HJ*, 30 (1987), 709–16, 31 (1988), 425–34, 921–31. The underlying

Parliament. The personal motive for this work is sufficiently notorious and does not need further comment. Nor are the specifically parliamentary aspects relevant here, except to note that Elton's approach to the parliamentary history of Elizabeth's reign both subsumed his old distinction between serious business and ephemeral politics within the wider revisionist emphasis on the greater importance of parliamentary business as opposed to constitutional or political conflict and combined it with his new interest in factional politics. Political conflict was now to be explained by the activities of court factions taking their opposition into the parliamentary arena. As he put it:

> Without the monarch, the Lords and Commons had no power; without the Council, they even lacked the means for organising themselves for any political purpose or for initiating a policy. This degree of powerlessness, this dependence on sources of power outside itself, had always been the truth about the Parliament as a participant in national politics.[50]

Leaving aside the wider aspects of this interpretation of parliamentary politics, what needs examination here is the argument that, to quote from 'Arthur Hall', 'Like so many other parliamentary events in the reign of Elizabeth, the demolition and restoration of Arthur Hall reflected the politics of Council factions rather than strictly House of Commons matters.'[51] Or to quote from his essay on 'Parliament' in Christopher Haigh's collection *The Reign of Elizabeth I*:

> The agitation over the Queen's marriage and the uncertain succession even more clearly demonstrates the real meaning of protest in Parliament. In 1563 and 1566, led by councillors despairing of any chance of pressing their policy in Council, both Houses were mobilised to urge the Queen to act ... Similarly, the pressure for the executions of Norfolk and the Queen of Scots ... exhibits not the opposition of religious extremists, but a rift within the government itself, as some courtiers and councillors, having failed at Court, tried to use Parliament to press their policies upon the Queen.[52]

Elton's motive for seeking to discredit what he termed 'the myth of opposition' needs no discussion here. Our concern is with the positive case he made for the court factional explanation. He did so in three

---

issue is the distinction between court and government. Both Elton's criticism of Starkey for writing the history of the Tudor court solely in terms of the Privy Chamber and Starkey's argument that the Tudor revolution was one-sided are valid.

[50] *Parliament*, 377.

[51] 'Arthur Hall', *Studies* 3 (39), 266.

[52] *Reign of Elizabeth I*, 99. As I observed in my review of *Studies* 4 (see n. 17 above), no reason is given for the omission of this essay from that volume.

specific instances: 'Arthur Hall' and the accounts of the debates on the succession in 1563 and 1566 in the section 'Great Affairs' in *Parliament*. His arguments rest not only on his own wider theories about court factions, but also on two new interpretations of Elizabeth parliamentary history advanced very much under his influence. The first was N. L. Jones's reappraisal of the religious settlement of 1559 and the second M. A. R. Graves's 'men of business' thesis.[53]

In his 'grasp of historical context' Arthur Hall is a true Eltonian hero. Yet what Elton wished to explain in 'Arthur Hall' was the hostility to Hall in the Commons in 1581, and specifically that of Thomas Norton. While admitting that 'the hunting of Arthur Hall sprang from motives linked to the obscure politics of the City [of London]', Elton, very much influenced by Graves's argument that Norton was the privy council's man-of-business, also detected the council's hand at work.[54] However, the ample evidence that Burghley had a soft spot for Hall and that the attack on Hall was led by Sir Thomas Wilson and Sir Walter Mildmay, with Sir Christopher Hatton playing a somewhat obscure role in the background, suggested a factional rather than a conciliar explanation. Hall was the victim of factional politics within the council: 'This would seem to clinch it: the real target for the Council group in pursuit of Hall was Hall's sole friend in high places, Burghley himself.'[55]

Ironically, given his reliance on the man-of-business thesis, Elton's interpretation of this affair has caused Graves considerable difficulties. In his recent biography of Norton Graves has emphasized Norton's connection to Burghley, and therefore he has had to work hard to find a convincing explanation for Norton's siding with Burghley's enemies on this occasion.[56] No less problematic is the composition of Elton's conciliar faction. If Sir Thomas Wilson had an established connection with the earl of Leicester, and Hatton was very much his own man, Mildmay was not the most obvious participant in an intrigue against Burghley. Elton finds the explanation for his involvement in somewhat mysterious disagreements with Burghley over the Anjou marriage.[57] Yet even if they held different views over the Anjou marriage, there was a general appreciation among the Elizabethan council that disagreements over policy were legitimate and Mildmay worked closely with Burghley for many years both before and after 1581. No more obvious is the

---

[53] N. L. Jones, *Faith by Statute: Parliament and the Settlement of Religion 1559*, Royal Historical Society, Studies in History, xxxii (1982). The latest version of Graves's thesis can be found in *Thomas Norton the Parliament Man* (Oxford, 1994).

[54] 'Arthur Hall', 260.

[55] *Ibid.*, 262.

[56] *Thomas Norton*, 361–2.

[57] 'Arthur Hall', 261.

answer to the question what—if their target was Burghley—did the faction hope to gain by attacking Hall? All Elton could come up with was 'if Hall had had to suffer the punishment imposed by the House the loss of face would certainly have extended to his patron'.[58] This raises the immediate supplementary questions what did 'loss of face' mean and how would it have extended to Burghley? It is difficult to avoid the suspicion that an elaborate framework is being erected on some rather shaky foundations.

The succession debates in 1563 and 1566 are notoriously difficult affairs and on one level Elton's interpretations are as valid as any of the others advanced to date. The possibility that there was a genuine faction involved in the 1563 debates in the form of various Seymour partisans advancing the case for Lady Catherine Grey Elton rejected out of hand. He did so partly (one suspects) because Sir John Neale had suggested there was parliamentary agitation in favour of the Grey claim, but also because the very existence of this type of faction assumed a degree of political organization within the Commons not directly instigated by a member of the council.[59] Instead Elton placed Lord Robert Dudley at the centre: 'the future earl of Leicester and his supporters offer themselves as the most likely Council faction to work up steam for the general hope [sic] that Elizabeth might act' and 'the "party" calling for action came together from a mixture of motives and under the guidance of a councillor (Dudley) who was not even a member'.[60] Lord Robert's motive in mobilizing support in the Commons was marriage: 'Lord Robert had reason to think that a call to the Queen to marry might promote himself into a royal consort.'[61] His evidence for the 'Dudley faction', on the other hand, consists of the suggestion that Alexander Nowell, the Dean of St Paul's, who preached at the opening of parliament, 'belonged to the clientage of the Dudley family', and that the release Lord Stafford obtained from the Lords for ill health was obtained by Dudley.[62]

This line of argument involves conflating the debate on the succession with the pressure on the queen to marry. It is instructive to compare Elton's case with the more recent treatment by Susan Doran. She too sees Dudley at the centre of the agitation, but criticizes her predecessors,

[58] Ibid., 266.

[59] J. E. Neale, Elizabeth I and her Parliaments I. 1559–1581 (1965 edn), 103–4. See also the discussion of the numerous Grey supporters sitting for Seymour seats in 1563 in S. T. Bindoff's chapter, 'Parliamentary History 1529–1688', in The Victoria History of Wiltshire, V (1957), 129.

[60] Parliament, 358–60.

[61] Ibid., 358.

[62] Ibid., 358, 361. Elton does not identify the peer, but he was clearly the 11th Lord Stafford. 'The Dudley faction' is referred to on p. 362.

including Elton, for failing to appreciate that marriage rather than the succession was the issue at stake.[63] Her case rests primarily on sources that Elton did not employ, and she is less persuaded of the involvement of a Dudley faction.[64] She argues that if Nowell was acting for anyone, it was for the council rather than Dudley himself, but (like Michael Graves) she draws attention to the role played by Richard Gallys, the mayor of Windsor, whom she identifies as one of Dudley's men of business.[65] However, Gallys is said to have initiated a debate on the succession on 16 January 1563. Doran's explanation of how a debate on the succession resulted in a petition to marry by the 26th is an idiosyncratic one: the assumption that marriage (in general terms) was less contentious an issue than the succession.[66]

One central conundrum that neither Elton, Doran nor Graves has been able to resolve was the role of Thomas Norton, who read the Commons draft petition to the House, but who was also the author of *Gorboduc* a year earlier.[67] The traditional reading of *Gorboduc* as a succession commentary would place Norton among the Grey supporters.[68] More recently discovered evidence suggests that *Gorboduc* may have been a marriage tract written in Dudley's favour.[69] This would cast Norton as a possible supporter of a Dudley marriage in 1563, but his long and active career supplies no other evidence of an association with Dudley.[70] Including him in a Dudley faction is highly debatable.

The high politics of the parliament are central to any argument for conciliar factions. The parliament was summoned to raise money for the Le Havre expedition, and Elizabeth's unwillingness to have either marriage or the succession discussed publicly was well established and clearly known to her councillors. From her perspective the parliament was therefore a calculated risk, particularly given her desire at this

[63] Susan Doran, *Monarchy and Matrimony: The Courtships of Elizabeth I* (1996), 60.

[64] *Ibid.*, 60–1, 64. She relies heavily on the reports of the Spanish ambassador, Alvaro de La Quadra, particularly that of 15 November 1562. Elton was sceptical of ambassadors as sources for parliamentary proceedings, see his comments on Chapuys's reports on the parliament of 1532 in 'Commons Supplication', *Studies* 2 (25), 112–13. Doran's caution about the Dudley faction was derived in part from my conclusions in 'The Dudley Clientele and the House of Commons, 1559–1586', *Parliamentary History*, 8 (1989), 216–39.

[65] *Monarchy and Matrimony*, 61, 64. *Norton*, 106.

[66] *Monarchy and Matrimony*, 64.

[67] *Parliament*, 358–9. *Monarchy and Matrimony*, 56–7, 61–2. *Norton*, 95–7.

[68] Marie Axton, *The Queen's Two Bodies: Drama and the Elizabethan Succession*, RHS Studies in History (1977), 46.

[69] See Adams, 'The Release of Lord Darnley and the Failure of the Amity', in *Mary Stewart: Queen in Three Kingdoms*, ed. Michael Lynch (Oxford, 1988), 137 n. 117, and *Monarchy and Matrimony*, 55–7.

[70] Graves accepts the connection between Dudley and *Gorboduc* and denies categorically that Norton and Sackville were members of a Grey faction (p. 97), but other than that Dudley appears only peripherally in *Norton*. See my review, *History*, 81 (1996), 656–7.

juncture to maintain friendly relations with the Queen of Scots, whose interests were most threatened by a possible limitation of the succession. Given Dudley's apparent commitment to the Queen of Scots's interests and Cecil's equally well-established caution, the council had no desire to rock the boat.[71] The earl of Huntingdon's surviving letter on the subject makes clear his unhappiness at his name being used.[72] The only people to have a clear interest in making the succession a public issue were those who wished to bar Mary.[73] The case for Dudley rests solely on the assumption that he had an interest in encouraging agitation for Elizabeth to marry. Yet neither Elton nor Doran are able to discover evidence for a sustained campaign to pressure the queen into agreeing to marry—indeed Doran's concession that the ultimate petition for marriage represented an evasion of the difficulties posed by the succession blunts the thrust of her argument. Moreover, given Elizabeth's dislike of this type of public debate, open encouragement of parliamentary agitation would do Dudley's chances little good, as Elton recognized in his further suggestion that the proposal of Dudley as a husband to Mary was 'one of Elizabeth's cruel jokes' to pay him back. Unfortunately this argument is difficult to maintain in the face of Elizabeth's sustained commitment to this scheme in 1564–5.[74]

The situation in 1566 is far more confused—indeed I must confess that I still do not fully understand it. Elton claimed that initially the 'great matter [the succession] which everyone expected to come up again remained dormant ... The real cause appears to have been a division in the Privy Council where Leicester apparently favoured the Queen of Scots while Norfolk supported Catherine Grey.[75] This situation was transformed by Molyneux's motion. In a novel argument, Elton suggested that Molyneux's motion was engineered by Cecil in 'a conciliar manoeuvre which accepted that if the money bill was to go forward marriage and the succession would have to be allowed back on the agenda'.[76] His general argument, that the course of the session was punctuated by a series of Cecilian manoeuvres, has been convincingly challenged by J. D. Alsop.[77] However, Alsop's claim that 'Few, if any, scholars would accept the [Spanish ambassador's] assertion that Elizabeth had not dared summon Parliament in the years following the

---

[71] This argument can be found in 'Release of Darnley', 136–7.
[72] Ibid., 137 n. 117.
[73] Ibid., 136.
[74] Parliament, 33. Cf. 'Release of Darnley', 128, 138–42.
[75] Parliament, 365.
[76] Ibid., 367.
[77] J. D. Alsop, 'Reinterpreting the Elizabethan Commons: The Parliamentary Session of 1566', JBS, 29 (1990), 216–40.

1563 session' can be queried.[78] On the contrary, Elizabeth's desire to avoid a revival of parliamentary pressure on the succession is the best explanation for the prorogations of parliament between 1563 and 1566. The reactions of the Queen of Scots are very revealing. She took parliament's possible role in the succession so seriously that as soon as she learnt that one was about to meet, she immediately sent an ambassador to London to safeguard her interests. This was why Maitland of Lethington was sent in 1563 and Robert Melville in 1566, but it was also the real reason for the well-known embassy of Melville's brother James Melville of Halhill in the autumn of 1564.[79] The decision to summon parliament in the autumn of 1566, when the birth of the future James VI had if anything heightened the tension surrounding the Stuart succession, therefore becomes all the more curious, and Elton's argument that financial needs forced the Crown to take a calculated risk (or uncalculated gamble) over the succession becomes more substantial.

By associating the MP John Molyneux with Cecil, Elton revised an earlier tentative identification of him as a follower of Leicester's. In his reinterpretation of the 1566 session, Alsop has reopened this question: 'In view of the fact that Molyneux's brother was secretary to Sir Henry Sidney in the later 1560s, it may be worth considering the possibility that his concerns lay with the Leicester clique.'[80] As with Richard Gallys in 1563, Molyneux's possible associations have a direct bearing on any factional interpretation of parliamentary politics. In Gallys's case the fact that he also initiated the debate on the Queen of Scots in 1572 is significant, for here we have a clearly active parliamentarian. The more difficult issue is the nature of his association with Leicester. Both Doran and Graves have rested their case that Gallys was one of Leicester's 'men-of-business' on the biography in *The History of Parliament*, but this does not mention any connection to Leicester.[81] In 1563 Gallys was mayor of New Windsor, and in that office signed the patent appointing Dudley, who had been granted the constableship of Windsor Castle the previous autumn, high steward of the borough on 9 September 1563.[82] Gallys was also a tenant of the castle, but the only evidence suggestive of a closer relationship is a reference in the 1588

---

[78] *Ibid.*, 221.

[79] 'Release of Darnley', pp. 126, 138. For Robert Melville, see also Neale, *Elizabeth and her Parliaments I*, 158–9.

[80] 'Reinterpreting the Commons', 239. Wallace MacCaffrey suggested that Molyneux may have been a partisan of Leicester's in *The Shaping of the Elizabethan Regime* (Princeton, 1968), 211.

[81] P. W. Hasler, ed., *The House of Commons 1558–1603* (3 vols., 1981), II, 163.

[82] The original of the patent is now Longleat House, Dudley Papers, Box II, art. 12. The Dudley Papers are cited with the kind permission of the marquess of Bath.

inventory of Leicester's wardrobe to a short sword 'which was Gallecies of Windsor'.[83] Leicester certainly exercised electoral patronage at Windsor, but Gallys's stature in the borough did not make him dependent on it.[84] Molyneux presents a greater problem, for a 'Molynex' is included in Cecil's well-known list of Leicester's friends of 1565–7.[85] However, no further evidence has yet been discovered to establish the connection, nor even to supply 'Molynex's' christian name, despite the survival of two long lists of men given Leicester's badge and livery in 1567.[86]

In 'The Dudley Clientele and the House of Commons' I concluded by noting that while certain of Leicester's followers (William Grice, Thomas Digges and Robert Snagge in particular) were very active parliamentarians, the great majority—including his leading household officers and servants—left little or no trace in the records of the Commons, and therefore the existence of an organized 'Dudley faction' was doubtful.[87] In essays published at roughly the same time on the House of Lords in the 1640s and the parliamentary patronage of Robert Cecil, earl of Salisbury, both J. S. A. Adamson and Stephen Hollings reached strikingly similar conclusions. To quote Adamson:

> Indeed, there is no evidence that peers ever attempted to demand the adherence (or the votes) of M.P.s who were their servants and stewards ... Far more important as potential allies of peers were those members of the Commons who were figures of standing and repute within their own House.[88]

[83] For Gallys's tenancy, see the Windsor Castle accounts for the period 1562–74, Public Record Office, Special Collections 6/Elizabeth I/136–47. Gallys is not found among the officers of the Castle listed in these accounts. For the reference to his sword, see Longleat, Dudley Papers XIII, fol. 21.

[84] This was my conclusion in 'Dudley Clientele and the Commons', 225–7, 233. Given the disappearance of the New Windsor records for the reign of Elizabeth I, we are dependent on Elias Ashmole's transcriptions (Bodleian Library, MS Ashmole 1126). Ashmole (fol. 46) notes the election in 1572 of Gallys and Edmund Dockwra, lieutenant of the Castle, and a letter of recommendation from Leicester. This certainly applied to Dockwra, but it is not clear whether it included Gallys as well.

[85] Hatfield House, Cecil Papers, MS 155, art. 28 (cited with the kind permission of the marquess of Salisbury). See the discussion in Adams, 'The Dudley Clientèle, 1553–1563', in *The Tudor Nobility*, ed. G. W. Bernard (Manchester, 1992), 240–1, in which I suggested Mollynex was probably Edmund rather than John. On the basis of further study of the internal evidence, I would now date this document to 1565.

[86] The lists are published in Adams, ed., *Household Accounts and Disbursement Books of Robert Dudley, Earl of Leicester, 1558–61, 1584–86*, Camden Society, 5th ser., vi (1995), 432–8. To be fair, Molyneux's absence from these lists proves only that he was not a member of Leicester's household.

[87] 'Dudley Clientele and the Commons', 231.

[88] J. S. A. Adamson, 'Parliamentary Management, Men-of-Business and the House of Lord, 1640–49', in *A Pillar of the Constitution. The House of Lords in British Politics, 1640–1784*, ed. Clive Jones (1989), 21–50, see 45–6.

Hollings's verdict was more or less the same: 'Being a client of the Earl of Salisbury did not commit you to support the Earl or government in Parliament, and ... this was understood by both the Earl and his clients.'[89]

Slightly earlier in his essay Adamson supplied a reason for his conclusion:

It was in the nature of such arrangements that peers should strive to leave the independence of the privilege-conscious House of Commons apparently unviolated. It hardly availed an M.P., when moving a question in the Commons, to announce that he had been put up to making his speech at the request of a member of the Lords. Sponsors of legislation in which they had a vested interest took pains to cover their tracks.[90]

There is some early Stuart evidence to support this argument, notably Robert Cecil's possible regular use of unofficial agents to raise matters in the Commons.[91] There is also the negative example of 'Goring's motion' in 1621.[92] However, Adamson's argument raises the broader question: if their servants were so unimportant, why then did the peers go to such lengths to get them elected to the Commons?

In Leicester's case a basic reliability may have been the reason. His electioneering in 1571–2 was undertaken partly under the umbrella of a general conciliar instruction that lords-lieutenants should ensure the election of reliable men in their counties. There is also evidence that in 1584 he and Walsingham engaged in an extensive electioneering campaign to ensure support for intervention in the Netherlands in the Commons.[93] On one level Gallys and Molyneux would appear to be suitable agents for theories of parliamentary intervention through indirect means, though one could also ask why—if indirect means were being employed—Leicester would use men with any connection at all? More important, though, is the question what did Leicester hope to

---

[89] Stephen Hollings, 'Court Patronage, County Governors and the Early Stuart Parliaments', *Parergon*, n.s. 6 (1988), 121–35, see 122–3.

[90] 'Parliamentary Management', 32.

[91] N. R. N. Tyacke, 'Wroth, Cecil and the Parliamentary Session of 1604', and Pauline Croft, 'Serving the Archduke: Robert Cecil's Management of the Parliamentary Session of 1606', *Historical Research*, 50 (1977), 120–5, and 64 (1991), 289–304.

[92] Negative in the sense that Goring was immediately identified as speaking on Buckingham's behalf. See Adams, 'Foreign Policy and the Parliaments of 1621 and 1624', in *Faction and Parliament*, ed. Kevin Sharpe (Oxford, 1978), 163, Conrad Russell, *Parliaments and English politics 1621–1629* (Oxford, 1979), 133–5, and Roger Lockyer, *Buckingham* (1981), 108–11.

[93] 'Dudley Clientele and the Commons', 219, 232. I intend to explore the 1584 electioneering in further detail in my planned study *The Decision to Intervene: England and the Revolt of the Netherlands 1584–85*.

gain by having these motions moved? In arguing for the attribution of the 1566 speech on the succession to Molyneux, Alsop has noted that here too, as he did in his account of 1563, Elton conflated marriage and the succession.[94] While we might argue for a personal interest on Leicester's part in bringing marriage forward, his attitude towards to the succession is less clear. There is sufficient evidence to suggest that until 1571–2 Leicester was more willing to come to terms with Mary than Cecil. Therefore there is some substance in the argument that Leicester took Mary's side in the succession debates. But in 1566, as in 1563, Mary's interests were best served by avoiding discussion. Thus Leicester, on the face of it, would have had no interest in stimulating a debate on this subject.

For all the difficulties of the factional explanation of Elizabethan parliamentary politics, Elton's separation of politics from business has led—almost by accident—to a reconsideration of a hitherto neglected subject, the national politics of the corporate towns. This took the form of a series of battles both against each other and against London for commercial interests and monopolies, battles that were fought out in parliament, before the council, at court and in the law courts. One aspect, the 'decline of the outports', has long been known, but Neale's assumption of the electoral supineness of the towns has helped to obscure the full extent of the urban dimension.[95] In his study of the Yarmouth interest at work in 'Piscatorial Politics' Elton has provided a valuable description of one parliamentary campaign.[96] The earl of Leicester's patronage of boroughs reveals how interweaved urban interests were with the wider politics of aristocratic clienteles and factions.[97] The whole subject deserves investigation.

The 'Points of Contact' articles are now twenty years old, but the study of Tudor factions and interests is still in its infancy. However, Elton's general theory about factional politics, at least in the terms in which he framed it, can be challenged. There is a final paradox here, in that Elton was at his boldest and most adventurous in a subject— Elizabethan politics—in which his command of the sources and evidence was at its weakest. By seeking to reduce all political discontent and

[94] 'Reinterpreting the Commons', 239.

[95] See the famous chapter on the 'invasion of the boroughs by the country gentlemen', in J. E. Neale, *The Elizabethan House of Commons* (1963 edn), 133–54.

[96] 'Piscatorial Politics', *Studies* 4 (54), 112–13, 124–5. See also Robert Tittler, 'Elizabethan Towns and the "Points of Contact": Parliament', and David Dean, 'London Lobbies and Parliament: The Case of the Brewers and Coopers in the Parliament of 1593', *Parl. Hist.*, 8 (1989), 275–88, 341–65.

[97] 'Dudley Clientele and the Commons', 220–3. I have explored this subject further in a paper, 'The Elizabethan Earl of Leicester as a Patron of Boroughs', delivered to the Tudor seminar at Cambridge University in 1991. It will be published in a forthcoming collection of my essays and papers.

'opposition' to the workings of obscure aristocratic intrigues and court factions he ran the risk of erecting complex edificies on shaky foundations. Not only did he make little effort to study the factions themselves, but the explanations he supplied for their motives, as in 'Arthur Hall', were on a level that he would have been the first to criticize if advanced by anyone else. Possibly at the heart of the problem is the fact that Elton never escaped the influence of his early distinction between government and politics. He was never particularly interested in political behaviour as such and made no real attempt to explore it. He never examined the problems of patronage and his conception of factions was quite basic and old-fashioned. Yet despite the critical tone to this paper, the Eltonian legacy is not, overall, a negative one. At the end of the day Elton was a true heavy-weight; he can always be read for profit and even when he is wrong his errors are stimulating. The questions he posed are questions that need addressing and the issues he tackled are important ones. This seriousness of purpose is his true legacy. He is still the ultimate reader of any scholarly work of Tudor history.

G. R. ELTON AS A LEGAL HISTORIAN

By Clive Holmes

READ 28 MARCH 1996 AT THE INSTITUTE OF HISTORICAL RESEARCH LONDON

'I AM not', Geoffrey Elton insisted, 'I am not a legal historian.' The provenance of this solemn denial is curious. Elton was giving a lecture in the Old Hall of Lincoln's Inn to the Selden Society, the pre-eminent learned society for the study of legal history in England, in 1978. He had been invited to join its Council in the previous year, and was to preside over the Society from 1982 to 1985. Even from that eminence, writing his study of F.W.Maitland, Elton persisted in his earlier denial: he was not 'a historian of law'.[1] Manifestly this was not an opinion shared by his colleagues in the Selden Society who invited him to lecture in 1978, and elected him to their presidency five years later. And it is certainly easy to discount Elton's denial as a false modesty. He was the mentor of a cadre of distinguished scholars whose work, more obviously than his own, centred on the study of courts, legal procedures or doctrines. He had emphasised in all his writings that those historians—particularly those *social* historians—who had plundered the rich records generated by the courts, were obliged to recognise that the 'stifling formality' of the latter could conceal essential issues, and badly mislead the neophyte. 'Critical analysis of the available sources' was imperative; 'only a precise knowledge of the machinery can really unlock the meaning of the record'.[2] And, most important, Elton was a distinguished historian in his own right of an instrument of critical importance, one of the three Maine modes of juridical change,[3] for constitutional and legal development and innovation: he was a pre-eminent student of legislation, more specifically, of parliamentary statute.

We should perhaps remind ourselves of how much of Elton's emphasis on the importance of statute for Henry VIII and Cromwell, once so original, has now become part of the accepted account of the early Tudor period. Statutes were used to determine matters which, previously, had never or very infrequently been the subject of government

---

[1] 'English Law', *Studies* 3(40), 274; *Maitland*, vii.

[2] 'Crime', *Studies* 3(41), 290, 300, 303.

[3] Sir Henry Maine suggested three 'instrumentalities' 'by which Law is brought into harmony with society': legal fictions, equity, and legislation (*Ancient Law* (Everyman edn, 1917), 15).

interference, like the royal succession or religious doctrine. They were also employed, perhaps more significantly, where other, prerogative, instruments had been utilised earlier: meat prices were now regulated by statute; the authority of commissioners of sewers was warranted by statute; central administrative agencies were established by statute; even royal proclamations were validated by statute.[4] Thomas Cromwell seems a man intoxicated by the possibilities that inhered in parliamentary legislation.[5] We owe these insights to Geoffrey Elton: no wonder his professional standing was recognised by the Selden Society.

And yet Elton denied that he was a legal historian. How are we to understand this apparent paradox? We get some insight, I think, if we pursue the language of his Selden Society lecture: 'I am not a legal historian, I am not a lawyer.' For an amateur to address a group 'so eminent in those particular ways' was an embarrassment certainly, but also a 'pleasure', because 'at least I can talk history, perhaps teach history, to lawyers'.[6] For Elton, legal history was—or had been—the domain of the lawyers, and while he never issued a missionary injunction to historians to rescue 'legal history out of the hands of the lawyers' as did Christopher Hill,[7] he was equally suspicious of the genre. When lawyers, Elton informed a distinguished gathering of that tribe at the Illinois College of Law in 1989, raise themselves above 'their more customary preoccupations with pettifoggery' to scholarly pursuits, 'they do not commonly think historically'.[8] This manifests itself in what Elton called 'traditional lawyers' legal history' in a number of ways. First, in an excessive preoccupation with the narrow technicalities of the law. Second, in a predilection for basing their studies on a single document, or class of documents, defined unreflectingly as authoritative; these self-validating mandarin texts are then employed with a deference that precludes proper source criticism. In conjunction, these first two characteristics lead to a third. Law is divorced from the social, political and administrative circumstances in which it was developed, and in which it operated. Legal historians had failed to do 'the work on the ground'

---

[4]For meat prices, see H. W. Heinze, 'The Pricing of Meat: A Study in the Use of Royal Proclamations in the Reign of Henry VIII', *Historical Journal* 12 (1969), 595. For sewers, see H. C. Richardson, 'The Early History of the Commissions of Sewers', *English Historical Review* [hereafter *EHR*] 34 (1919), 385–93; Clive Holmes, 'Statutory Interpretation in the Early Seventeenth Century: The Courts, the Council, and the Commissioners of Sewers', in *Law and Social Change in British History*, ed. J. A. Guy and H. G. Beale (1984), 107–17 [hereafter, Holmes, 'Statutory Interpretation']. For statutory agencies, see *Tudor Revolution*, 189–223. For proclamations, 'Proclamations', *Studies* 1(19); R. W. Heinze, *The Proclamations of the Tudor Kings* (Cambridge, 1976), chap. 6.

[5]'Political Creed', *Studies* 2(31), 226.

[6]'English Law', *Studies* 3(40), 274.

[7]Christopher Hill, *Puritanism and Revolution* (1958), p. 28.

[8]'Human Rights', *Studies* 4(51), 69.

that would enable them to understand the actual creation and enforcement of legal norms. 'If legal history is ever to grow up into a branch
of real history', it must free itself from the professional assumptions
that induced such flaws, Elton insisted.[9]

But Elton had another, more fundamental, criticism of 'lawyers' legal
history'; he convicted them of a serious intellectual failure that 'ruins
genuine history'. This was the 'teleological pre-occupation' that led
lawyers to value past legal forms 'only inasmuch as they persist and
have a life in the present'. Legal historians 'were led to believe that
their task lay in explaining the present rather than the past'. The so-
called 'Whig interpretation' of history denounced by Butterfield was,
in fact, nothing of the kind; it was simply 'the lawyers' interpretation
of the history of law, government and the constitution'. This was an
insight upon which Sir Herbert did not sufficiently reflect when his
own scholarly interests moved into the field of the history of science.
His insistent, triumphalist concern with the genesis of modern discoveries and theory rendered his work akin to that of 'a good lawyer
historian ... a faithful disciple of Sir Edward Coke'. Lawyers not only
limited their concerns to those aspects of the past that could be viewed
as precursors of modern doctrine or practice: worse, they read the
records of the past in the light of that modern doctrine, guaranteeing
that a proper approach to historical context would not be achieved.[10]
So Leonard Levy, studying the dispute over the oath *ex officio* in the
High Commission, 'reads' the latter in the light of the Fifth Amendment:
he has, in Elton's suave rebuke, 'got rather carried away by his laudable
conviction that he was investigating one of the great principles of
liberty'.[11]

And so Elton excoriated much that passed for legal history. Its
premises and methods ensured that it was not 'a branch of real history';
most particularly, its teleological preoccupation was subversive of proper
historical method. This was the substance of the indictment, which was
then tricked out with swipes at the 'pompous jargon' affected by
some scholars in the field; by battering its deified practitioners, like
Holdsworth and Radzinowicz; by caustic jibes at the tenor of its
periodicals, not least the flagship *Law Quarterly Review*: 'an austere
journal in which incomprehensible problems so regularly receive incom-

[9] Elton, reviews of *Lawyers in Early-Modern Europe and America*, ed. W. R. Prest, in *Times Literary Supplement* [hereafter *TLS*], 6 March 1981, 262; of J. H. Langbein, *Torture and the Law of Proof: Europe and England in the Ancien Régime* in *J. of Modern History* 50 (1978), 737–8; of L. W. Levy, *Origins of the Fifth Amendment* in *EHR*, 84 (1969), 839–40; 'Crime', *Studies* 3(41), 289.
[10] *Maitland*, 35; 'Butterfield', *Studies* 4(63), 267, 276.
[11] Elton, review of L. W. Levy, *Origins of the Fifth Amendment*, in *EHR*, 84 (1969), 839.

prehensible solutions'.[12] The hostility was, in some measure, reciprocated. J. M. Kaye, criticizing *Reform and Renewal*, in, of course, the *Law Quarterly Review*, argued that two of Elton's key assumptions, Thomas Cromwell's genuine commitment to, and the significance of the 1530s for, law reform, were questionable. Historians had said no less in their reviews of the work, but a significant sub-text of Kaye's essay was a professional suspicion both of programmes of legal reform and of the utility of statute as an instrument of significant legal change of almost Blackstoneian proportions. Statutes were usually the product of lobbying and special pleading by narrow interest groups; statutes normally 'led only to muddle and complexity'. Kaye concluded, sardonically, that amongst the welter of legislation in the 1530s it might be possible to pick out, 'here and there', an act 'which may seem to have been based on the idea of doing some disinterested good'; and he mooted the claims of 23 Henry VIII c. 4, forbidding brewers to make their own barrels.[13] Reform and renewal, indeed! Elton's elevation by the Selden Society, 'whose publications', he wrote, 'have shaped the nature of English legal history' (a double edged compliment, given his excoriation of so much of its product), seems very odd.

And yet Elton's presidency makes sense, and not just because of his own standing as a student of an essential aspect of legal change: legislation. From the late 1970s Elton, while still savaging its older practice and practitioners, acknowledged that legal history was experiencing a brilliant transformation. 'The present renaissance of legal history is one of the most cheering prospects on the historical scene'; topics were being 'wrestled from the dead hand of traditional lawyers' legal history'; Holdsworth's name no longer figured in the footnotes to major studies in the field.[14]

And this new product was not merely welcomed, it was employed by Elton in his own overviews of the period. In his earlier writings, Elton had tended to view the common law administered in the ancient courts as both ossified and passive: it was itself unable to provide new remedies for perceived ills and had to rely on statute to rectify its problems. Not until the 1580s did the common law courts begin 'to revive in the hands of men who valued the old law ... but saw the need for change'.[15] By the late 1970s this view of the ancient courts had shifted markedly to accommodate the work of the new, approved,

---

[12] Style: Elton, review of J. H. Langbein, *Prosecuting Crime in the Renaissance*, in *TLS*, 20 Sept. 1974, 991. Holdsworth and Radzinowicz: 'English Law', *Studies* 3(40), 276–7; 'Crime', *Studies* 3(41), 289, 296 n. 5, 302; *Maitland*, 29. Journals: *ibid.*, 2, 76.

[13] J. M. Kaye, review of *Reform and Renewal*, in *Law Quarterly Review*, 90 (1974), 573–5.

[14] Elton, review of *Lawyers in Early Modern Europe and America*, ed. W. R. Prest, in *TLS*, 6 March 1981, 262.

[15] *Tudors* (1955), 417.

generation of legal historians, notably John Baker. The common law, Elton acknowledged *was* 'flexible enough to meet changing circumstances' in the early sixteenth century; it possessed 'a self-renewing power'. Indeed, legal change was achieved 'much more commonly' by courts than by parliamentary enactment, through 'the action of counsel and judges anxious to accommodate outdated concepts to a changing society'. This last comment is from the second (1982) edition of *The Tudor Constitution*, and the influence and incorporation of the new research is most apparent in the revisions to sections of this volume: the discussion of the common law, Elton himself wrote, had 'changed out of recognition' since the first (1960) edition. This overstates the case, however. In the second edition of the *Tudor Constitution*, the reader is confronted with two revolutions in early Tudor England. We have 'the revolution described by Dr Baker', those substantive and procedural developments generated from within the common law system. And we have Elton's own Cromwellian revolution, with its emphasis on the transformation of the perception and role of statute, and the concomitant statutory transformation of law and legal institutions. But Elton found nothing repugnant in this duplication: the two revolutions were functionally related. Much of the Cromwellian legislation affirmed and codified the new principles and practices devised piecemeal by the lawyers. In this sense, the act of parliament was the 'ultimate instrument' of the common lawyers, establishing 'a certainty far more definite than the precedents created by judgements'.[16]

The lion shall lay down with the lamb. Elton was a distinguished commentator on aspects of legal procedure and practice in Tudor England. While he had savaged the absurdities of 'traditional lawyers' legal history', he had welcomed a revised form of the genre, much of it produced by his own students or those working under his influence, and he had incorporated its conclusions into his own overview of the period. Hence the appropriateness of the accolades of the Selden Society. And yet the denial still resonates awkwardly: 'I am not a legal historian.'

I want at this point, to shift the focus of this discussion from analysis of Elton's intellectual trajectory with relation to the practice of legal history, towards a critique of his own substantive contribution to that field. I want to argue that, because Elton was never fully at ease with legal questions, his central contribution not only on law but on parliamentary legislation itself, requires serious modification. As a corollary, I will suggest that Elton's endeavour to incorporate the new legal history into his synthesis is flawed: that Baker's work, in particular,

---

[16] *Constitution* (1982), xii, 148, 150–1; *Maitland*, 84, 86–7; 'Lex', *Studies* 4(50), 37, 48.

is far more subversive of his paradigm than he recognised. Two revolutions in the early Tudor period are too many.

But before beginning this critique, we must make one more foray into Elton's attitudes to lawyers and the law. For Elton, law continued to be 'that most arcane of all systems of knowledge'. He found it much easier 'to understand the thought processes of physicists or biologists, analysing their problems empirically', he wrote, than those of lawyers, seeking guides to present action from precedent. 'In their acquired mental characteristics' lawyers and historians are poles apart, and their concerns are irreconcilable. Elton found the 'teleological pre-occupation' of the legal professional not merely dangerous as a guide to historical investigation, not merely rebarbative, but intellectually impenetrable.[17] But this is no attitude for the historian, even the political or constitutional historian, enjoined 'to do the work on the ground'. The mind-set of the legal profession, its paradigms, even its ahistorical assumptions however derisory, are as crucial an element in the context of law enforcement as are 'the social and administrative circumstances' which Elton berated legal historians for neglecting in their work. So Lord Chancellor Nottingham's artificial doctrine that the Statute of Uses was only intended to apply to such equitable interests as fell within the purlieu of the earlier act of 1 Richard III c.1 is palpable nonsense as history: but we must seek to understand it if we hope to analyse Chancery's revival of equitable estates in the seventeenth century.[18] This need to comprehend the thought processes of the legal profession sympathetically is essential to any proper reading of legislation in the early modern period, and Elton's failure to achieve this is a major weakness in his work.

Let us begin this substantive analysis in high rhetorical vein, by considering a sonorous and didactic passage addressed to the bench by Francis Bacon, pleading in Chudleigh's case in 1594:

> For, as you my lords judges better know, so, with modesty, I may put it in your remembrance, that your authority over the ... statutes of this realm is not such as the Papists affirm the Church to have over the Scriptures, to make them a shipman's hose or a nose of wax; but such as we say the Church has over them, *scil.* to expound them faithfully and apply them properly.[19]

The statutes as Holy Writ: a simile very agreeable to Geoffrey Elton's

---

[17] Elton, review of *Lawyers in early modern Europe and America*, ed. W. R. Prest, in *TLS*, 6 March 1981, 262; *Maitland*, 35.

[18] See D. E. C. Yale, 'The Revival of Equitable Estates in the Seventeenth Century: An Explanation by Lord Nottingham', *Cambridge Law J.* (1957), 72–84.

[19] *The Works of Francis Bacon*, ed. J. Spedding, R. L. Ellis and D. D. Heath (7 vols., 1892), VII, 623 [hereafter, *Bacon's Works*].

views on parliamentary legislation in the sixteenth century, a period which 'established the supremacy and omnicompetency of statute'. The judges, faced with carefully drafted instruments, validated by an authoritative parliamentary sanction, were no longer able to undertake the boldly creative extravagances that had typified the performance of their fourteenth-century predecessors.[20] Statutes were like scripture. But as sixteenth-century Englishmen came to know only too well, scripture could be opaque. And the same is equally true of statutes, even of enactments drafted under the aegis of Thomas Cromwell. Sergeant Callis found 23 Henry VIII c. 5 ('of Sewers') 'dark and intricate'; the words of 32 Henry VIII c. 9 (against maintenance) 'are obscure', argued Sergeant Saunders; Judge Bromley thought some of the provisions of 31 Henry VIII c. 13, concerning the property of the greater monasteries, 'contrary to reason'.[21] Obscure points necessitated interpretation, yet given the authoritative aura that surrounded the statutes, the judges could not appear to be idiosyncratic or cavalier in their exegesis. The consequence was the development of rules of construction by the courts by which to interpret and to justify interpretation of 'dark and intricate' passages. So penal statutes or those in derogation of the common law were to be interpreted strictly; conversely, statutes that affirmed common law principles, or that were 'of evident utility publick' could be extended. And we may agree with Elton, and with S. E. Thorne, that the need for such rules powerfully manifests the judiciary's 'novel respect' for parliament.[22]

But, while the rules formed a grid within which any interpretation of statutory language had to be set, they did not, any more than the supposedly authoritative text, guarantee uniform interpretation. This point Elton was reluctant to concede, yet it is clear that parliamentary legislation, if not quite Bacon's 'nose of wax', was often plastic. In 1532 parliament passed 'the Great Statute of Sewers, Cromwell's work';[23] a century later this enactment had produced a cacophony of disagreement as to its meaning. Had the commissioners of sewers authority to build new drainage works? (a question that only arose by virtue of some

---

[20] *Tudors* (1955), 167–9; *Constitution* (1982), 236–40.

[21] Holmes, 'Statutory Interpretation', 109; 1 Plowden 82 (Partridge v. Strange and Croker); 109 (Fulmerston v. Steward) in *The English Reports* (177 vols., 1900–1930), LXXV, 129–31, 170–2 [hereafter *ER*].

[22] Sir Christopher Hatton, *A Treatise concerning Statutes* (1677); *A Discourse upon the Exposicion and Understanding of Statutes*, ed. S. E. Thorne (San Marino, 1942): Elton's account was, as he acknowledged, heavily dependent upon Thorne's introduction to this work, see *Constitution* (1982), 238–9, and nn 30, 31. The best recent survey is *Reports from the Lost Notebooks of Sir James Dyer* ed. J. H. Baker, 2 vols., Selden Soc., vols. 109–10 (1994), I, lix-lxi (hereafter *Dyer's Reports*).

[23] *Reform and Reformation*, 147. The statute was clearly Cromwell's work – see S. E. Lehmberg, *The Reformation Parliament, 1529–36* (Cambridge, 1970), 155–6.

lamentable drafting of the statute—by Cromwell?—a simple failure to provide an accurate translation of the previous latin commission). Could they levy assessments on a township without apportioning the sums on individual landholders? How wide were the discretionary powers granted the commissioners by the Act? Sir Edward Coke answered the first two questions in the negative, and severely circumscribed the discretionary latitude of the commissioners. Other eminent lawyers, like Sir John Popham, Coke's predecessor as Lord Chief Justice of the King's Bench, disagreed totally: the commissioners could build new works, they could levy general taxes; their discretionary authority was 'a very endlesse power such as hath neither breeth nor length'. Both sides appealed to the rules of statutory interpretation to justify their antithetic readings. So for Coke the Statute was penal in that it affected property rights, and must be construed strictly. For his opponents, the Act 'tends so much to the advancement of the commonwealth' that it was an obvious candidate for equitable extension.[24]

How is it that neither sacrosanct text nor rules of interpretation produced a common understanding of the enactment? I have argued that one context for the disagreement is as a side-show in the long-running dispute between Coke and Egerton over the standing of *res judicata* in Chancery. Such an interpretation was appealing to Elton. For him most of the supposedly titanic constitutional conflicts of the seventeenth century were ultimately reducible to trivial squabbles of personality and interest.[25] But there is more than pique to Coke's opposition to the commissioners of sewers, and to understand this we should first return to Bacon's pleading in Chudleigh's case.

The case turned on the Statute of Uses (27 Henry VIII c. 10): this Act was, for Bacon, the acme of the parliamentary draftsman's art. It was, he said, in his formal Reading on the Statute at Grey's Inn in 1600, 'the most perfectly and exactly conceived and penned of any law in the book ... the best pondered in all the words and clauses of it of any statute that I can find'. And yet, Bacon continued, it was an enactment 'whereupon the inheritances of this realm are tossed at this day, as upon a sea, in such sort that it is hard to say which barks will sink, and which will get to the haven'. And, pleading in Chudleigh, he remarked 'having made the statute clear, or at least favourably ambiguous for my side'.[26] How had the interpretation of this masterpiece of legislation become so convoluted by the end of the sixteenth century? Here reflection on a point made by Coke, arguing in the same case, may help our understanding: 'If any case be doubtful on a statute, it is

[24] Holmes, 'Statutory Interpretation', 107–8, 110–11.
[25] 'High Road', *Studies* 2(28), 165.
[26] *Bacon's Works*, VII, 395, 418, 618.

good to construe it according to the reason of the common law.'[27] Coke, somewhat naively, believed that the 'reason of the common law', if properly applied, would clarify the obscurities of the Statute. In fact, it was the judges' attempts in the half-century since the passage of the Act to do precisely what Coke enjoined, to 'read' the Statute in the light of previous common law rules, that had led to the uncertainties remarked by both lawyers. If we are to understand, specifically, the convoluted history of the application of the Statute of Uses in the courts, or, more generally, the wider question of statutory interpretation in the sixteenth century, we must seek to comprehend those assumptions derived from existing legal practice that informed the judges' understanding of legislation.

Elton had difficulties with the Statute of Uses, which grew over time as he sought to incorporate the scholarship of Ives, Bean and, finally, Baker. He persisted in arguing that Uses and the 1540 Statute of Wills 'revolutionised' the land law, terminating 'the truly feudal era in its history', and in suggesting that this 'fundamental reform of the land law' embodied in the two statutes, was the overall intention of Thomas Cromwell.[28] Such a reading is, I think, implausible, though this is not the occasion to review it thoroughly. But some points in Elton's analysis must be discussed.

First, Elton's understanding of the role of uses in the early sixteenth century was flawed, largely because he accepted Cromwellian propaganda far too uncritically. Uses were not devious devices spun by shady and nefarious lawyers to defraud creditors and the crown's 'just claims'. Nor were they the occasion of a persistent struggle between the common lawyers (or even the common law courts) and Chancery. Two late fifteenth-century statutes (1 Rich. III c. 1; 4 Henry VII c. 17) gave tacit acceptance to uses. The common law courts had accepted Chancery's protection of uses before this legislation, and the latter brought more cases directly to their cognizance. The suggestion that uses were 'le common ley del terre', rejected as a heresy by the Common Pleas in the 1460s, was increasingly expressed without rebuke—indeed, expressed from the bench: uses, said Justice Broke in an early Henrician case, are a product of 'common reason, which is common law'. We may even catch something of Bacon's suggestion in his 1600 Reading, that 'the learning of uses is not to be matched with other learnings', in this 1522 case when Broke suggested that the Chief Justice, Brudenell, was over-elaborating an already complex issue for his own intellectual amusement. Certainly, as Baker has argued, the 'staid' common law

---

[27] 1 Co. Rep., 134a in *ER*, LXXVI, 303
[28] 'English Law', *Studies* 3 (40), 284–5; *Reform and Reformation*, 228–9, 290–1; *Reform and Renewal*, 143–4, 160.

judges were beginning to invest general practices employed in the settlement of landed estates with a rational common law heritage.[29]

As a corollary of this, it must be noted that the vigorous campaign against uses conducted by the crown's lawyers did not carry all before it. In the case chosen as a test and carefully manipulated by the crown, counsel for the feoffees of Lord Dacre of the South could argue that 'it has been held for many years that a use was at common law by the common opinion of the whole realm'. Five of the judges whose opinion was sought initially agreed; only three accepted the position taken by the crown lawyers and by Chancellor Audley and Cromwell as Master of the Rolls. Direct pressure from Henry—who promised his 'hearty thanks' to those who supported him—and some tactical, or tactful, illness among the judges secured formal unanimity: the judiciary agreed that it was against the nature of land at common law to be devisable by will. The role of Thomas Cromwell in what Elton recognised as a 'savage legal trick' is worth remarking. So, in the early sixteenth century uses were 'at common law', and the lawyers, not just the landowning classes, were 'stunned' by the outcome of the Lord Dacre of the South case. As Sergeant Montague had insisted, pleading for the feoffees, 'many inheritances in this realm depend today on uses', and 'great confusion' would follow from a decision for the crown. It was to remedy this problem, *inter alia*, that the Statute of Uses was passed, outlawing devises for the future but upholding the wills of those who died before 1 May 1536.[30]

But the common lawyers, it soon proved, were not the subservient puppets of government. First, while there were some who sought to argue that the preamble to the Statute indicated that the legislature had intended to outlaw all enfeoffments to use—the position maintained fiercely by Coke in *Chudleigh*—this was not, as Bacon recognised, the dominant opinion in the immediate aftermath of the legislation.[31] The judges argued that the Statute had not outlawed enfeoffments to use; it permitted them, but immediately 'transubstantiated' the feoffees interest so created into a legal estate in *cestuy qui use*. Indeed, so reluctant were the courts to see legislation violate the sanctity of property, rights

[29] *The Reports of Sir John Spelman*, ed. J. H. Baker, 2 vols., Selden Soc., vols. 93–4 (1977–8), II, 192–200 [hereafter, *Spelman's Reports*]; J. M. W. Bean, *The Decline of English Feudalism, 1215–1540* (Manchester, 1968), 235–56 [hereafter Bean, *Decline*]; A. W. B. Simpson, 'The Equitable Doctrine of Consideration and the Law of Uses', *U. of Toronto Law J.*, 16 (1965), 3, 26, 35. Also *Les Reports des Cases en Ley que furent argues en temps du Roy Edward le Quart* (1680) Pasch., 4 Edw. IV, fol. 8, pl. 9; *Bacon's Works*, VII, 402.

[30] *Spelman's Reports*, I, 228–30; II, 195–203; Bean, *Decline*, 273–83; E. W. Ives, 'The Genesis of the Statute of Uses', *EHR*, 82 (1967), 673–97: Ives's suggestion that the Case of Lord Dacre was decided by 'the partisan interests of the common-law judges' (686–7) seriously underestimates the pressure brought to bear on them by the crown.

[31] 1 Co. Rep. 124a-5a, 129b-30a in *ER*, LXXVI, 281–7, 295–7; *Bacon's Works*, VII, 423.

of ownership and contractual obligation that they preferred to view the Statute, not as obliterating the feoffees and the whole process by which they had been established, but rather as obliging the feoffees to make a re-conveyance of the land to the beneficial owner. 'What the Parliament did', said Lord Chief Justice Montague in a case in 1547, 'was only a conveyance of land from one to another.'[32] Montague, as a Sergeant, had pleaded against the crown's arguments in the case of Lord Dacre of the South—the case that made the Statute necessary. So uses survived the Statute, which, from the first was read narrowly, indeed, unsympathetically, by the courts. It was ruled that the Statute did not apply to uses upon a term of years, because it only spoke of feoffees *seised* to the use of another, and a lease, of whatever duration, was only a chattel interest. It did not cover 'active' uses, where the feoffees had agreed to undertake immediate and continuing duties, such as collecting rents, on behalf of *cestui qui use*. The feoffees, in such circumstances, could not have conveyed the land to another without breach of trust, and the Statute, in the reading advanced by Montague, only obliged the feofees to undertake an act, re-conveyance, that they could have done privately before the compulsion exercized by the Statute. Moreover, uses brought with them into the common law courts not only the learning devised in those courts when they had dealt with uses in the early sixteenth century, but much that had developed in the 'alien' environment of Chancery prior to the passage of the Statute. This importation is probably explained initially by the common law courts having to determine cases that turned on wills and settlements that had been established before 1536. And so it became feasible, despite the Statute, to undertake actions that were impossible under the pristine rules of common law.[33] The early years of Elizabeth's reign see the development of a variety of executory interests, assisted by judges who took a minimalist view of the Statute, and argued that uses 'are not directed by the rules of the common law, but by the will of the owner of the lands: for the use is in his hands as clay is in the hands of the potter, which he in whose hands it is may put into whatever form he pleases'.[34] Later in Elizabeth's reign Coke's vast erudition was deployed, in Shelley's case (1581) and Chudleigh (1595) to argue for the destruction of executory interests, 'upstart and wild provisos and limitations such as the common law never knew', by insisting that a proper reading of the Statute obliged the maintenance

---

[32] 1 Plowden 59 in *ER*, LXXV, 94. And see J. W. Gough, *Fundamental Law in English Constitutional History* (Oxford, 1955), 25–6; A. W. B. Simpson, *An Introduction to the History of the Land Law* (Oxford, 1961), 174–5 [hereafter, Simpson, *Land Law*].

[33] Simpson, *Land Law*, 174, 182, 183, 184–5; *Dyer's Reports*, pp. 292, 426, 451.

[34] Manwood in Brent's case (1575): *Sources of English Legal History: Private Law to 1750*, ed. J. H. Baker and S. F. C. Milsom (1986), 137.

of the old rules that governed the limitation of estates. He was victorious, and the luxuriant growth of executory interests and the possibility of perpetuities was temporarily checked. But subsequent developments in real property law were to validate Bacon's position, that the Statute could not be construed independent of the understanding that three generations of lawyers had imposed upon it before 1595. The 'tree of uses' had not been hacked down in 1536, only 'lopped and ordered' by the Statute, and since then had enjoyed a flourishing 'new growth'.[35] No wonder Coke frequently expressed his reservations concerning legislative interventions, of statutes 'many times of a sudden penned ... by men of none or very little judgement in the law', that introduced 'uncertainties' and 'mischiefs' into the mandarin world of legal ratiocination.[36]

This analysis of the history of 23 Henry VIII c. 5, 'of Sewers', and 27 Henry VIII c. 10, the Statute of Uses, suggests a number of conclusions. Neither a sacrosanct text, nor generally agreed rules of interpretation, guaranteed a uniform reading of an enactment. Legislation had meaning only insofar as it was interpreted by lawyers. To understand that interpretation, the historian must make the mental effort to comprehend their assumptions.

Here it seems appropriate to introduce a lawyer: Sir Edward Coke. Both my specific examples, from the law of sewers and that governing uses, concluded with discussion of his typically vigorous opinions. Geoffrey Elton had little good to say of Sir Edward. He was an abysmal historian who had badly misled modern lawyer-historians; his clashes with James I were 'personal battles', only 'dressed up' as 'titanic conflicts of principle'; his 'tub-thumping' was self-interested and self-promoting. There is a softer note in 1981; Coke, despite 'his bigotry', was 'far from being the blind idiot that some historians of ideas have tried to make him'. But this is isolated, and one suspects that Coke's momentary redemption is largely a stick with which to beat J. G. A. Pocock. In general in the Eltonian canon, Coke is venal, opinionated and wrong.[37]

And yet in 1955, in *England under the Tudors*, Elton had written a more measured judgement on the Lord Chief Justice; a judgement which, unmodified in subsequent editions of that work, provides a counterpoint to the occasional pyrotechnic denunciation. Coke, he wrote, 'unat-

---

[35] Simpson, *Land Law*, 204–6; J. H. Baker, *An Introduction to English Legal History* (3rd edn, 1990), 322–7. 1 Co. Rep. 124b-5a, 129b-30a in *ER*, LXXVI, 281–7, 295–7; *Bacon's Works*, VII, 397.

[36] Stephen D. White, *Sir Edward Coke and the Grievances of the Commonwealth* (Manchester, 1979), 49, 79; Glenn Burgess, *Absolute Monarchy and the Stuart Constitution* (1996), 174–93.

[37] *Maitland*, 85; 'Early-Tudor Council', *Studies* 1(18), 327; 'High Road', *Studies* 2(28), 165; 'England & the Continent', *Studies* 3 (42), 309; review of A. B. Ferguson, *Clio Unbound*, *Studies* 3(II e), 470–1; 'The State', *Studies* 4(49), 11–12; 'Butterfield', *Studies* 4(63), 276.

tractive but impressive', had 'identified the law of ... reason with the English common law and thus translated the inherent moral restraints on behaviour into the highly practical restraint of the positive law of the land'.[38] Coke had questioned theoretical claims for the omnicompetence of royal or parliamentary enactments, and had done so practically, not by advancing the vague moral imperatives favoured by More. For Coke, legislation—a regrettable necessity—had to be interpreted in the light of 'common right and reason', which Coke saw as those substantive principles that could be adduced from the common law. It was for this reason that he found the powers claimed by the commissioners of sewers under the Henrician Statute so obnoxious— and he did so before his private vendetta against Egerton had gathered steam. The copious references in the Statute to the discretionary powers of the commissioners had troubled Coke in the late 1590s. Discretion, he insisted, 'is a science ... and not to do according to their wills and private affections'; in consequence the commissioners' proceedings must be 'bound by law', and must be reviewable in the courts.[39]

Coke was insisting on the 'practical restraint' of 'the law of the land' against individuals and institutions that claimed an authority by virtue of statute or royal grant that was not subject to judicial interrogation. His claims were based on a textual exegesis that was partial, and a derisory antiquarian scholarship. Yet when another king followed Henry VIII down the path of fiscal feudalism, when apparachik royal lawyers, like Cromwell previously, argued that the king had a residual authority which he might exercise contrary to the usual rules, when certain courts again claimed to rule on fiscal matters according to principles that advanced the crown's interests 'although they seem to cross the common law', then Coke's ideas took on a singular power.[40] 'The highly practical restraint of the positive law of the land' had been magisterially defined and defended. It was precisely the kind of process that Geoffrey Elton recommended to American lawyers: rights must have 'ascertainable certainty' if they are to be protected; as such, they should 'grow out of law, not out of philosophical abstractions'.[41] This is a classically Eltonian insight. Where I have criticised Geoffrey Elton is in his failure of empathy, his refusal to try and comprehend the legal ratiocination, from which such checks were devised, because he found the history that was adduced in support of them in the early modern period so flawed, and the professional discourse in which they were defended so incomprehensible.

[38] *England* (1955), 401, 417.
[39] 5 Co. Rep. 99b–100a in *ER*, LXXVII, 210; Holmes, 'Statutory Interpretation', 112.
[40] Clive Holmes, 'Parliament, Liberty, Taxation, and Property', in *Parliament & Liberty from the Reign of Elizabeth to the English Civil War*, ed. J. H. Hexter (Stanford, 1992), 142–4.
[41] 'Human Rights', *Studies* 4(51), 71–2, 74, 76.

RELIGION

By Christopher Haigh

READ 28 MARCH 1996 AT THE INSTITUTE OF HISTORICAL RESEARCH LONDON

'OH, A paper on Geoffrey and religion', sneered a friend: 'that won't take you long!' But it did: it took ages. For many of us, I am sure, thinking about Elton's work and influence has been an autobiographical experience, surveying our own intellectual development in relation to his. For the first time, I read right through the fat file of twenty-five years of letters from Geoffrey (and I will be quoting from some of them). I recalled the first visit of the man my little daughters called 'The Teddy Bear', and how he delighted them with a description of Disneyland. Elton in Disneyland is indeed a thought to conjure with! And I was reminded of all I owed to him. Although this conference has been dubbed 'Oxford's revenge' and Geoffrey's graduate students are not giving papers, many here stand in his debt: my own life as a historian was a constant epistolary debate with Geoffrey, and it has been a lengthy and nostalgic business trying to sort it out.

Contrary to my sneering friend (it was David Starkey, of course!), there *is* a lot of Elton on religion. There was at least enough for the Ecclesiastical History Society to elect him its president for 1983, though the prospect made him uncomfortable: 'I *am* oddly placed among all those Christians.' David Knowles thought that Geoffrey did not really understand religion, but that was unfair: he wrote sensitively about the private religion of Thomas More and Oliver Cromwell, for example.[1] Although Geoffrey rarely wrote in detail about spiritual needs and experiences, he insisted on their authenticity and would not have them reduced to marxist cloaks for economic interests.[2] He wrote much more about religious institutions and the mechanisms of religious change: about 40 per cent of his publications on early modern history relate directly or substantially to religious topics, and 40 per cent of Geoffrey is a career's-worth for anybody else—forty-odd new books and articles, and I have re-read them all. I have tried to work out what he has said, and how it related to what others were doing. At first I decided that Geoffrey did not read any secondary works but the dissertations he

---

[1] Elton to Haigh, 16 September 1981; M. D. Knowles, review of *Tudors* (1955), *Cambridge Historical Journal*, 12 (1956), 92; M. D. Knowles, review of *Studies* 1 & 2, *Historical Journal* [hereafter *HJ*], 17 (1974), 871; *Studies* 3, 454–60, 479–83.
[2] *Cambridge Modern* (1958), 2–4; *Reformation*, 274–9, 311–18.

supervised or examined—but later I concluded that was unfair: he did read, he just did not take much notice!

Of course, we are not the first generation to learn how to write respectable history—but I was surprised to be reminded just how primitive English Reformation historiography was when Geoffrey began. The intellectual framework was still set by A. F. Pollard, and the Reformation was a national revolt of Crown and people against foreign authority bolstered by foreign superstition.[3] (Eurosceptics must be told about this.) The Reformation's detailed story was told by Maynard Smith, who was lightweight even by the standards of the 1940s.[4] In the bibliography of the first edition of *England under the Tudors* (1955) there were forty-five items on the church and Reformation politics: on average, they were twenty-four years old, and twelve were more than forty years old (I note, of course, that *England under the Tudors* is itself now forty-one years old!). Geoffrey's early writings on Reformation topics—the articles on the Act of Appeals (1949), the Supplication (1951), and Cromwell's influence (1954, 1962), together with *England under the Tudors* and *The Tudor Constitution* (1960)—brought evidential rigour, hard-nosed realism, drive and excitement into Reformation studies. His crisp account of 'The Reformation in England' in *The New Cambridge Modern History*, vol. II (1958), was an astonishing advance on (say) Tom Parker's little book of 1950, and was almost a research-agenda for the next thirty years.

Pollard's Reformation had been a national event, A. G. Dickens's Reformation was to be a Protestant event: Elton's Reformation was a constitutional event. 'The Man behind the Henrician Reformation' was, of course, Thomas Cromwell—but the Henrician Reformation, in that article, ended in 1533 with the Act of Appeals. 'It is necessary to keep in mind what the "Henrician Reformation" really meant ...: the definition of independent national sovereignty achieved by the destruction of the papal jurisdiction in England.'[5] It was a Reformation made possible by the power of anticlericalism, the destructive influence of Wolsey and Henry's demand for a new wife, but it was achieved by the ineffable genius of Thomas the Great—the most incredible innovator, administrator, statesman and all-round good-guy who ever lived. (It is well known that Kitson Clark claimed Elton was a reincarnation of Cromwell: 'too much honour!', said Geoffrey.[6]) By comparison, Henry

---

[3] A. F. Pollard, *Henry VIII* (1902); *idem, Thomas Cranmer and the English Reformation* (1904); *idem, Wolsey* (1929).

[4] H. Maynard Smith, *Pre-Reformation England* (1938); *idem, Henry VIII and the Reformation* (1948).

[5] 'King or Minister?', *Studies* I, (9), 177–8 (1954).

[6] Elton to Haigh, 9 April 1978.

VIII was nowhere: 'it is doubtful if he was the architect of anything, least of all of the English Reformation'.[7]

Religion does not seem to have been very important in all this. The constitutional revolution 'may even have been assisted by the supposed spread of new and reformist ideas, whether Lutheran or humanist, though here the present writer [in 1954] would advocate the utmost caution'.[8] (As (in 1996) would the present writer!) Indeed, for the early Elton religion was either lukewarm and ineffectual or sincere and impractical. Pre- Reformation Catholicism had 'little spiritual zeal', and 'the old ways were eminently distinguished by the absence of real conviction or genuine faith'.[9] The men of zeal were the Fishers and Mores, who were crushed in the cause of progress; the Hoopers and Knoxes, who made nuisances of themselves; and the Bonners and Poles, who killed for ideas. The woman of zeal was Mary, who finally discredited Catholicism and made Protestantisation possible. The achievers were the 'secular' realists, who did not allow religion to get in the way of practical politics: Cromwell made the revolution, and Elizabeth made it safe.[10] Geoffrey later decided that Cromwell was not so secular, and conformist religion was not so bad, but in his early work he was unable to recognise that simple faith and customary practice could matter. And he never escaped the conviction that pre-Tridentine Catholicism was so much hocus-pocus: though persuaded (by Eamon Duffy) of its strength, 'yet I have to admit that to me much of it still looks like somewhat desperate superstition'.[11]

When I compiled my notorious grid of Reformation historiography, Geoffrey was one of the few who did not complain of mis-representation:[12] 'fast Reformation from above'—how could it have been otherwise, in the age of Thomas Cromwell? But I had not then noticed that Geoffrey's Reformation was slower in the 1950s than it was to be in the 1970s. By 1553 'England was now a Protestant country', but only in law: 'the changes at the top had as yet made little impression', and it would take 'a prolonged course of propaganda and enforcement' for the novelties 'to be inculcated in the nation'.[13] In 1558, despite the best efforts of Cranmer and the worst of Pole, England 'was

---

[7] *Henry VIII: An Essay in Revision* (1962), 27.

[8] 'King or Minister?', *Studies* 1 (9), 178 (1954).

[9] *Cambridge Modern* (1958), 239, 249.

[10] *Tudors* (1955), 127, 134, 151, 219–20, 263, 276; *Cambridge Modern* (1958), 249–50.

[11] G. R. Elton, review of Eamon Duffy, *The Stripping of the Altars* [hereafter Duffy, *Stripping*], *Journal of Ecclesiastical History* [hereafter *JEH*], 44 (1993), 719.

[12] C. Haigh, 'The Recent Historiography of the English Reformation' (original version published in 1979), in *The English Reformation Revised*, ed. C. Haigh (Cambridge, 1987) [hereafter *English Reformation Revised*], 19–33; Elton to Haigh, 1 January 1980: 'very interesting and largely convincing, but it makes me sound (and feel) about eighty!'

[13] *Cambridge Modern* (1958), 245.

predominantly Catholic; of this there can be no doubt.'[14] Later, there *was* doubt, and it was Dickens's *English Reformation* (1964) which created it—helped perhaps by the writing of *Reformation Europe* (1963), where Geoffrey showed himself sensitive to the power of liberating ideas.[15] From 1964 onwards, there was more Protestantism in Geoffrey's Reformation. But, with that exception, it was all clear by *England under the Tudors* in 1955, and it stayed the same for nearly twenty years. It was repeated over and over again. On the Reformation, as on the Tudor Revolution, Geoffrey followed the first law of historiographical fame—do not retract, do not apologise, just keep shouting. For if you say the same thing loudly enough and often enough, the teachers will believe you, your books will sell, and you will be an issue! Geoffrey was always an issue.

But in the 1970s the Eltonian Reformation got into difficulties. They were partly of his own making, from all the work which led to *Policy and Police* (1972). Geoffrey said that his friends could be divided into those who thought *Policy and Police* his best book, and those who thought it was *Reform and Renewal* (1973): I have always rooted for *Policy and Police*—but then I would. Geoffrey showed that there was widespread, frequent and mounting hostility to the break with Rome and religious change—however, this was 'the age of Thomas Cromwell', and, against all the odds and oddballs, he succeeded: by 1540 'the realm had accepted the new situation and was, for the moment, obedient as instructed'.[16] (More probably, of course, the Act of Six Articles and the fall of Cromwell reduced the cause for and level of complaint.) Others also discovered determined and sometimes effective opposition: Michael Kelly and Jack Scarisbrick found it among churchmen, and I found it in Lancashire.[17] If Reformation seemed less popular, it also seemed less necessary: Margaret Bowker and Peter Heath looked at parish clergy, Mrs Bowker also looked at church courts, and the merry band assembled by O'Day and Heal looked here, there and everywhere—we all found a church which worked pretty well, and anticlericalism began to look a mite overdone.[18] Keith Thomas looked at magical religion, and gave good reasons and good evidence for attachment to conventional parish

[14] *Tudors* (1955), 287.

[15] G. R. Elton, review of A. G. Dickens, *The English Reformation*, *The Listener*, 1 October 1964, 515–16; *Reformation*, 15–22, 30–4, 210–22.

[16] *Policy and Police*, 1.

[17] M. J. Kelly, 'The Submission of the Clergy', *supra*, 5th ser., XV (1965), 97–119; J. J. Scarisbrick, *Henry VIII* (Harmondsworth, 1971 edn), 329–31, 358–63, 387–93; C. Haigh, *Reformation and Resistance in Tudor Lancashire* (Cambridge, 1975).

[18] M. Bowker, *The Secular Clergy in the Diocese of Lincoln, 1495–1520* (Cambridge, 1968); P. Heath, *The English Parish Clergy on the Eve of the Reformation* (1969); M. Bowker, 'The "Commons Supplication against the Ordinaries" in the Light of Some Archidiaconal Acta', *supra*, 5th ser., XXI (1971), 61–77; *Continuity and Change: Personnel and Administration of the Church in England 1500–1640*, ed. R. O'Day and F. Heal (Leicester, 1976).

religion.[19] And Eric Ives and David Starkey rediscovered faction—
helped, perhaps, by Elton's own picture of an inattentive and man-
ipulable Henry VIII. Geoffrey, of course, always maintained that faction
had been his idea, in 'Thomas Cromwell's decline and fall' (1951).[20]

Out of all this came *Reform and Reformation* (1977), a version of politics
and religious change rather different from *England under the Tudors*,
supported by background and related articles. Cromwell was again at
the centre, but his motives and achievements had changed. Cromwell's
'cast of mind was less determinedly secular and less ruthlessly radical
than I once supposed',[21] his hostility to clerical power was based on
positive religious principle, and he became more Lutheran through the
1530s: he was willing to take political risks for religion, to act inde-
pendently of the king.[22] Geoffrey had found a flaw in Cromwell, that
'ultimate surrender to the corrupting—and in his case fatal—appeal of
idealism I find myself regretting'.[23] Geoffrey now confessed he had made
'extravagant claims' for Cromwell: 'I singled out Thomas Cromwell too
much and overemphasised the originality of his ideas'.[24] But if this looks
like a breach of the first law of historiographical fame, Elton was merely
following the second: you may have to say you recant, but you do not
actually have to do it. Graham Nicholson had discovered the *Collectanea*,
and Scarisbrick had shown a new policy direction from the autumn of
1530—so Geoffrey coolly shifted Cromwell's influence six months earlier,
and rewrote the events of 1530–2 with Cromwell as a consummate
political strategist and tactician.[25] And he rewrote the political events
of 1532–40 in much the same way: faction had given another opportunity
to display Cromwell's skill. Geoffrey always managed to have his cake
while eating his humble pie.

[19] Keith Thomas, *Religion and the Decline of Magic* (1971).

[20] E. W. Ives, 'Faction at the Court of Henry VIII: The Fall of Anne Boleyn', *History*,
47 (1972), 169–88; D. R. Starkey, 'The King's Privy Chamber, 1485–1547' (PhD thesis,
Cambridge University, 1973); 'Decline and Fall', *Studies* 1 (10), 189–230 (1951); 'Court',
Studies 3 (33:3), 49–56 (1976); Elton to Haigh, 18 November 1993.

[21] *Reform and Renewal*, vii–viii.

[22] *Reform and Reformation*, 171–2, 282–3, 293. Although Elton hinted from the start that
Cromwell may have been genuinely reformist in religion ('Decline and Fall', *Studies* 1
(10), 212 (1951); *Tudors* (1955), 151n), he had usually presented Cromwell as a man of
'essentially secular temper' ('Cromwell, Thomas', *Encyclopedia Britannica*, 15th edn (1975),
II, 749; *Tudors* (1955), 127, 151). He seems to have been persuaded of Cromwell's religious
commitment by Dr John Oliver (*Reform and Renewal*, 26–8, 34) and A. G. Dickens, *Thomas
Cromwell and the English Reformation* (1959) (cf. Elton's review of Dickens in *The Listener*, 31
December 1959, 1167–8; *Thomas Cromwell* (Bangor, 1991), 35–6, 41). The new Cromwell
was displayed in *Reform and Reformation*, 171–2, and 'Redivivus', *Studies* 3 (46), 377–8 (1977),
one of the very few examples of Elton recycling paragraphs verbatim.

[23] Elton to Haigh, 13 September 1976.

[24] 'Redivivus', *Studies* 3 (46), 373 (1977); *Reform and Reformation*, 103n.

[25] G. Nicholson, 'The Nature and Function of Historical Argument in the Henrician

The same was true of Reformation: if it was difficult, then Cromwell's success was all the greater. The conventional piety of the old religion was hard to break, Wolsey had not softened the church up for Cromwell, the higher clergy put up vigorous resistance, there was organised opposition in parliament, the priests ranted against schism and heresy, and the people moaned and groaned.[26] But anticlericalism was still there to help, fitted out in new clothes. Geoffrey had to accept that the church was not as bad as had been supposed, but the laity still disliked the clergy because they thought it was. Anticlericalism was now a matter of perception rather than a response to reality, and an aspiration rather than a grievance. Having lost many of the reasons for old-version anticlericalism, Elton (like Claire Cross in *Church and People*, 1976) was coming to see anticlericalism as a positive demand for direct access to God and political control of the church. 'I am willing to regard the fact that the priesthood became the ministry and the laity moved on to power-sharing (as it were) in the Church as the most significant single thing about the ecclesiastical history' of the sixteenth and seventeenth centuries.[27]

Cromwell and anticlericalism made the Henrician Reformation, and made a truly Protestant Reformation possible. By 1977 Elton was convinced that the Edwardian Reformation had been underestimated: it 'was within limits a real Reformation', and, famously, 'the fact is that by 1553 England was almost certainly nearer to being a Protestant country than to anything else'.[28] In *Reform and Reformation* the reasoning behind this conclusion is neither clear nor persuasive: there had been twenty years of reformist exhortation, some priests married, there was not much rebellion, and the Marian reaction ran into trouble. But for Geoffrey, I think, two long-held assumptions were decisive: weak-kneed Catholicism represented the past, and Cromwell's vibrant vision represented the future. 'The actively religious part of the nation had turned to the reform', which 'alone had dynamic life in it': 'whereas the new people stood up to be counted (and burned), those of the older persuasion did as a rule acquiesce whatever happened'.[29] And those who did not care enough about religion cared about the Cromwellian

---

Reformation' (PhD thesis, Cambridge University, 1977); Scarisbrick, *Henry VIII*, 341–3; *Reform and Reformation*, 103n, 129–56.

[26] *Reform and Reformation*, 119–20, 146; 'Thomas More: 2', *Studies* 1 (8), 155–72 (1968); *Policy and Police*, 1–170.

[27] *Constitution* (1982), 219, 327–8; Elton to Haigh, 26 March 1977. Both Elton and Cross used the term 'triumph of the laity': *Reform and Reformation*, 199; C. Cross, *Church and People, 1450–1660: The Triumph of the Laity in the English Church* (1976).

[28] *Reform and Reformation*, 370–1.

[29] Elton to Haigh, 22 February 1978. Elton did, however, concede 'that I seem to be arguing backwards from success and offending my own canons of historical investigation'!

state: 'The majority of the political nation might still not be Protestant in any meaningful sense, ... but they remained attached to the political revolution out of which Protestantism had grown and which Protestantism protected.' I have to confess that I have never had much idea what that meant.[30]

The 1970s Eltonian Reformation was much more sophisticated than the 1950s Mark 1 version. The 'Points of Contact' essays (1974–6) established a political structure for events, and 'Thomas Cromwell Redivivus' (1977) made the bureaucrat a dreamer. 'Politics and the Pilgrimage of Grace' (1980, though written in 1975) showed that Geoffrey knew a lot about Westminster and Whitehall, and nothing much about the north—but it cleverly relocated the Pilgrimage in the Reformation story. The Mark 2 Reformation was based on the latest research, generously acknowledged: if you lay Scarisbrick, Kelly, Nicholson, Starkey, Joyce Youings, Michael Bush, Dale Hoak, Glen Lemasters, Rex Pogson and David Loades end-to-end, you get a lot of *Reform and Reformation*! Geoffrey's determination to write a political narrative imposed a linear, progressive sequence, and the self- conscious navel-watching footnotes on whether he had or had not altered his views do get embarrassing. But *Reform and Reformation* is a book with force, imagination and sensitivity—less dismissive than before of Wolsey, and others who had the misfortune not to be Cromwell; more sympathetic towards Cranmer, and other moderates who changed, or could not make up, their minds; less contemptuous of liberal-minded sympathy for rebels and underdogs. It proved to be as far as Geoffrey was willing to go in print to accommodate new research and revision.

By 1979 Geoffrey was getting touchy, by 1983 he was digging his heels in, and by 1986 he was deep in the bunker. It was not all David Starkey's fault—but some of it was! Starkey's aggressive emphasis on faction as the driving force of politics, and the rise of the Privy Chamber at the expense of the Privy Council, diminished the achievement of Cromwell, made the whole Reformation contingent, and destroyed the Tudor Revolution in Government—while Penry Williams's *Tudor Regime* (1979) now offered an alternative model of government and politics (one uncomfortably close to 'Points of Contact'?).[31] So it was back to the Tudor Revolution in Government in something like its original crudity, and Geoffrey broke the third law of historiographical fame— do not retract your retractions, it only makes you look silly.[32] Unwittingly,

---

[30] *Reform and Reformation*, 388–9.

[31] See Elton's review of Penry Williams, *The Tudor Regime* (Oxford, 1979), in *Times Literary Supplement*, 15 February 1980, 183.

[32] 'Stop press: the latest news is that the Tudor revolution in government may be on the way back' ('Revisionism Reassessed: The Tudor Revolution a Generation Later', *Encounter*, July–August 1986, 41n.) It was not. Hearing the Tudor revolution defended by

he had already prepared his retreat: 'It will not do to overrate Starkey, not a thinker of the first rank or teeming with original ideas; yet he had a good and interesting mind, wrote with force and instructed passion, proved himself independent and willing to speak frankly, and added quite a powerful rational dimension to the turmoil of ideas'— that was in *Reform and Reformation*, though about Thomas Starkey, not David.[33] Geoffrey insisted again that the post-Cromwellian state was solidly bureaucratic, and could enforce its will: government was more than magnates, patronage and informal links. As he protested in 1985, 'I have often enough said that I exaggerated in 1953—but I did not invent!'[34]

For Geoffrey, the Reformation was going to the dogs too. Ralph Houlbrooke had shown that church courts were busy and effective, and Margaret Bowker that Longland fought heresy and fended off reform in Lincoln. Alan Kreider, as Elton noted, demonstrated that the piety which produced chantry-foundations remained strong until crushed by the Reformation's attack on purgatory.[35] I argued for 'slow Reformation from above', and suggested that anticlericalism was a result rather than a cause of Reformation.[36] Worst of all, Scarisbrick's sentimentalization of pre-Reformation religion, and what Elton saw as special pleading, made him cross. At the third of Scarisbrick's Ford Lectures in 1982, Geoffrey could barely contain his irritation and went grumpily to sleep. In preparation for the *Lutherjahr*, Geoffrey himself had been working on Luther's influence, with rising impatience towards those, in Germany and in England, who questioned the success of the Reformation: 'The principle seems to be that the Reformation can be called successful only if it led pretty immediately to a total transformation in faith as well as society', he spluttered.[37] Nevertheless, he did encourage me to publish *The English Reformation Revised* (1987), and rightly predicted 'Geoff Dickens will blow a gasket!'[38] But Geoffrey now needed a stick

---

two American colleagues 'made me re-read my first book and I discovered that I had indeed been ready to surrender too soon!' (*Thomas Cromwell*, 23n)

[33] *Reform and Reformation*, 168.

[34] Elton to Haigh, 16 September 1985.

[35] R. Houlbrooke, *Church Courts and the People during the English Reformation, 1520–1570* (Oxford, 1979) (cf. Elton's review in *JEH*, 31 (1980), 232–3); M. Bowker, *The Henrician Reformation: The Diocese of Lincoln under John Longland, 1521–1547* (Cambridge, 1981); A. Kreider, *English Chantries: The Road to Dissolution* (Cambridge, MA, 1979); see Elton's comments in *Times Literary Supplement*, 23 November 1979, 27.

[36] Haigh in *English Reformation Revised*, 19–33 (earlier versions published 1979, 1982), 56–74 (first published 1983).

[37] Elton to Haigh, 20 April 1984; *idem*, 7 September 1981; *JEH*, 39 (1988), 610; 'Lex', *Studies* 4 (50), 38 (1984, 1990).

[38] Elton to Haigh, 12 June 1987.

to beat the Reformation revisionists, and he found it in Lollards and the significance of their ideas.

Geoffrey had read—or at least cited—J. F. Davis's 1968 thesis on Lollard influence in the south-east by 1979, and used it to argue that religious change in England grew from native roots. He helped with the revision of the thesis, and sponsored publication of Davis's *Heresy and Reformation* in 1983. He then contested the view that the English Reformation was imposed from above on a reluctant people, and claimed that the Lollard movement provided support for the attack on church wealth and the provision of an English Bible, and pushed England into a 'Swiss' rather than 'German' Reformation (1986).[39] Of course, Geoffrey had known about Lollards from Margaret Aston, J. A. F. Thomson and Dickens,[40] but did not make anything of them until he needed some supporters for the Reformation. For now we are into the Eltonian Reformation Mark 3—no longer just a jurisdictional adjustment, more than the religious aspect of commonwealth reform, and a real Reformation of ideas. 'I am reluctantly getting to believe in the English Reformation more than I used to. Must be old age.'[41]

Mark 3 Reformation was more than a constitutional adjustment: it was a national religious revolution. The attention to Lollardy and the work on Luther had contributed to a view of the Reformation (and the Counter-Reformation too) as an opportunity to escape from the priest-ridden medieval mind-set to a more thoughtful and immediate relation-ship with God.[42] But, despite the role of Lollardy and Swiss ideas, it was *still* the Henrician (or Cromwellian) Reformation which mattered, which brought the victory of common law over canon law,[43] and which really worked. Elton asked whether by Reformation we meant the wholesale conversion of the nation to ardent Protestantism (an 'incon-ceivable situation'), or 'the casting off of the papacy'?—in which sense, he said, 'the vast bulk of the country was "reformed" by 1559'. By then, indeed, the Cromwellian Reformation was irreversible and 'there was no chance of a return to Rome'.[44] This was not quite the same as the view which Dickens expressed, that Protestant victory was assured (though not complete) by 1558. Elton had suggested (1984) that Prot-estantism was not safe in England until after the Civil War, and he

[39] 'England and the Continent in the Sixteenth Century', *Studies* 3, 316–17 (1979); 'Die europaische Reformation: Mit oder ohne Luther?', *Studies* 4 (62), 253–63 (1986); J. F. Davis, *Heresy and Reformation in the South East of England* (1983) [hereafter Davis, *Heresy and Reformation*]; Elton to Haigh, 13 November 1983; *idem*, 26 November 1983.
[40] *Reform and Reformation*, 11, 74–5, 404.
[41] Elton to Haigh, 29 September 1988.
[42] Elton to Haigh, 20 May 1984.
[43] 'Lex', *Studies* 4 (50), 37–57 (1990).
[44] Elton to Haigh, 16 September 1985; *idem*, 17 April 1983.

again distinguished (as he had done in *England under the Tudors*) between the rapid success of the political Reformation and the much slower success of Protestantism. The English had regained their 'national independence' in 1559, and would not surrender it again: religion was another, and rather trickier, matter.[45]

In *The English* (1992), the constitutional revolution of 1532–4 was decisive and entrenched: it was guaranteed by the work of Cromwell, and by the spread of Protestantism. The Marian restoration was therefore doomed, as no one in their senses was going to return church lands or return to the cloister. But the progress of Protestantism was a slower business: the people were, it seems, willing enough to abandon the old religion, but reluctant to be dragooned into the new—or, at least, into the enthusiasts' version of it. 'These less than passionate Christians' were 'moderate men and women', who went to church and did their duty: 'they were people governed by good sense', 'unwilling to become instruments of an intolerant persecution'—they were, it seems, Pat Collinson's 'rustic pelagians' (perhaps my own 'parish anglicans'?), and had no cause to be ashamed of it.[46] Nearly forty years on from *England under the Tudors*, the once-despised conformists have come into their own; the dullards who had needed a Reformation to wake them up are allowed to slumber on, and good order and moderation are the key virtues of religion. Perhaps it was an element in Geoffrey's anglicization that he was becoming an admirer of Anglicanism! In a strange address in memory of Lancelot Andrewes (1990), Cranmer was praised as the inventor of good, sensible Anglicanism: 'The essence of the Anglican reality lies in the absence of fanaticism regularly denounced by the more ardent and half-witted spirits as merely Laodicean. That was the note Cranmer struck at the start of it all.'[47] This was pretty bad history, I think, but it tells us something about the man as he neared seventy.

In 1990 Geoffrey published a second edition of his volume in *The New Cambridge Modern History*, and in 1991 a third edition of *England under the Tudors*. The changes are few but illuminating. The main text of *England under the Tudors* remained as it was in 1955, with the addition of a chapter of 'Revisions' and a new bibliography. 'It is indeed clear', I

[45] A. G. Dickens, 'The Early Expansion of Protestantism in England, 1520–1558', *Archiv für Reformationsgeschichte*, 78 (1987) [hereafter Dickens, 'Early Expansion'], 189, 219–21; *idem*, *The English Reformation* (1989 edn), 313–15, 333–4; 'Auseinandersetzung und Zusammenarbeit zwischen Renaissance under Reformation in England', *Studies* 4 (59), 199–200 (1984); 'The Tudor Regime' (recorded discussion, Sussex Tapes, 1980), side 2.

[46] *English*, 114–19; P. Collinson, *The Elizabethan Puritan Movement* (London, 1967), 37; C. Haigh, 'The Church of England, the Catholics and the People', in *The Reign of Elizabeth I* (Basingstoke, 1984), 218–19.

[47] 'Andrewes', *Studies* 4 (57) 172 (1990).

was glad to see, 'that the true Reformation[48] took much longer to triumph than we used to suppose—something like three generations'— I could not quarrel with that.[49] However, 'the revisionist views make it difficult to see how England ever got Protestant'—or perhaps I could. (Elsewhere, Elton took a general swipe at revisionists: 'in demonstrating the errors that had been adduced in teleologically explaining later events, they come close to making it impossible to see how those later events and conditions could ever have come about'.[50] But note the saving 'come close'.) The 1955 bibliography had had forty-five items on Reformation politics and the church: in the 1991 version there are eighty-four. Only eight works survive from 1955, and at least twenty-nine new items were published by Elton, his pupils and others he had helped. It is a whole new historiographical world, a world substantially remade under Elton's influence.

In the revised *New Cambridge Modern History*, the introductory chapter on 'The Age of the Reformation' stands unchanged, except for the addition of a parenthetical '(and woman)'[51]—perhaps Geoffrey's only recorded concession to political correctness. But 'The Reformation in England' has been carefully (if very selectively) revised. A sentence on the 'barrenness' of Wolsey's rule has gone (well done, John Guy!). A sentence on the *Collectanea* comes in, and a couple more describe Cromwell making a reality of existing ideas rather than dreaming up a new policy and polity. Cromwell is no longer 'forthrightly secular', but 'shared the preference for a reform in religion which could lead to a Protestant Reformation'. Somerset pinches the lands of Bath and Wells (thanks to Felicity Heal), and Northumberland is briskly (Dale) Hoak-ed. The only dramatic shift is down to David Loades. The 'sterility' of Mary's reign had been in 1958 'a verdict from which only the earnest partisan will find it easy to dissent'—'but more recent studies of the age have clearly demonstrated the error of that verdict'! The earnest partisans were right after all. ('At the same time, some recent assessments have been a bit too indulgent', so Professor Loades should not be complacent.) And in 1559 the Protestants in Parliament no longer 'pushed the queen farther and faster', but found the government 'anxious to lead them in the direction they meant to go'.[52] Nice one, Norman Jones!

---

[48] In 1954, the Henrician Reformation 'really meant' the break with Rome. In 1977 the Edwardian Reformation was 'a real Reformation', and by 1991 'the true Reformation' was the substantial protestantization of the nation, achieved only by the 1580s.

[49] *Tudors* (1991), 481. Cf. *Thomas Cromwell*, 19.

[50] *English*, 161.

[51] *Cambridge Modern* (1990), 15. For what follows, cf. *Cambridge Modern* (1958), 226–50, with *Cambridge Modern* (1990), 262–87.

[52] *Cambridge Modern* (1958), 244, 250; *Cambridge Modern* (1990), 284, 287.

The obvious winners are John Guy, Graham Nicholson, Michael Bush, David Loades and Norman Jones. Just one person earns a specific, but anonymous, refutation, in one of only two new footnotes (the second being a reference to *Policy and Police*). 'Recent attempts to deny a role to anticlerical feelings have been sufficiently answered by A. G. Dickens, "The shape of anticlericalism and the English Reformation".'[53] However, I do not believe it *is* a sufficient answer to string together, as Dickens did, occasional examples of satire and moral exhortation drawn from two centuries, without attention to context or motive, or to select comments on the clergy from writers who also condemned the failings of other social groups. Diarmaid MacCulloch has suggested that court-peers and common lawyers were anti-prelatical, and, after Wolsey, wanted to reduce the jurisdiction of the churchmen; there may have been, as I have said before, particular reasons why specific groups criticised clerical power at specific moments.[54] But that does not prove an endemic anticlericalism which made the English ready for Reformation. Peter Marshall has shown how high was the ideal of a sacrificing priesthood, and how attitudes towards the clergy changed when the Reformation undermined their status.[55] The Reformation made the English ready for anticlericalism.

On other issues, Elton's changes in *New Cambridge Modern History* were no more than tinkering. Wolsey now 'paid lip-service to' rather than supported the pope in foreign policy. Church courts are 'supposedly' rather than 'notoriously' corrupt: not a big shift for all those months Bowker, Houlbrooke, Stephen Lander and the rest of us spent on almost-indecipherable court books. Lollardy played 'only a small' rather than 'no part in the Reformation' (it seems, as we shall see, that Geoffrey had lost faith in J. F. Davis's interpretation, rather than that he could not face any substantial reworking). The evidence at Thomas More's trial is 'doubtful' rather than 'perjured', which must be a relief to Richard Riche. Henry now 'refused to' authorise the 'Bishops' Book' (correcting an earlier error), and the book 'tried to build on' (rather than 'withdrew even from') the position of the Ten Articles. Somerset is only 'ostensibly' willing to help the poor. Perhaps a 'supposedly' here, an 'ostensibly' there, and three deletions of 'secular' (describing

---

[53] *Cambridge Modern* (1990), 263n; A. G. Dickens, 'The Shape of Anticlericalism and the English Reformation', in *Politics and Society in Reformation Europe*, ed. E. I. Kouri and T. Scott (1987), 379–410.

[54] Diarmaid MacCulloch, 'Henry VIII and the Reform of the Church', in *The Reign of Henry VIII: Politics, Policy and Piety*, ed. D. MacCulloch (Basingstoke, 1995) [hereafter *Reign of Henry VIII*], 166–7 (cf. Dickens, *Thomas Cromwell*, 179); Haigh, *English Reformation Revised*, 73; *idem*, 'The English Reformation: Church, People and Origins', *Early Modern History*, 1(2) (1992), 21–4.

[55] Peter Marshall, *The Catholic Priesthood and the English Reformation* (Oxford, 1994).

Cromwell) do not amount to a great advance after thirty-two years of fast and often furious scholarship. Those of us who thought we were turning the Reformation up-side down were obviously wrong.

In truth, through forty years of collective historical endeavour Geoffrey never really changed his mind on essentials—or rather, when he did, as with the much-regretted flirtation with Starkeyism in the 1970s, he soon changed it back again. On the main issues of Reformation historiography—what it was, how it happened, how far and how fast it went—there was little movement. When he came to revise his books—*The Tudor Constitution* in 1982, *The New Cambridge Modern History* in 1990, *England under the Tudors* for a second time in 1991—he left things substantially as they were, not out of laziness but because he thought he had been right the first time. In *The Tudor Constitution*, the sections on ordinary ecclesiastical courts and 'Grievances against the Clergy' were given new footnotes to Bowker, Heath, Houlbrooke and others, and tiny insertions to say that contemporary critics may have exaggerated. The text on the royal supremacy and the secularization of lands is as it was, with up-dated notes—especially to Joyce Youings. In the account of religious change, the authorities were Clebsch, Dickens, Jordan and Loades, in place of Pollard and Maynard Smith, but except for a Norman Jones version of 1559 the text is identical.[56] In the whole book, the only sections which were substantially rewritten were those on the common law, parliament and puritanism. It looks as if J. H. Baker, Sheila Lambert and Patrick Collinson were the only people who ever shifted Geoffrey—and the last two had the ghost of J. E. Neale to help them!

So, for all our efforts, the rest of us did not make much difference to what Elton thought, or, more precisely, what he printed: we provided the footnotes which did not support his text. But what difference did he make to us? For me, as for many, his early influence was crucial. At Cambridge in 1965–6 I did the undergraduate special subject which became *Policy and Police*. I was not sure I believed in the wonder-working Cromwell, and went off to look at Lancashire as a testing test-case: I hope I would still think as I do if I had worked on Surrey instead! Thereafter, Geoffrey and I rarely agreed, except on the virtues of home-grown vegetables, the defects of English cricket and the importance of historical debate. Nevertheless, he was a constant cor-respondent and commentator on my work, who helped me sharpen my ideas and always encouraged me to publish them. Now I know

---

[56] Cf. *Constitution* (1960), 214–16, 318–21, 329–36, 369–74, 385–9, with *Constitution* (1982), 218–21, 327–30, 338–45, 378–83, 395–9; N. L. Jones, *Faith by Statute: Parliament and the Settlement of Religion* (1982). Richard Hunne's death was 'pretty certainly murder' in 1960, but 'possibly an accident' by 1982.

that Elton has sponsored publication of some pretty dreadful stuff when it suited his own purposes, and his enemy's enemy always got support.[57] But Elton never led a school of slavish followers, and there was a lot to be said for Starkey's distinction between the Eltonians and the Eltonettes—those who copied the method and those who copied the ideas. Many of Elton's pupils came to disagree with him: Brendan Bradshaw on More; John Guy on the making of the Privy Council; David Starkey on the importance of household rather than bureaucracy; Michael Bush on the Pilgrimage of Grace; David Loades on Mary; Rex Pogson on Cardinal Pole—Jack Scarisbrick on almost everything![58]—and most of them disagreed without forfeiting friendship or support or Glenfiddich.

Many of the Reformation-related issues Geoffrey wrote about are still current, and ideas which he floated or furthered are debated in recent books and journals. He agreed we could no longer use 'anticlericalism' as a convenient shorthand for lay attitudes towards the pre-Reformation church—'but I still think you play it down too much'.[59] Elton's own rather crude, monolithic version has had its day: it was refined out of existence by Peter Marshall, dismissed by Richard Rex, almost ignored by Diarmaid MacCulloch and reduced 'from a movement to a moment' by Richard Hoyle.[60] The most satisfying account of the intellectual origins and political implementation of the royal supremacy now comes from John Guy, and it is a far cry from Thomas Cromwell inventing the sovereign nation state and everyone else saying 'Let's go for it!' On the suppression of the monasteries, it is hard to know which of the two most recent versions Elton would dislike more—Richard Hoyle's, that confiscation was proposed by the conservative nobility in 1529, but Cromwell botched it in 1534 and again in 1536; or Richard Rex's, that Cromwell had to rush in to wholesale suppression to stop the monks flogging off what was left. In

[57] Elton vigorously defended R. M. Warnicke, *The Rise and Fall of Anne Boleyn* (Cambridge, 1989), e.g. in Elton to Haigh, 9 and 18 September 1990.

[58] Brendan Bradshaw, 'The Controversial Thomas More', *JEH*, 36 (1985), 535–69; J. A. Guy, 'The Privy Council: Revolution or Evolution', in *Revolution Reassessed*, ed. C. Coleman and D. Starkey (Oxford, 1986), 59–85; David Starkey, 'Court and Government', in *Revolution Reassessed*, ed. Coleman and Starkey, 29–58; Michael Bush, *The Pilgrimage of Grace* (Manchester, 1996); D. M. Loades, *Mary Tudor: A Life* (Oxford, 1989); R. H. Pogson, 'Revival and Reform in Mary Tudor's Church', reprinted in *English Reformation Revised*, 139–56; Scarisbrick, *Henry VIII*; idem, *The Reformation and the English People* (Oxford, 1984).

[59] Elton to Haigh, 12 January 1992.

[60] Marshall, *Catholic Priesthood and the English Reformation*; Richard Rex, *Henry VIII and the English Reformation* (Basingstoke, 1993), 46–7, 50–5; MacCulloch, 'Henry VIII and the Reform of the Church', 166–7; R. W. Hoyle, 'The Origins of the Dissolution of the Monasteries', *HJ*, 38 (1995) [hereafter Hoyle, 'Origins of the Dissolution'], 289.

neither case was the dissolution the smooth bureaucratic process which showed the genius of our hero.[61]

Lollardy has grown in stature and social status since Geoffrey took it up in 1979. Anne Hudson has demonstrated the range and respectability of its intellectual heritage, and argued, as J. F. Davis had done, that it revived in the sixteenth century and influenced the early reformers. Andrew Hope and Derek Plumb have found dense clusters of Lollard sympathisers in some Chiltern towns and villages, sometimes among community leaders. But we should be cautious, as Geoffrey himself became: 'native heresy at best contributed to such willingness as there was to receive the reformed religion'.[62] In those few localities where their presence was most substantial, Lollards and fellow-suspects were fewer than one tenth of the population in 1521: they were a tiny, tiny fraction of the nation as a whole, and in their religion a secretive and introspective one. Lollardy was a series of networks of families rather than a platform of ideas, constrained and weakened by hostility and persecution. There is, as yet, no convincing evidence that Lollards actually influenced the academics and future-bishops who carried forward the Reformation of belief.[63]

We now seem to have passed beyond Elton's rewriting of the Pilgrimage of Grace. Perhaps he explained Lord Darcy's motives, perhaps even Robert Aske's—but he did not explain why and how seven northern counties rebelled. Cliff Davies has already shown the significance of popular religion for the rising, and Michael Bush has argued for the importance of fiscal grievances: in both respects, the Pilgrimage was a protest against Cromwellian policy. Elton tried to make the rebellion monocausal and monolithic, and denied that it was an authentic popular protest: he would never recognise that unrest broke out at different times and in different places; and that

---

[61]John Guy, 'Thomas Cromwell and the Intellectual Origins of the Henrician Revolution', in *Reassessing the Henrician Age*, ed. A. Fox and J.A. Guy (Oxford, 1986), 151–78; John Guy, *Tudor England* (Oxford, 1988), 122–36; Hoyle, 'Origins of the Dissolution', 275–301; Rex, *Henry VIII and the English Reformation*, 59–66.

[62]Ann Hudson, *The Premature Reformation* (Oxford, 1988); Davis, *Heresy and Reformation*, 26–97; Andrew Hope, 'Lollardy: The stone the Builders Rejected', in *Protestantism and the National Church in Sixteenth Century England*, ed. P. Lake and M. Dowling (1987), 1–36; Derek Plumb, 'The Social and Economic Status of the Later Lollards', in *The World of Rural Dissenters, 1520–1725*, ed. Margaret Spufford (Cambridge, 1995) [hereafter Plumb, 'Social and Economic Status'], 103–31; *Tudors* (1991), 477.

[63]According to Plumb, 'Social and Economic Status', 114, 'certain' and 'probable' Lollards were 8.5 per cent of taxpayers in eighteen mid-Thames parishes (his unreliable category of 'possible' Lollards would contribute another 6.5 per cent); Hope, 'Lollardy', 4; R. G. Davies, 'Lollardy and Locality', *supra*, 6th ser., I, 191–212; Diarmaid MacCulloch, 'England', in *The Early Reformation in Europe*, ed. Andrew Pettegree (Cambridge, 1992), 172–3.

localities had their own particular complaints which were incorporated into common Articles of petition. These points are, at last, carefully documented in Bush's new book, and the conspiracy theory is nailed in the process.[64] 'Politics and the Pilgrimage' was a wonderfully exciting piece: when I first saw a draft in 1975, I told Geoffrey I disagreed completely but wished I had written it. But it was wrong-headed and narrow in its vision. It showed what could be achieved by careful analysis of crucial texts—Chapuys's reports, Aske's examinations and the Pontefract Articles; but it also showed what a mess you get into if evidence is taken out of context. Elton had not worked through the mass of evidence of events in the north in the months of the Pilgrimage: he never knew what happened there, and never really cared.

The problem Elton posed in 1954, 'King or Minister? the man behind the Henrician Reformation', later became a three-way split—king, minister or factions, with not many supporters for the minister. The structure of Henrician politics has a direct bearing on the nature of the early Reformation—was it a cautious and developing answer to the king's practical problems and responsibilities (Scarisbrick and Glyn Redworth); the deliberate implementation of a ministerial blueprint (Elton alone?); or the meandering and accidental consequence of competition between factions which may (Starkey and Joseph Block) or may not (Eric Ives) have had ideological commitments.[65] From 1983 at the latest, Geoffrey back-pedalled fiercely on the significance of faction, and again stressed Cromwell's role as the omnicompetent implementer.[66] But with no one else pressing Cromwell's claim, the argument is, as Steven Gunn put it, 'between the king's men and the factionalists': the issue has kept the *Historical Journal* and the *English Historical Review* busy for years. Was there a Boleyn faction, and did its success promote the Reformation?—Ives and Block say 'yes' to both questions; George Bernard and Retha Warnicke say 'no'; and Steven Gunn (if I understand him aright) says it all depends.[67] No doubt he is right. I hope our

---

[64] C. S. L. Davies, 'Popular Religion and the Pilgrimage of Grace', in *Order and Disorder in Early Modern England*, ed. A. Fletcher and J. Stevenson (Cambridge, 1985), 58–91; M. L. Bush, '"Up for the Commonweal": The Significance of Tax Grievances in the English Rebellions of 1536', *English Historical Review*, 106 (1991) [hereafter *EHR*], 299–318; Bush, *Pilgrimage*.

[65] Scarisbrick, *Henry VIII*; Glyn Redworth, *In Defence of the Church Catholic: The Life of Stephen Gardiner* (Oxford, 1990); D. Starkey, *The Reign of Henry VIII: Personalities and Politics* (1985); J. S. Block, *Factional Politics and the English Reformation, 1520–1540* (1993); E. W. Ives, *Faction in Tudor England* (2nd edn, 1986).

[66] Elton to Haigh, 17 April 1983; *idem*, 12 June 1987; 'Revisionism Reassessed', 38 ; 'Tudor Government', *HJ*, 31 (1988), 428; *Thomas Cromwell*, 15–40.

[67] Steven Gunn, 'The Structures of Politics in Early Tudor England', *supra*, 6th ser., V, 59–90, quotation at p. 60; G. W. Bernard, 'The Fall of Anne Boleyn', *EHR*, 106 (1991),

litmus-tests for the presence of faction will not be so exacting that no effective alliance could ever be found, nor so loose that 'faction' becomes a synonym for 'politics'.

Policy and Police was followed by a range of studies on the local impact of the Reformation—Henrician and later. But few have investigated the detailed interaction between central enforcement and local government. Mary Robertson has tried to show how Thomas Cromwell managed the west country—rewarding the leading local gentry, taking their sons into his household, receiving regular reports and intervening when, as he thought, things were going wrong. It was a neat well-ordered argument for neat and well-ordered rule: Thomas Cromwell would have liked it, and Geoffrey Elton did. But Helen Speight retorted that effective central control was impossible, and when tried was counter- productive: Cromwell had little room for manoeuvre in selecting local magistrates and officials, and central interference threatened stable county government. For Dr Robertson, good local government meant following the centre's priorities; for Dr Speight, local government could only be good if it was left to balance the centre's priorities and its own.[68] As Steven Gunn might say, it all depends. For Reformation historians, the question is crucial, but probably unanswerable. If county magistrates had a practical veto on law-enforcement, if they concealed disobedience and evasion in the interests of order, then the Reformation was a slow and almost voluntary process. But if they did, we will hardly ever know. Only if magistrates broke ranks, as some did in the west country in 1537–9, will concealment come to light. Otherwise, we are as well-informed—or as ill-informed—as Cromwell was.

Finally, we may examine the problem of the speed at which the Reformation happened. Once more, it all depends: what do we mean by Reformation?—changing the laws, changing public behaviour or changing private belief? For years, Geoffrey was impatient with the question: once the laws were changed, the rest would follow in due course and perhaps it did not matter (and we could not measure) how rapidly. But he was finally persuaded that competent studies of response to the Reformation could be written, and that the response was generally hostile—though he was more willing to accept the detail than

---

584–610; *idem*, 'Anne Boleyn's Religion', *HJ*, 36 (1993), 1–20; R. M. Warnicke, *The Rise and Fall of Anne Boleyn* (Cambridge, 1989), 105–13, 135–62.

[68] Mary L. Robertson, ' "The Art of the Possible": Thomas Cromwell's Management of West Country Government', *HJ*, 32 (1989), 793–816; *idem*, 'A Reply to Helen Speight', *HJ*, 37 (1994), 639–41; *Thomas Cromwell*, 34–5; Helen M. Speight, ' "The Politics of Good Governance": Thomas Cromwell and the Government of the Southwest of England', *HJ*, 37 (1994), 623–38.

to envisage any revisionist Mark 4 Eltonian Reformation.[69] Geoffrey reluctantly agreed that the progress of religious change in the localities is a legitimate and important question. But it also happens to be a very difficult one, and passions have run high. Lots of us have counted will-preambles, and recent methods are much more refined;[70] Geoffrey Dickens counts heretics;[71] Richard Rex counts 'the new learning, as they call it'; Claire Cross counts bequests; Robert Whiting counts gilds and images; Ronald Hutton counts church-ales and processions; I count altars and church-incomes—and we all hope our calculations mean something. The solution, of course, is to fit everything together—but that seems to lead to either crude simplification or the prospect of mind-boggling confusion.[72]

But we have to try, and to do it with humanity and sensitivity: we must not only chart change, crunching our numbers, but seek to understand the experience of it. We need to write about religion in a way that Elton rarely managed, with the kind of sympathy Susan Brigden has shown on evangelicals and Eamon Duffy has shown on traditionalists.[73] We need to know what it felt like to be there. The Reformation was much more than the jurisdictional revolution to which Geoffrey once reduced it, and more too that the bright new idea which freed the laity from their priests: it could be a shattering experience, which mattered a bit to everyone and a lot to very many. Of course, Reformation did not all happen at once, and perhaps there were Reformations, but the mounting sense that the world was in ferment loosened certainties and brought doubts and fears.

Perhaps the piecemeal dismantling of traditional religion was rather like the right's piecemeal dismantling of the consensual post-war welfare

---

[69] Elton to Haigh, 18 November 1993; Elton's review of Duffy, *Stripping*, *JEH*, 44 (1993), 719–21.

[70] Caroline Litzenberger, 'Local Responses to Changes in Religious Policy Based on Evidence from Gloucestershire Wills (1540–1580)', *Continuity and Change*, 8 (1993), 417–39. As in Christopher Haigh, *English Reformations: Religion, Politics and Society under the Tudors* (Oxford, 1993), 199–202, I remain cautious about the use of soul-bequests even when a 'slow Reformation' view is supported!

[71] Dickens, 'Early Expansion', 198–212. Much of the evidence cited there is, it seems to me, stretched well beyond its proper significance. Many modern historians have looser definitions of heresy than early Tudor bishops!

[72] Richard Rex, 'The New Learning', *JEH*, 44 (1993), 26–44; Claire Cross, 'Monasticism and Society in the Diocese of York, 1520–1540', *supra*, 5th ser., XXXVIII (1988), 131–45; Robert Whiting, *The Blind Devotion of the People: Popular Religion and the English Reformation* (Cambridge, 1989); Ronald Hutton, 'The Local Impact of the Tudor Reformations', in *English Reformation Revised*, 114–38; Haigh, *English Reformations*, esp. 206–13, 244–7. For a recent example of crudity see Robert Whiting, 'Local Responses to the Henrician Reformation', in *Reign of Henry VIII*, ed. MacCulloch, 203–26.

[73] Susan Brigden, *London and the Reformation* (Oxford, 1989), esp. 398–422, 458–87; Duffy, *Stripping*.

state and Keynesian economy. At first it seems only the contracting-out of refuse-collection, but ultimately it is recognised as a wholesale attack on conventional structures, conduct and attitudes. There are zealots who drive on (and thrive on) change, and winners who find the new culture a liberating environment for personal fulfilment; there are reluctant conformists, who admit change is needed, or accept it is coming, but are uncomfortable, often irritated, nostalgic and far from certain that the future will be better; there are bewildered bystanders who can make no sense of what is happening around them, but know they did not ask for it; and there are die-hards, who fight to sustain old ways, or at least duck down to avoid complying with the new ones. Even the opposition has to move with the times. But whether social values can so quickly be remade remains to be seen.

We need to know about, and to understand, all sorts of responses to the Reformation—not focus, as we once did, on the progressivist zealots who got things done. For the change which actually happened was made by those who did not want it as well as by those who did, and those who just stood by had something to do with it too. There are colleagues who feel this will all go too far (or are sure it already has): that the Protestants will be forgotten, that it will be supposed that some opposition to Reformation means no support for Reformation. Geoffrey shared this view: 'I sometimes feel that the recovery of the truth from behind the skirts of John Foxe tends to drift into the opposite extreme—more so in Duffy than in Haigh, but still a bit there too.'[74] But I trust we will not be *so* afraid of Robert Persons that we stick too close to John Foxe—or, if I may put it thus, so afraid of Eamon Duffy or Jack Scarisbrick that we stay too close to A. G. Dickens or G. R. Elton. Reformation studies came a long way during Geoffrey's academic life. There is no way back to *England under the Tudors*: but how lucky we were to be able to start there.

[74] Elton to Haigh, 18 November 1993. Cf. Elton's similar comment that 'Duffy justly rewrites a history too long dominated by the likes of John Bale and John Foxe, but he too overbalances – in the opposite direction', *JEH*, 44 (1993), 721.

SIR GEOFFREY ELTON AND THE PRACTICE OF HISTORY

By Quentin Skinner

READ 28 MARCH 1996 AT THE INSTITUTE OF HISTORICAL RESEARCH LONDON

A REVEALING metaphor runs throughout *The Practice of History*, Sir Geoffrey Elton's first and fullest consideration of the methods and purposes of historical study.[1] The aspiring historian is pictured as an apprentice—at one point specifically as an apprentice carpenter (p. 214)—who is aiming to produce a first piece of work to be inspected and judged by a master craftsman. Elton repeatedly speaks of the need for the young scholar to undergo 'a proper apprenticeship' (p. 103). He must acknowledge that 'his life is that of an apprentice learning a craft', and that he requires to be 'instructed, guided, and trained'.[2]

Two aspects of this image seem especially worth spelling out. One is that teacher and student are both assumed to be male, an assumption sustained throughout Elton's later writings on history, up to and including his final thoughts on the subject in his Cook Lectures of 1990, published in *Return to Essentials* in 1991.[3] (I mention this because I shall sometimes find myself obliged, in the course of laying out Elton's arguments, to follow him in writing 'he' when what I mean—and what he means—is 'he or she'.) A second and pivotal assumption is that teachers and writers of history are best viewed as practitioners of a *techne* who have mastered a distinctive set of skills and are thus in a position to pass on what Elton describes as 'the truths of practice and experience'.[4] This commitment is strongly reinforced by the authorial voice we hear throughout Elton's writings on historical method. The tone is very much that of someone who has rules to impart, rules that an apprentice will do well to read and mark if he is to 'train himself to his trade' (p. 113).

The first important lesson the apprentice learns from the opening Chapter of *The Practice of History* is that 'history deals in events, not

---

[1] G. R. Elton, *The Practice of History* (Sydney, 1967). My quotations are taken from the revised edition published in the Fontana Library (1969). Page references are hereafter given so far as possible within the body of the text.

[2] *Ibid.*, 213, 221. Cf. 144, 159, 215.

[3] G. R. Elton, *Return to Essentials* (Cambridge, 1991), 5 *et passim*. Again, page references are hereafter given so far as possible within the body of the text.

[4] Elton, *Practice*, 19. Cf. 34, 160, 187.

states; it investigates things that happen and not things that are' (p. 22). From this it is said to follow that historians must think of their analyses 'as steps in a chain of events, as matters explanatory of a sequence of happenings' (p. 22). They must therefore 'concentrate on understanding change, which is the essential content of historical analysis and description' (p. 22). Subsequently this activity is equated with providing explanations of events. The historian's basic duty is to explain,[5] and this ability is in turn identified with the process of 'deducing consequences from disparate facts' (p. 129).

I am not sure how much headway we are to imagine that the apprentice may already have made in his historical studies. But he will not need to have read very much to know that all these contentions are somewhat questionable. Suppose he has at least turned the pages of some works in the history of art or philosophy. In that case he will know that by no means all historians are preoccupied with explanation, especially if by that process we mean the deducing of consequences. Some are concerned with the provision of interpretations, and thus with the process of placing texts and other such objects within fields of meaning from which their own individual meanings can arguably be derived. If, in addition, the apprentice has read anything on religious or economic history, he will know that even historians concerned with explanation are by no means always interested in explaining events. Some are interested in explaining such matters as the prevalence of particular belief-systems or the ways in which past economic systems have worked.

I suppose we are not to imagine that the apprentice will have read any works in the philosophy of history. Certainly he will not have done so if he has been following the lessons of the master, for Elton explicitly assures us in the Preface to *The Practice of History* that 'a philosophic concern with such problems as the reality of historical knowledge or the nature of historical thought only hinders the practice of history' (p. vii). Nevertheless, our imagined apprentice might surely be a sufficiently reflective person to wonder how it can possibly be the case that, as Elton maintains, the way in which historians explain events is by 'deducing consequences from disparate facts' (p. 129). It is true that a knowledge of consequences may sometimes lead an historian to reconsider the significance of an event. But the result of doing so will not of course to explain it; it will merely be to re-identify what stands to be explained. When it comes to explanation, the historian surely needs to focus not on the outcome of events but on the causal conditions of their occurrence.

These considerations might lead one to conclude that Elton must

---

[5] *Ibid.*, 128. Cf. 37, 166.

simply have made a slip at this point, and that what he meant to write was that historians explain events by way of assigning their causes. He insists, however, that 'events are not the product of simple causes' and that 'to suppose that causal relationships are the main content of history is an error'.[6] So he evidently has no wish to be rescued in this way. But in that case I am bound to confess that I cannot make sense of his view of historical explanation, simply because I cannot see how the act of tracing the consequences of an event has any bearing upon the explanatory task of giving an account of why it occurred.

If we turn, however, to Elton's second book on the study of history, we encounter a more sophisticated and extended analysis of historical explanation in which the emphasis is placed entirely on causes rather than on consequences. I am referring to *Political History: Principles and Practice*, which Elton originally published in 1970.[7] The first three chapters are largely given over to a more genial if less incisive development of a number of claims already advanced in *The Practice of History* about the alleged primacy of politics in historical studies. But in chapter 4, entitled 'Explanation and Cause', Elton breaks a considerable amount of new ground. He also breaks a considerable number of lances, tilting at the entire philosophical literature on historical explanation with exhilarating self-confidence.

While the outcome is polemically spectacular, the argument seems to me weakened by Elton's insistence that good theory in this area amounts to nothing other than a reflection and restatement of practice.[8] Since it is historians who provide historical explanations, he repeatedly proclaims, it is for them to tell us what what makes a good explanation, rather than listening to what he describes as philosophers' nonsense (p. 129). What is needed is an account of 'what the historian does', an analysis of 'the historian's concept of cause', an investigation into 'what the historian might mean by talking about causes'.[9]

Elton may well be right to stress the pragmatic element in the notion of explanation, an element perhaps best captured by saying that good explanations are those which succeed in removing puzzles about the occurrence of facts or events. But it hardly follows that good historical explanations consist of anything that practising historians may care to offer us in the way of attempting to resolve such puzzles. Historical explanations cannot be immune from assessment as explanations, and the question of what properly counts as an explanation is inescapably

[6] *Ibid.*, 23, 129.

[7] G. R. Elton, *Political History: Principles and Practice* (1970). Once again, page references are hereafter given so far as possible within the body of the text.

[8] See *ibid.*, esp. 135, and cf. Elton, *Return*, esp. 3, 34, 51, 54, 61.

[9] Elton, *Political History*, 125, 136, 145.

a philosophical one. The question cannot be what historians say; the question must be whether what they say makes any sense.

This is not to deny that Elton may be justified in claiming that the philosophers he discusses imposed too stringent a model by making it a requirement of good historical explanations that they be nomological in form, such that the task of the historian is held to be that of deducing facts and events from covering laws of which they can be shown to be instances.[10] Nevertheless, the philosophers in question were surely right to insist that the provision of causal explanations in history must to some extent depend on our capacity to relate particular instances to wider generalities. Elton strongly disagrees, arguing that generalizations are 'no help at all' in the search for historical explanations, since historians are always concerned with 'the particular event'.[11] But the *non sequitur* here is blatant: even if it were true that historians are only concerned with particular events, it certainly does not follow that they are under no obligation to investigate causal uniformities in order to explain them. Despite Elton's assurances, moreover, I cannot myself see how historians can hope to solve any puzzles about the occurrence of facts or events without making some attempt to relate such particulars to a broader explanatory background.

If we now return, however, to the point at which we left Elton's argument in *The Practice of History*, we find that none of these considerations matter much after all, since these are not the problems that Elton really wants the apprentice to address. At the end of chapter 1 he suddenly introduces a new and different claim about the objectives of history. The apprentice is now told that history, 'to be worthy of itself and beyond itself, must concentrate on one thing', namely the extraction from all the available evidence of what Elton later calls the true facts.[12] This is not perhaps a very felicitous way of introducing the argument, since it subsequently emerges that, for Elton, a true statement *is* a statement of fact, so that the concept of a true fact turns out to be a pleonasm. Nevertheless, the new and contrasting claim he wishes to advance is not in doubt: it is that historians are basically engaged in what he describes as 'a search for the truth' (p. 70).

Elton's later pronouncements about historical method admittedly involve some shifting back and forth between these two perspectives. His first Inaugural Lecture of 1968, reprinted in *Return to Essentials*, begins by reverting to the claim that 'the essence of all history is change' (p. 80). The second Inaugural of 1983, reprinted in the same

[10] For Elton's attack on attempts to apply hypothetico-deductive models of explanation to history, see *ibid.*, esp. 125–8.

[11] *Ibid.*, 132, 151–2. Cf. 127.

[12] Elton, *Practice*, 68, 86.

volume, speaks even more emphatically about 'the inadequacy of any historical analysis which is not predominantly directed towards an understanding of change through time' (p. 120). But on the whole it is the idea of extracting the truth from the facts that wins the day. The first Inaugural demands that historians must 'consider all the evidence', adding that this is because they are 'concerned with one thing only: to discover the truth'.[13] Chapter 3 of *Political History*, which is actually entitled 'Evidence', speaks again about the bodies of material studied by historians and promises that 'something like the truth can be extracted from them' (p. 84). The second Inaugural ends by repeating once more that the sole aim of the historian is that of 'telling the truth about the past'.[14] Finally, these are precisely the 'essentials' to which Elton recalls us in his *Return to Essentials* of 1991. The apprentice must acquire 'a professional training' in 'the treatment of the historical evidence' about every event he investigates, with the eventual aim of arriving at 'the truth of the event and all that surrounds it' (pp. 30, 54).

The second chapter of *The Practice of History* adds some examples to clarify what Elton means by speaking about items of historical evidence.[15] The sort of thing he has in mind, he says, is something like a financial account, or the record of a court case, or one of the material relics of the past, such as a house. These are 'far and away the most important and common' types of evidence that the apprentice can expect to meet, and these are the sorts of relics and documents from which he must extract the truth (p. 101).

I imagine the apprentice exhibiting a certain surprise at this point. Perhaps these forms of evidence are the most common, but is it so obvious that they are 'far and away the most important'? What about the major works of theology, philosophy and science that adorn our libraries? What about the heritage of great paintings and other works of art that fill our museums and galleries? Elton gives his answer in the concluding chapter of *The Practice of History*. The apprentice must learn to distinguish between optional aspects of historical study and 'real' or 'hard' history.[16] The 'hard outline' of historical research and teaching 'must consist of the actions of governments and governed in the public life of the time', this being the only theme 'sufficiently dominant to carry others along with it'.[17] But as long as this forms the backbone of

---

[13] Elton, *Return*, 86n. and 91.

[14] *Ibid.*, 125.

[15] The points are repeated in Elton, *Political History*, 12–13.

[16] Elton, *Practice*, 190, 197, 199. On 'real' history see also Elton, *Political History*, esp. 22, 32.

[17] Elton, *Practice*, 172, 199. The same point is even more emphatically made in Elton, *Political History*, esp. 7, 65, 157, 177. He recurs to it yet again at the end of his second Inaugural lecture. See Elton, *Return*, 123.

our historical studies,[18] there is no harm in adding such optional extras as intellectual history or the history of art, although the latter admittedly encourages 'woolliness and pretence' (p. 190). Elton even allows that some kinds of intellectual history—for example, the history of political thought—may have a positive value, since this type of investigation 'bears directly on a main part of the student's "hard" history' through its connection with 'political organization and action'.[19] By the time Elton came to publish *Return to Essentials,* however, he had noticed that in the meantime the history of ideas had been 'suddenly promoted from the scullery to the drawing room' (p. 12). To cope with this impertinence, he takes more care in this later work to warn the apprentice that intellectual history is not 'real' history at all. 'By its very nature' it is 'liable to lose contact with reality', and is indeed 'removed from real life'.[20]

The apprentice is thus left with some very definite instructions about what to study and how to study it. He must concentrate on 'hard' history, and thus on the type of evidence originally singled out in chapter 2 of *The Practice of History:* the evidence provided by such things as the record of a court case or a material relic such as a house. He should then make it his business to extract the facts, and thus the truth, from such forms of evidence. He must remember, as chapter 2 later puts it, that 'historical method is no more than a recognised and tested way of extracting from what the past has left the true facts and events of that past' (p. 86). Nor need he have any doubt 'that the truth can be extracted from the evidence by the application of proper principles of criticism' (p. 97). He can be certain that, properly approached, the evidence will 'tell him the truth'.[21]

By this stage I imagine the apprentice beginning to feel slightly bewildered. Elton has offered him the example of a house as an instance of the type of evidence from which he is expected to extract the facts in such a way as to arrive at the truth. But how can one hope to go about seeking the truth, *simpliciter,* about such a thing as a house? Won't it be necessary to approach the study of the house with some sense of why I am studying it, why it might be of interest, before I can tell how best to set about examining it?

Elton has of course foreseen the worry, and offers an interesting response. The opening chapter of *The Practice of History* introduces a

---

[18] Elton, *Practice,* 197. Cf. Elton, *Political History,* insisting (p. 73) on the 'primacy' of political history and singling it out (p. 68) as 'the most important' subject of historical research.

[19] Elton, *Practice,* 190. For a repetition and enlargement of this argument see Elton, *Political History,* 43–53.

[20] Elton, *Return,* 27, 60.

[21] Elton, *Practice,* 101. Cf. 117.

distinction betwen 'real' historians and amateurs.[22] Amateurs such as Lord Acton or G. M. Trevelyan (who was 'a really fine amateur') intrude themselves and their enthusiasms upon the past (p. 31). By contrast, real historians wait for the evidence to suggest questions by itself. As Elton later puts it, the questions a real historian asks are never 'forced by him upon the material'; rather they are forced by the material upon the historian (p. 83). The real historian remains the servant of his evidence, of which he 'should ask no specific questions until he has absorbed what it says' (p. 83). The distinction recurs in chapter 3, in which we are again told that the questions we ask as historians must 'arise out of the work' and 'not be sovereignly imposed on it' (p. 121).

This kind of injunction has been central to the German tradition of hermeneutics, and is prominent in the writings of Hans-Georg Gadamer, especially his *Wahrheit und Methode* of 1960.[23] It is true that Gadamer makes no appearance in *The Practice of History*, and that when Elton later invokes him in *Return to Essentials* it is only to dismiss him as ponderous and confused (pp. 29, 38). It seems to me, however, that Elton is not only echoing one of Gadamer's most characteristic themes, but that the argument they are both putting forward embodies a salutary warning about the need to avoid fitting the evidence we read as historians into pre-existing patterns of interpretation and explanation. Moreover, the reminder seems all the more valuable in view of the fact that the premature consignment of unfamiliar evidence to familiar categories is so hard to avoid, as even apprentice historians know.

There remain some difficulties, however, about applying this rule in practice. Gadamer would certainly not approve, in the first place, of the positivistic confidence with which Elton asserts it. Consider again Elton's example of a house as an instance of the sort of evidence that an apprentice might confront. Gadamer would point out that Elton has already begged the question by characterizing the object under investigation as a house. It will be unwise for Elton to retort that the object must be a house because it is described as such in all relevant documents. The House of Commons is described as a house in all relevant documents, but it is not a house. Nor will Elton fare much better if he replies that the object must be a house because it looks like a house. On the one hand, an object might look nothing like a house and nevertheless be a house. (Think of Martello Towers now used as houses.) On the other hand, an object might look very like a house and nevertheless not be a house. (Think of the mausoleums designed by Vanburgh.) As Gadamer always stresses, but Elton scarcely acknow-

[22] *Ibid.*, pp. 29–36.
[23] Hans-Georg Gadamer, *Wahrheit und Methode* (Tübingen, 1960).

ledges, we are already caught up in the process of interpretation as soon as we begin to describe any aspect of our evidence in words.

A second and more intractable problem arises as soon as we ask how far we can hope to carry Elton's idea of confronting something like a house and allowing it, as he repeatedly asks, to force its questions upon us. I can see that, if we found ourselves confronting a very odd house, some questions might spontaneously arise. ('If that's a house, why are there no windows?') But I cannot see that this approach will take us any great distance. More broadly, I cannot see how the basic idea of seeking 'the truth' about something like a house can be rendered intelligible. Elton is adamant that 'the only proper ambition' for an historian is 'to know all the evidence' that 'may conceivably be relevant to his enquiry'.[24] Historians must begin by acquiring 'total acquaintance with the relevant material' if they are to end up with the truth.[25] But what would it be like to acquire total acquaintance with an item of evidence such as a house? Consider, for example, the project of acquiring total acquaintance with Chatsworth House, and thereby arriving at the truth about that principal residence of the dukes of Devonshire. A complete study of all the facts about Chatsworth would be literally endless. It would take a lifetime for the apprentice to accumulate a full description (whatever that may mean) of the house itself, without even entering its muniment room and staring glassily at the scores of manuscript volumes relating to the lives of its owners and the process of building it.

As Elton's discussion proceeds, however, he evidently begins to see this difficulty, or at least he undoubtedly begins to shift his ground, although admittedly at the cost of introducing some contradictions into his argument. In chapter 3 of *The Practice of History* he is still assuring us that we can hope to reach 'the truth' about the objects of our research (p. 117). But in chapter 4 he replaces this contention with the very different and rather more modest claim that we can hope to arrive at some particular truths. Whereas chapter 2 had spoken of recovering 'the truth' about 'past realities', chapter 4 instead speaks of the historian's capacity to 'establish new footholds in the territory of truth'—that is, to find out new truths.[26]

It subsequently turns out that this more modest account of the historian's task is what really matters to Elton. It is because of his sense that, as he puts it in chapter 3 of *The Practice of History*, there are many

[24] Elton, *Practice*, 87.

[25] *Ibid.*, 96. Cf. 88, 92, 109.

[26] *Ibid.*, 74, 177. Cf. 207. But at some points Elton continues to insist that the aim must be to disover 'the truth' and not merely particular truths. See *Ibid.*, 179, 205–6, 221, and cf. Elton, *Political History*, 105.

things that historians 'know beyond doubt' and 'can say with certainty' that he later savages the Deconstructionists and their scepticism about facts with such extraordinary confidence (pp. 107,111). Elton knows beyond question 'who the eldest surviving child of Henry VIII was'; this is one of an 'enormous number' of historical facts 'on which no dispute is possible'.[27] It follows that, when he finds himself obliged to confront such deconstructionist critics as Dominick LaCapra with their claim that 'there cannot be any ascertainable certainties in history', Elton is in no doubt about how to respond.[28] Although he does not know how to spell Professor LaCapra's name, he knows for a fact that LaCapra is merely exhibiting 'the mindless arrogance of the self-satisfied' if he is attempting 'to deny the existence of facts' (pp. 58–9).

It is true that Elton's confidence betrays him into some further contradictions. In *Return to Essentials* he informs us that the historian 'must be a professional sceptic',[29] and in *The Practice of History* he similarly asserts that the historian's function must be 'to cast doubt upon the possibility that in historical studies anyone will ever be finally "right"'' (p. 206). Yet he is even more emphatic that that 'some historical writing is simply and obviously right', his reason being that 'increasing knowledge genuinely produces increasing agreed certainty', giving rise to a body of knowledge which cannot possibly be called in doubt.[30]

Elton's restatement of his ideal is far from coherent, but his ideal itself is surely clear and unexceptionable. If we now return to Chatsworth with no higher ambition than to say a number of true things about it, we can surely hope to succeed. We may be able to determine such matters as its overall height, the size of its grounds and perhaps even the number of its rooms with absolute finality, so long as we take care to avoid any problems of an interpretative kind (such as, for example, what is to count as a room). If this is all that is meant by the quest for the truth—that is, the capacity to find out and state a number of things that are true—it can certainly be granted to Elton that, as he puts it in chapter 3 of *The Practice of History*, historians are often able to end up by offering statements 'of manifest and incontrovertible truth' (p. 176).

Unlike his initial demand, Elton's more modest proposal at least has the merit of suggesting a research programme that could in principle be carried out. It is not clear, however, that this will necessarily alleviate the anxiety originally expressed by our imagined apprentice. He now knows that his job is to find out a number of facts about Chatsworth

[27] Elton, *Practice*, 80.
[28] For the discussion of LaCapra's views see *Return*, 58–61.
[29] Elton, *Return*, 23–4. Cf. Elton, *Practice*, 55, 103, 205.
[30] Elton, *Practice*, 81–2, 123.

with the eventual aim of stating a corresponding number of truths about it. But he also knows that the facts about Chatsworth are so numerous that he will never be able to find out more than a fraction of them. (If he stupidly decides, for example, to start by finding out how many stones went into its construction, he will certainly never finish his thesis on time.) Moreover, since every fact he discovers will have to be expressed in words, and since Foucault has by now familiarised even apprentice historians with the thought that all classificatory schemes are subject to endless challenge and revision, he may even begin to wonder how many genuinely incontrovertible facts he can hope to enunciate. Suppose, for example, he decides to catalogue the works of art contained in Chatsworth. He wants to know whether he should include the furniture. The correct answer, obviously, is that he should include only those items of furniture which are also works of art. But what is it for something to be a work of art? On the one hand, the question clearly has no simple answer, perhaps no answer at all. But on the other hand, the apprentice needs to answer it if he is going to be able to state as a matter of incontrovertible fact how many works of art Chatsworth contains. Perhaps there are fewer incontrovertible facts than he has been led to believe.

The apprentice need not despair, however, for Elton is on hand to reassure him that (as he remarks in speaking of my own writings on this subject) these are unduly high-falutin doubts.[31] But even if the apprentice feels duly reassured, he is still in need of some advice about how to start work on his thesis about Chatsworth. What sort of incontrovertible facts should he be looking for? What sort of things should he be trying to find out?

One obvious way of replying would be to revert to the somewhat Socratic approach I initially suggested. What first attracted you, one might ask in return, to the idea of studying Chatsworth? What made you think that a thesis on Chatsworth might be of any interest? I think this would certainly be my own response. I would expect the apprentice to have some views about why it might be of some value—here and now, to himself and others—to know more about Chatsworth and its history. I would urge him, in other words, to solve the problem of how to approach his study of Chatsworth by first asking himself what might be the point or purpose of studying it at all.

If our imagined apprentice is expecting some such answer from Elton, however, he is in for a rude shock. It is Elton's view that asking such questions is the quickest way of revealing that you have failed to understand the nature of the historian's craft. He insists in *The Practice of History* that our historical studies must be kept entirely separate from

[31] Elton, *Return*, 42.

any such personal concerns (p. 65), and in *Return to Essentials* he reiterates the point with even greater vehemence. 'The fundamental questions we put to the evidence' must remain 'independent of the concerns of the questioner' (p. 55). We must recognise that Chatsworth—or any other relic of the past—must be studied 'for its own sake', and that this constitutes 'the first principle of historical understanding'.[32] What distinguishes a true practitioner of history is a willingness to 'cultivate a respect for the past in its own right'.[33]

It might be supposed that what Elton means is that, once we have selected a topic for investigation, we must be sure to treat it in its own terms, even though the topic we initially select will of course have been chosen on the grounds that it seemed to us to possess some inherent value and importance. This would be to say—to cite an epigram of John Dunn's—that the historian should be Whig as to subject-matter, Tory as to truth.[34] But to assume that this is Elton's position would be seriously to underestimate the sweep of his argument in *The Practice of History* about the need to approach the past 'in its own right, for its own sake, and on its own terms' (p. 86). It is Elton's view that we must take the greatest care *not* to select our topics on the grounds that they seem to us to have some current interest or (worse still) some contemporary social relevance or importance. The point is made with the utmost firmness, and with Elton's habitual repetitiousness, in every chapter of the book. To proceed in this way is to commit 'the cardinal error' (p. 86). The historian must avoid any attempt 'to justify his activity as a social utility' (p. vii). He must recognise that his entire pursuit 'involves, above all, the deliberate abandonment of the present' (p. 66). The same point is made yet again, with even greater assurance, in *Return to Essentials*. The entire project of historical reseach ('all of it') must be completely divorced from the 'needs and concerns of the present' (p. 72).

By this stage I imagine the apprentice becoming seriously bewildered, perhaps even a touch desperate. Does this mean that all the facts I might discover about Chatsworth are of equal interest? Am I just to go there and start making a list of anything it occurs to me to say about it? If this is all I am expected to do, might I just as well be studying something else, perhaps anything else?

If the apprentice is insolently attempting a *reductio ad absurdum* he is in for another rude shock, for it turns out that this is exactly what Elton believes. When he addresses the question of teaching in the

---

[32] Elton, *Practice*, 18, 86. Cf. 65, 66.

[33] Elton, *Return*, 24. Cf. 9, 52.

[34] See John Dunn, 'The Identity of the History of Ideas', in *Political Obligation in its Historical Context* (Cambridge, 1980), 13–28.

closing chapter of *The Practice of History*, he goes so far as to declare that the actual content of what we teach, and *a fortiori* what we study as historians, 'matters in essence very little' (p. 188). True historians, as he had earlier put it, are not marked out by 'the problems they study' but by 'the manner of their study' (p. 69). Their problems may indeed seem 'narrow or petty', but they gain their importance from 'the techniques of study' they teach (p. 34). This is a truth that needs to be grasped not merely by teachers of history but by 'anyone concerning himself with historical studies in any form' (p. 186). The purpose of our studies must be sought 'in the intellectual training they provide' (p. 186). And it is because 'all history, properly deployed' can supply this training that 'it matters in essence very little what particular sections of it are taught' (p. 188).

I imagine the apprentice stunned at this point into incredulity. Surely Elton cannot want to say that all the ideas and information we might acquire from a study of the past are irrelevant to the basic reason we have for studying it? But this is exactly what he does want to say. 'The University', he patiently explains, 'must train the mind, not fill the untrained mind with multi-coloured information and undigested ideas, and only the proper study of an identifiable discipline according to the rules and practices of that discipline can accomplish that fundamental purpose.'[35] But what of our ability to learn from the past about unfamiliar social structures, about the development of art, religion and philosophy, about the conditions and mechanisms of economic change? Some of these examples are Elton's, but they leave him unmoved. 'This is nothing to do with the framing of courses for study and examination, with the real work of intellectual training.'[36] But what about his earlier insistence that it matters very much what kind of history we learn and teach, since 'the actions of governments and governed' alone provide us with a backbone of 'real' or 'hard' history? Here I do not know what to say, for as far as I can see Elton makes no effort to reconcile the apparently blank contradiction between this argument and his no less strongly voiced belief in the supreme importance of technique.[37]

It is surely worth pausing at this sensational moment to reflect on the completeness of the disjunction that Elton eventually draws between the content and the justification of our historical studies. What could

[35] Elton, *Practice*, 199.

[36] *Ibid.*, 200.

[37] One possible reconciliation might take the form of saying that the required technical skills can best be gained from studying certain types of document, and that the most suitable types on which to practise are those concerned with English central government. So far as I am aware Elton never explicitly suggested this reconciliation, although he arguably hints at it in G. R. Elton, *England 1200–1640*, Sources of History (Cambridge, 1969), 33. I owe this suggestion to Glenn Burgess.

have prompted so great a scholar to paint himself into such a dark and dismal corner? The clue lies, I believe, in considering the nature of the intellectual crisis so painfully reflected in the pages of *The Practice of History*. By the time Elton came to publish this manual in 1967, he had issued some of his best-known technical scholarship as well as two of his most widely used textbooks. As *The Practice of History* makes clear, he not only thought highly of this *œuvre*[38] but had managed to persuade himself that the kind of research in which he himself specialised called for the exercise of exceptional human powers. He speaks of the need for a searching intelligence, for sympathy and judgement, for 'imagination controlled by learning and scholarship'.[39] He even speaks in an uncharacteristic moment of pomposity of the historian's 'obligations as an artist' as well.[40]

Elton was acutely aware, however, that a number of prominent historians had meanwhile ceased to believe in the validity or importance of the sort of administrative and political history in which he had made his name. Among those particularly singled out in *The Practice of History* for arguing that such preoccupations have 'ceased to be valid' are Richard Southern and Keith Thomas.[41] As Elton concedes, both acknowledge that political history retained its importance so long as the teaching of history in British universities remained closely tied to the training of a political elite and of a civil service capable of running a great empire. With the loss of these social conditions, however, Southern and Thomas were led to conclude that the justification for singling out this kind of history had come to an end as well. Both accordingly enter what Elton describes as unacceptable pleas for a new sense of why history might matter to our society, together with a call for the cultivation of new forms of historical enquiry—a call for more intellectual history in the case of Southern, more social history in the case of Thomas.[42]

A surprising feature of *The Practice of History* is that Elton makes almost no attempt to respond to these arguments by seeking to vindicate the social value or cultural significance of his own very different kind of research. He could surely have attempted—as several of his obituarists did—to convey some sense of why the study of administrative and constitutional history might still be thought to matter even in a post-imperial culture dominated by the social sciences. It is true that, a couple of years later, he offers some gestures in this direction in his

---

[38] See for example Elton, *Practice*, 174–6.

[39] *Ibid.*, 112, 177. On the exceptional skills needed to write political history see also Elton, *Political History*, esp. 108.

[40] Elton, *Practice*, 158–9. Cf. 124.

[41] See *Ibid.*, 17–18, 185.

[42] For a discussion of these claims see *Ibid.*, esp. 17–18, 185–6.

first Inaugural Lecture. But it is striking that he almost instantly stops short, apologizing for starting to speak in such a 'very vague and rather vapoury' way.[43] Faced with the question of how a knowledge of history might help the world, he preferred to advise historians to 'abandon and resign' such aspirations altogether.[44]

Why was Elton so doubtful about assigning any social value or utility to his own brand of history? I confess that I am not altogether sure, although the answer must certainly be connected with his curious but persistent belief that any attempt to vindicate the usefulness of studying the past must include a demonstration of the historian's capacity to issue predictions.[45] This is particularly a theme of Elton's first Inaugural Lecture. 'We are told', he confides, that what historians must do if they are to be socially useful is to answer the question 'What help can the past offer to the future?'[46] But who tells us this? It is hard to think of any contemporary historian or philosopher of history who has advanced this argument, and Elton himself mentions no names. He can scarcely have in mind his two *bêtes noires*, Southern and Thomas, both of whom are exclusively concerned with the question of how the past might be made relevant to the present. Nor can he be thinking of the Marxist historian he most frequently attacks, Christopher Hill, for while it was undoubtedly an aspiration of classical Marxism to make use of historical materials to formulate predictive social laws, Christopher Hill has never exhibited anything more than a passing interest in that aspect of Marxist philosophy.

There remains something of a mystery surrounding the sources of Elton's scepticism about the broader educational value of his own studies. About the fact of his scepticism, however, he leaves us in no possible doubt. His second Inaugural Lecture robustly declares that 'we should not trouble ourselves too much' about the alleged lessons of history, since this would be to study the past for an 'inappropriate and usually misleading purpose'.[47] Eight years later, in the version of his Cook Lectures published in *Return to Essentials*, his mood had become even more dismissive. He begins by stigmatizing the nineteenth-century belief in the lessons of history as little more than an influential absurdity, and goes on to warn us against the 'temptation' of believing that the study of history is of any essential relevance either to our future or our present state (pp. 4, 9).

Elton clearly recognised, however, that these commitments left him

---

[43] Elton, *Return*, 93.

[44] *Ibid.*, 96.

[45] The same anxiety afflicted J. H. Hexter at much the same time, but he responded by attempting to vindicate the historian's predictive powers. See *The History Primer* (1971), esp. 36–42.

[46] Elton, *Return*, 84.

[47] *Ibid.*, 114.

with only two possible ways of convincing us—as he always remained anxious to do—that the study of history should nevertheless be recognised, as *The Practice of History* puts it, as a vocation 'appropriate to the highest abilities of the human reason' (p. 16n). One alternative would be to abandon any attempt to vindicate the social value of his own kind of history in favour of claiming that the value of the subject somehow lies in the study of the past as a whole. This is the line he begins to follow in *Return to Essentials*, and especially in the three Cook Lectures included in that book. The first lecture opens by informing us that 'history teaches a great deal about the existence of free will' (pp. 7–8). The second adds that a professional assessment of the past can be used to demolish a number of comfortable myths (pp. 45–6). The third concludes that history can tell us about the unexpected and, again, about the reality of human freedom (p. 73).

These are not perhaps very promising lines of thought, and it seems to me to Elton's credit that he never makes any effort to explain or develop them. He was undoubtedly aware that the past has always been studied for a myriad of changing reasons, and that any attempt to summarise them will almost inevitably degenerate into just such a string of clichés. But this leaves him with only one means of vindicating the importance of his own studies. As we have already seen, he is forced into arguing that any attempt to offer a social justification of history is an irrelevance, the reason being that what matters in history is not the content of our studies but the range of techniques we deploy in practising them. This is the conclusion which, in effect, supplies him with the theme of both the Inaugural Lectures reprinted in *Return to Essentials*. The second proclaims that the value of historical study lies entirely in the 'mind-training capacity' it provides (p. 108). Even more bluntly, the first concludes that what historians 'are here to teach the world' is nothing other than 'the proper assessment and proper study of evidence' (p. 89).

We can now see what makes Elton's image of the historian as a master carpenter such a deeply revealing one. What matters, he believes, is not whether we are engaged in making tables, chairs or wooden spoons; what matters is the nature of the craft skills equally required for engaging in any of these activities. The discoveries made by historians are of less importance than the techniques by which their discoveries are made.

By now I would expect the apprentice to have given up his thesis on Chatsworth, perhaps devoting himself instead to a career in retailing (as Elton appears to advise at one point in his second Inaugural Lecture).[48] I fear that some such feeling of discouragement would

---

[48] *Ibid.*, 94.

certainly have been my own response, although it is important to add that Elton's outstanding success as a teacher, especially of graduate students, suggests that there must be some way in which I am failing to respond with adequate appreciation to his advice to neophytes. Be that as it may, I should like to summon my imagined apprentice back once more to ask Elton if he does not fear that something of broader educational significance may have been forfeited by his unrelenting insistence on technique at the expense of content. It turns out, however, that Elton has no regrets, since he is not sure about the value of a broader liberal education in any case. This darkest vein of scepticism surfaces—without preamble or explanation—in his first Inaugural Lecture, in the course of which Sir Richard Morison, one of Henry VIII's propagandists, is approvingly cited for the view that education is a great cause of sedition and other mischiefs in commonwealths. Elton follows up the quotation with a disconcerting flurry of questions. 'Should we', he suddenly asks, 'really be practising education? Are we not overestimating it as a power for good, or possibly underestimating it as a power for evil? Ought we not sometimes to stand away from the whole question of education?' Even more disconcerting is his response. Education 'is a livelihood', he concedes, 'but it may be a folly', and it is undoubtedly a cause of mischief in commonwealths.[49]

Elton's fundamental reason for wishing to emphasise technique over content appears to have been a deeply ironic one: a fear that historical study might have the power to transform us, to help us think more effectively about our society and its possible need for reform and reformation. Although it strikes me as strange in the case of someone who spent his life as a professional educator, Elton clearly felt that this was a consummation devoutly to be stopped.[50]

[49] *Ibid.*, 85.
[50] For commenting on earlier drafts I am deeply grateful to Susan James and John Thompson.

ELTON ON *THE ENGLISH*: A DISCUSSION
Patrick Wormald, John Gillingham, Colin Richmond

27 MARCH 1996 AT UNIVERSITY COLLEGE LONDON

SIR GEOFFREY ELTON'S *ENGLISH*: A VIEW FROM THE EARLY MIDDLE AGES

By Patrick Wormald

SIR Geoffrey Elton begins his 'essay' on *The English* in 927, 'the year in which Æthelstan, king of Wessex and Mercia, took over the Danish and English parts of Northumbria and thereby in effect also accepted the existence of a separate kingdom of Scotland'. It was a characteristic moment to choose. This is the date given by the *Handbook of British Chronology*, evidently the consideration foremost in Sir Geoffrey's mind. Æthelstan was the first to declare (in effect) that 'this realm of England is an empire', which one might have suspected to be a factor too, had Elton not soon explicitly denied any Anglo-Saxon meaning to 'such noise'.[1] More pertinently, Æthelstan was actually the first king of about all of what is now England, and the first so to style himself officially. By any standards except his grandfather's he was one of the most gifted and well-counselled rulers in English history, whom only the quirks of surviving evidence and historiographical fashion have denied the status of a William the Conqueror or an Edward I.[2]

Elton's choice of Æthelstan's Northumbrian *démarche* for his launch-pad is thus characteristic in another way. There is a lot more in the first chapter of *The English* that is right than is wrong. Whatever the experience of specialists in other ages (and one does not have to be a

---

[1] G. Elton, *The English* (henceforth *English*), xi, 1, 20. On the editors' instructions (and by their good grace) I reproduce this sketch almost exactly as delivered at the *Eltonfest* of March 1996. The annotation now provided is designed only to support what assertions of substance I offer, and to direct interested readers to the best detailed treatment of the early medieval topics I raise. I owe my usual debt to the acuity and encouragement of Dr Jenny Wormald.

[2] There is no fully satisfactory treatment of Æthelstan's reign, and probably never can be. Best results to date are to be had from conflating the different but complementary studies of M. Wood, 'The Making of King Æthelstan's Empire: An English Charlemagne?', in *Ideal and Reality in Frankish and Anglo-Saxon Society. Studies Presented to J. M. Wallace-Hadrill*, ed. P. Wormald, D. Bullough and R. Collins (Oxford, 1983), pp. 250–72; and D. Dumville: 'Between Alfred the Great and Edgar the Peacemaker: Æthelstan, First King of England', in his *Wessex and England: From Alfred to Edgar* (Woodbridge, 1992), pp. 141–71. Æthelstan's mistake, from the point of view of his historiographical fortunes, was to be at odds with the Winchester establishment who were the effective guardians of English historical tradition in the tenth century. However, a forthcoming paper by Mr Wood gives better grounds than any yet for taking seriously the (?tenth-century, ??Malmesbury) account of the king that was reproduced by William of Malmesbury: W. Stubbs, ed., *Willelmi Malmesbiriensis ... De Gestis Regum Anglorum*, 2 vols., Rolls Series 90 (1887–9), chs. 132–5, I, 144–52.

Tudor *afficionado* to sense that Thomas Cromwell's entry in the index, which outstrips that for any king including Henry VIII, transcends the bounds of self-caricature), the Anglo-Saxonist has relatively little to complain about. I would add that, so far as I am concerned, and though the province is really John Gillingham's, the same goes for the account of the Norman Conquest and its consequences. In fact I would go further than that. In the three abiding themes of the whole book— that the history of the English is marked by extraordinary continuity; that this continuity resided above all in an enduring system of government; and that this system's endurance rested on the unusual size of a political nation whose depth and coherence was in turn sustained by the access of its members to the king's law—there seems to me to be fundamental truth. Those who deny that the story of the English is inseparable from that of a state which has now lasted thirty-five generations may still accept that it is truer for the English than almost any of the world's other peoples.[3] Granted that Elton had the best possible mentor in Mr Campbell (and granted too that I would think that, having sat at the same feet), it is no small thing for early medievalists to see what amounts to the doctrine of Stubbs revived in a one-volume History of the English, after a century when such works have rarely done justice to the early English period. For this to be done by a Renaissance–Reformation expert, whom I know on the evidence of another Cambridge historian less than ten years his senior to have been educated in the tradition that little could be known before 1066, even supposing it were worth knowing, shows a flexibility of intellect that is the mark of a great historian. Elton had in fact come to terms with the problem that must henceforward dog all historians of the English: that so much of what mattered had happened before there is nearly enough evidence of how it happened. Our subject thrives (in fact lives) on revision and reappraisal. There must be controversy and refinement ahead in the assessment of the Anglo-Saxons. But I doubt whether they will ever again join the Romans and Celts in the musty, artefact-strewn vestibule of English history proper.

What more is there for me to say? Something; because, if Elton rightly perceived the defining role of events from the ninth to eleventh centuries for the English experience, he was not so sensitive to their inner dynamics. Specifically (and unsurprisingly), he misconceived the nature of power in the early middle ages: he was pessimistic about what was not done by kings, and correspondingly optimistic about what was. But a word should first be said about inhabitants of these islands

---

[3] G. E. Aylmer, 'The Peculiarities of the English State', *Journal of Historical Sociology*, 3 (1990), 91–108: Professor Aylmer wrote from the significant standpoint of an editor in the European Science Foundation project on 'La genese de l'etat moderne'.

who are denied more than cameo (and usually burlesque) parts in the drama. Whatever the Anglo-Saxonist's contentment, one would hardly expect Scots or Welshmen, let alone Irishmen, to be able to read this book without wearing out their teeth. His indifference or worse to the periphery is perhaps Elton's most typically 'English' feature, where his Francophobia has a Germanic flavour about it (it is certainly unmatched by a single swipe at Germans). Examples include silly, indeed offensive, remarks about the Celtic capacity for disorder, plain error about the ancestral Labour debt to a Scots heartland, or a comment on the unpropitious effects of empire-building within the British Isles, which sure enough, turn out unfortunate not for the victims but for the English themselves. It should not have escaped your notice that Scotland comes into being in the book's opening sentence by virtue of an Æthelstanian *congé*; another predictable touch is that Thomas Cromwell's 'failure' in Ireland was the one respect in which his namesake outdid him, and was like that of 'any English statesman over the centuries'.[4]

In the period that is my business, this attitude leads to serious neglect of an abiding English debt to Irish and latterly even Welsh or Breton influences down to at least 950.[5] Elton says much of the virtues of the English language. He never admits the likelihood that it owed its early florescence to the example of an Irish Christian culture that instantly developed its own vernacular. When we say that English art remained 'insular', as it emphatically did until *c.* 950, and to a degree till 1066 itself, we are speaking of a culture province shared by Teuton and Celt, however much easier it was becoming to distinguish their life-styles.[6] Nor are Celts the only other characters worth a place on the stage. The English can hardly be anatomised without considering their settlement pattern. Yet faith in their essentially 'Germanic' culture, which is eminently justified, and inconceivable without a substantial level of immigration, would a generation ago have gone along with an image of the clearing of the forests by Germanic axes and heavy ploughs that can no longer be sustained. On the contrary, it seems more than likely that the advance of an 'English' regime depended not

[4] *English*, 229, 224, 70–1, 139, 159.

[5] Irish influences have of course been much discussed (and not infrequently mispresented) by specialists; for the particular point made here, compare the important paper by C. Donahue, '*Beowulf*, Ireland and the Naturally Good', *Traditio*, 7 (1949–51), 263–77, with modern views represented by K. McCone, *Pagan Past and Christian Present in Early Irish Literature*, Maynooth Monographs 3 (Naas, 1990). Welsh and Breton influences have been generally neglected, but are the subject of Dr Dumville's promised *England the Celtic World in the Ninth and Tenth Centuries* (O'Donnell Lectures, 1978 & 1981).

[6] See, for example, L. Webster and J. Backhouse, eds., *The Making of England*, British Museum, London (1991), especially the sections on manuscripts.

just on the smallish area involved and its lack of natural obstacles, but also on man's removal of forest cover in the two millennia before the Romans arrived. Already in AD 43, lowland Britain was perhaps the least wooded part of Europe north of the Alps.[7] More immediately, patterns of Anglo-Saxon settlement were unquestionably dictated by indigenous traditions, down to their very housing; which is what underlies the current fantasy that there was no such thing as a Germanic invasion. English experience has a *'longue durée'* (not of course a phrase in Elton's vocabulary) which is ignored only at the cost of the necessary perspective in depth. Concentration on the English, even in 'essay' form, is no excuse for glib cracks at their neighbours. Informed comparison is what brings out the true distinctiveness of their stories— which, in this (or, I would argue, any) period, is a prime justification for *British* history.[8]

This point has a perhaps unexpected bearing on the way we interpret the keeping of order and the exercise of power among Englishmen before the making of England. Elton sees the early Anglo-Saxons as 'diverse tribesmen' under 'quasi-rulers', quite distinct from the 'later reality' of a kingship that he cannot detect until the eighth century. He does find in the early Anglo-Saxon laws 'a society which managed to organise itself from within its own conventions and resources'. But he leaves no doubt that in this 'mixture of the primitive and sophisticated', royal action is what is identified with sophistication. The upshot is that pre-unification society is 'far from civilised', 'still distinctly rude and barbaric'; unification comes in with 'a really strong monarchy ... true kings not glorified chieftains': 'royal rule took over from the kindred and the realm became governable'.[9] Now, it is no surprise that a scholar whose highest praise for Maitland was that he opened the road to the Public Record Office finds the tracks of effective and beneficent government only in a trail of expanding documentation.[10] And to regard the prevalence of fighting and plundering in seventh- and eighth-century England as an uncivilized state of affairs is fair enough. The trouble is that an Eltonian mind-set equates civilization with ordered, and even bureaucratic, government. Not only are kings and peoples who did a lot of killing denied the capacity for the sort of self-generated

---

[7] Cf. P. H. Sawyer, ed., *English Medieval Settlement* (revised edn, 1979); and for a different view of the Anglo-Saxon invasions from that taken above, R. Hodges, *The Anglo-Saxon Achievement* (1989), ch. 2; or N. Higham, *Rome, Britain and the Anglo-Saxons* (1992). I hope to substantiate my provocative remarks in a future paper on 'The Anglo-Saxon *Adventus*: Fact or Figment?'

[8] So R. R. Davies, 'In Praise of British History', in *The British Isles 1100–1500. Comparisons, Contrasts and Connections*, ed. R. R. Davies (Edinburgh, 1988), 9–26.

[9] *English*, 4–5, 8, 10–11, 13, 17, 19–20, 75.

[10] *English*, 229; cf. G. R. Elton, *F. W. Maitland* (1985), 7–8, 21, 25–6, 97–8.

social order, founded on kin, feud and surety, that is the glory of Celtic legal systems (not to mention those of a wide cross-section of the world's other 'tribal' societies).[11] The resources of kingship are also understated because undocumented. In giving a passing nod to Offa's Dyke, Elton fails to note that this kind of structure had been erected in north-west Europe for thousands of years, aeons before there can have been any question of the sort of government he is ready to recognise. It is quite wrong to regard the early kingdoms as loose congeries of kin-groups and warbands, or to identify the appearance of a single English kingdom with 'real' kingship. It was in fact the early kingdoms (and their near continental neighbours) who had the very coining of the word 'king' to their credit.[12] The enduring success of these kingdoms is what renders the creation of a durable single kingdom so remarkable.

Thus, when he does come to the actual making of an English kingdom, Elton misses some of the crucial sinews in the power that kings could exert. Typically, almost his only mention of government machinery at this early stage focuses on the increasingly tired 'Chancery' debate, so on *central* government. No less predictable is that he sides with Dr Chaplais rather than Dr Keynes—his Light Blue loyalties eclipsed by his well-developed ear for the sounds that an active government agency will emit.[13] But the real phenomenon of later Anglo-Saxon government was the shire.[14] The detailed operations and even prosopography of some shires can be reconstructed out of unique survivals from Fenland abbey archives.[15] Shires were the *fora* for most

[11] Now magisterially deployed in T. M. Charles-Edwards, *Early Irish and Welsh Kinship* (Oxford, 1993); see also R. Chapman Stacey, *The Road to Judgement. From Custom to Court in Medieval Ireland and Wales* (Philadelphia, 1994); and the essays by W. Davies and D. B. Walters in *Lawyers and Laymen. Studies in the History of Law Presented to Professor Dafydd Jenkins on his Seventy-Fifth Birthday*, ed. T. M. Charles-Edwards, M. E. Owen and D. B. Walters (Cardiff, 1986). For the wider anthropological picture, it is only necessary to cite M. Gluckman, *Politics, Law and Ritual in Tribal Society* (Oxford, 1965).

[12] J. M. Wallace-Hedrill, *Early Germanic Kingship in England and on the Continent* (Oxford, 1971), 13–16; I return to this issue in my chapter on 'Kings and Kingship' for P. Fouracre, ed., *The New Cambridge Medieval History, I: c. 500–c. 700* (Cambridge, forthcoming).

[13] *English*, 20–1. For the latest statements by the protagonists, see P. Chaplais, 'The Royal Anglo-Saxon "Chancery" of the Tenth Century Revisited', in *Studies in Medieval History presented to R. H. C. Davis*, ed. R. I. Moore and H. Mayr-Harting 1985), 41–51; and S. Keynes, 'Regenbald the Chancellor [*sic*]', *Anglo-Norman Studies*, 10 (1988), 185–222.

[14] Among studies of Anglo-Saxon shires (which tend to be studies of society and economy in the area rather than institutional, let alone political, histories of the unit) are C. Heighway, *Anglo-Saxon Gloucestershire* (Gloucester, 1987); J. Blair, *Early Medieval Surrey. Landholding, Church and Settlement before 1300* (Stroud, 1991); and J. Blair, *Anglo-Saxon Oxfordshire* (Oxford, 1994). The one institutional study is of a lost unit: J. Whybra, *A Lost English County. Winchcombeshire in the 10th and 11th Centuries* (Woodbridge, 1990).

[15] P. Wormald, 'A Handlist of Anglo-Saxon Lawsuits', *Anglo-Saxon England*, 17 (1988), 279–80; A. Kennedy, 'Law and Litigation in the *Libellus Æthelwoldi episcopi*', *Anglo-Saxon England*, 24 (1995), 131–83.

recorded litigation in the early English kingdom, or such as was not taken straight to the *curia regis*. They were also, as revealed by the Northamptonshire Geld-roll (a post-1066 text but in Old English), the arena for apportionment of liability for the Geld.[16] Elton does naturally describe this imposing tax system, on which John Gillingham has broken a lance or two. But the shire gets into his story only in chapter 2's account of the Norman inheritance; and it is not long before it is the subject of well-deserved suspicion from the bureaucrats of the centre.[17] Government power before 1066, and of course in some sense for a very long time afterwards, rested on the relationship of king and shire. This relationship did not necessarily depend on a ceaseless stream of long-lost instructions from the court. Insofar as it did not, it drew on a tradition of communal organisation which, though the shires themselves were mostly fashioned in the tenth century, was already ancient.

An element of consensus, and at a level well below the elite, was a *sine qua non* of the Making of England. It was not on royal orders, nor in any way that I can envisage in response to ruling-class 'propaganda', that the notion of Englishness displaced older identities. Historians have recently rediscovered a respect for the ability of early medieval peoples to develop and retain an ethnicity spontaneously and regardless of leads from above; this is partly the outcome of decades of trying to prove the exact opposite.[18] But Elton was well aware of this, and I have said quite enough about it recently. Instead, I wish to spotlight something of which he and many others do not make nearly enough. The kingdom of the English was also built by force. What little we can see of the process suggests that it may have involved expropriation on a par with that of the Norman Conquest itself.[19] It was then sustained for its first century and a half of existence by a brutality that may come as a shock to those disposed to belief in immemorial English gentleness. One respect in which Elton's otherwise agreeably unconventional account of the development of English law certainly errs is in his assertion, derived from Maitland, that 'the curious Anglo-Saxon belief in money fines' (a misnomer in itself) did not altogether withstand the savage

[16] Most conveniently consulted in D. Douglas, ed. *English Historical Documents, II: 1042–1139* (2nd edn, 1980), no. 61. The most important modern study is C. R. Hart, *The Hidation of Northamptonshire*, Department of English Local History, Occasional Papers 2nd series no. 3 (Leicester, 1970). See also J. Campbell, 'The Late Anglo-Saxon State: A Maximum View', *Proceedings of the British Academy*, 87 (1994), 40–65 (and his forthcoming Ford Lectures on the same theme, especially chs. II–III).

[17] *English*, 21, 47, 58.

[18] 'Ethnogenesis' is now not far short of an obsession in German and French early medieval studies. But see P. Heather, *Goths and Romans 332–489* (Oxford, 1991), 322–30.

[19] See the crucial, if inevitably isolated, evidence in E. O. Blake ed., *Liber Eliensis*, Camden Society, 3rd series XCII (1962), bk II, ch. 25, 98–9.

habits brought over by the Normans'. He means that only after 1066 did mutilation and death become sanctions enforced upon criminals, and felonies emerge. On any reading of the laws themselves (apart from the misleading because misled *Leges Henrici Primi*), never mind the charters that show a string of property forfeitures for crime, and narratives reporting a wealth of bloody trials political and otherwise, this is just not true.[20] So far as society's upper echelons were concerned, it is, as John Gillingham shows, the reverse of the truth.[21] Anglo-Saxon kings regularly enforced death, or mutilations to which death may well have been preferable, on even leading subjects. When they held back from the supreme penalty, this was often because their victims were able to redeem their lives by paying what was literally its price: the *wergeld* that would once have been payable to their kin for their murder. It follows that the first kings of the English had the resources and/or the support with which to coerce even the overmighty subject that is the Tudor historian's traditional bogeyman. I shall say no more for now about how this was done.[22] I observe merely that to follow a gut-feeling that it cannot have been possible is to indulge a *de haut en bas* approach to the past every bit as unacceptable as the imposition of our values upon it. That it patently was possible is proof of the formation of a new kind of society. But one answer to scepticism is to point out that this may not be quite the break it looks. Kings were not so much 'taking over from the kindred' as intruding themselves and their claim to defend the communal interest into the primordial rhythms of dispute and redress. Wergeld became the king's because the peace did.

Sir Geoffrey defends himself at the outset from charges 'that I have painted an unduly favourable picture of the English', by pleading that his is an outsider's view formed by what he has found since he came among us aged seventeen. His enterprise may perhaps be understood as that of one of a long and illustrious line of foreigners, from Hume through Ranke and Guizot to Namier, who have approached the story of the English and their institutions in a spirit compounded of bemusement and admiration, who have seen a shape to things that the English themselves either could not see or were disqualified by their

---

[20] *English*, 56. I have argued against Maitland's position (and its *Leges Henrici* inspiration) in my 'Maitland and Anglo-Saxon Law: Beyond Domesday Book', in *The History of English Law. Centenary Essays on 'Pollock and Maitland*, ed. J. Hudson, Proceedings of the British Academy 89 (1996), 13–17.

[21] J. Gillingham, '1066 and the Introduction of Chivalry into England', in *Law and Government in Medieval England and Normandy. Essays in honour of Sir James Holt*, ed. G. Garnett and J. Hudson (Cambridge, 1994), 31–55.

[22] Cf. my '*Engla Lond*: The Making of an Allegiance', *Journal of Historical Sociology*, 7 (1994), 5–16; and 'Giving God and King their Due: Conflict and its Regulation in the Early English State', *Settimane di Studio del Centro italiano di Studi sull' alto Medioevo*, 44 (1997).

complacency from proclaiming convincingly. Judging by his low opinion of the analyses of Montesquieu and Voltaire, it is not an image he would have relished.[23] Still, he is to be acquitted both of teleological optimism, a confidence that all was scheduled to produce a felicitous present, and on the other hand of curmudgeonly gloom that all is not what it was, *ergo* should be again. He concludes that the irrepressible English may be about to 're-emerge from their British phase' (a characteristic formulation, as we have seen).[24] But we may possibly see another cycle in their story. Englishmen have lived as something like a nation-state for a millennium. That they experienced a form of organisation which did not come to most of humanity until much more recently and in very different circumstances is no grounds for self-congratulation, any more than is its failure to happen so soon elsewhere a reason for denying that it happened here. It merely reminds us that nation-states are historical contingencies like any other. That being so, even antiquity is no guarantee of permanence. The English came into existence at a time when they were unlike most of the rest of the west, and were arguably justified in finding their experience preferable. For 350 years after their conquest they were no longer set apart, becoming deeply embroiled in the conflicts and culture of western Europe. Defeat and dissent led to another half millennium of distinctiveness, when the English lot was again on the whole enviable. But God no longer seems particularly English. English institutions now look far from juster and freer than their neighbours'. Elton's book is at its most successful when handling not only the third phase that is his speciality but also, significantly, the first. Yet, as Otto von Hapsburg was with imperial grace suggesting to the audience of the *Today* programme on the morn of this conference, the prototype nation-state may now be due for another more cosmopolitan phase.

[23] *English*, xii, 193, 210–12.
[24] *Ibid.*, 233–4.

1066 AND ALL THAT ELTON

By John Gillingham

1066, wrote Elton, 'opened an age which called in doubt the very existence of an English nation' p. (32). For a historian who famously proclaimed that within a few months of his arrival in England in 1939 he decided that this was the country in which he ought to have been born, the Norman Conquest has to be the great crisis of English history, threatening to deprive him of his chosen homeland nearly 900 years before he got there. Given that the best, perhaps the only, justification for paying attention to his views on medieval English history lies in the hope that they might expose his underlying assumptions even more starkly than do his more learned writings on his own period; given that, as he not quite disarmingly states, *The English* is a book which 'tries to pay a debt of gratitude'; given that in it he identifies 'Francomania' as a 'long-standing affliction' (p. 37); and given that he chose to regard 'continuity' as an essential feature of all English history up until the nineteenth century; for all these reasons we might expect his treatment of the disruptively French period of English history to be the most revealing of all.

In this comment I note five assumptions, two which he explicitly avowed and three which are merely blatant. The first explicit assumption is his top-down approach, his belief that 'the enduring features of the English' owed most to the monarchy and to 'the administration and law which that monarchy provided' throughout a thousand years of virtually unbroken existence: 'two mechanisms which imposed themselves upon the people rather than emerged from them' (pp. 213–4). Hence the second avowed assumption, his patriotism, is founded on the conviction that in the service of a strong English monarchy lay perfect freedom. Although he entered a defence against the anticipated charge that his was 'an unthinking and somewhat old-fashioned patriotism', he acknowledged that it had been 'reinforced by two and a half years spent in the ranks of His Majesty's Army' (p. xii), and not surprisingly there is a strong flavour of the 1940s about it.[1] Consider the book's last sentence. 'Perhaps they [the English] will retain the ability to tolerate variety and will once again come to respect the rights of the individual: the rights not of Man but of English men and

---

[1] We in England have been fortunate and we must remember our good fortune, for we have actually drawn strength from the continuity of our history', H. Butterfield, *The Englishman and his History* (Cambridge, 1944), v.

women.'[2] That his last word should be 'women' is comically ironic in view of the implicit assumption that this was a story in which women hardly mattered—not until page 204 in a 235 page book did he concede that it was 'high time a word was said about women'.[3] The second implicit assumption is the Germanist one which Patrick Wormald has highlighted.[4] The third is Elton's faith that in the making of the English the Tudor state was of central importance.[5] All five assumptions are conventional enough and three of them might be found in the practice of the historian of either sex and any period, but the Germanist as well as the Tudor one may come more naturally to sixteenth-century specialists, concerned not only with their own view of 'their' century, but also with that century's view of its own past and hence with what has been termed 'The Rise of Anglo-Saxonism'.[6]

Elton took the view that on the eve of 1066 there existed 'an English kingdom peopled by an English nation ... organised and ruled by just about the most advanced and richest monarchy of the West, united to a degree quite unknown at this time in either France or Germany' (pp. 27–8). A nation-state in all but name? Perhaps.[7] But the term is not used. Inevitably Elton believed that even in the fifteenth century 'the English nation-state was by no means yet safely constructed' (p. 112). After 1066 insofar as there was a state in these 'higgledy-piggledy dominions' (p. 64) it had, regrettably and like the church, 'turned Latin and continental' (p. 37). Equally regrettably this impeded the fulfilment of England's manifest destiny: to rule the British Isles—for although Henry II, a great lawyer-king, did his best 'to establish the English king as *positive* [my italics] ruler of all the British Isles', in general 'dreams of empire on the continent took precedence over *genuine* [my italics]

---

[2] 'It is regrettable sometimes that we should construe so English a system as ours in terms of continental political theory', *ibid.*, 116.

[3] Perhaps he would have argued that women ought not to figure in a brief survey narrowly focused on presenting the English 'through their public lives and outward experience' (xi).

[4] 'unimpeachably English, teutonic and historically rooted, with no taint of abstract cosmopolitan arguments from metaphysical rights of man'—phrases which characterise Elton's sympathies rather well but which are in fact a description of E. A. Freeman's, J. W. Burrow, '"The Village Community" and the Uses of History in Late Nineteenth-Century England', in N. McKendrick, *Historical Perspectives*, ed. N. McKendrick (London, 1974), 264–5.

[5] 'the role of the Tudors was an absolute necessity', 'Butterfield, *The Englishman and his History*, 8.

[6] The title of the second chapter of Hugh A. MacDougall, *The Racial Myth in English History* (Montreal, 1982).

[7] Cf. 'Let me state a certainty. Late Anglo-Saxon England was a nation state', James Campbell, 'The Late Anglo-Saxon State: A Maximum View', *Proceedings of the British Academy*, 87 (1995), 47.

rule in the Isles' (pp. 67–8).[8] So England became marginal to the interests of its 'most definitely foreign kings' and, given his view of the determinative role of rulers, it followed that 'this could not but affect the self-awareness of the people of England as Englishmen' (p. 32).

One disquietingly Latin and continental development in this period was the threat to the state posed by a reformed and aggressive papacy. 'What had been territorial Churches well integrated with princely rule turned all over Europe into more or less obedient sectors of the Universal Church ruled by the successors of St Peter' (p. 61). Thereafter 'the authority of king and common law in England was always potentially rivalled by the claims of the Universal Church' (p. 113) and he repeated the conventional belief that 'universal rule ... reached its height in the reign of Innocent III, the pope who accepted King John's offer of vassalage' (p. 93). However he dealt with the highpoint of this threat in a single sentence, referring to John becoming Rome's vassal in an attempt to avert rebellion and French invasion (p. 62). Perhaps if he had dealt with it at marginally greater length he might have noted that the pope's support did not stop either the barons from rebelling or the French from invading. Of course, if the Universal Church, even at its height under Innocent III, was as ineffectual as this, then the significance of the Cromwellian breach with Rome is somewhat diminished—not something a defender of the Tudor faith could readily countenance.

Despite Norman occupation and papal interference by 1272 England had recovered its rightful place as 'the most advanced polity of the age' (p. 68). Indeed this lamentably cosmopolitan interlude turns out to have been the period responsible for precisely those two achievements about which Elton was at his most eloquently patriotic: the common law and the English language. The common law he describes as 'the only other system that ever was to rival the law of Rome. In the course of time the common law of England was to serve far vaster areas of population and litigation than Rome could ever have considered' (p. 57). As we might expect, he gives due weight to developments in the administration of the law in this period, though naturally without mentioning Paul Hyams's suggestion that the common law might usefully be thought of as one of the western group of French customary laws.[9]

For Elton the English language was 'easily the most adaptable and most varied means of communication ever put together by man' (p.

[8] After the Reformation there was a marked rise in Henry II's reputation thanks to his brush with Rome and his invasion of Ireland.

[9] P. Hyams, 'The Common Law and the French Connection', *Anglo-Norman Studies*, 4 (1981).

55) and he dealt with its emergence as Middle English in a section entitled: The Englishing of Normans. Given his view that the Norman Conquest called in doubt the very existence of an English nation, the Englishing of the Normans is presumably crucial. His treatment of this key topic is fascinatingly Eltonian. It begins with a page on the emergence of Exchequer and Chancery because an expanding royal bureaucracy apparently had to be 'recruited from people of English descent for the simple reason that there were far too few Normans around to fill the need. In any case, time did its work of removing the distinction '(p. 51). And this is all. So it seems that what was not the requirements of an expanding bureaucracy, was just the passage of time; and with no further explanation of how 'time did its work'—except that it was 'by stages'. 'The knighthood and baronage of England by stages accepted their English origins and even learned the language' (pp. 51–2). This is curiously perfunctory. Was this brevity a way of avoiding saying that Englishness, far from being imposed from above, had somehow seeped up from below?

The language at any rate they must have acquired partly by normal everyday contact with 'the people'—whose language, of course, had always remained English—but primarily through intermarriage with Englishwomen. In their earliest years children were brought up by women, and it was assumed that women would teach children how to speak. Thus we have the famous case of Orderic Vitalis, the Shropshire lad born in 1075, son of a French father, Odelerius of Orleans. In Orderic's own words,

> O glorious God who didst command Abraham to depart from his country and his kindred and his father's house, thou didst inspire my father Odelerius to renounce me utterly, and submit me in all things to thy governance. So, weeping, he gave me, a weeping child, into the care of monks ... And so, a boy of ten I crossed the English Channel and came to Normandy ... where I heard a language which I did not understand.[10]

Orderic never mentions his mother. He clearly loved his father and believed that he was loved by him. Yet it was only his anonymous mother's language that he could speak. According to Elton, 'by the middle of the thirteen century the mother tongue of the feudal classes had become English' (p. 52). But Old Mother Time probably worked much faster than he thought. 'As early as the second or third post-1066 generations ... English needs to be viewed as the class-inclusive

[10] Orderic Vitalis, *The Ecclesiastical History*, ed. M. Chibnall (Oxford, 1969–80), VI, 553–5.

vernacular not only of the native population, but also of members of the French-speaking minority.'[11]

Of course Englishness is much more than the acquisition of a language. There is also the matter of perception of identity, and the recovery of a sense of the English past as being 'our past'. One aspect of the recovery of the English past was the matter of giving it status. In the early twelfth century this meant making it available in the languages of culture and it is at least arguable that the work of recovering the past through translation owed much to the stimulus of women's patronage. The earliest post-1066 Latin version of English history is William of Malmesbury's masterpiece, the *Deeds of the Kings of England*, finished by 1125 and commissioned by Queen Matilda. The earliest English history in French—indeed the earliest history of any country written in French—is Geoffrey Gaimair's *Estoire des Engleis*, composed in the late 1130s and commissioned by Constance FitzGilbert, wife of a Lincolnshire landowner. Elton's omission of women's role in what was, on his own terms, the great crisis of Englishness, is paralleled by his comment in a footnote to his discussion of the early Anglo-Saxons. 'I find recent arguments saddling the Anglo-Saxons with Celtic wives and inherited institutions less (than) persuasive' (p. 2 n. 4).

Clearly a twelfth-century sense of English identity could not be merely a recovery of an earlier identity. I have argued elsewhere that the new sense of Englishness which emerged in the 1140s already contained what Elton regarded as the characteristic English mixture of superiority and xenophobia—but that mixture which he associated with anti-French feeling and the Hundred Years War, I put two hundred years earlier and in the more virulent and damaging form of a condescending view of the 'barbarous' Irish, Scots and Welsh.[12] True, surviving twelfth-century expressions of English identity were not written in English. Elton's linguistic patriotism evidently led him to share the widespread assumption that the only right and proper vehicle for Englishness is English. The English, unlike some other peoples, now feel uncomfortable with bilingualism, let alone trilingualism, but this may make us misinterpret the twelfth and thirteenth centuries.[13] Indeed

[11] I. Short, '*Tam Angli quam Franci*: Self-Definition in Anglo-Norman England', *Anglo-Norman Studies*, 18 (1995), 156.

[12] J. Gillingham, 'The Beginnings of English Imperialism', *Journal of Historical Sociology*, 5 (1992); and 'Foundations of a Disunited Kingdom', in *Uniting the Kingdom? The Making of British History*, ed. A. Grant and K.J. Stringer (1995).

[13] I. Short, 'Patrons and Polyglots: French Literature in Twelfth-Century England', *Anglo-Norman Studies*, 14 (1991), 246–8. See also T. Turville-Petre, *England the Nation. Language, Literature and National Identity, 1290–1340* (Oxford, 1996), especially chapter 6 'Three Languages'.

it was the Frenchness of the twelfth-century English which helped them to the comfortable assumption that they were an advanced and civilised people—a subject on which Colin Richmond has something to say.

ELTON'S *THE ENGLISH*

By Colin Richmond

GEOFFREY Elton's *The English* is not a book the author took seriously. The reader does not need to either. The author regarded the English later middle ages with scornful amusement; reading chapter 3, therefore, is a non-event, the chapter ending, 'In essence, nothing much has altered since the days of Edward I or even Henry II.' There is an exception: 'England had become beyond doubt or limitation the realm of the English nation.' The stage is set for the entrance of the author's dynamic hero. After a long lull, the whirlwind.

Patrick Wormald has identified the principal Eltonian heresy. 'The trouble is', he writes, 'that an Eltonian mind-set equates civilisation with ordered, even with bureaucratic, government.' Such an attitude is not only perverse—how can an historian living in the twentieth century not see that government, especially bureaucratic government, is tyrannical and barbaric?—it is also self-revealing. The author tells us that the fourteenth and fifteenth centuries 'in both the secular sphere and the sphere of religion ... were remarkably full of noise and upheaval', which has to be at odds with his 'nothing much had altered' if 'upheaval' is to mean what it normally means; yet, he continues, 'despite that age of ever-renewed disturbance, the monarchy continued to build up both its means of rule and the organised state of England'. In other words, whatever else was going on (or not going on), civilisation advanced. English civilisation, that is. The gist of the difficulty for this reader lies precisely there: how civilised was English government? *Is* English government, for that matter? If we are not simply to bandy terms, comparisons have to be made. Elton, I am sure, was making them; just as Sir John Fortescue, whom he approved of for getting down to fundamentals, made comparisons between English and French government in the fifteenth century. English government was not despotic, at home its barbarities were infrequent, none the less it was government by the very few, for the advantage of the few, and without benefit, even in the fifteenth century, to the many. There is more to this, in other words, than comparisons, but let us first get them out of the way.

I cannot understand where Elton's Jewishness went. Even if it was only residual, which, given his upbringing and environment, one supposes it was, why did it not revive with the events which brought Geoffrey Elton to England in 1939, the *Shoah* itself, and with his own fight against Nazism and his experience of it in those Germans he interrogated after the war? Were there not comparisons to be made throughout that time between the power of governments and the powerlessness of those whom they choose to victimise? I do understand that England was a haven in 1939 and that the government of England between 1940 and 1945 fought a good fight, although not on behalf of European Jewry. In such circumstances the author's 'debt of gratitude' is entirely credible. The book, he continues, tries to repay that debt, 'but it does so after careful reflection and after personal experience of other peoples'. The comparisons (and contrasts) it appears, have been made. I do not doubt it. For a home-grown Englishman sees things differently, not more clearly, not more acutely, but differently. At this juncture recognition has also to be given to motes and beams, even if the parable's meaning needs to be reversed. For English men and women who turn out to be historians the beam in the eye of the authorial beholder of the English and their past are all too plain to see. How absurd: that the history of the English is a history of their government. Or, if not absurd, as it is after all a Stubbsian point of view, then so cockeyed (or so partial a vision) as to demand explanation. And the explanation is obvious: a wholehearted conversion to Anglophilism invariably strikes the longsuffering English as risible. Especially if it is a conversion from Judaism, or, if not a conversion from, then a choice of Englishness over Jewishness. That, however, is a personal mystery I can do no more than remark. What is remarkable beyond the personal is Geoffrey Elton's conversion to the idea that English government did anybody besides those who governed any good.

It is not a question of class. It is a question of rulers and ruled. When the author writes that the monarchy survived the 'upheaval' of the later middle ages, and 'even improved the machinery of government', no irony is intended. How can an intelligent observer of, and participant in, the 'upheaval' of the twentieth century write approvingly of improved government machinery? Improved for whom we have to ask? The example he offers poses the dilemma precisely. Bishop Stapledon in the 1320s, says Elton, 'thoroughly reformed the Exchequer (thereby arousing the hatred of the Londoners which caused him to be lynched)'. Lynched for reforming the Exchequer: those *were* the good old days. No one lynched Reginald Bray or Thomas Lovell for their financial 'reforms' two hundred years later—which goes to show that a great deal has changed in the interim. What Bruce McFarlane famously said of the 'chastened, indeed craven, mood in which those who had served Edward IV and lived through the events of 1483–5 greeted yet another new dynasty ... [theirs] was not the spirit of 1297 or 1311', might be applied more widely, even at large. Paradigm shifts, as they say, might be discovered here: in the relation of the governors to government on the one hand, and in that of the governed to the governors on the other. Why, for example, did the Pilgrims of Grace accept the lying assurances of Henry VIII and not carry on to London to lynch Thomas Cromwell, Thomas Cranmer and the rest of the rogues in office? They were not the rebels of 1381 or 1450, to go no further back in time. Was it because they had gentry leaders? Are the gentry the greatest (and therefore) the crucial turncoats? Those who had sold out to government lock, stock, and barrel between the 1330s and the 1530s? More conventionally phrased: the gentry in that two hundred years had become more than allies of the organised state, they *were* the organised state. This, surely, is what makes possible the Cromwellian Reformation. God alone knows what further steps on the descent into tyranny they would have allowed Thomas Cromwell to implement had his rivals not cut him down.

Put another way: who are the hooligans? In an interesting passage on the 'hard to govern' English the author notes that 'the freedom-loving commons of England included a sizeable number of straightforward hooligans'; such men who were the hardcore of English armies in France and the backbone of 'the bands led by disaffected or plainly criminal members of the lesser nobility who practised their marauding in England itself'. There is a singular conjuncture of opposites here: Thomas More, the saint whom Elton could not stand, offered in *Utopia* Book I, the same analysis of criminal England, only he called the noble-led bands noble retinues. There are, however, hooligans and hooligans. When it comes to the sort who do the most damage we have to wait until the end of *Utopia*, Book II, where the 'so-called gentry' are named among those who have 'given their extortion the form of law, and thus [they] have palmed injustice off as legal', and it is they 'who are fattening up their own interests under the name and title of the commonwealth'. Can Thomas More's 'commonwealth' be Geoffrey Elton's 'organised state'? It is easy to see where their sympathies lie: no meeting of minds there. Any more than there was when Thomas Cromwell confronted Thomas More in 1535; each, one has to suppose, regarded the other as the hooligan, while Thomas Cranmer saw both sides of their arguments. The historian makes his choice. Elton plumped for Thomas Cromwell and the organised state; I opt for Thomas More and the commonwealth. Which logically leaves me regarding Geoffrey Elton as a hooligan of English historiography. A highly placed hooligan of course, but that is exactly where Thomas More has taught me to look for them.

Not that our author is inevitably wrong, any more than Thomas More was inevitably right—Geoffrey Elton, indeed, hacked at the hagiographic plaster with a zeal which puts Tudor historians forever in his debt. If, for instance, he is plainly wrong in telling us 'that the first signs of peasant unrest appeared only after the disruption caused by the Black Death', or that 'lords knew well that their exploitation of their lands depended on a reasonably contented peasantry', and only half right when he talks about the 'political insignificance of Parliament, and especially of the Commons', he is patently correct to characterise the English Lollards as 'sober and restrained'. Or is he? Oldcastle's Rising was a reckless adventure; or so it seems half a millennium later. Moreover, to say that the late medieval English mystics were 'markedly marginal in influence' may not win him friends among the historians of English literature. Nevertheless, I think he does have a point about the 'low-key' tone of English religious devotion and religious dissent in the later middle ages. There is no Dorothy of Montau among English mystics: Margarey Kempe never gets beyond a thoroughly respectable (and socially acceptable) hysteria. And there are no Drummers of Nicklashausen among English popular preachers: Reginald Pecock never stirred any crowds, let alone to repentance. Can it truly be said that there was an Anglican spirit already inhabiting the *Ecclesia Anglicana* before the Reformation? That there was an Englishness of English Religion just as there was an Englishness of English Art? If there was, as our author rightly tells us in concluding his late medieval chapter, an England that 'had become beyond doubt or limitation the realm of the English nation', why should it not truly be said?

What of Parliament, and especially the Commons in Parliament with their 'pompous and fruitless efforts at interference'? We are faced here, and not for the first time, with the author's love of tilting at English idols, especially English liberal idols. Whatever his motivation, he does nail half a truth: the Commons never succeeded in tying down, let alone tying up, king and council for very long. Half-truths, it hardly needs saying, are dangerous. Kings and their councillors could not ignore Parliament, especially (and this too hardly needs saying) where taxation was concerned, and after (at the latest) 1341 they never sought confrontation. Parliament, especially the Commons, the gentry-dominated Commons, had become a not-negligible part (organ? arm?) of government by (at the latest) 1376. Yet, and yet, there was, as Professor Roskell long ago taught us, a decline in the role of Parliament in government after 1413: a kind of withering of that arm of government. There are too many reasons why this was so for them all to be gone into here. Chief among them, however, is the one which is identified above and which Elton believed advantageous, namely the loss of confidence of the gentry, or, put another way, their increased willingness to be managed in and out of Parliament by king and council. Elton appears, all along, to equate, I would say, confuse, better management with better government. He seems, all along, not to articulate that essential reservation all twentieth-century historians have to make concerning bureaucratic government, that it is only more efficient from a managerial point of view and is only beneficent in the sense that more petty thieves get hanged, which, as Thomas More pointed out, is a sure sign that non-petty theft is being committed wholesale by the hangmen, otherwise known as the High and Mighty, or to themselves as the Great and the Good. It was, I would suggest, not so much a loss of confidence on the part of the late medieval English gentry, more an ever keener awareness that the side on which their bread was most generously buttered was the government side. If, that is, they at all saw this as a question of sides, at any rate after (at the earliest) 1341, or 1413 (at the latest). I am convinced that there is some greater attention on their part to acquisitiveness, that the shift which does take place in England in the later middle ages is a cultural one—and it is seismic. It is not a change (from one complete set of attitudes to another complete set) but it is a shift of sufficient dimensions to be termed paradigmatic. The plunder of the *Ecclesia Anglicana*, still disinformationally known as the English Reformation, was not the inauguration of the Acquisitive Society; it was a consequence of a greed already dominant in English upper-class hearts and minds (and probably souls). Thomas More never lived to see his nightmare come true: the perverted idea of commonwealth own the day—and convince so many, both then and subsequently (even to this day), that it was not perverse at all.

Geoffrey Elton was among those convinced. In his case it is not hard to see why. A sleight of hand which so many Englishmen have been taken in by, a German Jew in flight from a Europe gone raving mad was only too ready to fall for: England, once Churchill had replaced Chamberlain, did stand for sanity. It is to Elton's credit that, in those circumstances, he did not fall for the extra illusion which had been added in later centuries, that England was a Liberal Nation. Whatever Elton's England, the one he came to love, it was not that counterfeit one. But, and in conclusion, I return to my starting point: the mystery of omission. It is no mystery that he admires Edward I—that king's 'clear-sighted energy and unprincipled ruthlessness'—as Edward Plantagenet is so evidently a prototype Thomas Cromwell; it is strange that the Jews, who require to be included in a book on *The English*, get only a single mention and a back-handed sort of mention at that. Discussing the Black Death the author comments, 'The English could not blame the Jews for supposedly poisoning wells and massacre them in revenge: they had driven all Jews out of the realm in 1290'—the premier example, it has to be said, though it is not said here, of Edward I's 'clear-sighted energy and unprincipled ruthlessness'.

THE ROYAL HISTORICAL SOCIETY
REPORT OF COUNCIL, SESSION 1996–1997

THE Council of the Royal Historical Society has the honour to present the following report to the Anniversary Meeting.

1. Developments within the Society during the year

a) The new Editorial Board for *Studies in History*, announced in last year's Report, has made a most successful start, commissioning a number of volumes for the new series. It is hoped to launch four of them at the reception after the 1997 Anniversary Meeting. Three more will be launched at the Society's spring 1998 conference at the University of Sussex.

b) The Society slightly increased the amount which it allocates to support postgraduate research. 72 individual grants were made on the advice of the Research Support Committee to postgraduates and some others to attend training courses and conferences and to undertake visits essential for their research and to the organisers of certain conferences, primarily to enable younger scholars to attend them. Supplements were paid to 4 holders of awards under the Overseas Research Scheme. The Society continues to provide a Centenary Fellowship at the Institute of Historical Research for a student in the last year of his or her research. It has also made a contribution to the Institute's introductory course in research methods. An appeal to the Fellowship has been launched for contributions towards a new fund to support the work of part-time research students. It is hoped that Fellows, Associates and Members might be willing to make covenants with the Society for their subscriptions, enabling the money recovered from tax in this way to go to that fund.

c) Publications in all the Society's series, *Transactions, Camden Series, Camden Reprints* and *Guides and Handbooks*, appeared on schedule during the year through the Cambridge University Press, now established as the Society's publisher. It is too early to have received any critical response to this year's crop, but the reception in the past twelve months of previous years' volumes has been gratifying. John Vincent's selection from the *The Derby Diaries* has drawn particularly enthusiastic comment. Yet for all the well-attested quality of the Society's publications, sale figures remain disappointing. Academic publishing appears to be yet again going through a difficult period. The decline in sales in the United States is a particular cause for concern.

d) The card catalogue of the Society's library has now been completely revised and updated; consideration is being given to how best to make it available to Fellows and other inquirers. Substantial progress with the necessary high-quality binding work on the Society's holdings of pre-1850 books, in implemen-

337

tation of Council's agreed policy of conservation, continues to be made.

e) The Society has this year vigorously pursued its long-standing policy of fostering close contacts with historians in other countries. Among other measures to achieve this end, the decision of Council to expand the size of the Society's corresponding fellowship, primarily to include scholars with a wider range of expertise and drawn from a wider geographical area, has been carried forward, the *Camden* series is to include future volumes edited at the German Historical Institute and joint lectures have been arranged with representatives of the Spanish embassy. The British National Committee, with which the Society is closely associated, has supported British representatives at conferences overseas.

f) The Society's activities to promote the cause of history in this country include further representations to the Economic and Social Research Council on its policy of Thematic Priorities, replying, as an interested 'stakeholder' to the Prior Options Questionnaire about the future running of the Public Record Office and to the Humanities Research Board Review of Funding Needs in Subject Areas.

2. Bibliographies

a) The data for the first stage of the *British and Irish History Bibliographies* is currently being worked on by the software engineers for the publication in the near future of the CD-ROM. Selected printed volumes will follow.

b) The new bibliographical project, to produce a second edition of titles published down to 2000, announced in last year's Report, was launched on schedule on 1 January 1997 under the general editorship of Dr. Julian Hoppit with the assistance of Mr. Peter Salt, who works on the electronic data base, and Dr. Austin Gee, who edits the *Annual Bibliography of British and Irish History*. Accommodation for the project has been provided at the Institute of Historical Research. Funding for the initial work has been obtained thanks to a most generous grant from the Andrew W. Mellon Foundation and further funding is being actively pursued.

c) The Society is committed to the continuing publication of the *Annual Bibliography* in book form and to funding this project itself. Dr. Gee continues as editor. The Society owes him a debt of gratitude for his admirable work in developing and improving the series. It is also much in the debt of those of its Fellows who generously give their time to editing sections within the volume.

3. Meetings of the Society

The Society held six Council meetings, and paper readings and receptions in London, which were generally well attended. A Reception was held at the Borthwick Institute, York, in September 1996, to mark the incorporation of the books of Sir Geoffrey Elton into the Library. The Society has arranged to meet at St Andrews and Norwich during the 1997–1998 session.

A well-attended Annual Reception was held for members and guests in the Upper Hall at University College London on 2 July 1996.

A two-day conference, 'Gendering History' was held at the University of York in September 1996, attended by almost 100 people.

A further two-day conference, 'Anglo-American Attitudes', organised jointly with the North American Conference on British Studies with financial support of the British Council and other benefactors, was held at Harvard University on 5 and 6 April 1997.

During the 1997–1998 session, a two-day conference, 'Empire and Identities since 1500' is to be held at the Institute of Historical Research, London, on 26 and 27 September 1997; a Colloquium on William Camden is to be held at Westminster School, London, on 7 October 1997, and a further two-day conference, 'Oral History, Memory and Written Tradition' is to be held at the University of Sussex on 26 and 27 March 1998.

4. Prizes

This year has seen important developments in the Society's ability to award prizes for historical scholarship.

a) The established prizes, the Whitfield Prize for a first book on British history and the Alexander Prize for an essay by a younger scholar, both attracted excellent fields, which were highly commended by the assessors.

The Whitfield Prize was awarded to Dr. Paul D. Griffiths for his book, *Youth and Authority: Formative Experiences in England, 1560–1640* (Oxford University Press).

> The idea of a separate age of youth in early modern England is no longer disputed, but in much of the writing on this subject youth emerges as a passive construct of the adult society. This book offers a more positive image of young people, showing that they had a creative presence, shared identity, and historical significance. Their responses to authority and the ideal place for them in the social order as understood by magistrates and moralists are discussed through close examination of the nature of youth culture, religious commitment, juvenile delinquency, master/servant relations, and a social milieu of masterless youth. Contemporaries called youth 'the choosing time', and the best time to inculcate conformity and sound religion. Yet the idea of choice was double-edged. This ambiguity is a theme of this book which demonstrates that although there was a politics of age at this time, young people developed their own initiatives and strategies and grew up in all sorts of ways.

The Alexander Prize for 1997 was awarded to Dr. Steve Hindle for his essay 'The Problem of Pauper Marriage in Seventeenth Century England'.

b) Leave was obtained from the Charity Commissioners to alter what have proved to be the excessively restrictive conditions attached to the David Berry Prize. Instead of being confined to Scottish history within the reigns of James I and James VI, it is now to be open to any approved topic in Scottish history.

c) A generous donation from the Gladstone Memorial Trust has enabled the Society to announce the creation of a new prize to be called The Gladstone History Book Prize. This is to be awarded to a first book published in Britain on any topic that is not primarily British history.

5. Publications

Transactions, Sixth Series, Volume 6 was published during the session, and *Transactions*, Sixth Series, Volume 7 went to press, to be published in 1997.

Seventeenth-Century Political and Financial Papers, Miscellany XXXIII (Camden, Fifth Series Volume 7) and *The Plumpton Letters and Papers*, ed. J.W. Kirby (Camden, Fifth Series, Volume 8) were published during the session. *Lord Kimberley's Journal, 1862–1902*, ed. J. Powell and A. Hawkins (Camden, Fifth Series, Volume 9) went to press during the session, to be published in 1997.

A Guide to the Papers of British Cabinet Ministers, 1990–1964, ed. Cameron Hazlehurst and Sally Whitehead with Christine Woodland (Guides and Handbooks No. 19) was published during the session.

The Society's *Annual Bibliography of British and Irish History, Publications of 1995*, was published by Oxford University Press during the session, and the *Annual Bibliography of British and Irish History, Publications of 1996* went to press, to be published in 1997.

In the *Studies in History* series Lorna Lloyd, *Peace through Law* (Volume 74) was published during the session. Seven volumes are currently in the press for a launch later in 1997/1998.

6. Papers read

At the ordinary meetings of the Society the following papers were read:

'England, Britain and the Audit of War'
Professor Kenneth Morgan (2 July 1996: Prothero Lecture)
'Against "Englishness": English Culture and the Limits to Rural Nostalgia, 1850–1940'
Dr. Peter Mandler (25 October 1996)
'The Hereford Map: its Author, Two Scenes and a Border'
Professor Valerie Flint (24 January 1997)
'Constitutionalism in Ireland'
Professor Charles Townshend (7 March 1997)
'An Age of Uncertainty: Britain in the Early Nineteenth Century'
Professor David Eastwood (16 May 1997)

At the Anniversary meeting on 22 November 1996, the President, Professor R.R. Davies, delivered an address on 'The Peoples of Britain and Ireland, 1100–1400: IV. Language and Historical Mythology'.

At the two-day conference entitled 'Gendering History' held at the University of York on 27 and 28 September 1996, the following plenary papers were read:

'Gendering Conquest: eleventh-century England' Professor Pauline Stafford
'History by default' Professor Marilyn Strathern
'Seeing St. Cecilia: Imagining in Late Eighteenth-Century England' Professor Marcia Pointon.
'Something Old, Something New, Something Borrowed: Plutarch, Advice to the Bride and the Groom' Professor Sarah Pomeroy
'The Problem with Separate Spheres' Dr. Bob Shoemaker

Theme sessions were held on:

Gender, Production and Reproduction
Gender, Science and Medicine
Gender, Empire and Monarchy
Gender and War

At the two-day conference entitled 'Anglo-American Attitudes' held at Harvard University on 5 and 6 April 1997, the following scholars from Britain and the United States delivered papers:

Professor Walter Arnstein
Professor Christine Bolt
Professor Kathleen Burk
Professor James Epstein
Assistant Professor Eliga Gould
Associate Professor Peter Hahn
Associate Professor David Hancock
Dr. Anthony Howe
Professor Paul Langford
Professor D. LeMahieu
Professor Fred Leventhal
Professor P. J. Marshall
Dr. Roland Quinault
Dr. Alan O'Day
Professor Reba Soffer

7. Finance

The Society is in a healthy financial state overall, as the invested endowment continues to grow, from £1,750,000 in 1996 to £1,870,000 in 1997. Council, however, shared the Treasurer's concern as the continuing operating deficit, which, while falling from £25,000 in 1996 to £24,600 in 1997, was still nearly 1.5% of the endowment. This deficit has arisen because Council has been carrying out the purposes and obligations of the Society, but nevertheless Council reaffirmed that it was their duty to future generations not to allow the continuing effective erosion of the endowment. Therefore decisions have been taken to increase income and control expenditure in the following manner.

a) Income will be increased by modifying the investment strategy: we have realised some of the profits made in our equity investments and re-invested the proceeds in income-generating instruments. We will also propose to the Anniversary Meeting, to be held on 21 November 1997, the raising of the yearly subscriptions, which have remained unchanged for three years, by £4 for Fellows and Associates and by £2 for others.

b) Expenditure will be controlled primarily by modifying our publications programme, which has generated most of the deficit. We will also more tightly control travel and other costs as far as possible without crippling the activities of Council.

8. Membership

Council records with regret the deaths of 30 Fellows, 4 Corresponding Fellows and 3 Associates. They include Professor H. Hearder, Professor W. E. Minchinton, Dame Veronica Wedgwood and Professor R. M. T. Hill.

The resignations of 6 Fellows, 2 Associates and 1 Member were received. 56 Fellows, 22 Members and 4 Corresponding Fellows were elected. 26 Fellows transferred to the category of Retired Fellow. The membership of the Society on 30 June 1997 numbered 2315 (including 29 Life, 377 Retired, 50 Corresponding Fellows, 125 Associates and 66 Members).

The Society exchanged publications with 15 Societies, British and Foreign.

9. Officers and Council

At the Anniversary Meeting on 22 November 1996, Professor P. J. Marshall succeeded Professor R. R. Davies as President from 1 December 1996, Professor K. Burk was elected to succeed Professor P. M. Thane as Honorary Treasurer; the remaining Officers of the Society were re-elected.

The Vice-Presidents retiring under By-law XVII were Professor R. A. Griffiths and Dr. J. S. Morrill. Professor M. J. Daunton and Professor P. J. Hennessy were elected to replace them.

The members of Council retiring under By-law XX were Dr. G. W. Bernard, Professor K. Burk, Professor A. J. Fletcher and Dr. F. Heal. Following a ballot of Fellows, Professor J. M. Black, Dr. C. R. J. Currie, Professor A. E. Goodman and Dr. J. P. Martindale were elected in their place.

MacIntyre and Company were appointed auditors for the year 1996–1997 under By-law XXXIX.

10. Representatives of the Society

The representation of the Society upon various bodies was as follows:

Mr. M. Roper, Professor P. H. Sawyer and Mr. C. P. Wormald on the Joint Committee of the Society and the British Academy established to prepare an edition of Anglo-Saxon charters;

Professor H. R. Loyn on a committee to promote the publication of photographic records of the more significant collections of British Coins;

Professor G. H. Martin on the Council of the British Records Association;

Emeritus Professor M. R. D. Foot on the Committee to advise the publishers of *The Annual Register*;

Dr. G. W. Bernard on the History at the Universities Defence Group;

Professor C. J. Holdsworth on the Court of the University of Exeter;

Professor D. d'Avray on the Anthony Panizzi Foundation;

Professor M. C. Cross on the Council of the British Association for Local History; and on the British Sub-Commission of the Commission International d'Histoire Ecclesiastique Comparée;

Miss V. Cromwell on the Advisory Board of the Computers in Teaching Initiative Centre for History; and on the Advisory Committee of the TLTP History Courseware Consortium;

Dr. A. M. S. Prochaska on the National Council on Archives; and on the

Advisory Council of the reviewing committee on the Export of Works of Art;

Professor R. A. Griffiths on the Court of Governors of the University of Wales Swansea;

Professor A. L. Brown on the University of Stirling Conference;

Professor W. Davies on the Court of the University of Birmingham;

Professor R. D. McKitterick on a committee to regulate British co-operation in the preparation of a new repertory of medieval sources to replace Potthast's *Bibliotheca Historica Medii Aevi*;

Dr. S. R. B. Smith on the ESRC Working Group on *Quality and Data Collection*; and Professor J. Breuilly on the steering committee of the proposed British Centre for Historical Research in Germany.

Council received reports from its representatives.

During the year, Professor N. P. Brooks agreed to succeed Professor H. R. Loyn on a committee to promote the publication of photographic records of the more significant collections of British Coins.

25 September 1997

ACCOUNTS

PREPARED IN ACCORDANCE WITH THE STATEMENT OF RECOMMENDED PRACTICE OF CHARITIES

THE ROYAL HISTORICAL SOCIETY

AS AT 30 JUNE 1997

MacIntyre & Co
Chartered Accountants
Registered Auditors
London

LEGAL AND ADMINISTRATIVE INFORMATION

Registered Office: University College London
                                            Gower Street
                                            London
                                            WC1E 6BT

Charity registration number: 206888

The Honorary Treasurer: Professor K Burk, MA, DPhil

The Honorary Secretary: R E Quinault, MA, DPhil

Auditors: MacIntyre & Co
                                            Chartered Accountants
                                            28 Ely Place
                                            London EC1N 6RL

Investment managers: Cazenove Fund Management Limited
                                            3 Copthall Avenue
                                            London
                                            EC2R 7BH

Bankers: Barclays Bank plc
                                            27 Soho Square
                                            London
                                            WC1A 4WA

A full list of trustees is given in the Trustees' Report.

THE ROYAL HISTORICAL SOCIETY
REPORT OF THE COUNCIL OF TRUSTEES
FOR THE YEAR ENDED 30 JUNE 1997

The members of the Council present their report and audited accounts for the year ended 30 June 1997.

PRINCIPAL ACTIVITIES AND REVIEW OF THE YEAR

The Society exists for the promotion and support of historical research and its dissemination to historians and the wider community.

The Society expects to continue with these aims in the future.

RESULTS

During the year the Fund's income from members contributions, donations and bequests totalled £129,316, an increase of £59,954 from that received in 1996. Expenditure and grants relating directly to charitable activities totalled £166,963, an increase of £31,584 on that expended in 1996.

The Society's deficit before surplus from investment activities was £22,488 (1996: £25,173).

FIXED ASSETS

Information relating to changes in fixed assets is given in notes 2 and 3 to the accounts.

INVESTMENTS

During the year the investment objective of the society was altered to increase investment income streams and therefore to make capital appreciation a secondary objective. Accordingly a portion of the Society's equity investments were sold and reinvested in higher yielding securities.

DONATIONS

The Society made donations to other charities in the year of £200.

STATEMENT OF TRUSTEES' RESPONSIBILITIES

The Council is required to prepare accounts for each financial year which give a true and fair view of the state of affairs of the Society and of the surplus or deficit of income over expenditure of the Fund for that year. In preparing these accounts, the Trustees are required to:

- select suitable accounting policies and then apply them consistently;
- make judgements and estimates that are reasonable and prudent;
- state whether applicable accounting standards have been followed, subject to any material departures disclosed and explained in the accounts;
- prepare the accounts on the going concern basis unless it is inappropriate to presume that the Fund will continue in business.

The Trustees are responsible for keeping proper accounting records which disclose with reasonable accuracy at any time the financial position of the Society. They are also responsible for safeguarding the assets of the Society and hence for taking reasonable steps for the prevention and detection of fraud and other irregularities.

MEMBERS OF THE COUNCIL

Professor P J Marshall, MA, DPhil, FBA	– President
R E Quinault, MA, DPhil	– Honorary Secretary
Professor D S Eastwood, MA, DPhil	– Literary Director
Professor M C E Jones, MA, DPhil, FSA	– Literary Director
Professor K Burk, MA, DPhil	– Honorary Treasurer
D A L Morgan, MA, FSA	– Honorary Librarian
Professor M D Biddiss, MA, PhD	– Vice-President
Professor P Collinson, MA, PhD, DLitt, DUniv, FBA, FAHA	– Vice-President
Professor M J Daunton, PhD, FBA	– Vice-President
Professor R A Griffiths, PhD, DLitt	– Vice-President
Professor P J Hennessy, PhD	– Vice-President
Professor R D McKitterick, MA, PhD, LittD	– Vice-President
Professor H C G Matthew, MA, DPhil, FBA	– Vice-President
A M S Prochaska, MA, DPhil	– Vice-President

Professor D Bates, PhD	– Member of Council
Professor R C Bridges, PhD	– Member of Council
Professor P J Corfield, MA, PhD	– Member of Council
Professor P R Coss, PhD, FSA	– Member of Council
A E Curry, MA, PhD	– Member of Council
Professor J A Guy, MA, PhD	– Member of Council
Professor L J Jordanova, MA, PhD, MA	– Member of Council
Professor R I Moore, MA	– Member of Council
Professor J L Nelson, PhD	– Member of Council
Professor F O'Gorman, PhD	– Member of Council
Professor P A Stafford, DPhil	– Member of Council
J R Studd, PhD	– Member of Council
Professor J M Black, MA, PhD	– Member of Council
C R J Currie, MA, DPhil	– Member of Council
Professor A E Goodman, MA	– Member of Council
J P Martindale, MA, DPhil	– Member of Council

MEMBERS OF THE COUNCIL

At the Anniversary Meeting on 22 November 1996, the Officers of the Society were re-elected.

The Vice-Presidents retiring under By-law XVII were Professor R. A. Griffiths and Dr. J. S. Morrill. Professor M. J. Daunton and Professor P. J. Hennessy were elected to replace them.

Professor P. J. Marshall was elected President in accordance with By-law XVI, replacing Professor R. R. Davies. Professor K. Burk was elected Honorary Treasurer in accordance with By-law XVIII, replacing Professor P. M. Thane.

The members of Council retiring under By-law XX were Dr. G. W. Bernard, Professor K. Burk, Professor A. J. Fletcher, and Dr. F. Heal. Following a ballot of Fellows, Professor J. M. Black, Dr. C. R. J. Currie, Professor A. E. Goodman and Dr. J. P. Martindale were elected in their place.

STANDING COMMITTEES 1997

The Society was operated through the following Committees during 1997:—

Finance Committee:
Professor R. C. Bridges
Mr. P. J. C. Firth   – non Council Member
Professor L. Jordanova
Professor P. Mathias   – non Council Member
Professor R. I. Moore
Dr. A. M. S. Prochaska
The six Officers

General Purposes Committee:
Professor M. D. Biddiss
Professor P. Coss
Professor J. Guy
Professor P. J. Hennessy
Professor R. D. McKitterick
The six officers

Membership Committee:
Professor M. D. Biddiss
Professor P. J. Corfield
Professor A. E. Goodman
Professor F. O'Gorman
Professor P. A. Stafford
The six officers

Publications Committee:
Professor D. Bates
Professor P. Collinson
Dr. C. R. J. Currie
Professor M. J. Daunton
Dr. J. P. Martindale
Professor H. C. G. Matthew
The six officers

Research Support Committee:
Professor J. M. Black
Miss V. Cromwell
Dr. A. Curry
Professor J. L. Nelson
Dr. J. R. Studd
The six officers

Studies in History
Editorial Board:

Professor M.J. Daunton (Convenor)
Dr. S. Gunn   – non Council Member
Professor C. Jones   – non Council Member
Dr. P. Mandler   – non Council Member
Dr. S. Walker   – non Council Member
A Literary Director
The Honorary Treasurer

The Society is financially responsible for the *Studies in History* series and has two representatives on the Board.

Election of Officers
Subcommittee:
(Literary Director)

The President
Non-retiring Literary Director
Professor R. McKitterick
Professor J. A. Guy

Corresponding Fellows
Subcommittee:

The President
The Honorary Secretary
The Honorary Treasurer
Literary Director
Professor M. Biddiss
Professor J. Black

AUDITORS

MacIntyre and Company were appointed auditors for the year 1996–1997 under By-law XXXIX. A resolution to re-appoint Messrs MacIntyre & Co will be submitted to the Anniversary Meeting.

By Order of the Council
Honorary Secretary

REPORT OF THE AUDITORS

TO THE MEMBERS OF ROYAL HISTORICAL SOCIETY

We have audited the accounts on pages 344 to 355 which have been prepared under the historical cost convention, as modified by the revaluation of fixed asset investments, and the accounting policies set out on page 351.

RESPECTIVE RESPONSIBILITIES OF THE COUNCIL OF TRUSTEES

As described on page 1 the Trustees are responsible for the preparation of accounts. It is our responsibility to form an independent opinion, based on our audit, on those accounts and to report our opinion to you.

BASIS OF OPINION

We conducted our audit in accordance with Auditing Standards issued by the Auditing Practices Board. An audit includes examination, on a test basis, of evidence relevant to the amounts and disclosures in the accounts. It also includes an assessment of the significant estimates and judgements made by the Board of Trustees in the preparation of the accounts, and of whether the accounting policies are appropriate to the Society's circumstances, consistently applied and adequately disclosed.

We planned and performed our audit so as to obtain all the information and explanations which we considered necessary in order to provide us with sufficient evidence to give reasonable assurance that the accounts are free from material misstatement, whether caused by fraud or other irregularity or error. In forming our opinion we also evaluated the overall adequacy of the presentation of information in the accounts.

OPINION

In our opinion the accounts give a true and fair view of the state of the Society's affairs as at 30 June 1997 and of its surplus of income over expenditure for the year then ended.

MacIntyre & Co
Chartered Accountants
Registered Auditors

28 Ely Place
London
EC1N 6RL

THE ROYAL HISTORICAL SOCIETY

Balance Sheet as at 30th June 1997

	Notes	£ 1997 £	£ 1996 £
Fixed Assets			
Tangible assets	2	4,438	504
Investments	3	2,112,412	1,884,318
		2,116,850	1,884,822
Current Assets			
Stocks	1(c)	26,025	5,264
Debtors	4	35,558	29,983
Cash at bank and in hand	5	74,718	12,814
		136,301	48,061
Less: Creditors			
Amount due within one year	6	(89,096)	(60,536)
Net Current Assets (Liabilities)		47,205	(12,475)
Net Assets		2,164,055	1,872,347
Represented by:			
Unrestricted – General Fund		2,002,048	1,767,543
Unrestricted – *Studies in History*		(9,295)	(4,892)
Restricted – Miss E.M. Robinson Bequest		79,914	73,250
Restricted – A.S. Whitfield Prize Fund		39,072	36,446
Restricted – Andrew Mellon Fund		52,316	—
		2,164,055	1,872,347

Approved by the Council on 25 September 1997

President: P. J. Marshall

Honorary Treasurer K. Burk

The attached notes form an integral part of these financial statements.

THE ROYAL HISTORICAL SOCIETY

Consolidated Statement of Financial Activities for the Year Ended 30 June 1997

	Notes	Unrestricted Funds General Fund £	Studies in History £	Restricted Funds E M Robinson Bequest £	A S Whitfield Prize Fund £	Andrew Mellon Fund £	1997 Total £	1996 Total £
INCOMING RESOURCES								
a) VOLUNTARY								
Members subscriptions								
net		50,233					50,233	58,917
tax recovered on Deeds of Covenant		2,566					2,566	2,456
		52,799					52,799	61,373
Donations and legacies	7	12,397				64,120	76,517	7,989
Total Voluntary Income		65,196				64,120	129,316	69,362
b) OTHER INCOME								
Investment income		69,340	476	3,457	1,225	1,834	76,332	81,125
Royalties and reproduction fees		46,803	598				47,401	11,689
Total Other Income		116,143	1,074	3,457	1,225	1,834	123,733	92,814
Gross Incoming Resources in the Year		181,339	1,074	3,457	1,225	65,954	253,049	162,176
RESOURCES USED								
Grants and prizes payable	8	(25,765)		(4,500)	(1,000)		(31,265)	(22,906)
Direct charitable expenditure	9	(148,653)	(5,477)		(40)	(12,793)	(166,963)	(135,379)
Administration expenses	10	(31,488)				(845)	(32,333)	(29,064)
Total Resources used		(205,906)	(5,477)	(4,500)	(1,040)	(13,638)	(230,561)	(187,349)
Net Incoming/(Outgoing) Resources		(24,567)	(4,403)	(1,043)	185	52,316	22,488	(25,173)
Gains and Losses on Investment Assets								
Realised on Investments		42,121		486			42,607	(11,238)
Unrealised		216,951		7,221	2,441		226,613	155,445
Net Movement in Resources in Year		234,505	(4,403)	6,664	2,626	52,316	291,708	119,034
Balance Brought Forward at 1 July 1996		1,767,543	(4,892)	73,250	36,446		1,872,347	1,753,313
Balance Carried Forward at 30 June 1997		2,002,048	(9,295)	79,914	39,072	52,316	2,164,055	1,872,347
Unrealised Surpluses included in above balances		743,629		15,905	14,717		774,251	793,310

351

THE ROYAL HISTORICAL SOCIETY

Notes to the Accounts for the Year Ended 30 June 1997

1. Accounting Policies
   (a) *Basis of accounting*
   The accounts have been prepared under the historical cost convention as modified by the revaluation of quoted investments to market value.
   (b) *Depreciation*
   Depreciation is calculated by reference to the cost of fixed assets using a straight line basis at rates considered appropriate having regard to the expected lives of the fixed assets.
   The annual rates of depreciation in use are:
Furniture and equipment	10%
Computer equipment	25%
   (c) *Stocks*
   Stock is valued at the lower of cost and net realisable value.
   (d) *Library and archives*
   The cost of additions to the library and archives is written off in the year of purchase.
   (e) *Subscription Income*
   Subscription Income is recognised in the year it became receivable with a provision against any subscription not received.
   (f) *Investments*
   Investments are stated at market value. Any surplus arising on revaluation is charged to the income and expenditure account.
   Dividend income is accounted for on a received basis.
   (g) *Publication costs*
   Publication costs are transferred in stock and released to the income and expenditure account as stocks are depleted.
   (h) *E.M. Robinson bequest*
   Income from the E.M. Robinson bequest is used to provide grants to the Dulwich Picture Gallery.
   (i) *A.S. Whitfield Prize Fund*
   The A.S. Whitfield Prize Fund is used to provide an annual prize for the best first monograph for British history published in the calendar year.
   (j) *Donations and other voluntary income*
   Donations are recognised on a received basis.
   (k) *Grants payable*
   Grants payable are recognised in the year in which they are paid.
   (l) *Allocation of administration costs*
   Administration costs are allocated between direct charitable expenditure and administration costs on the basis of the work done by the Executive Secretary.

2. Tangible Fixed Assets

	Computer Equipment £	Furniture and Equipment £	Total £
Cost			
At 1st July 996	10,215	1,173	11,388
Additions	4,896	—	4,896
At 30th June 1997	15,111	1,173	16,284
Depreciation			
At 1st July 1996	10,215	669	10,884
Charge for the year	845	117	962
At 30th June 1997	11,060	786	11,846
Net book value			
At 30th June 1997	4,051	387	4,438
At 30th June 1996	—	504	504

All tangible fixed assets are used in the furtherance of the Society's objectives.

3. INVESTMENTS

	General Fund £	Robinson Bequest £	Whitfield Prize Fund	Total £
Cost at 1.7.96	904,599	56,689	17,571	978,859
Additions	536,320	13,621	—	549,941
Disposals	(300,050)	(10,975)	—	(311,025)
Cost at 30.6.97	1,140,869	59,335	17,571	1,217,775
Surplus in revaluation	743,629	15,905	14,717	774,251
Quoted Securities at market value	1,884,498	75,240	32,288	1,992,026
Cash awaiting investment	98,542	13,787	8,057	120,386
	1,983,040	89,027	40,345	2,112,412
Market value at 1.7.96	1,675,184	67,138	29,847	1,772,169
Additions	536,320	—	—	549,941
Disposals	(543,957)	(12,740)	—	(556,697)
Unrealised gain on investments	216,951	7,221	2,441	226,613
Market value at 30.6.97	1,884,498	75,240	32,288	1,992,026

4. DEBTORS

	1997 £	1996 £
Trade debtors	30,462	18,464
Sundry debtors	—	8,300
Prepayments	5,096	3,219
	35,558	29,983

5. CASH AT BANK AND IN HAND

	1997 £	1996 £
Deposit accounts	82,423	12,507
Current accounts	(7,705)	307
	74,718	12,814

6. CREDITORS: Amounts due within one year

	1997 £	1996 £
Trade creditors	62,319	48,086
Sundry creditors	3,050	1,000
Subscriptions received in advance	1,823	1,758
Accruals	21,904	6,692
Provision for publications in progress	—	3,000
	89,096	60,536

7. DONATIONS AND LEGACIES

	1997 £	1996 £
A. Browning Royalties	527	—
G.R. Elton Bequest	4,606	4,111
Donations and sundry income	1,016	3,878
Conference fees and funding	6,248	—
	12,397	7,989

8. Grant and Prizes Payable

	Unrestricted Funds £	Restricted Funds £	Total 1997 £	Total 1996 £
Alexander Prize	568	—	568	163
Grants	2,650	—	2,650	114
Research support grants	13,920	—	13,920	13,321
Young Historian Scheme	1,852	—	1,852	2,500
Centenary fellowship	5,975	—	5,975	4,908
A Level prizes	800	—	800	900
A.S. Whitfield Prize	—	1,000	1,000	1,000
Miss E.M. Robinson Bequest				
— Grant to Dulwich Picture Library	—	4,500	4,500	—
	25,765	5,500	31,265	22,906

9. Direct Charitable Expenditure

	Unrestricted Funds £	Restricted Funds £	Total 1997 £	Total 1996 £
Publishing costs	99,161	—	99,161	79,837
Provision for publication in progress	—	—	—	3,000
Purchase of books and publications	3,053	—	3,053	2,349
Binding	4,044	—	4,044	5,288
Prothero lecture	349	—	349	274
Donations and sundry expenses	55	—	55	768
A.S. Whitfield Prize Fund	—	40	40	164
Miss E.M. Robinson Bequest—				
Studies in History				
— Executive Editor's honorarium	3,500	—	3,500	3,500
— Executive Editor's expenses	1,289	—	1,289	1,031
— Sundry expenses	688	—	688	402
Other publications (Note 17)	7,678	—	7,678	9,191
British Bibliographies	—	12,793	12,793	
Salaries, pensions and social security	11,210	—	11,210	10,616
Computer consumables, printing and stationery	8,060	—	8,060	6,172
Meetings and travel	9,428	—	9,428	10,744
Conference costs	5,615	—	5,615	2,043
	154,130	12,833	166,963	135,379

10. Administration Expenses

	Unrestricted Funds £	Restricted Funds £	Total 1997 £	Total 1996 £
Saleries, pensions and social security	15,711	—	15,711	15,925
Postage and telephone	1,635	—	1,635	1,635
Bank charges	1,356	—	1,356	1,190
Audit and accountancy	5,611	—	5,611	3,126
Insurance	943	—	943	933
Repairs and renewals			—	875
Depreciation	117	845	962	1,124
Circulation costs	5,767	—	5,767	4,257
Sundry	348		348	—
	31,488	845	32,333	29,065

11. Insurance Policies

	1997 £	1996 £
The Society was charged with the following amounts relating to committee and employees liability:		
Employees liability	88	88
Public liability	87	86
	175	172

12. Councillors' Expenses

During the year travel expenses were reimbursed to 31 Councillors attending Council meetings as a cost of £4,782.

13. Auditor's Remuneration

	1997 £	1996 £
Audit fee	5,581	3,126
Consultancy fees	520	—
	6,101	3,126

14. Grants Paid

During the year the Society awarded grants to a value of £13,920 (1996: £13,321) to 72 (1996: 58) individuals.

In addition £2,600 (1996: £Nil) was awarded to the Institute of Historical Research and a further £4,500 (1996: £Nil) to the Dulwich Picture Gallery.

15. Publications

	Transactions Sixth Series 5, 6 £	Camden Fifth Series 5, 6, 7, 8 £	Classic Reprints £	1997 Guides and Handbooks Reprint Costs £	Total £
Cambridge University Press: Costs					
Opening stock	830	4,434	—	—	5,264
Printing	12,705	29,789	—	17,838	60,332
Offprints	1,023	—	—	—	1,023
Reprints	—	—	17,425	—	17,425
Carriage	541	1,170	—	—	1,711
Airfreight	—	81	—	—	81
Society's costs	3,744	2,872	—	—	6,616
	18,843	38,346	17,425	17,838	92,452
Closing stock	(2,928)	(4,739)	(10,014)	(8,344)	(26,025)
Paper					18,619
Sales commission					14,115
					99,161

16. Publications

	1997 £	1996 £
Provisions for publications in progress		
List of Fellows	—	3,000
	—	3,000

17. Publications

	1997 £	1996 £
Other publications costs		
Annual Bibliography	11,268	10,543
Less: royalties received	(3,590)	(1,352)
	7,678	9,191

18. Lease Commitments

The Society has the following annual commitments under non-cancellable operating leases which expire:

	1997 £	1996 £
Within 1–2 years	1,006	—
Within 2–5 years	2,517	3,523
	3,523	3,523

19. Life Members

The Society has on-going commitments to provide membership services to 29 Life Members on a cost of approximately £28 each year.

20. UNCAPITALISED ASSETS

The Society owns a library the cost of which is written off to the income and expenditure account at the time of purchase.

This library is insured for £150,000 and is used for reference purposes by the membership of the Society.

21. ANALYSIS OF NET ASSETS BETWEEN FUNDS

	General Fund £	Studies in History £	E.M. Robinson Bequest Fund £	A.S. Whitfield Prize Fund £	Andrew Mellon Fund £	Total £
Fixed Assets	387	—	—	—	4,051	4,438
Investments	1,983,040	—	89,027	40,345	—	2,112,412
	1,983,427	—	89,027	40,345	4,051	2,116,850
Current Assets						
Stocks	26,025	—	—	—	—	26,025
Debtors	35,558	—	—	—	—	35,558
Cash at bank and in hand	23,685	—	—	—	51,033	74,718
	85,268	—	—	—	51,033	136,301
Less: Creditors	(66,647)	(9,295)	(9,113)	(1,273)	(2,768)	(89,096)
Net Current Assets	18,621	(9,295)	(9,113)	(1,273)	48,265	47,205
Net Assets	2,002,048	(9,295)	79,914	39,072	52,316	2,164,055

THE ROYAL HISTORICAL SOCIETY
THE DAVID BERRY ESSAY TRUST

BALANCE SHEET AS AT 30TH JUNE 1997

	1997 £	1997 £	1996 £	1996 £
FIXED ASSETS				
1,117.63 units in the Charities Official Investment Fund (Market Value £9,524: 1996 £8,163)		1,530		1,530
CURRENT ASSETS				
Bank Deposit Account	7,706		11,186	
LESS: CREDITORS				
Amounts falling due within one year	—		(4,126)	
NET CURRENT ASSETS		7,060		7,060
REPRESENTED BY:		9,236		8,590
Capital fund		1,000		1,000
Income and expenditure reserve		8,236		7,590
		9,236		8,590

INCOME AND EXPENDITURE ACCOUNT

	1997 £	1997 £	1997 £	1997 £
INCOME				
Dividends		387		366
Bank Interest Receivable		259		320
		646		686
EXPENDITURE				
Adjudicator's Fee		—		—
Excess of income over expenditure for the year		646		686
Balance brought forward		7,590		6,904
Balance carried forward		8,236		7,590

The fund has no recognised gains or losses apart from the results for the above financial periods.

1. ACCOUNTING POLICIES
  Basis of accounting.
    The accounts have been prepared under the historical cost convention. The late David Berry, by his Will dated 23rd April 1926, left £1,000 to provide in every three years a gold medal and prize money for the best essay on the Earl of Bothwell or, at the discretion of the Trustees, on Scottish History of the James Stuarts I to VI, in memory of his father the late Rev. David Berry.
    The Trust is regulated by a scheme sanctioned by the Chancery Division of the High Court of Justice dated 23rd January 1930, and made in action 1927 A 1233 David Anderson Berry deceased, Hunter and Another v. Robertson and Another and since modified by an order of the Charity Commissioners made on 11 January 1978 removing the necessity to provide a medal.
    The Royal Historical Society is now the Trustee. The investment consists of 1117.63 Charities Official Investment Fund Income with units. The Trustee will in every second year of the three year period advertise inviting essays.

REPORT OF THE AUDITORS TO THE TRUSTEES OF THE DAVID BERRY ESSAY TRUST

We have audited the accounts on page 356 which have been prepared under the historical cost convention and the accounting policies set out on page 356.

Respective responsibilities of the Council and Auditors

The Trustees are required to prepare accounts for each financial year which give a true and fair view of the state of affairs of the Trust and of the surplus or deficit for that period.

In preparing the accounts, the Trustees are required to:
—select suitable accounting policies and then apply them consistently;
—make judgements and estimates that are reasonable and prudent;
—prepare the accounts on the going concern basis unless it is inappropriate to presume that the Trust will continue in business.

The Trustees are responsible for keeping proper accounting records which disclose with reasonable accuracy at any time the financial position of the Trust. They are also responsible for safeguarding the assets of the Trust and hence for taking reasonable steps for the prevention and detection of fraud and other irregularities.

As described above the Trustees are responsible for the preparation of accounts. It is our responsibility to form an independent opinion, based on our audit, on those accounts and to report our opinion to you.

Basis of opinion

We conducted our audit in accordance with Auditing Standards issued by the Auditing Practices Board. An audit includes examination, on a test basis, of evidence relevant to the amounts and disclosures in the accounts. It also includes an assessment of the significant estimates and judgements made by the Trustees in the preparation of the accounts, and of whether the accounting policies are appropriate to the Trust's circumstances, consistently applied and adequately disclosed.

We planned and performed our audit so as to obtain all the information and explanations which we considered necessary in order to provide us with sufficient evidence to give reasonable assurance that the accounts are free from material misstatement, whether caused by fraud or other irregularity or error. In forming our opinion we also evaluated the overall adequacy of the presentation of information in the accounts.

Opinion

In our opinion the accounts give a true and fair view of the state of the Trust's affairs as at 30th June 1997 and of its surplus for the year then ended.

MACINTYRE & CO
Chartered Accountants
Registered Auditors
London

25 September 1997